DIS-RUPT
Filipina Women: Rising
3.0

About the Filipina Leadership Global Summit

The Filipina Women's Network's (FWN) annual Filipina Leadership Global Summit brings together highly successful Filipina women global leaders, influencers, thought leaders and public figures for discussions, learning journeys, and kwentuhan sessions on how to succeed as multi-cultural professionals. At the summit, Filipina women discuss cooperative ventures and public and private partnerships. The high-powered gathering is a vital part of FWN's Pinay Power 2020 Mission: A Filipina leader in every sector of the economy. The Global Summit is the leading forum in the Filipina global community and contributes to an expanded understanding of the Filipino culture's influence.

www.filipinasummit.org

About the Global FWN100™ Awards

The global FWN100™ Awards is a strategy to execute FWN's Mission—a Filipina woman leader in every sector ot the global economy by 2020. The 100 Most Influential Filipina Women in the World Award™ recognizes women of Philippine ancestry who are influencing the face of leadership in the global workplace, having reached status for outstanding work in their respective professions, industries and communities. These distinguished women are recognized for their achievements and contributions to society, femtorship and legacy. What makes this award distinctive is the awardee's commitment to reinvent herself by paying forward to the future of the Filipina community by femtoring ONE young Filipina and thereby contributing to FWN's pipeline of qualified leaders and increasing the odds that some Filipina women will rise to the 'C-suite' position in all industry sectors.

www.filipinasummit.org/fwn100

About FEMtorMatch™

FEMtorMatchTM is the Filipina Women's Network's strategic tool for developing the next generation of Filipina leaders through local and global partnerships between female mentors, calle FEMtorsTM, and female mentees, called FEMteesTM. FEMtorMarchTM provides structured one-on-one mentoring that harnesses the power of the internet to broaden and deepen the reach of traditional mentoring. Thus, both FEMtorsTM and FEMteesTM can reside anywhere in the world.

www.femtormatch.org

DIS-RUPT

Filipina Women: Rising

3.0

The Third Book
on Leadership
by the Filipina
Women's Network

Edited by
MARIA AFRICA BEEBE

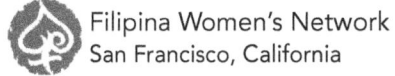
Filipina Women's Network
San Francisco, California

Copyright © 2018
by Filipina Women's Network
Manufactured in the United States of America.
Edited by Maria Africa Beebe, Ph.D.

All rights reserved under International
and Pan-American Copyright Conventions.

*No part of this publication may be reproduced or transmitted
by any form or by any means without prior permission
from the Editors, Publisher or Contributors.*

Contributing writers retain copyright to their work.

The statements and opinions contained in the individual chapters are solely those of the individual authors and not of FWN. The editors, contributing authors, and FWN shall have neither liability nor responsibility to any person or entity with respect to any loss or damage caused, or alleged to have been caused, directly or indirectly, by the information contained in this book.

Disrupt 3.0, 2nd Edition
ISBN-13: 978-0-9908093-3-3
Library of Congress Control Number: 2018953258

Cover Design: Lucille Tenazas, Tenazas Design/NY
Interior Design: Anne Quintos, PageJump Media

Published by
Filipina Women's Network
San Francisco, CA 94119 USA

http://filipinawomensnetwork.org
Email: filipina@ffwn.org

Babae Kami
We are Women
Somos Mujeres

Marra PL Lanot

Babae kami
Nagluluwal ng sanggol
Na tagapagmana ng mundo
Marunong kaming umaninag
Ng hugis sa araw at gabi
Marunong maghimay
Ng kulay ng bahaghari

Marunong sumalo
Sa kaluluwang babagsak
Marunong magmahal
Sa pusong maalalahanin
Marunong lumaban
At magwasto ng baligtad
Habang naghahardin
Sa ikagaganda ng daigdig.

We are women
Bearer of babes
Inheritors of the world
We know how to discern
Shapes during day or night
We can separate
The colors of the rainbow

We know how to catch
A soul about to fall
We know how to love
A thoughtful heart
We know how to fight
And straighten the crooked
While doing gardening
To beautify the world.

Somos mujeres
damos nacimiento a los bebés
que son los herederos del mundo
sabemos ver
figuras por día y por la noche
sabemos nombrar
los colores del arco.

Sabemos salvar
un alma que está cayendo
Sabemos amar
un corazón considerado
Sabemos luchar
y corregir injusticia
mientras cultivamos un huerto
para un mundo bello.

CONTENTS

FOREWORD — XI
Marily Mondejar

PREFACE — XI
Angelica Berrie

INTRODUCTION — XV
Maria Africa Beebe, Ph.D.

FWN Rising

1. **MARILY MONDEJAR** — 27
   Marily: Rising

2. **SUSIE QUESADA** — 52
   Sisterhood, Dialogue, and Impact

3. **GEORGITTA 'BENG' PIMENTEL PUYAT** — 58
   Rising to the FWN Challenge

Developing Leadership

4. **LEAH L. LAXAMANA** — 65
   Journey to Being Present: Making Friends with Fear and Uncertainty

5. **ANA BEL MAYO** — 73
   Five Dollars in My Pocket

6. **JOANNE MICHELLE FERNANDEZ OCAMPO** — 79
   The Dynamics of Defining Success and Failure

7. **RACHEL U. SALINEL** — 90
   Purpose, Passion, and Pass It On

8. **EDITHA TIJAMO WINTERHALTER, Ed.D.** — 98
   Sangandaan

9. MYRNA P. YOUNG, MSN, RN, CNOR	109
Big Dreams, Broken Glass	
10. GERI ALUMIT ZELDES, Ph.D.	116
Was It Murder? Leadership in My Quest for Truth	

Building Leadership Legacy

11. JOJI ILAGAN BIAN	129
Dreaming Big, Giving the Best	
12. REBECCA MURRY	140
Redefining Pathways	
13. DINA DELA PAZ STALDER	154
Blow. Fall. Bounce.	
14. MILA EUSTAQUIO-SYME with MA. VICTORIA E. AÑONUEVO	163
Success Amidst Adversities	
15. CATHERINE TEH, M.D.	171
Turning Struggles into Strengths	

Leadership and Entrepreneurship

16. MYLENE ROMUALDEZ ABIVA	189
Filipina Champion of the Geeks	
17. CRISTINA CALAGUIAN	196
The Road to My Ikigai	
18. JANETTE NELLIE GO-CHIU	207
Innovator By Happenstance	
19. SANDY SANCHEZ MONTANO	218
Intensity 7	
20. ANNE QUINTOS	230
Butterflies in the Gut: Leading Outside Comfort Zones	

21. ROWENA ROMULO — 238
   Nothing is Impossible: From Banker to Restaurateur

22. NIKKI TANG — 251
   No Way to Go but Up

Being First and Foremost

23. CYNTHIA BARKER — 263
   Building My Political Backbone

24. MARIA ROSA 'BING' NIEVA CARRION, Ph.D. — 278
   What Makes an Effective Leader

25. JENNIFER MARIE B. JOSÉ, M.D. — 286
   The Woman's Room

26. JUSLYN C. MANALO — 294
   If at First You Don't Succeed

27. ROXANE MARTIN NEGRILLO — 302
   Moving Mountains

28. GEORGITTA 'BENG' PIMENTEL PUYAT — 314
   Volunteerism: A Life's Journey

29. LUCILLE TENAZAS — 329
   A Class of Her Own

30. LILY TORRES-SAMORANOS — 344
   A Hymn of Praise to Failure

31. LEONOR S. VINTERVOLL — 354
   Janteloven and Leadership

Leading for Impact

32. CHRISTINE AMOUR-LEVAR — 369
    Finding Your Profession of the Heart

33. HON. THELMA B. BOAC — 382
    Filipina: Leave Footprints That Last

34. WILMA 'AMY' EISMA — 395
    Moving Beyond Power and Position

35. ANNABELLE MISA HEFTI — 404
    Stepping over Stolpersteine

36. CATHY SALCEDA ILETO — 414
    Filipina Delikadesa = Waves of Positive Change

37. WAFA 'MARILYN' R. QASIMIEH, Ph.D. — 422
    Ambassador of Peace and Humanity

SYNTHESIS — 430
Maria Africa Beebe, Ph.D.

ACKNOWLEDGEMENTS — 439

Appendices

Appendix A: References — 443

Appendix B: Additional Web-Based Resources — 451

Appendix C: Suggestions for Workshop Activities — 453

Appendix D: FWN Award Categories — 456

Biographies — 458

FOREWORD

Marily Mondejar

FOUNDATION FOUNDER AND CEO, FILIPINA WOMEN'S NETWORK

The DISRUPT Filipina leadership book series is needed to fill the gap in the current leadership literature. The practical leadership lessons learned by the authors from their successes and victories over poverty, domestic violence, oppression, harassment, and workplace micro-aggressions shaped their worldview about power and influence. Their leadership has heart. Their experiences mirror what is being taught by career coaches on ways to avoid executive derailment but instead to seek career advancement. This collection of lessons from the global experiences of the authors include leadership qualities and styles developed from early childhood through learning at school and at work. Schools, universities, corporations, and government training centers need to add this book in their teaching toolkit because it is about achieving success. The book is about change.

I know all the 38 authors of the chapters in this book. They now call ten countries their home. I have met each one of the authors at a Filipina Leadership Global Summit in San Francisco (USA), Manila and Cebu (Philippines), and Toronto (Canada). I read their significant contributions in their communities, organizations, and industries as part of their nomination for the Most Influential Filipina Women in the World Award. I was moved to hear about their dreams. I am honored that they have shared their innermost thoughts and secrets.

I travel a lot and make a point of stopping by the airport bookstores to check on the latest fiction and non-fiction books. There are very few books authored by women, books about women, and zero books about women of color. As I browsed the best sellers, I realized that the themes of the best-selling books are the same themes that these 38 authors have written about. These themes are about developing leadership, building leadership legacy, innovation, social entrepreneurship, exceeding expectations, leading for impact, and giving back.

As I read each of the chapters, I sensed a pattern. Something extraordinary is going on here. It is a quiet revolution of Filipina women in the diaspora influencing the world.

As I reviewed the stories of the previous two books again, *DISRUPT. Filipina Women: Proud. Loud. Leading Without A Doubt.* and *DISRUPT 2.0. Filipina Women: Daring to Lead*; this book, *DISRUPT 3.0. Filipina Women: Rising* provides additional evidence that we should not be invisible any longer. These authors are agents of change. Filipina women have risen.

PREFACE
FILIPINA POWER

Angelica Berrie

PRESIDENT, THE RUSSELL BERRIE FOUNDATION

"A woman with a voice is by definition a strong woman but the search to find that voice can be remarkably difficult."
- **Melinda Gates**

I am a great believer in the heroic power of women, in the power of one to make a difference, and the power of a network to raise its collective voice and create positive change wherever we are in the world! I have had the privilege of meeting women in the Filipina Women's Network who triumphed over adversity, whose example empowered others to rise in wisdom and grace. American poet Maya Angelou calls these women "She-roes!"

This is a book full of stories from Filipina "She-roes" whose resilience, true grit, and creativity strengthen the larger narrative of Filipino peoplehood, womanhood, and nation-building. Thirty-eight women living in nine countries sharing their leadership journeys; change-makers connected by a common identity as Filipinas.

Their mythic journeys resonate with all of us who had to find our inner voice, who learned to speak from our bravest and most authentic self, and who mastered the art of telling the story of who we are and what we stand for.

We celebrate women who exercise their influence to be a force for good, whose lives remind us that leadership requires disruption, reinvention, and fearlessness. These women answered the call to lead by asking of themselves, "How can we use our life to create a better world?"

As transformative leaders, we bring all of who we are, all of who we are becoming, to where we are going. We discover our better selves as we share life lessons that empower others along the way. Navigating that distance within ourselves is a journey of self-transformation.

One of the common traits of these remarkable women is their ability to lean into the challenges of personal growth, transmuting experiences that changed them into a gift of spirit that enabled them to rise, enriching those of us who have the honor of bearing witness to their incredible journey! In their journey toward transformation, they develop the capacity to transform the world.

As we celebrate their success, we are conscious that we stand on the shoulders of those who came before us, women who dared, nameless women who contributed to our national resilience in hard earned ways. We honor those women by paving the way for those who will come after us, a new generation of women leading in their own unique ways.

Filipina Power demands more of us, to be bolder as we rise to fulfill our highest purpose. Every woman has this power to transcend, to stand for truth, justice and humanity, to use our voice to transform not just our circumstances but the community in which we live.

Nobel Prize Laureate Leymah Gbowee urges us to "do one thing every day that everyone else is scared to do" because "everything is within our power, and our power is within us."

More power to rising Filipinas, wherever you are.

INTRODUCTION

Maria Africa Beebe, PH.D.

DISRUPT 3.0. Filipina Women: Rising celebrates Filipina women who have emerged as global leaders despite varying levels of challenges. Some challenges were major setbacks while other challenges were minor. The same challenge was viewed as a failure by some and only an inconvenience by others. In this book Filipina women discuss their responses to challenges and their actions that led to success. They discuss the significance of their success and the implications of their leadership for their *kapwa tao* [fellow humans]. The book is the third in a series on leadership by the Filipina Women's Network (FWN). As part of the strategy of FWN to recognize Filipina woman leaders in the global environment, FWN first established the US FWN100™ awards and in 2013 the Global FWN100™ awards. Almost 100 of the awardees have shared their leadership stories in the three DISRUPT books published by FWN. The books celebrate Filipina women leaders who have had an impact beyond the boundaries of the Philippines. The goal of the FWN books was to make the stories of the women leaders accessible to next-generation leaders while contributing to the scholarship on women and leadership.

The purpose of *DISRUPT 3.0*, similar to the purpose of *DISRUPT 1.0* and *DISRUPT 2.0*, is to inspire, motivate, and nurture the leadership of not only Filipina women but also non-Filipina women worldwide. These are women who have leadership responsibilities in cross-cultural and global situations and leadership positions in the diaspora. The explicit goal of the book is to teach leadership in a way that not only informs but also transforms.

Leadership and Global Leadership

The Filipina women whose stories are told in this book are leaders first and then global leaders. The concept of leadership is understood in different ways by different people. The purpose of this section is to explore some of these meanings and how they provide a foundation for global leadership and then explore concepts of global leadership that are unique to Filipinas and Filipinos.

The Bass Handbook of Leadership: Theory, Research and Managerial Applications (2008) 4th edition reflects changes in the way leadership is understood. These changes include the increasing importance of cognitive models as well as behavioral models, the return of older concepts such as personal traits of leadership bolstered by the belief that leaders are both born and made, and the emergence of new terms and concepts, such as strategic and virtual leadership, ethics of leadership, transformational, visionary, and value-based leadership.

Follett distinguished between "power-over" and "power-with" (coercive vs. co-active power) as essential characteristics of leadership. She suggested that organizations function on the principle of "power-with" rather than "power-over." For her, "power-with is what democracy should mean in politics or industry" (Follett 1924 p.187). Leadership is not defined by the exercise of power but by the capacity to increase the sense of power among those led. The most essential work of the leader is to create more leaders (attributed to Follett, 1924).

The Sage Handbook of Leadership (Bryman, Collinson, Grint, Jackson, & Uhl-Bien, 2011) considered leadership scholarship from numerous angles and concluded with an optimistic look at the future of leaders, followers, and their place in organizations and society at large.

Trying to define leadership is further complicated by the differences in mental models people from different parts of the world bring to the workplace (Gentry & Eckert, 2012) although the challenges leaders face around the world seem more similar than different (Gentry et al., 2016).

Leadership research has been conducted predominantly from a Western viewpoint. Researchers have begun to engage in the systematic exploration of the cross-cultural aspects of leadership and the vast, diverse cultures and organizations from which leadership emanates (Hernandez et al., 2011). One such study is the Global Leadership and Organizational Behavior Effectiveness (GLOBE). GLOBE has sought to address the gap in cross-cultural leadership studies with their research on culture and leadership in 61 countries (House, Javidan, Hanges, & Dorfman, 2002).

Global leaders are defined as: "individuals who effect significant positive change in organizations by building communities through the development of trust and the arrangement of organizational structures and processes in a context involving multiple cross-boundary stakeholders, multiple sources of external cross-boundary authority, and multiple cultures under conditions of temporal, geographical, and cultural complexity" (Mendenhall, 2008, p.17). Global leaders "value transparency, authenticity, collaboration, action, and integrity" and work closely with individuals of various cultures and backgrounds (Pless, Maak, & Stahl, 2011, p.1). A Global Mindset is a critical aspect of being able to lead globally. According to Javidan (2010), having a Global Mindset requires: (a) intellectual capital, including global business savvy, cognitive complexity, and a cosmopolitan outlook; (b) psychological capital, including passion for diversity, eagerness for adventure, and self-assurance; and (c) social capital, including intercultural empathy, a history of interpersonal impact, and diplomacy skills. In *Global Leadership: Research, Practice, and Development* (2018), global leadership is defined as "the processes and actions through which an individual influences a range of internal and external constituents from multiple national cultures and jurisdictions in a context characterized by significant levels of task and relationship complexity" (Reiche, Bird, Mendenhall, & Osland, 2017, p. 553).

In the Global Leadership study, the Philippines was considered part of the Southeast Asia cluster and was described as high in power distance and group and family collectivism practices (Gupta, Surei, Javidan & Chhokhar, 2002). Gupta et al. indicated that Filipinos have "the highest scores on four societal practices: groupism, collectivism, humanism, and gender egalitarianism" (p. 22).

The significance of culture is underscored by the Global Competence Model (Hunter & Hunter, 2018) that defines global competence as "Having flexible, respectful attitudes, including self-perspective, and applying knowledge of the historical, geographic, and societal factors that influence cultures in order to effectively interact and build relationships with people around the world." Another global leadership assessment is the Global Competencies Inventory (GCI) proposed by Stevens, Bird, Mendenhall, and Oddou (2014). The GCI measures "the degree to which individuals possess the intercultural competencies that are associated with global leader effectiveness" (p. 115).

Filipina Leadership

DISRUPT 1.0 Filipina Women: Proud. Loud. Leading without a Doubt (2015) and *DISRUPT 2.0* started the process of identifying the leadership repertoire of Filipina women leaders. Each author of a chapter in *DISRUPT 1.0* identified their tips for leadership. In *DISRUPT 2.0. Filipina Women: Daring to Lead* (2016) chapter authors focused on the leadership competencies that they have mastered over time.

Ethnocentrism, valuing of cultural aspects, loyalty to the national community, and commitments to the role requirements of citizenship are identified as patterns of Filipino national identity (Doronila, 1989, 46-47). These patterns appear to inform the identity of Filipinas, no matter where they are in the world, and appear to be foundational to the leadership of Filipinas, including their desire to give back to society.

Another contributing factor to the leadership of Filipinas could be the overall gender gap score in indicating that the Philippines is second in the East Asia and the Pacific region and among the top ten countries out of 144 countries in addressing gender discrimination in 2017. The Philippines is among the first in closing the gender gap in educational attainment and health and survival, fourth in closing the gender gap in economic participation and opportunity, and sixteenth in terms of the ratio of women in politics.

A summary of the key findings from four studies about Filipino leadership in the Philippines provides a link between the leadership narratives of the US and Global FWN100™ Filipina women and the broader discourse on leadership.

DISRUPT 1.0. Filipina Women: Proud. Loud. Leading without a Doubt (2015) made a significant contribution to redefining how Filipina women in the diaspora are perceived. The themes articulated by Filipina women in their leadership stories in *DISRUPT 1.0* concern the **how** and **why** of leadership that make up their leadership repertoires (Beebe, 2017). The **how** of leadership consisted of actions that emphasized the centrality of relationships, the significance of values, and self-transcendence. The **why** of leadership for most of these women referenced finding purpose and meaning in life, achieving impact in their work, and giving back to their local communities. At the center of their leadership repertoires is the Philippine cultural value, *kapwa*. Translations for *kapwa* include "shared humanity," "unity of the self and the others," "shared inner self," and "together with the person." *Kapwa* is said to be the core value that guides all forms interpersonal relations and of social interaction among Filipinos. It stands to reason that *kapwa* would play a central role in their leadership which is the result of human interaction and negotiations.

DISRUPT 2.0. Filipina Women: Daring to Lead (2016) is an affirmation of the leadership competencies of Filipina women leaders (FWL) with a global mindset. The global FWL referenced competencies that were relevant in various global settings. Using the "Benchmarks by Design" (Center for Creative Leadership (CCL), 2015), the competencies can be organized into: (1) Leading yourself – Filipina women leaders showed an awareness of their strengths and the capacity to adapt, learn, and cope in both the Philippines and in international environments; (2) Leading others – Filipina women leaders have shown that effectively leading others could be done as part of a team or as part of an organization; (3) Leading the organization – The Filipina women leaders have carried out their leadership roles for setting vision and direction, building commitment, and creating alignment.

Cuyegkeng and Palma-Angeles (2011) defined Filipino leadership as visionary with the ability to engender meaningful change and transform individuals and their institutions through gradual reforms. According to Cuyegkeng and Palma-Angeles (2011), Filipino leadership depends on good judgment in choosing a team to formulate strategy and the ability to negotiate cooperation and build trust and relationships while showing humility.

In one of the few studies examining the leadership of Filipina women, Roffey (1999) identified six competencies needed by Filipina women for effective leadership and management of businesses based in Metro Manila. These competencies are: (a) interpersonal; (b) leading by example; (c) initiating; (d) external public relations; (e) market and customer orientation; and (f) integrity and honesty. Roffey noted that in contrast to research on western-based business leadership, Filipina leaders view the organization as an "extended family." In the extended family model leaders have "personal responsibility for the social and psychological well-being of their employees" and employees expect to be "looked after by their managers" (p. 383). Roffey concluded that effective Filipina leaders in subsidiaries of multinational corporations demonstrated professional skills and transformed strategic vision into operational reality. In examining the role of family kinship, including fictive kinship, Roffey concluded that effective leaders were able to navigate the "contradictions between contemporary professional and managerial expectations and cultural dynamics" (p. 388). Effective leaders used their networks with integrity and practiced ethical business with their kinship networks.

Power is generally recognized as an element of leadership. Carmen 'Pinky' Valdes (2017) indicated that Filipina women avoid discussing power. Valdes provided a list which identifies the role of power in the leadership of Filipina women (p. 57). You have power, if your decisions affect the lives of others, if people want your approval, if you understand problems better than others, and if your opinions are listened to. You have power if you have a network of resources or connections, people are attracted to you, if people follow you, if people want to please you, and if people love you. You have power, if your business position has a budget and if your family is financially well-off. You have power, if your creativity makes things happen, if you have innovative ideas that work, if you can see the intangible and the ethereal, if your skills surpass others in your field, and if you have an exceptional talent in any field. Valdes has issued a challenge to women to claim that power, to do something with the power they have, and create meaning with that power. Women who have created meaning with their power set a positive energy in motion, according to Valdes (p. 84). As Filipina women leaders, graduates of Assumption College, Miriam (formerly Maryknoll) College, and St. Scholastica's College demonstrated the following leadership qualities. They place people as the first priority; offer others the opportunity to use their talents and grow their self-confidence; give others access to resources, which promotes independence and autonomy; and entrust control and power to others within their sphere of influence. They are vulnerable because accepting wounds and weaknesses opens the door to others to have more courage to do the same. They establish a place where people are respected for themselves, and not just for their usefulness to the enterprise. They create a space where negative criticism and bullying behavior are not allowed and where people assume their responsibility with the beautiful Filipino value—*malasakit* (dedicated caring even beyond the call of duty) (Valdes, 2017, p. 84).

One Purpose, Shared Future: Bridges of Peace in Mindanao (AIM, Center for Bridging Leadership, 2015) highlighted the experiences of bridging leaders in Mindanao, the southern Philippines who co-created communities of change. These leaders shared their "deepening personal ownership of an issue and the response to it; moving from the self to build co-ownership of the issue among stakeholders; and finally, mobilizing stakeholders into collaborative action for the co-creation of a new reality" (p. 13). Among the leaders are women who have contributed to meeting the challenges building peace in Mindanao.

Understanding how to lead better as global leaders requires self-awareness, self-transformation, and self-transcendence. Judging by the stories shared by the Filipina women in, *DISRUPT 2.0*, and now in this book, they have shown attentiveness to experience, intelligence in understanding that experience, fairness in judging that experience, and responsibility in deciding how to use that experience in leadership.

Socio-cultural Context

Like most countries in the world today, the Philippines is characterized by cultural diversity. The Ethnologue[1] listed the number of individual languages in the Philippines as 187. Tagalog was chosen as the national language in 1937 and renamed Filipino in 1987 to incorporate other Philippine languages.

These different languages define the main ethnolinguistic groups in the Philippines. The earliest settlers in the Philippines are the Aetas. Most Filipinos are Malay people. Other ethnic groups include the Japanese, Kokkien and Cantonese from China, Punjabi, Tamil and Kerala from India.

What is now known as the Philippines was originally small maritime states or independent *barangays* (villages) In 1521, Spain colonized and named the islands after King Philip of Spain. Spanish colonialization established the Catholic church. Spanish colonization started the process of large scale out-migration. Filipinos who

[1] https://www.ethnologue.com/country/PH

served as navigators for the Spanish galleons, beginning in the 1760s jumped ship on the shores of Lake Borgne, east of New Orleans in an area that later became part of the United States (Bautista, 2002). As early as 1788, Filipino seamen are recorded as having contact with indigenous Alaskans (Buchholdt, 1996). In the late eighteenth century, Mexicans were forced to join the Spanish armies deployed to the Philippines and became a cultural influence (Mehl, 2016).

Spain did not encourage the use of the Spanish language in the Philippines. One of the most important influences of Spain on the Philippines was the rise of the *Ilustrados*. Many of the *Ilustrados* were mixed-race and made up the elite. These Filipino elites studied in Spain during the late 19th century and presented their demands for assimilation, good governance, and representation in the Spanish government administration. After a hard-fought revolution, the Filipinos declared independence from Spain in 1896. However, in 1898 Spain ceded the Philippines to the US for $20 million. The subsequent American rule was contested by the Philippine Republic resulting in thousands of deaths among Filipinos. Although the war ended in 1902, veterans of the *katipuneros* [revolutionaries] who fought against Spain continued to battle the American forces until 1913. The US occupation of the Philippines changed the cultural landscape in the Philippines through the introduction of English as an official language of government and education and the establishment of public schools initially staffed by American teachers called Thomasites. The Philippines gained independence from the US in 1946.

The first wave of Filipino immigration to the U.S. started during this period. In 1909 Filipinos from different ethnic groups were recruited to work on the Hawaiian sugar plantations. In 1921, farmers in California and canning factories in Alaska began recruiting Filipino workers.

MIGRATION AND DIASPORA EXPERIENCE: FILIPINOS IN THE WORLD

In 2018, the Philippine population was estimated at 106,512,070 million people. Of these, approximately 11 million are overseas. A majority of the overseas Filipinos are women. A significant portion of the overseas Filipinos are workers, identified as Overseas Filipino Workers (OFWs). OFWs can be found in 170 countries, with one million in Saudi Arabia alone, followed by the United Arab Emirates, Malaysia, and Canada. The U.S. is an important destination for OFWs and is the top destination for immigration. As of December 2013, the number of overseas Filipinos totaled slightly more than 10 million, including some 4.9 million permanent settlers in other countries. It is estimated that 64 percent of the permanent settlers are in the

United States. There are an estimated 1.2 million unauthorized migrants worldwide, primarily in Malaysia and the United States.

The 2015 CFO Statistics on Philippine International Migration contains information on registered (1) Filipino emigrants leaving the Philippines permanently for family reunification, (2) spouses and partners of foreign nationals, (3) immigrant workers, (4) Exchange Visitor Program participants, and (5) au pairs. Of registered Filipino emigrants from 2005 to 2015, 60% were female, 49% were college graduates, and 39% were professionals or technical workers prior to migration.

Filipinos marriage migrants leave the Philippines to join their foreign spouse or partner overseas. Filipinos are most likely to marry citizens from the US, Japan, and Australia. Marriage migrants are 92% female, 36% college graduates, and 34% high school graduates. Sixty two percent had no professional experience prior to migration, 19% were housewives, and 58% had no knowledge of the country they are migrating to. Twenty-five percent of the marriage migrants met their partner through the Internet or other social media, and 30% through personal introduction.

Filipino immigrant workers are qualified to stay long-term or permanently in their host country. They are 75% female. The Top three destinations of immigrant workers are US, Canada, and Australia.

Filipino au pairs are 18 to 30 years old, unmarried and without children. They are supposed to be enrolled in a cultural exchange program and are placed with a host family for a maximum of two years. Ninety-seven percent of Filipino au pairs are female and are mainly bound for Denmark, Norway, and The Netherlands. Nurses and service workers are the top occupation of Filipino au pairs prior to migration.

Book Organization

The context for the rest of the book is provided by the information in this introduction, especially the information on the variety of global leadership demonstrated by Filipina women, the themes in *DISRUPT 1.0* and *DISRUPT 2.0* on the leadership repertoire of Filipina women, and the implications of history, culture, and migration on Filipina women's leadership. *DISRUPT 3.0. Filipina Women: Rising* has thirty-eight first person narratives organized into five sections:

The Filipina Women's Network (FWN) Rising. This section discusses the leadership role of the FWN in networking Filipina women leaders from around the world and the rationale for the leadership summits and the FWN100™ Global leadership awards.

Developing Leadership. The chapters in this section share the themes of how the Filipina Women Leaders have developed their leadership expertise and how these women have femtored, coached, and developed leadership of their *kapwa*.

Building Leadership Legacy. In the chapters in this section select Filipina Women Leaders discuss leadership values and qualities that have transferred from one generation to the next generation and their hope that the next generation will surpass their legacy.

Leadership and Entrepreneurship. The chapters in this section discuss how the Filipina Women Leaders became entrepreneurs, and the link between being entrepreneurial and being a leader.

First and Foremost. In this section, Filipina Women Leaders discuss their journeys of exceeding expectations, disrupting the status quo, and breaking the glass ceiling as they became first and foremost in their fields.

Leading for Impact. The chapters in this section discuss the leadership reach of Filipina Women Leaders beyond their professional fields to include their advocacies. The chapters end with a summary of their impact.

Finally, a **Synthesis** provides the leadership themes articulated by the chapter authors who are *Filipina Women Rising*. The themes include recognition of Philippine values such as *malasakit* and *delikadesa*, of rising from failures, rising to face challenges, and rising to celebrate success.

FWN Rising

MARILY MONDEJAR

Founder & CEO, Filipina Women's Network (FWN)
President, Commission on Community Investment and Infrastructure
Keeper of the Flame (2007-2018)

Marily: Rising

I arrived in San Francisco in 1980 not knowing anyone, to escape an abusive spouse, get a divorce since there was no divorce in the Philippines and in order to start a new life. With only $200 in my pocket, I was rich in contacts in America and determined to start a new life for myself and my sons.

I lied to my sons about the reason for my travel and promised I would soon return for them. I do not think they quite believed me especially my younger son, Ganie. Franklin, however, gave me a look that I interpreted as, "I believe you, Mommy."

At that time, I was already traveling for Time Life Books Asia, lived in Bangkok, Thailand, and was involved in the launch of the Time Life Books distributorship. This was one of the business ventures of Bill Heinecke, the president of Minor Holdings. My sons had lived with me in Bangkok during one of their summer vacations, so I had some credibility talking about my promised return. I had always involved my sons in my work bringing them along on business trips and to work events. I wanted to share with them my work ethic and why I wanted to be independent and earn my own money.

The Bangkok distributorship launch was so successful that Bill Heinecke offered me a trip to Hong Kong to attend the Time Life Books distributors conference. He also offered me the opportunity to launch the distributorship of Helene Curtis, his new business venture. I turned this down because I had unfinished business;

getting a divorce and starting a new career unshackled from the spiral of violence that permeated by marriage "and the culture of violence ingrained in the Filipino culture." I wanted to get my personal life in order and to advance my career.

Two sisters, Bessie and Eppie Bangalan, whom I had not met, and activist friends of my late brother, Noel Mondejar, welcomed me into their home in San Francisco, with no questions asked. I shared with them my personal story, career plans, and life goals. I asked if I could stay at least six months until I could find a job and figure out what I wanted to do for the rest of my life. They were very kind and told me that I could stay as long as I wanted to, rent-free. I also sensed that they felt I was too ambitious, but they wanted to give me a chance to find out about life in America.

I scoured the classifieds, contacted employment agencies, and explored opportunities with my U.S. contacts. One of the talent managers of an employment agency who interviewed me saw my career potential and enlightened me about two things: 1) I needed to apply to positions consistent with my experience; (2) I had to change my career strategy and focus on "networking," a strange word that I had not heard as a job search strategy. I have never heard about it. She said that the high-paying jobs are found through the people you know; the "insiders" who can open doors that would not otherwise be known since they are not published but only "whispered" about. She invited me to join a women's organization, the Embarcadero Center Forum. A whole new world opened for me. I met amazing women who were involved in advancing their careers, dressing for success, forming alliances, and getting their "foot-in-the-door" and their "seat-at-the-table." I did not quite understand all this information. I did not know how to navigate this corporate world of networking. But I knew that this is how I could succeed. I just did not know how to put it all together. I tucked all this information deep into my consciousness until I needed it for the Filipina Women's Network.

I was accepted into a bank management program based on a Fortune 500 corporation's strategy for recruiting, training, and fast-tracking "high potentials" or "Hi-Po's" to become their future executives. I was assigned a Management Development Officer whose only job was to discover my strengths and weaknesses through endless assessments, on-the-job assignments, multiple one-on-one personal development meetings, and coaching me on how to leverage my talents to become an executive. I felt very special. I talked about this experience with my roommates and the very few Filipina women friends I had met. They did not quite know what I was talking about. I slowly became aware that I did not look like my corporate world. I wanted to find other Filipina women who would be able to relate with what I was experiencing. There were none. There were many occasions when my culture and values were not in sync with my new world of work. As my network expanded, I was the only Filipina woman on a fast track. I looked for the Filipina women career professionals.

I later learned that the women who have become members of the Filipina Women's Network also were looking for successful Filipina career professionals.

Balancing career and home life are difficult. I was determined to succeed, so I returned to school at night and weekends to earn my bachelor's and master's degrees in organization development and leadership from New College of California, graduate studies in public relations at Golden Gate University, and doctoral coursework in organizational psychology at Alliant International University. Being a single mom made it even more challenging. I will always be grateful to my Mom who allowed me to thrive while she took care of my sons. She had 13 children and ran a successful printing business. I do not think she ever did anything for herself.

Parallel worlds

As I was seeking or thinking about founding an organization for Filipina career women, Cora Manase Tellez was also gathering Filipina women in management to create a support network of management rising stars. At that time, Cora was herself a rising executive in the healthcare industry. She was Vice President and Regional Manager, Hawaii Region for Kaiser Foundation Health Plan and Hospitals. She organized a lunch at the San Francisco City Club in 1996. Virna S. Tintiangco, then a recent college graduate, was there and continued the group's networking. The goal was "to provide a unique space for Filipina women to discuss concerns and issues related to their personal and professional lives." She operated under an informal structure with volunteers chairing ad hoc planning committees for each meeting.

I was not at the lunch that Cora Tellez hosted at the City Club in 1996. I did not know Cora then. At that time, I had my own successful image consulting and career coaching practice. I had a lucrative practice preparing witnesses for depositions and court appearances. I had finished my undergrad and master's degrees in leadership, image development, and organizational change and was working on my doctorate in organizational psychology. I developed a 360-degree image assessment based on the seven aspects of image development that I was utilizing in my career coaching practice. I was traveling for Fortune 500 clients and a global cement company. My kids were grown and home was an empty nest.

In 1998, Virna invited me to speak on one of my company's workshops, "Transitions: Life Planning." At that meeting, Virna announced she was moving to Oregon and wanted someone to take over this loosely organized network. I also met Tessie Guillermo, who was then President and CEO of Asian American Health Forum. It was also in 1998 when Cora Manase Tellez became the first Filipina woman to break the Fortune 500 "glass ceiling" when she became the President and CEO of Health Net (NYSE:HNT).

So, one day, it happened. I think I was ready when I met Virna and the timing could not have been more perfect. I found Filipina women who shared my career needs, a network of women who were looking for ways to succeed in their professional paths.

The following two feature articles capture my journey and the founding of the Filipina Women's Network. I will end this chapter with a photo essay about FWN: Rising.

※

This chapter is dedicated to my two sons, Franklin Ricarte and Gani Ricarte. FWN would not have risen without their support especially Franklin who should be celebrating his 15th year at Filipina Women's Network. He has been the rock of FWN.

KUWENTO KUWENTO: MARILY'S MISSION

Benjamin Pimentel, INQUIRER.net
Posted date: October 25, 2007

Google "Filipina" and you will likely find Web sites about mail order brides or international dating—online destinations that typically bring to mind the many stories of Filipinas being exploited or abused.

Marily Mondejar wants to change that.

The first time we met, she was trying to do it by producing and promoting Eve Ensler's internationally renowned play about female sexuality, *The Vagina Monologues*. Not only was the production composed of an all Filipina-cast, but it was also in Tagalog.

I interviewed Marily, who is president of the Filipina Women's Network, on Pinoy Pod, the San Francisco Chronicle's podcast focused on the Filipino American community. (The feature marked the first time that the Tagalog word for the female organ was published on a major U. S. metropolitan newspaper's Web site. You can check it out at https://blog.sfgate.com/chroncast/2006/06/06/usaping-puki-the-vagina-monologues-in-tagalog/).

Marily is trying to overhaul the image of Filipina women again this year by identifying the 100 most influential Filipinas in the United States.

"We want to be showing on the first page of any Yahoo or Google search with the meaning for 'Filipina' as 'someone doing influential things,'" she said.

The idea for the campaign, which culminates this week at the organization's 5th Filipina Summit in Washington DC., came to Marily and her group last year during the celebration of the centennial of Filipino migration to the United States.

That commemoration had focused largely on the Filipino men who came to America as migrant farm workers. "There were very few women mentioned, just the war brides," Marily said.

For the bicentennial celebration of Filipino presence in America, she said, her group "wants to make sure there are at least 100 Filipinas" mentioned in the stories about the Filipino American journey.

For this to happen, FWN wanted to find influential Filipinas willing to take part in a campaign to reshape their public image. Marily and her team didn't want another popularity contest or another feel-good schmooze-fest for the rich and famous.

"We did not want that," Marily said. "You may be high society; you may come from a wealthy family. But we want to make sure that's not your only claim to fame."

And making it to the list is just the first step. Each honoree has a job to do.

"We want you to promise to be a womentor, " she quipped, using FWNspeak for "mentor." Each honoree must commit to helping younger Filipinas as they begin their careers or take on other challenges in their community and beyond. "The goal is to change the face of power in America," she said.

The organization solicited nominations from all over America, from the world of business, the arts, education, and nonprofits. After the list is completed, Marily said, FWN will then launch a mentorship program that it hopes to become fully-developed by 2012.

It's a tough challenge, she acknowledged.

While there is much excitement now about the campaign to identify the 100 Pinas, sustaining that energy will be difficult even for an established organization like FWN with its 500 active members and a network of 5,000 supporters throughout the United States.

"The fear is obviously sustainability," she said. "Are we going to get the support of the community? Is the program going to get the support of the community?"

But for the 57-year-old business consultant and single mother, it's worth a shot. A native of Tacloban who grew up in San Juan, Metro Manila, Marily married young, had two sons and got divorced after moving to the United States in the early 1980s. She later built a successful career as a business development and image consultant, but she did not play an active role in Filipino issues.

"I had been here 20 years but never got involved," she said.

That changed in 2000 when she signed up for FWN which she has turned into a vibrant civic organization.

"This is my legacy to the community," Marily said. "That's all I ask for." Laughing, she added, "I don't even have a daughter. That's probably why I'm involved in this."

FILIPINA WOMEN'S NETWORK IN US MARKS GLASS-CEILING BREAKTHROUGH

By Lito Gutierrez, Philippine Daily Inquirer
First Posted 09:56:00 08/23/2010

Organization-image specialist Marily Mondejar was doing a pretty good job consulting for a mayoral candidate in San Francisco several years ago.

Her team had been tasked to dig up dirt on the incumbent administration. One of the sitting mayor's appointees had allegedly approved a construction contract certification for a crony. The media had a feeding frenzy that threatened to topple the Hizzoner.

"The name of the official sounded foreign," she says, recalling the episode. "After further research, I found out she was a Filipina, and I began to wonder why she was being hung out to dry."

The mayor would be re-elected, but at the cost of the job of this Filipina official. Mondejar was appalled, not because her candidate lost, but because she felt the official had been thrown under the bus to redeem the re-electionist's image. She named the official but requested anonymity for her.

"Very few came to her defense," Mondejar says.

A support group

Thus, it became the mission of the Filipina Women's Network (FWN), a volunteer, non-profit organization to "level the professional and business playing field for Filipinas across America."

FWN was conceived in 2001 after a lunch in 1996 organized by Cora Tellez, then the chief executive officer of one of America's biggest health-care providers, Healthnet. Many in her circle of friends were in management positions themselves. Mondejar, who had taken on image consultancy work for a giant Mexican cement maker, and Virna Tintiangco, then a college student.

Tintiangco continued the group's informal networking, but when she moved to Oregon in 2000, Mondejar took over.

"We want to open doors," says Mondejar. "We want to let America know that Filipinas have the skills to compete at all levels in all areas." She enlisted Filipinas who had proven their mettle in the upper reaches of the different branches of government as well as the private sector.

Successful women

Today FWN has some 800 active members. Its success can also be gleaned in the names of more than 100 people who have signified their intention to attend the 7th Filipina Leadership Summit in Las Vegas in October. Among them: former White House physician, retired Rear Admiral Connie Mariano; California Appeals Court Judge Tani Gorre Cantil-Sakauye, who has been nominated by California Governor Arnold Schwarzenegger to be chief justice of the state Supreme Court; California Lieutenant Governor Mona Pasquil; Nevada Judge Cheryl Moss; Davis, California Mayor Dr. Ruth Asmundson; and information technology tycoon Zeny Cunanan.

Over the years, FWN has been associated with such social issues as domestic violence.

Mondejar said significant impediments for women seeking to move their careers forward are issues at home, particularly violence inflicted by spouses or partners.

It is an issue close to Mondejar's heart, having herself been a victim of domestic violence. In fact, the reason she came to America in 1980 was to seek a divorce from her abusive husband. Her tale of woe is typical. When she told her friends what her husband was doing to her, she would be told: "It is your fate," and "Try not to make him angry."

Marily's own struggle

She initially brought her two sons to the US, but since she could not afford to support them yet, she brought them back home to live with her mother for a few years or until she became financially stable. She recalls the pain the divorce inflicted on her children, one of whom blamed her for not sticking it out. She says it took some doing to make them understand. Now she says she has "a great relationship" with them.

In California, Mondejar found her feet. She got bachelor's and master's degrees in Humanities and is finishing her thesis for a doctorate in Organizational Psychology. After 13 years as an image builder for the cement company, she eventually resigned to run FWN as a full-time career.

It is important for women, Mondejar says, to understand the cycle of domestic violence. "It took me years to understand that," she adds. "I kept getting into abusive situations and did not know how to break the cycle and seek help."

FWN has also become known for its women's rights activities as part of its business networking agenda. Its most popular program is its adoption of "The Vagina Monologues," the off-Broadway stage phenomenon going into its 10th year, whose theme "the vagina as a tool for female empowerment" has become a rallying point of women the world over. It has been translated into 45 languages, and when its Tagalog version, "Usaping Puki," was staged in Manila in 2002, church groups raised a howl, which helped ensure its success, she said.

FWN will present it again during its Vegas summit in October, which is Domestic Violence Awareness Month.

FWN itself does not provide logistical support for abuse victims. What it offers are education and moral support.

For instance, FWN members were at the murder trial of William Corpuz, who was convicted by a jury of murder for slitting his wife's throat.

> It is important for women, Mondejar says, to understand the cycle of domestic violence. "It took me years to understand that," she adds. "I kept getting into abusive situations and did not know how to break the cycle and seek help."

Mondejar says she is also mobilizing her members to support the confirmation of Cantil Sakauye, who would if elected in November, be the first Asian-American Chief Justice of the California Supreme Court. Sakauye is an FWN member.

Not mail-order brides

Despite the number of high-caliber women in FWN's roster, Mondejar acknowledges that Filipinas have a long way to go in breaking the glass ceiling.

Google "Filipina" and most of the 3.77 million results are links to matchmaking, dating, and adult-entertainment sites.

"Initially, American men thought we were some mail-order-bride organization, and we would get requests to meet Filipina women," Mondejar says. In fact, she adds, "many mail-order-bride and matchmaking groups still link to our website and we would have to back-trace them and remove their links."

This was why FWN launched its "Shaping the Filipina image" campaign, which, she says, is just another step to create a positive image and open up leadership opportunities for Filipinas in the US.

100 Most Influential Pinays

During the Vegas gathering, Mondejar says she will push FWN's "womentoring" and leadership program, and the selection of the "100 Most Influential Filipinas in the US."

She hopes each of the 200 "most influential" Filipino women selected in 2007 and 2009 would take at least one Filipina under her wing and teach her what it takes to make it in the American workplace.

"Can you imagine?" she says rhetorically. "By 2012 (in time for a planned Pinay Power reunion) we'd have 600 more successful Filipinas after the final FWN 100 are selected next year?

To be sure, FWN faces many challenges. For one, "funding and keeping the FWN mission alive," she says.

But she draws her energy from FWN's members and what they have so far achieved. She still remembers the first summit in 2002 when she was selling the idea to a group of women in San Francisco. After her spiel, one of them stood up, saying: "I'm in. I want to be part of this group. I have never been in the same room with so many accomplished women. Here's my check!"

Then just about everybody else took out their checkbooks and signed up.

FWN: RISING

This photo essay celebrates the rise of the Filipina Women's Network (FWN). FWN has succeeded in elevating the status of Filipina women in the global environment. However, more work is needed from us to achieve gender equality.

2001: Launch of FWN

Marily Mondejar wrote a plan that identified the goals for the Filipina Women's Network (FWN). These goals included creating a professional identity for FWN, ensuring leadership succession, providing programs that meet the professional needs of the members; and creating a vision of the role of FWN in the Filipino community.

The first group of amazing Filipina women who helped "steer" and birthed FWN were: Anna Bantug, Anna Villena, Judy Nipay Gee, Laarni San Juan, Victoria Urbi and Marily Mondejar. Thereafter, the elected founding board members were: Anna Villena, Christina Macabenta Dunham, Dina Guingona, Elaine Serina, Katherine Zarate, Laarni San Juan, Marily Mondejar, Maya Ruiz and Thelma Estrada. The Steering Committee worked to incorporate in California as a not-for-profit professional association. The founding board members held a board retreat to articulate the strategic plan and sharpen the vision for FWN. Organizational coach, Kelsey Escoto facilitated the retreat at the vacation home of board member, Christina Macabenta Dunham.

FWN was committed to the use of technology and required member to have email accounts and to receive announcements via Yahoo Group and e-blasts. FWN utilized WebEx as the board's video meeting online platform and documents storage before "cloud" was even talked about.

2002: First Filipina Conference

The First Filipina Conference, now called the Filipina Leadership Summit was at the Moscone Convention Center in San Francisco and had a standing-room-only audience. The first ever Filipina Women CEO Forum showcased the three Filipina women who had broken Fortune 500 glass ceilings: Cora Tellez, President and CEO of HealthNet, Evelyn Dilsaver, President and CEO of Charles Schwab Investments, and Marissa Peterson, Executive Vice President, Worldwide Operations for Sun

Microsystems Inc. They were joined by Tessie Guillermo, CEO of Community Technology Foundation of California, a public foundation based on partnership of 134 community organizations and leaders from the merger of Pacific Bell and SBC Communications who were committed to the use of community technology for access, equity, and social justice for California's underserved communities. They were also joined by Mona Lisa Yuchengco, Publisher of Filipinas Magazine, the first glossy magazine to chronicle the Filipino community in the U.S. The conference evaluations indicated a need for more career-oriented sessions and the celebration of Filipina women who had succeeded in the corporate workplace.

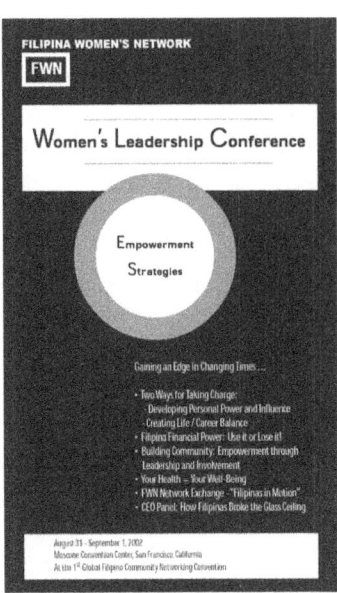

2002: FILIPINAS IN MOTION

FWN expanded its membership targeting Filipina women in multiple industries and professional fields in both the private and public sectors. "Filipinas in Motion" described the many roles of Filipina women. The name also suggested Filipina women were constantly growing, transforming, innovating, and changing themselves as they secured their place in the workforce. It celebrated Filipina women who shared stories, strategies, and passed on their insights to those needing inspiration. Filipinas in Motion is about "what it means to be a Filipina woman."

FWN hosted small discussion groups of Filipina women who shared similar experiences in their professional areas of expertise. Each group had a Discussion Leader who facilitated the flow of ideas and ensured participant sharing and empowerment. Topics covered career strategies and real-life stories of triumphs and struggles as well as best practices on how to "arrive, survive, and thrive" in the world of work.

2002: Professional Development Series

FWN's professional development philosophy is based on the Farren Associates 12 Life Areas of Empowerment. Participants complete the Life Empowerment Overview exercises that provides a practical foundation for career and life planning.

Mondejar offered this 12-week cycle workshop in 1998 and again in 2002 at the first Filipina Conference. The 12 Life Areas are:

Community	Participating, volunteering, helping others in the community
Economic Security	Managing personal resources, income, budgeting, savings, investments, insurance
Environment and Safety	Taking care of your physical surroundings, including recycling, pollution, and waste removal
Family	Caring for life partners, marriages, children, parents, extended family
Health and Well-Being	Mental, emotional and physical health, feeling good about yourself and others
Home and Shelter	Caring for and improving personal space, such as home, office, cars
Learning	Acquiring and applying new knowledge, skills, and abilities to different areas of life
Leisure	Diversifying interests and renewing energy through sports, hobbies, entertainment
Social Relationships	Getting along with all types of people, nurturing friends, making new acquaintances
Spirituality	Exploring the meaning of life through philosophy, religion, humor, the arts, nature
Transportation and Mobility	Moving from place to place to take care of needs as well as families and friends
Work and Career	Choosing a field, feeling satisfied, contributing to society, creating balance

2003: Launch of FWN's Iconic Logo

Christina Macabenta Dunham who was FWN's Board Vice President for Communications led the team that created the FWN logo. The logo represented energy, movement, and the modern Filipina woman. The FWN logo is a registered service mark. The FWN logo is circular in a mostly desaturated purple color with jagged edges and a central stylized character which represents "woman" in Alibata, also known as Baybayin, the Philippine ancient alphabet known as the Tagalog script. The traditional female symbol is styled as an inverted heart-shape with a curving cross and features inward spirals joining at bottom-center. The stylized character is an important design element because it was the symbol of a woman in the pre-Hispanic Philippine writing system and is believed to have been in use as early as the 14th century. The jagged soft edges represent Filipina women in motion, always redefining themselves, disrupting the status quo as they constantly re-invent themselves in their home and adopted countries.

2003: Shape the Filipina Image Campaign

The plan was to focus on the Filipina women's accomplishments, leadership positions, and economic contributions to the corporate world, the private sector, and the public sector. This campaign was driven when a Google search for the word "Filipina" yielded 3,770,000 results. Yahoo yielded 5,530,000. Ask.com yielded 565,800. These millions of search results listed hundreds of website links to dating, matchmaking, "exotic" and "submissive" girls, and personal ads for mail-order brides. These sites defined Filipina women on the web at that time. FWN wanted to change that.

2004: FWN Against Violence

Eve Ensler, the author of *The Vagina Monologues* convinced Marily Mondejar in 2004 to produce The Vagina Monologues. In March 2004, FWN premiered the first all-Filipina women cast production of The Vagina Monologues in collaboration with V-Day at a sold-out show at the Herbst Theatre in San Francisco. This was a signature event to celebrate Women's History Month.

This annual production became an important social justice campaign of the FWN after it was discovered that 40 percent of women murdered by their partners in San Francisco were Filipina women (1998 Homicide Survey, San Francisco District Attorney's Office). Part of FWN's mission is to raise awareness through theatre, popular culture, and education about the high incidence of violence in Asian homes and intimate partner relationships. FWN has sought to encourage Filipina women in abusive homes and relationships to take action and seek help.

What Mondejar thought was a simple play became FWN's Anti-Violence Awareness Campaign despite opposition from some of the Filipino American community because of the V-word.

In 2000, a 22-year old Filipina woman Claire Joyce Tempongko was stabbed multiple times by her ex-boyfriend in front of her two young children, ages five and ten years old. FWN was instrumental in bringing the man to justice. The Tempongko case was instrumental in the City of San Francisco's overhaul of its systemwide response to domestic violence. Mayor Willie Brown convened the Justice and Courage Oversight Committee to implement City Attorney Louise Renné's 12-point recommendations to improve the City's process in responding to domestic violence cases after the City was found liable for Tempongko's murder. Mondejar was appointed to the Oversight Committee. Tari Ramirez, Tempongko's murderer was apprehended in Mexico, extradited, convicted of second-degree murder, sentenced to 16 years to life in prison in 2008, overturned on appeal in 2009, and reached the California Supreme Court which confirmed the sentence of the San Francisco County Superior Court in 2010. The case was successfully prosecuted by then District Attorney Kamala Harris, now a US Senator. It took almost 10 years for justice to be served in Tempongko's murder.

FWN continues to present The Vagina Monologues as part of its annual anti-violence awareness campaign. FWN has taken the show to Filipino communities in New York, Washington DC, and Las

Vegas. The FWN Board has decided to include the production in its annual Filipina Leadership Summit first in Toronto, Canada in 2017 and then in London, U.K. in 2018. FWN has produced 35 productions of *The Vagina Monologues* with a cast of over 700 and reached an audience of thousands, raising almost $300,000 to benefit local domestic violence efforts. The campaign includes CourtWatch of cases involving Filipina women, anti-domestic violence workshops, and most recently the Comfort Women Justice Coalition that installed a memorial in San Francisco.

2005: V-DIARIES: ANTI-VIOLENCE RESOURCE GUIDE

The premiere issue of the *V-Diaries* was published in conjunction with the Filipina Women's Network's all-Filipina cast and crew production of Eve Ensler's *The Vagina Monologues, Usaping Puki,* its Filipino language version, and *A Memory, A Monologue, A Rant and A Prayer.* The *V-Diaries* includes information on how and where to look for shelters, counseling, legal restraining orders, and resources, including organizations for violence victims and survivors. It is also the Playbill of the TVM productions.

2005: FWN MAGAZINE

The Filipina Conference became the Filipina Leadership Summit. The Premiere issue of the FWN Magazine was published in conjunction with the 3rd Filipina Summit: Filipina First: Reinventing Ourselves featuring Evelyn Dilsaver, President and CEO of Charles Schwab Investments. The FWN Magazine is an annual publication that features the Most Influential Filipina Women in the World Awardees and serves as the souvenir program for the Filipina Leadership Summit.

2006: FUTURE SEARCH: FILIPINA POWER 2012

"Never again forget the role of Filipina women in the building of America."
- **Marily Mondejar** (2006)

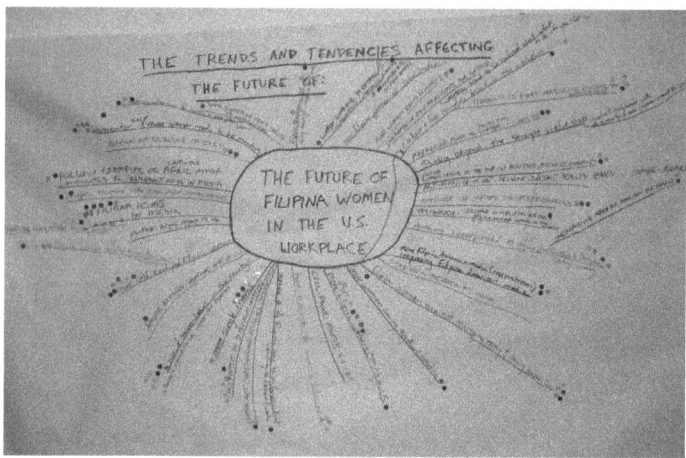

When the Filipino American community had a year-long celebration of the centennial of Filipino migration to the U.S., all the presentations and exhibitions featured the accomplishments of Filipino men. The contributions of Filipina women were not acknowledged. There was agreement that FWN was missing an important aspect of its work and decided to initiate a Future Search process for the 2006 Filipina Leadership Summit. In October 2006, FWN met for a Future Search Conference with one task: develop a plan on how to advance Filipina women in the U.S. workplace. Working through a carefully-designed format facilitated by future search experts, FWN noted strong reasons to build community, made commitments, and set a clear direction that will propel Filipina women to Pinay Power by 2012. FWN generated a comprehensive set of issues and opportunities, analyzed data, and articulated a common vision of how Filipina women should be perceived by the next generation. These action items set the groundwork for a collective understanding of where FWN has been, what was happening, and where FWN as an organization should go. From being San-Francisco-Bay-Area-centric, FWN wanted to know about fellow Filipina sisters and their contributions to communities in America. San Francisco Consul General Rowena Sanchez hosted the summit at the Philippine Consulate.

The major outcome of Future Search was the launch of FWN's nationwide search for the 100 Most Influential Filipina Women in the United States. The campaign was called Pinay Power 2012.

2006 December 4: Inspiration from Nicole

The Makati, Philippines Regional Trial Court found US serviceman Lance Corporal Daniel Smith guilty of rape against "Nicole" and the three other defendants were acquitted. The court sentenced Smith to *reclusion perpetua*. Mondejar attended the sentencing, along with the late Senator Letitia Shahani, Monique Wilson (Global FWN100™ 2014), Lisa Masa, and many other activists representing Gabriela and women's rights organizations.

"Nicole" sparked an international dialogue about women's rights, national sovereignty, and international law, as she steadfastly pursued justice against her rapists. Nicole is the inspiration for one of the award categories in the Most Influential Filipina Women in the World Award. FWN helped raise funds to support Justice for Nicole.

2007: Premiere of 100 Most Influential Filipina Women in the United States Awards

The 5th Filipina Leadership Summit featured the first 100 Most Influential Filipina Women in the United States Awards in Washington DC. The award showcased Filipina women who exemplified innovation, mentorship, professionalism, gender empowerment and leadership.

Lieutenant Colonel Shirley Saoit Raguindin of the Arizona National Guard, now Colonel of the US Air National Guard, indicated:

> Being honored as one of the 100 Most Influential Filipina Women in the United States had introduced me to a network of women who recognize your achievements and who want to help in any way they can to ensure that you remain a success. This award, and the recognition that comes with it, has really given me the urge to propel forward with more vigor than ever before.

2009 JANUARY: FILIPINA SALO SALO FEATURING THE *ADOBO* CRAWL

When the Great Recession in 2008 hit, many Filipino owned businesses struggled. FWN wanted to help and decided to bring their business meetings to the Filipino restaurants in the San Francisco Bay Area. The Great Recession was notably severe in several respects. GDP fell 4.3 percent. The unemployment rate, which was 5 percent in December 2007, rose to 9.5 percent in June 2009, and peaked at 10 percent in October 2009 (Rich, 2013).

FWN launched the Filipina Salo Salo with two goals: (1) celebrate Filipino heritage and cuisine in collaboration with 12 highly acclaimed restaurants; and (2) introduce Filipino food to the mainstream market. It was a year-round culinary adventure celebrating the many flavors, exotic ingredients, cultural and regional influences, as well as the cooking and dining traditions associated with Filipino food. Each featured restaurant highlighted its unique version of *adobo* as the main entree. The following year, we featured the *sabaw* [soup] as the main dish.

2009 JUNE 28: SHEROES MONOLOGUES: WOMEN OF THE PHILIPPINE REVOLUTION

To honor Philippine Independence Day at the FWN Salo Salo, Elena Mangahas, Gloria Ramos, Maya Ong Escudero, Sol Manaay, and Marily Mondejar wrote a unique Taglish performance featuring the women of the Philippine Revolution. The play was set in a typical living room of a Filipino home and based on the imagined conversation of women revolutionaries to end the Spanish colonial rule. The conversation was among the following women revolutionaries: Agueda Esteban, Agueda Kahabagan, Espiridiona Bonifacio, Gleceria Marella Villavicencio, Gregoria de Jesus Nakpil, Gregoria Montoyo, Hilaria Del Rosario-Aguinaldo, Marcela Marino Agoncillo, Melchora Aquino, Patrocinio Gamboa, Teodora Alonzo, Trinidad Perez Tecson.

2009 SEPTEMBER 12: NOTABLE FIRST

Ana "The Hurricane" Julaton, US FWN100™ 2009 became the first Filipina American to capture the IBA World Championship. This championship was captured and defended five times by the great Laila Ali, daughter of Muhammad Ali.

2009 November 4: Notable First

Mona Pasquil, US FWN100™ 2007 became the 47th and Acting Lieutenant Governor of California.

2011 January 3: Notable First

Chief Justice Tani Gorre Cantil-Sakauye, US FWN100™ 2007 was sworn in as the 28th Chief Justice of the State of California. She is the first Asian-Filipina American and the second woman to serve as the state's chief justice. Former Governor Arnold Schwarzenegger nominated her as Chief Justice in 2010 and in the general election in 2010, an overwhelming majority of voters elected her to the position.

*Mondejar representing the Filipina Women's Network testified at Chief Tani's confirmation hearing. Her testimony (and FWN's) is now in the audio, print and video history of the California Supreme Court.

2011 October 14: First Pinay Speed Femtoring @ the Filipina Summit

Pinay Speed Femtoring is an annual learning event during which femtees and protégés could ask the Global FWN100™ Awardees, also known as Femtors,

the "everything-you've-always-wanted-to-know-but-didn't-know-whom-to-ask" questions. Femtees have the opportunity to interact for over an hour with Femtors during the session by moving to different topic tables every 15 minutes.

New in 2011 was the "FWN Gives Back," the FWN way of giving back to the host country for the summit. This program is integral to FWN's FemtorMatch™, our campaign to increase FWN's talent pipeline and the active development of the next generation of leaders. This session is now part of the FWN Leadership Summit.

2012 DECEMBER 13: NOTABLE FIRST

Judge Lorna Schofield, Global FWN100™ 2015 is the first Filipino American in the history of the United States to serve as an Article III federal judge. She was nominated by President Obama in 2012 to serve as a United States District Judge for the United States District Court for the Southern District of New York. The Senate confirmed Schofield on December 13, 2012 by a 91-0 vote.

2013 OCTOBER 24: FWN GOES GLOBAL

FWN premiered the 100 Most Influential Filipina Women in the World Awards to reach out to the sisters in the diaspora and to Filipinas in the Philippines with global competence. The board voted to convene the annual Filipina Leadership Global Summit at various geographic locations: 2014 (Manila

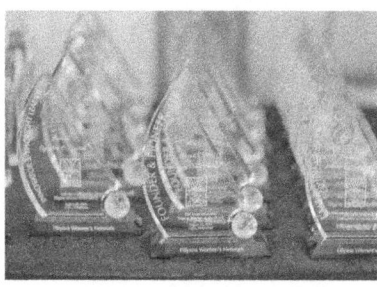

Philippines), 2015 (San Francisco), 2016 (Cebu, Philippines), 2017 (Toronto, Canada), 2018 (London, United Kingdom), 2019 (Dubai, United Arab Emirates), and 2020 (Washington, DC, US) for the Pinay Power 2020 Reunion of all the Most Influential Filipina Women in the United States and the World.

FEMTORMATCH LAUNCHED AT THE FILIPINA LEADERSHIP SUMMIT

FEMtorMatch™ is the FWN's program for developing the next generation of Filipina leaders through local and global partnerships between female mentors, FEMtors™, and female mentees, FEMtees™. FEMtorMatch™ provides structured one-on-one mentoring that harnesses the power of the Internet to broaden and deepen the reach of traditional mentoring anywhere in the world.

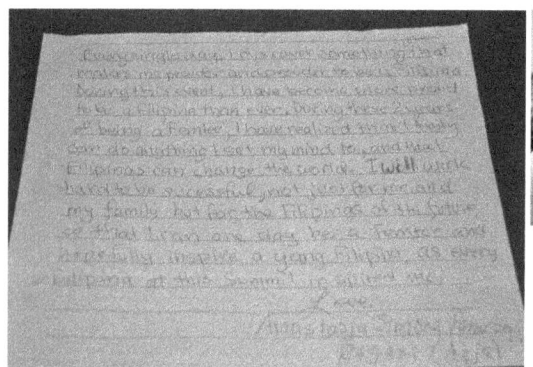

2013 FEBRUARY 14: V-DAY ONE BILLION RISING

FWN CEO Marily Mondejar was the executive producer of the first V-Day One Billion Rising dance protest held in front of the San Francisco City Hall. The event was attended by San Francisco Mayor Ed Lee, Board of Supervisors, all branches of city and national government, and over 4,000 women, girls, men and boys.

2014 OCTOBER 5-8: FWN GOES HOME TO THE PHILIPPINES!

For the first time in FWN's history, the annual summit was convened outside of the United States in Makati, Philippines.

The FWN Filipina Leadership Book Series was also launched to fill the gap in the leadership literature about the leadership competencies of women of Philippine ancestry. This is a ground-breaking series that documents the leadership stories of Filipina women who have become successful after overcoming serious disruptions, including migration. These disruptions shaped their world view, leader identity, life purpose, power, and influence. The book series is key to FWN's strategy of building a pipeline of qualified leaders that some will rise to fill leadership positions in all sectors of the economy.

2014 OCTOBER 5: DISRUPT. FILIPINA WOMEN: PROUD. LOUD. LEADING WITHOUT A DOUBT.

35 authors from 9 countries. 582 pages
Launched in Makati, Philippines

2015 OCTOBER 29-NOVEMBER 1: FACE OF GLOBAL PINAY POWER

Francine Maigue, Global FWN100™ 2015, became the Face of Global Pinay Power 2015 at the Filipina Leadership Summit in San Francisco.

2016 AUGUST: INFLUENCE. ACCELERATE. ACTION

The 2016 Filipina Leadership Global Summit was convened in Cebu, Philippines and chaired by Myrna Yao. The 2016 FWN Magazine cover women are Ace Itchon and Myrna Yao, both from the Philippines.

2016 AUGUST 22: DISRUPT 2.0. FILIPINA WOMEN: DARING TO LEAD.

35 authors from 5 countries. 497 pages
Launched at the University of San Carlos in Cebu and at the Asian Institute of Management, Makati, Philippines.

Global DISRUPTing Events

2014	October 07	DISRUPTing Manila
	November 03	DISRUPTing San Francisco
	November 23	DISRUPTing Las Vegas
	December 14	DISRUPTing Hollywood
2015	April 17	DISRUPTing Singapore
	June 12	DISRUPTing Las Vegas
	June 21	DISRUPTing Japan
	June 27	DISRUPTing Washington DC
	October	DISRUPTing Portland
2016	June 17	DISRUPTing Los Angeles
	August 22	DISRUPTing Cebu
	October 06	DISRUPTing San Francisco
	October 13	DISRUPTing San Diego
	December 10	DISRUPTing Beverly Hills
2017	January 07	DISRUPTing San Jose-Silicon Valley
	March 26	DISRUPTing Toronto
	March 28	DISRUPTing New York
	March 29	DISRUPTing Washington DC
	April 12	DISRUPTing Portland
	July 27	DISRUPTing Vancouver
2018	February 08	DISRUPTing Oxford

2017 September 22:
"Comfort Women" Column of Strength *(Bronze, Steel © 2017)*

The girl in the bandanna represents Filipina comfort women who were conscripted as young as 12 years old.

"Our worst fear is that our painful history during World War II will be forgotten."
- Comfort Woman survivor

The Comfort Women in the Philippines, young girls who were conscripted as sex slaves of the Japanese Imperial Army during World War II, is an important part of our women's history, raping women as weapons of war. In 2006, Eve Ensler wrote a powerful monologue to honor the comfort women survivors in the Philippines. The "Say It" monologue is in keeping Eve Ensler's promise to write about their painful story when she met the Filipina comfort women survivors in 2002. FWN includes this eloquent poem in its annual production of *The Vagina Monologues*.

In 2016, the Comfort Women Justice Coalition comprised of Chinese, Korean and Filipino women leaders came together to install a Comfort Women Memorial in St. Mary's Square in San Francisco. It was a difficult year-long process with hundreds of protests from the Japanese government and the Japanese American community obstructing its approval. It almost divided the Asian women leaders community. We prevailed. The memorial was unveiled on September 22, 2017. Special kudos to the coalition's co-chairs, Judge Lillian Sing and Judge Julie Tang.

2017 OCTOBER 25-29: FWN CONVENES FILIPINA SUMMIT IN TORONTO, CANADA!

Rowena Romulo, Global FWN100™ 2017 was selected Face of Global Pinay Power for 2017.

FWN Against Violence: The Vagina Monologues premiered outside of the United States.

The initial Power Meetup was launched with Amazing Filipina and Canadian Women Professionals. The 2017 FWN magazine cover women are Councillor Cynthia Barker (London, UK) and SBMA Chair snd Administrator Wilma 'Amy' Eisma (Subic, Philippines).

2018 AUGUST 15-30:
#FWN15CELEBRATION OF SUSTAINABLE DEVELOPMENT GOALS

#FWN15Celebration honors the significance, success, and relevance of what FWN members are doing to achieve the UN Sustainable Development Goals (SDG). The objectives of the #FWN15Celebration are to inspire others to take the lead and to create collective impact.

2018 SEPTEMBER 12-16:
FWN CONVENES FILIPINA SUMMIT IN LONDON, ENGLAND!

FWN Against Violence: The Vagina Monologues premieres in Europe.
Women Who ROCK: Power Meetup London with Filipina and British Women Professionals

2018 SEPTEMBER 13:
DISRUPT 3.0. FILIPINA WOMEN: RISING

38 authors from 9 countries. 479 pages
Launch 13 September 2018, UK Parliament, London, UK

FWN continues to re-invent itself to adapt to the changes in the global workplace, respond to the economic and political trends, and address the needs of Filipina women in the global environment.

SUSIE QUESADA

President, Ramar Foods International, USA
GLOBAL FWN100™ 2007

Sisterhood, Dialogue, and Impact

I always felt different growing up. I grew up in a mostly white American suburb in Northern California where I was only one of a handful of Asians at school. 99.9 percent of my teachers and coaches were white. In my seventh grade Spanish class, the teacher spoke to me in Spanish because of my last name and I was mortified because I did not understand Spanish. My name was different, my food was different, and my parents were different. I was made fun of for eating with a fork and spoon. I did not know my parents had an accent until a friend of mine mentioned it in middle school. I had a crush on the only Filipino boy at school in seventh grade. I was too nervous to get to know him, but I felt like if I did, we would have had a lot in common. Having things in common with others is what most kids are looking for as they grow up. They want to be accepted and have successful role models that look like them. Do not get me wrong. I had great friendships growing up. Friendships that endure even today but I knew I was very different from the other kids.

As I continued to navigate the world as a young adult, my parents instilled a strong sense of culture in me. Not only did my mom cook Filipino food six days out of seven but also we were lucky enough to go home to visit family in Manila every year. They were involved in the Filipino Community having pioneered one of the first and largest Filipino food manufacturing companies in the US. They sold *ube* ice cream, *lumpia,* and *longanisa* to the growing Filipino population, the second largest Asian population in the U.S.. They put up booths at local festivals organized by Filipino organizations. I started scooping ice cream at these events when I was 12 years old. Like a true family business, I worked at Ramar Foods on the weekends doing demos at Asian stores and during my summer breaks in the office or in production. My mom was also very involved in the University of the Philippines Alumni Association Berkeley Chapter and served on the board for many years. This organization was a way to network with other Filipino families in the area with a mission of giving Filipinos a voice in the greater American culture. As a kid, my mom always brought my brothers and me to help set up and take down their events. It was so nice to grow up around other Filipino families and their kids through my parents' involvement in the community. This had a big impact on me and my quest for helping other Filipinos not feel so different but rather to feel supported.

When I entered the workforce as an educator, I sought Filipino student populations. I wanted to make an impact on young Filipinos and be someone they could learn from and emulate as they navigated the world. I wanted every Filipino to have a broader circle of Filipinos in addition to family members and parents' friends. I taught Middle School in San Lorenzo which was not a high paying district, but it had the growing Filipino population I was looking for. I started the Diversity Club my first year teaching with a core group of Filipino kids who were in my classes. We planned the Multicultural Potluck Dinner every year complete with cultural entertainment and *lumpia*. When I started working for my parents at Ramar I saw the need to continue this personal mission as the kids of many of our Filipino employees were looking for guidance.

Sisterhood

In 2007, my aunt, Elena Mangahas, invited me to a Power Lunch hosted by the Filipina Women's Network, an organization she was active in based in San Francisco. On the panel was Nana Luz, an entrepreneur in the consulting space and Hydra Mendoza, President of the San Francisco Board of Education. Both of their stories were especially inspiring and encouraging as I had just shifted from teaching into my new role as Marketing Manager at Ramar Foods. By the end of the panel, I had met dozens of amazing Filipinas; women like me who were navigating the American work culture and pushing the glass ceiling further and further up. These women lit a fire under me.

We had an immediate natural sisterhood. We were in different careers and different industries yet we had much in common. We all wanted to reshape the Filipina Image, support our fellow Filipinas, and give back to the community.

That fall I was awarded the Most Influential Award in Washington, DC for my Behind the Scenes work as the Marketing Manager for Ramar Foods International. I shared a room in Washington, DC with two other women for my the very first FWN Summit. Again I was excited by the topics of the Summit that included STEM, Health Care, Public Policy, Leadership, Women in the Workplace, and Anti-Violence against women and girls.

The FWN considered critical issues for the Filipino Community and society as a whole. The panelists were the awardees themselves, so we were able to learn from each other and cultivate a camaraderie during the three-day conference. We toured the Capitol building. We shared our experiences. We shared our stories. It was a unique gathering and because of this incredible experience, I have not missed a Summit. From San Francisco to Berkeley to Las Vegas, I have attended every Summit and continued to meet more amazing Filipinas from all over the world.

In the beginning, I supported FWN with in-kind sponsorships. One of my favorite events was the All Filipina cast of the Vagina Monologues. I would provide the food for the cast and crew in the green room. The atmosphere was energetic. It was fascinating to watch the volunteer staff and cast come together and put together such a powerful performance. It was not until FWN that I realized that Eve Ensler and her play was not only entertaining but brought awareness to violence against girls all over the world. FWN issued the *Anti-Violence Resource Guide*, called the *V-Diaries* that included resources access to resources in the community. We would deliver these *Resource Guides* to the Filipino and Asian stores that were our customers. I educated my then mostly male sales team to ask the store owners if they would support this significant cause by distributing this resource to their customers and communities.

Back then, FWN was a US based organization founded by Marily Mondejar, and a majority of our members were in Northern California. Member engagement was high. In 2009 we started the *Salo-Salo Adobo* Crawl and gathered once a month. The *Adobo Crawl* gave us a reason to network with each other and to learn about topics that were relevant to the community. We were also supporting a local Filipino restaurant that cooked their version of *adobo* on slow weekday nights and thus promote their business. Some of the topics for meetings included joining boards and commissions or mentoring (what we have now re-labeled as FEMtoring) young Filipinas. The board at that time wrote the She-roes Monologues which was similar to Eve Ensler's format; it was a series of monologues by famous or not so famous Filipinas who contributed to the history of the Philippines. Each gathering was full of active dialogue on real issues and how we could solve them. It was so successful and had such a great turn out we did the *Sabaw* Crawl the following year and showcased traditional soups with a whole new set of topics. This helped engage our San Francisco Bay Area-based members. Our members from around the US wanted to have similar events in areas that also had a high concentration of members.

When Marily asked me to be on the board in 2010, I gladly accepted. What better way to give back than to donate my time. Besides as an awardee I pledged to Femtor a young Filipina and support the FWN Mission. With a voice on the board, I could help influence this organization to make an even greater impact. In 2011, we brought back the Power Lunch Series with new topics that centered around Filipina Voices. In 2012, we did an all Tagalog version of Vagina Monologues. In 2013, we joined V-Day San Francisco on Valentine's Day with a flash mob for One Billion Rising. We also started a Professional Tuesday's series to support our members' aspirations and life goals. Most of these events were based in the San Francisco Bay Area. I was always asking myself how to engage members in other parts of the US.

FWN is a sisterhood. At every Leadership Summit, we go through a transformation together. Since I have been active with FWN, we have been to Washington DC, Las Vegas, Berkeley, San Francisco, Manila, Cebu, and Toronto. We learn about the Filipino community in the communities where we hold the summit. We have learned from each other, about each other's industries, countries, issues, and concerns. I could travel in a handful of states in the US for work and reach out to my FWN sisters and connect. When we went global in 2013, the sisterhood expanded to 28 countries.

We also launched FEMtorMatch, a program that connects Filipina Mentees or FEMtees to our Awardees for a long-term FEMtorship. This program has helped dozens of young Filipinas as they navigate their careers all over the world.

Dialogue

At the FWN Summits, we have dialogue about issues that are relevant for our members. Some of my favorite panels include Make Me a Filipina CEO, Speed Pinay Femtoring, Make Me a Filipina Entrepreneur, and STEAM (Science, Technology, Engineering, Arts, Music.) These dialogues have evolved into projects in different countries. In Toronto in 2017 we kickstarted these projects. We keep the FWN Global sisterhood connected via Viber, Whatsapp, Instagram, and Facebook. We recently added a panel on the United Nations Sustainable Development Goals that led us to our 15 Year Anniversary Project. This year the Summit turns 15! So, we are celebrating this milestone by asking all of our members to share how their company or organization is supporting any of the 17 sustainable development goals. This weeklong event will take place all around the world prior to the Summit where our members will hold local events highlighting how their organizations are involved in addressing the 17 sustainable development goals.

IMPACT

In 2014, FWN published its first Leadership book, *Disrupt. Filipina Women: Loud, Proud and Leading without a Doubt*. It was a way to share the stories of our members and inspire others. Thirty-five authors shared their stories. Authors sponsored book readings all over the world and worked with other community leaders. In 2016, we published our second Leadership book, *Disrupt 2.0. Filipina Women: Daring to Lead*. Thirty-five more members shared their stores, and we launched the book at the University of Cebu and at the Asian Institute of Management in the Philippines. More book readings for both books ensued. And now we have *Disrupt 3.0. Filipina Women: Rising*. The dedication and commitment of our Editor Maria Beebe is amazing. To put out three books in four years is no small feat. The books are an important part of FWN's FEMtoring initiative.

We have the sisterhood and we have the dialogue so what is our impact? In 2015, we started the *FWN Impact Report*. This tracks the number of women we have FEMtored, the number of Anti Violence Resource guides we have printed, and the number of Filipinas we have engaged.

My goal as President of FWN is to ensure that the dialogue to continue so we can fulfill our 2020 mission: A Filipina Leader in every industry across all sectors and make the biggest Impact as possible. To do this we need to keep our members worldwide engaged and this has become easier with social media. However, social media cannot replace face to face networking. The energy that our members create when we gather is a force to be reckoned with. I believe Chapters are the way to fulfill this mission and keep our members engaged all over the world.

FWN is not immune to challenges. Like many organizations we are constantly exploring ways to engage our members and find sponsors, especially now that we are global. We need to keep the flame growing and impact our community as much as we can. We are currently working with our members in the Los Angeles area to pilot our first Chapter and we have interest to start local chapters in Orange County, San Diego, Toronto, Dubai, and Manila. Through local Chapters our members can continue to meet through programs like the *Adobo Crawl* or Power Lunch and thus find more Influential Filipinas who can become Femtors for the next generation. Through local Chapters we could have a greater presence in more cities and show our communities that Filipina women are involved in their communities. Through local Chapters we could network more often than just once a year. Instead of waiting for the Summit every year, we would engage members year-round. Through local Chapters we can support policy changes as an organization in multiple cities instead of being San Francisco centric. Through local Chapters we could have a Boards and Commissions event annually to increase the number of Filipinas on important community or corporate boards or commissions. We would keep the energy flowing year-round and this would increase our **Sisterhood**, our **Dialogue**, and our **Impact**.

For me, FWN is about the sisterhood, the dialogue and the impact. I longed for this sisterhood while growing up Filipina in America. I am happy to be part of an organization that continues to discuss how we as Filipinas can together impact the world. I ask you to support me in my last year as FWN President to launch these Chapters globally. By dedicating your time and commitment, together we can support the FWN Mission for 2020 and sustain the impact of FWN for the next 15 years.

GEORGITTA 'BENG' PIMENTEL PUYAT

Chairman, Philippine Orchard Corporation
Filipina Women's Network, Board Member (2018-2021)
Global FWN100™ 2017

Rising to the FWN Challenge

Amelia Earhart: Aviator, Author, Women's Advocate, and Member of Zonta International, once said, "The most difficult thing is the decision to act, the rest is merely tenacity. The fears are paper tigers. You can do anything you decide to do. You can act to change and control your life; and the procedure, the process is its own reward."

When I was first asked to accept a nomination for the "100 Most Influential Filipina Woman in the World Award™, I had to decline because I had too much on my plate. My work with the family business and with my Zonta club gave me little time for myself. When I was asked again, I felt I was not worthy of being included with such lofty company. In fact, I felt weary and wanted to go somewhere to de-stress. It was only after I was asked for a third time that I accepted the nomination. And later, I accepted to serve on the FWN Board.

Leadership in Volunteerism: Pitfalls and Success

In addition to my being Chair of the Philippine Orchard Corporation, I have served as a volunteer for the Sigma Delta Phi Alumnae Association, Inc. (SDPAA), SDP Outreach Trust Fund Inc., (OTFI), the Philippine Philharmonic Orchestra Society

Inc., (PPOSI), the UNIFEM Philippine National Committee (now UN Women), and Zonta International (ZI) for more than 32 years. I discussed my involvement with these organizations in Chapter 29. Volunteerism: A Life's Journey of this book.

My volunteer work was the driving force in my life but drew reactions from cynical friends and detractors who thought I was doing this work for an ulterior motive. Less altruistic minds can see volunteer work as a way to gain a better position in a socio-civic organization, or worse, as a way to enter Philippines politics. Allow me to relate some of the hurdles I have experienced in my volunteer work.

I have learned over time that you cannot expect cooperation from everybody. Every person has their own agenda that reflects their character and their motivations. It is unfortunate that some people are more malicious than others when it comes to meeting their goals. I have been hurt by people who I thought shared my best intentions at heart. Sometimes it has been greed and jealousy that lead to hurtful betrayals. Though it bewilders me why some people would invest time and energy to destroy another person's integrity, it is painful when anyone believes in the lies and the innuendoes being spread. In my personal experience, the more you resist the harpies, the more vicious they become in discrediting you and forcing you to become a pariah. I believe that you should defend yourself whenever possible but there are moments when you have to stay quiet. Eventually your defenders will take up your cause and spread the truth without you having to ask for it. The truth will always come out although it may take time, for an issue to be corrected. Your perseverance, patience, understanding, and humility will overcome all challenges.

Another problem that may come, especially in socio-civic organizations, is politicking. Politicking is defined as trying to persuade others to support a particular party or candidate by any means. In a perfect world, the process of elections would always be fair and untainted by politicking. However, when an agenda is being pushed by certain people for power no matter what the cost, their skullduggery knows no bounds. I have been the victim of politicking and each time was more heartbreaking than the last. I think I would have given up if it had not been for the support of my friends who believed in me. It is even more devastating because I do not seek positions for prestige, but because I feel it is the right thing to do. If there is a lesson to be learned from all the ugly politics, it may be part of God's plan for me to evolve into a better person. Some storms come to clear our path.

Challenges are a fact of life and we either overcome them or not. It is our response that builds us as capable and responsible people. We learn and grow from challenges, much like the seed that draws water and nutrients from the soil in order to become a beautiful tree. Eventually, all these lessons will build within us experiences that can prepare us for the future.

Despite adversities in volunteerism, it is the positive outcome and people-level impact that have kept me going. For example, when I was Governor of District 17 of Zonta International, we garnered all of the ZI Awards offered annually during my biennium term.

- The Young Women in Public Affairs Award- to encourage young women, ages 16-19, who demonstrate superior leadership skills and a commitment to public service and civic causes to continue their participation in public and political life.

- The Jane M. Klausman Women in Business Scholarship- to encourage more women to pursue education and careers in business.

- The Amelia Earhart Fellowship- Named in honor of Zonta's most illustrious member, this Fellowship is awarded annually to women pursuing Ph.D./Doctoral degrees in aerospace-related sciences or aerospace-related engineering around the globe.

- The Emma Conlon Service Awards- for Z/ Golden Z Clubs whose projects and programs best express the ideals of Zonta International to empower women through local and international service and advocacy.

Conductor at the Helm: Joy and Expectations

If I were to describe my style of leadership, it would be very much like a seasoned conductor at the helm of an orchestra. It is only with the common goal and cooperation of the musicians that a performance can be harmonious. Proper attention and due diligence to the work is key as well as giving them room to grow creatively. That and the occasional fellowship among members filled with singing, dancing, and merrymaking.

I had a limited understanding of what being part of the FWN really meant. At the Welcome Reception, I was both surprised and warmed by the enthusiasm of the members. This experience was different than the meetings that I was used to because I was dealing with other accomplished Filipina women, most of whom I had never met before. It was refreshing to meet these women from all over the world with a common heritage that binds us. I grew to appreciate the FWN by getting to know the members, attending the seminars, the learning journeys, and immersing myself in the culture of the organization. Despite the jetlag I was feeling, I powered through and gained much from this experience.

When I was presented in 2017 the FWN100™ Most Influential Filipina Woman in the World Award: Innovator and Thought Leader Category, I was overwhelmed, since I was not used to being recognized for my work. Volunteerism demands selflessness so this was something new. When asked to respond in ten words at my acceptance of the award, I said, "What truly matters in life is the joy of giving and serving others."

As I basked in the feelings of appreciation and joy, I thought of the life journey that got me to this point. I thought of all the service and advocacy projects that have helped hundreds of women and girls. The tough times and the good were all amazing experiences that shaped me as a person. The celebration that night was a validation that what we do is worthwhile and a reminder that the work we do is indeed great.

In hindsight, I believe that I made the right decision to serve in the FWN Board. Many of the qualities I value in a socio-civic organization are inherent in the FWN, such as the focus on the Success of the (Filipina) Woman in male dominated and gender biased areas and industries, Women supporting other Women on their own endeavors, and recognizing their own achievements and merits. The vision and goals of FWN are admirable in which it seeks to place Filipina Women in the Diaspora beyond the glass ceiling and become leaders in every sector of a working economy. As a member of the Board, I am hopeful that my many years of experience will be to the benefit of FWN and that I can share my knowledge with FWN members, whether they are established or new to the organization. In return, I hope to listen and learn from our collective membership in all its diverse and interesting facets.

I was reminded of a quote by Winston Churchill that I think sums up what my life in volunteerism is like, as well as my near future with FWN, "We make a living by what we get; but we make a life by what we give."

Developing Leadership

LEAH L. LAXAMANA

Liminalist
GLOBAL FWN100™ 2017

Journey to Being Present: Making Friends with Fear and Uncertainty

"I am brave...I do things even when I'm scared. I realize, though, that there aren't a lot of things I'm scared of anymore."
- **Leah L. Laxamana**, Author journal entry, 5/2/15

It was May 2014, and I found myself in month nine of unemployment following graduate school. I only had one job option at the time, and while the role was exciting and purpose-driven, it would have also meant having to take the fourth pay cut in my career. I was at the crossroads of getting to do meaningful work and urgently needing income, but ultimately, I knew I literally could not afford that job. I had no choice but to decline the offer even though it broke my heart.

Fast forward to a few weeks later when I ended up getting a dream job at Twitter doing social impact work. This was going to be a three-month assignment, but I was eventually hired full-time and even got to help craft my position description. Through this work, I connected with San Francisco like never before, met and collaborated with some of the smartest and passionate people I have ever known, and stretched my abilities beyond my imagination. I also got paid at the level I needed.

This journey from unemployed-and-worried to employed-and-thriving taught me two major lessons that could be helpful for anyone who has had limited practice in self-advocacy during a job search. First, it's important to acknowledge and be clear about our own needs and the minimum of what we want from a role, including pay. We should not feel guilty about taking care of ourselves before trying to help others. It's also critical to have the salary conversation sooner in the hiring process no matter how uncomfortable. Second, we have to be equally empowered about choosing our employers and not merely wait to be chosen. We need to see the job interview as an opportunity to assess who is hiring. This felt odd to me at first but eventually became liberating. Alignment is key, and instead of feeling deflated when prospects do not work out, I learned this simply means we are meant for something else. Before Twitter hired me, the recruitment process at other organizations I applied for was drawn out, and they made applicants jump through hoops, whereas with Twitter, all it took was a few earnest conversations and I had an offer seven days after the initial interview. I knew then that I had found a place that recognized what I could bring. Life was good.

Ironically, I would leave this job almost four years later. After careful reflection, I knew it was simply time to move on, and I could not go against my instincts. Soon after I left, I went back to Honduras to reconnect with the community where I served with the Peace Corps. I also traveled for a couple of months in the Philippines to finally get to know the country I grew up in, as well as, to spend quality time with my relatives and aging parents. Since returning to San Francisco, I intentionally became a tourist-in-my-backyard by exploring places I did not yet know in what had been my home for 17 years. I have also immersed myself in community work in the Tenderloin neighborhood, reconnected with people whom I have admired, and focused on activities that uplifted my spirit. And in between all of this, I have been continuously contemplating on where the world wants me to make an impact next. This period became my inadvertent, yet glorious, sabbatical, and created the space for me to review my professional life and to allow the next steps to unfold organically.

My Career Path: When the Journey is the Destination

> "For, in the end, it is impossible to have a great life unless it is a meaningful life. And it is very difficult to have a meaningful life without meaningful work."
>
> - Jim Collins

I did not think about college until it was time to apply and picked my course based on location and what sounded the most exciting to me — Social Sciences! I had no idea then about career development nor had professional role models to emulate, so it was not a surprise that I took the first job I could get right out of college. Until I gained more experience and access to career resources, most of my decision-making processes were based on gut call.

Here is the overview of my journey as a professional: My first ever employer was *(1) Pegasus*, an aircraft leasing company, where I developed my super administrative skills and a knack for doing a little bit of everything. Four years later, I went to *(2) The Natural Step*, an organization advocating for sustainable practices and gained my exposure to advocacy and nonprofit administration. Sadly, this organization closed down not long after I joined but after a temporary job, I was hired full-time by *(3) Korn/Ferry*, an executive recruitment firm. There, I refined my multi-tasking skills and ability to maintain grace under pressure. A year later, the call to do social impact work became stronger than ever, so I joined the *(4) Peace Corps* and served in Honduras, where I was awakened to my love for connecting with people and community development. When I returned to the U.S. in 2008, I had limited options due to the recession, and I ended up back at executive search firms working with *(5) m/Oppenheim Associates* and *Korn/Ferry*. This second round in the field further developed my ability to balance simultaneous projects and personalities delicately. While at Korn/Ferry, I became a part-time fellow with the *(6) Filipina Women's Network (FWN)* for a year, where my appreciation for my heritage and women's empowerment continued to strengthen. I then pursued my long-term goal of getting a graduate degree and ended up in New York to be part of the *(7) National Urban Fellows* (NUF) program. As part of the leadership development component, I was selected by the *Robert Wood Johnson Foundation* (RWJF) to launch its global health initiative; this opened my horizons to new possibilities and the strengths that I did not know I have. These attributes would later serve me well during the almost one year of unemployment that followed. The light at the end of the tunnel was when *(8) Twitter* hired me to help build on its philanthropic work. I even had the honor of creating a technology learning center for the community. During my first year at Twitter, I also held a second job at *(9) Target* as a contracted community resource specialist so I could make up for the lost income while I was unemployed. On November 2017, I left Twitter to start a new career chapter.

Whew, right? While this path at first felt all over the place, each experience built on the prior one and in the long run gave me an incredible cross-sector expertise eventually allowing me to adapt to, be effective with, and bridge diverse people and environments. I gained valuable insights from every field I was in and fostered positive relationships that helped shape my future path. However, every "*it all turned out great eventually*" experience was preceded with major bumps.

Growing, not Failing

"If you fall down, who cares? Just keep moving."

- **Mestra Márcia Treidler**, capoeira teacher

I rarely think of setbacks as failures, but rather, as opportunities to pause before finding a way forward using the same challenges as fuel to aim higher and be more courageous. Following are three epic lows in my professional life; at the time they happened, I felt like I was being gutted, but they ended up taking away a lot of my fear and turned into some of my best life lessons.

Almost a Dream Job

I left my corporate job of four years to pursue my long-term hope of working with a mission-driven organization only to be laid off not even a year into the role when the not-for-profit dissolved. This experience taught me that true leaders are the people who show up especially in the hardest times; the ones who maintain their composure and persevere to shepherd others through the finish line. I also witnessed there how regular staff members were the ones who stepped up and went over and beyond their call of duty. *Virtues cultivated: integrity and selflessness.*

Back to Dreaming, Part 2

Dream jobs do happen, and that is what I felt when I joined the Peace Corps and had my most exciting and transformative role yet. When I finished my service and returned to the U.S. in 2008 eager to continue doing social impact work, the recession had other ideas for me. I ended up going back to corporate roles, and even though the detour frustrated me at first, it eventually worked in my favor. Not only did it allow me to pay off a school loan and save money, but I also experienced an indirect leadership development training from my constant exposure to executives and the world of talent management. I was also able to keep my ties to the community by being a fellow with FWN, that I did part-time in conjunction with my role at Korn/Ferry. This would not have been possible without incredibly supportive managers. It was an experience that crystalized what it meant to have managers who not only treated me as an equal but championed me and allowed me to spread my wings. *Virtues cultivated: flexibility and empowerment.*

Back to Dreaming, Part 3

After graduate school and an exciting assignment with RWJF, I was unemployed for almost a year as I held out for a community-oriented role that could make my heart sing. The more time passed and as my bank account dried out, the more challenging it became to balance ambition with practical needs. Thankfully, the combination of my best friend letting me crash on her couch (for a year!), food stamps and contract work sustained me, and I eventually did get the job at Twitter. I am grateful I stayed focused on what I wanted and that my steadfast efforts to plant seeds and build relationships over the years bore fruit at the right moment. *Virtues cultivated: perseverance, initiative, and faith.*

Life's toughest moments can also be the greatest teachers. Through these experiences, I have developed a greater tolerance for ambiguity and learned not to take road bumps as personal nor allow them to be a trigger for self-doubt. I have also come to embrace the nonlinear path, and to be fully present to wherever I am and what it has to offer. I now have less fear of things not turning out as planned and greater trust that as long as I put in the hard work and treat people well, everything will work out. I have also become more proactive, resourceful, and diligent in finding and creating opportunities for myself instead of simply having dreams and waiting for them to fall into my lap. This has not been a solitary effort, and I am beyond blessed to have my own village of supporters and role models.

FINDING MYSELF, HONORING MY LEADERSHIP INFLUENCES AND PAYING IT FORWARD

> "You can do anything without batting an eyelash."
> - **Brenda Abille**, third-grade teacher

> "She has not only influenced me, but is helping to guide me to the person I aspire to become."
> - **Alex Palma**, my niece (writing about me on her college essay)

I once heard that success is personal and I could not agree more. What that looks like in my life has been guided by my purpose to love, serve, and dance. One of my biggest gifts to myself was to take the time to reflect on what motivates and fulfills me. Thanks to a long history of journaling since I was in the 5th grade, I was able to see the common thread of my hopes and the three themes that brought me the most joy: (1) *To love* — to see the best in everyone and all circumstances and to have a passion for all I do. (2) *To serve* — to be present for those who are hurting, whether the most marginalized or those in my immediate circle who simply need compassion and encouragement. (3) *To dance* — to move as a form of self-expression and to live life graciously, always striding gracefully through challenges and adversities.

How my purpose is manifested in my life constantly evolves. My aspirations for my vocation is to fully use my talents to impact the world positively and to grow continuously along the way. I welcome increased responsibilities and accolades that may result from my efforts, but they are not my driver. My purpose statement 'to love, serve, and dance' serves as my North Star guiding how I invest my full self and also anchoring me without restricting how I live out my calling.

It took a while for me to define leadership in a way that really resonated with me, but I have settled with: *the practice of bringing out the best in others, daring them to be more than they think possible, and paving the path for them*. I realized much later in life that my first real experience of being empowered was when my third-grade teacher told me with absolute conviction that I could do anything. This felt strange at the time as I was raised in a home with mostly old school elders who were more providers and authority figures than sources of positive reinforcement. I never sought out leadership positions while growing up but organically assumed them as happenstance, usually when peers and colleagues called for me to step up. In hindsight, others seem to have recognized my abilities, dependability, and how I gave my all into my work, way before I did.

In summary, my leadership journey started to unfold when my third-grade teacher planted the seed of self-confidence in me and was cultivated by school activities. My journey continued with jobs and my fellowships with FWN and NUF, experiences that transferred me to larger and larger roles and eventually, my work with the Peace Corps, RWJF and Twitter allowed me to flourish. Each career phase had many influences that contributed to my formation. Some of the key lessons I gained that others may find helpful include:

1. **Be curious and committed to growth.** I was exposed to diverse sources, models, and examples of leadership that shaped my development and introduced me to best practices. I have also cultivated over the years a support system made up of formal and informal relationships with femtors/mentors, leadership coaches, teachers, and various professionals with whom I regularly connect with and learn from. Fellowship programs like FWN and NUF also broadened my horizons exponentially and provided leadership frameworks and hands-on opportunities to apply them. Some of the concepts that greatly impacted my personal development and philosophy are: Jim Collins' level-five leadership (2005) that attributes success in companies to leaders who possess a blend of professional will and personal humility;

David Hutchens' series of allegories (2002) that challenge people's mental models and ability to listen; Peter Block's proposal (2009) that a community's transformation is rooted in seeing its gifts and generosity, and fostering accountability in its members; and Robert Greenleaf's assertion (2002) that the key to a leader's greatness is his ability to be a servant first.

2. **Listen more. Ask for feedback and help often.** I firmly believe it is in authentically listening and being fully present to people that allows new possibilities to happen. True leadership is not simply about doing but honoring where people are and being fine with letting them be. Additionally, the practice of asking for feedback and help regularly is freeing because it removes the pressure to be perfect. Feedback provides us a larger picture of ourselves and our work and in turn, creates space to improve and expand what is possible constantly. And when it comes to asking for help, if we are fine with getting "*no*" for a response, then we can practically ask for anything from the universe. This is powerful; how I remained unaffected when I did not get what I wanted and when the seemingly impossible things I *did* get for simply asking have dramatically shifted how I see and interact with the world.

3. **Honor who I am and how I function.** Often in the past, I have felt so strange compared to how most of the world operates. Then I discovered Susan Cain's book *Quiet* (2013), that spoke of the power of being an introvert and Marianne Cantwell's TED Talk on being a liminalist (2017)—one who does not try to find the world to fit into but creates it. These brave women encouraged me to harness what made me feel different instead of suppressing them or thinking something was wrong with me. I realized I need not be loud for the sake of it and can use my voice in my way and still be powerful and effective. I also learned to honor the eclectic mix of topics and activities that excite me, as well as, my passion for bridging different worlds; and making sure that fun and hard work go hand in hand. I used to know that I was different, but these days I actually like and embrace that and do my best to encourage others who do not quite fit the mold to embrace their difference.

4. **Have an anchor and build a community.** Knowing our unique purpose and leadership style is critical because they provide the roadmap for our self-actualization and moving toward a shared goal. From my experience, leadership is most rewarding and meaningful, and the challenges are

less daunting when it is built on mutual respect, authentic relationships, and bringing others along. The more we also engage and empower those impacted by our work, the better the results become. I am extremely fortunate to have had people who became my sources of strength, courage, and wisdom throughout my career. Thus, it is very important for me to show up in the same way for others and to be a pillar they can lean on. I give my all to support the next generation by passing on lessons, especially to my nephews and nieces, who are my biggest motivation to be my best self. Growing pains are a constant part of life, but they are less disconcerting when we have people to help keep our sails steady.

Now what?

"You're not here to change the world. You're here to love the world."
- **Anthony de Mello**

The question I posed to myself when I started a new life chapter a few months ago was: *What would it look like to be right where I want to be, in the company of people I would like to be with, and doing what I love?* I have been fortunate enough to actually live out the answer to this since then by being more present and deliberate than ever on a daily basis. I learned that living fully is not about having one big moment in time when all things align, but rather, it is about filling our lives with little moments when things feel right. To be in a space where setbacks, fear, and uncertainty become the fuel for maturity and surrender to bigger possibilities, this is my hope for everyone.

My career path has been a winding road, and perhaps it was meant to be that way so I could keep bringing my talents and gifts to places that need them the most at a given time. Sure, all the starting over and practical concerns were stress-inducing, but whenever I pause and look back at how uncertainties in my life turned out, I recognize that they were always beyond simply okay. Most were even amazing. Looking at it differently, there is something liberating and exciting about starting over, and I have come to accept that constant reinvention and taking regular leaps of faith are part of my DNA, so I no longer resist.

De Mello's (2012) mandate to simply love and the idea that the world is our oyster serve as my mantra while I navigate the path towards my calling. The universe knows my heart well, and how open I am, therefore I trust that my efforts and the right opportunities will align in due course to point me to where I need to show up next and love.

ANA BEL MAYO

PRESIDENT, *I COLORI DEL MONDO D'ADDA [THE COLORS OF THE WORLD]* ASSOCIATION

GLOBAL FWN100™ 2016

Five Dollars in My Pocket

While I was in Iraq, an Iraqi woman read my future in my cup of coffee and told me that I would find my destiny in a country with many flowers. It was 1984. At the middle of the Iran-Iraq war that started in 1980. I worked at the Information Center of the Meridian Hotel in Baghdad. Despite the war, or maybe because of the war, I obtained a working visa. It was my first overseas experience. I became an Overseas Filipino Worker (OFW) in order to improve the future of my children.

LEARNING TO BE RESILIENT

I was born in Pasig, Rizal. My father, Ramon Mayo, was a supervisor of a construction company and my mother, Milagros Lumibao, a housewife who attended to five children. Due to financial difficulties, my parents allowed my grandparents to take me to the province and live with them. I remember afternoons when I missed my parents so much I cried a lot. I have many fond memories of growing up with my grandparents, Lola Baing and Lolo Juan. My childhood days started with Lolo Juan's homemade breakfast made of fried rice with egg, freshly brewed local coffee with carabao's milk, and big hot *pandesal* from the nearby bakery.

Since there was no potable water in the house, fetching water from the water well was one of my daily chores to help my grandparents. There was no electricity, so we used a kerosene lamp. Moonlight from a full moon was joyous to my childhood friends and me as we could play *patentero* until late at night, followed by midnight snacks of rice cakes, *pinipig*, and other Philippine snacks.

I remember that at age five, I started attending elementary school as *saling pusa* [a temporary pupil]. Even though I was too young to enroll officially I was allowed to because I was tall compared to other kids of my age.

My *lolo* was very strict, and my *lola* was the opposite. But I loved them both equally. I remember that I enjoyed my childhood with my grandparents which was cut short because a car accident killed my Lolo Juan. I was ten years old. After my grandfather's untimely death, I was reunited with my parents, brothers, and sisters.

Coping with Marriage and Two Babies

I married young. My ignorance about sex education made me believe that "a kiss on the cheek can get you pregnant." When the kiss happened, I was afraid to go back home. I thought that my only choice was to elope. As a result, I had my first child when I was seventeen. I thought I could still study while taking care of my first born, but that was very hard. My ex-husband was a soldier, and his salary was not enough to feed the family and pay for my schooling. So I stopped going to school and looked for a job. My first job was as a lady guard assigned as the assistant to the general manager of the Manila International Airport (MIA). I was part of the security task force, with the code-named Vigilant of MIA. I was the youngest and the only woman. I made suggestions on how to improve airport services and lower the cost of management. During my time at MIA, I worked at the international zone where arriving international passengers have not yet formally entered the country since they have not cleared arrival customs and immigration controls and departing passengers have not formally exited the country because they have not yet cleared immigration control. I learned to interact with different personalities from different cultures and to help them solve their problems because of delayed flights or problems with departure. Interaction with different people and the ability to problem solve would become building blocks for my community leadership.

When I was 23, my husband and I separated. I became a single-parent with children. I questioned how I would be able to take care of the future of my children.

Taking Risks to Start My OFW Life

I made my way to Baghdad, Iraq. Working in Baghdad during the Iran-Iraq war presented unique challenges. There was no banking system. I was paid in Iraqi dinars which I had to convert to U.S. dollars in order to send to my children and my family in the Philippines. I had to use the black market and this meant being shortchanged. Despite the difficulties, I persevered. When I completed my contract, I had the opportunity to apply for a job in Cyprus, a country recovering from the war between the Turkish Cypriots and the Greek Cypriots. In 1986 when I arrived, Cyprus was under the control of international peacekeepers. It was a relatively peaceful time. And, the Cypriots spoke English making it easier to communicate. One of the things I did was to work with a manpower agency to recruit Filipino workers to come to Cyprus. I succeeded in bringing one batch that included some of my family members.

La Vida Bella: Paese con Molti Fiori
My Beautiful Life: a Country with Many Flowers

While I was back in the Philippines from Cyprus in 1988, I applied for a working visa to Italy as part of two groups, a total of 16 Filipino. I flew with the first group. Upon arrival in Rome, I thought that I would find an easy life. I was wrong. Thirty years ago nobody spoke English in Italy, outside the immigration office. Since I did not speak Italian, communication was a problem. In Italy, my educational background was not useful. Like many other Filipinos, I worked as a domestic servant, babysitter, or caregiver. I worked as all three without hesitation since I needed to send remittances to the family.

It was a double-edge hardship with long working hours and no day-offs. I sometimes felt like I should quit but I could not because of my responsibilities. With this inner drive, I just kept going and supported the needs of my family for years.

Today, home is Inzago, a municipality in the Province of Milan in the Italian region of Lombardy, located about 25 kilometers (16 miles) northeast of Milan. I am active in several associations in Inzago and in the greater Milan area in support of the local Filipino communities as well as the broader immigrant and the Italian community. Today I serve as a councillor and treasurer of the Città Mondo Association and president of the I Colori del Mondo d'Adda association. I am a member of the Inzago Volunteer Council, and member of the Filipina Women's Network. In my leadership story, I reflect on how I took control of my life to become a Filipina women leader.

Taking Control of My Life

Several factors were critical in my taking control of my life in Italy. Initially, I used sign language to communicate. Then, I started to learn Italian from television, cartoons, and magazine. I enrolled in Italian language classes. I also became a student at a European private academy and paid my tuition by installment. I showed up at meetings. Initially, to be present. And then, I started to find my voice and to speak out.

Fast forward, at a fiesta, with the help of my friends I was able to show my Filipino cultural identity through a Filipino dance and through showcasing Filipino handicrafts. I saw that the local community was interested in knowing my roots. With this experience, I made it a mission to show my inner-self and to prove I was more than just a good worker, but who I am as a Filipina.

In 1997, a group of us migrants in Italy started the *I colori delmondo adda* [The Colors of the World] group of migrants helping migrants. Our goal was to help newly arrived migrants, especially with food and shelter, helping them to find work, and assisting with documents. I became serious about knowing what is happening in my community. I attended almost all the meetings and conventions from the town level to provincial, regional, national, and international levels.

In 1998, I was elected as president of the *Consulta di Stranieri* at Inzago. We started working for integration, conducting dialogs with Italians, organizing fiestas like fiesta *di culture* in Inzago and *tutto mondo nel paese* in Cassano d Adda by showing different culture, food, handmade products, and music. In 2009 when planning started for the expo Milan 2015, I attended seminars to learn about being a volunteer but more importantly, about how to bring Philippine representatives to the expo Milan 2015. At the expo, our participation consisted of Milan based artist sculpture Richard Gabriel and the Filipino dance group during the opening celebration.

In 2000, opportunity knocked. I was accepted as kindergarten school helper and this started my journey as an educator, including being a mediator and a teacher.

In 2007, the *I Colori del Mondo Adda* was registered in the region of Lombardia. Town officials, parish priests, and politicians started to take notice of me as a community leader. I began to talk in my crooked Italian during meetings and conventions. I Colori del Mondo Adda started developing projects, like a school for learning the Italian language, called the abracadabra and an after-school tutoring program for children to complete their homework.

My work in *I Colori del Mondo Adda* led to my participation in 2009 in the Migrant Associations and Philippine Institutions for Development (MAPID) course, organized by the ISMU Foundation and promoted by the Scalabrini Migration Center. This effort was co-funded by the European Commission. My MAPID training was pivotal in my leadership development. What I learned from MAPID provided the framework to explain the migrant situation in Italy and provided the tools for working collaboratively with our Filipino migrant associations, the Italian government and Philippine institutions. My passion for volunteering for social causes blossomed after participating in the MAPID course. (See Box 1 for more information about MAPID.)

In 2011, the *Associazione Citta Mondo Milano* was established as a partnership between non-profit organizations and the city of Milan. The association includes 115 non-profit organizations and contributes to the growth and diversification of the city of Milan. The goal of the association is to help with the process of integration of the migrant population by highlighting social cohesion. The association stimulates the member bodies to share similar objectives. In 2014, the association elected me as one of the councillors and until now I serve in that capacity.

In 2012, the Filipino diaspora in Rome served as the secretariat for European Network of Filipino Diaspora (ENFiD). ENFiD includes Filipinos from about 17 countries in Europe and is growing. The aims of ENFiD include connecting, networking, and trying to have a unified voice on matters that are important to the organization. It was at ENFiD where I met for the first time Attorney Loida Nicolas Lewis who nominated me for the GLOBAL FWN100™ 2016 award. I am grateful that I was recognized for my social commitment and as a Filipina woman leader behind the scenes.

In 2014, along with Marie Luarca-Reyes of ENFiD and Michele Piacentini of *Les Artistes*, and I, representing The Colors of the World, organized a show based on Fibers Philippines, Eco-sustainability and Fashion in Cassano d'adda. The show was held in the presence of the outgoing Filipino Ambassador Virgilio A. Reyes Jr and the Vice Consul, welcome remarks were made by the Mayor, the Deputy Mayor, and the Councillor for Culture of Cassano d'Adda. The show brought to the Villa Maggi Ponti in Cassano d'Adda an original collection of the Filipino designers. The designers arrived in Italy for the occasion with their clothes made exclusively of natural fibers, to promote the eco-sustainability of textile production of Filipino origin. The Province of Milan, the Municipality of Cassano d'Adda, and the Municipality of Inzago supported the event. Famous Filipino designers including, Patis Tesoro, Jaki Penalosa, and Andrada were among the Filipino designers. Designers, such as Jaki Penalosa have sought my help for return engagements in Milan. They know from experience that they could count on me because, as they say in Italian, "*Conosco i miei polli*," or literally "I know my chickens," that actually means "I know what I'm talking about."

Last year we were able to host 500 youth who are ethnically Filipinos but who now carry passports from different European countries. We hosted the engagement of Eugenio Torre a chess grandmaster, considered as one of the best chess player the Philippines; and Jay Taruc who wrote the documentary, "From Manila to Milan" about two different countries, two different cultures, two different persons, sharing one mission of overcoming boundaries. In the documentary, Taruc documents the story of Marvin Aguda, a Filipino dishwasher-turned-pizza shop owner in Milan and Roberto Bellini, an Italian who established a restaurant in Cubao. Their success in overcoming boundaries resonates with me.

At these various events, my leadership skills in organizing and in bringing together multiple people with shared interests have become visible resulting in interviews with media and universities in Italy, Philippines, India, Japan, and other countries.

The consulate of Milan and municipality of Inzago have given me an award for the work done with migrants and for migrants.

Upon receiving news of the FWN award, I was very excited. I considered the award as an indication of gratitude. Thanks to MAPID, I had laid the foundation for my growth as a volunteer engaged in social work and in the promotion of intercultural dialogue and integration. I also thank the municipalities of Inzago, Cassano d'Adda, and Milan, with whom I had targeted projects with the Italian immigrant population residing in the province of Milan. Even after receiving this recognition, my goal remains to continue working to shape a positive image of the Filipino community in Italy. In an article about me, Vita.IT wrote that I beamed when I said: "The Filipino migrants are a mine of culture and human capital, not only an army of domestic workers."

My Lucky Charm

I married an Italian man, Giovanni Riva in 2004 who adopted my children and who took the responsibility for securing their future. With my husband's help, I continue to enjoy my advocacy work. Being married to Giovanni has given me new respectability in the eyes of the Italians. Giovanni only asks me if I am happy with what I am doing. I am very pleased.

With his help, I have secured a better future for my children. It took twenty years of hardship but I did it. My daughter, Lyanne Mayo Guillermo Riva graduated cum laude from the Pamantasan ng Maynila. Lyanne works as a board director for one of the leading Philippine companies and is based in Rotterdam, in the Netherlands. My son, Willie Guillermo Riva Jr. Riva graduated from the Philippine Aeronautics Technical School. Under the family reunification plan that I helped implement in Italy, Willie works at the Home for Aged Cooperatives in Milan; Willie, his wife Cristina Agustin Guillermo, and their daughter, 15-year old Chrisele Anne now live close to me.

The first time I went abroad in 1988, I had US five dollars in my pocket. I remember that the agency gave me US$23 as a cash advance and I gave my father US$17 to feed my family and my mother who was bed-ridden. I left the Philippines with one small baggage. I remember how difficult that decision was to leave my family and my young children, with only a hope that tomorrow would be better. It was like going to war without a gun.

Let me close with an Italian expression: "*Non tutte le ciambelle riescono col buco,*" or "Not all doughnuts come out with a hole." Sure, you might expect them to, but that is not the way the world works. Things do not always turn out as planned. Sometimes, things turn out better than anyone could ever imagine.

JOANNE MICHELLE FERNANDEZ OCAMPO

PROJECT DIRECTOR, GEORGETOWN UNIVERSITY
ADVISOR, NORWEGIAN INSTITUTE OF PUBLIC HEALTH
GLOBAL FWN100™ 2017

The Dynamics of Defining Success and Failure

THIS IS ME

Ancestral heritage: The Philippines (+).
Born and raised in: Norway.
Currently lives in: The United States.
Works: Globally.

In the late 70s/early 80s, my father decided, that for him to provide sufficiently for his family, he had to leave the Philippines. At the same time, while performing as a vocalist in Germany, his sister had met and fell in love with my uncle and moved to his native Norway. At the request of my aunt and uncle, my dad traveled to Norway on a cold winter day in 1986 for a new employment opportunity. About six months later, my mom and brother followed suit, and three years following that, I was born.

As a tropical islander welcomed to this world in the midst of a polar winter, I have always seen life from a slightly non-traditional point of view, and I bring this unique perspective with me wherever I go. This has (1) steered me towards a career path in scientific research that often challenges conventional wisdom, and (2) inspired me to pursue opportunities that others may find either incredibly daunting, such as, moving across the Atlantic Ocean eight times, or just flat out risky, such as diving to 30m depths, or walking canopy trails 30m above ground.

The reality is, by my existence alone, I already break normative barriers. And, at times, it has been pretty strenuous to realize that just because of who I am – I could never easily fit into the cultural lens that we traditionally view the world with. From this perspective, it is hard to make sense of me as a person. I mean, how can a someone look one way, speak like they are from some other place, live somewhere completely different, and then work just about everywhere? People do try to make sense of my identity by seeking answers to questions that might help them categorize me into one of the more traditional cultural boxes asking questions such as: "What country do you like the most?" For me, that is like making me choose between my left and my right arm. While different in their own way, they are both equal parts of who I am.

Many of us tend to forget that people lived their mobile lives across borders long before the notion of a country ever existed. I am a product of multiple cultures. I am a person who lives and breathes a life that shows that you can cherish different cultures across the globe. Cultural traits, especially from the Philippines, Norway, and the United States, have all helped shape who I am today. Take for example how the American work ethic has immensely improved my capacity and capability to drive my career forward, or how the humanitarian values from my Norwegian upbringing have shaped the motivational drivers behind why I do what I do. While I could elaborate more on the latter, this chapter focuses on my Filipino heritage and how this has contributed to my leadership story. Before continuing, I ask that the readers understand and appreciate that one cultural aspect of who I am does not, in any way, shape, or form take away from any other cultural aspect of who I am.

This is What I Studied

As an undergraduate student at a small liberal arts college in Eastern Connecticut, I studied biology, Latin for "the study of life." As most other biology students, it was essential for me to learn the basic concept of genetics, which rests on the central dogma of molecular biology. Oversimplified, Crick explains that "DNA is transcribed → into RNA, which is then translated → into protein" (Crick 1970, p. 561-563). I remember one of my college professors first introducing this linear relationship as the ultimate modern truth. And then thoroughly confusing me and my classmates, a few moments later, when he told us that well, it was the ultimate truth until scientists (like Gallo and Montagnier, 2003) found a new group of viruses (i.e., retroviruses like HIV) that had an enzyme (i.e., reverse transcriptase), that initiated the reverse process (i.e., going from RNA to DNA). The notion of challenging and modifying conventional wisdom made me appreciate biology even more and later became a key feature of my leadership style.

Science fit me. I loved the notion of building an evidence base for a new hypothesis, and then continuously challenging it to see if it could stand the test of time. Because of this, I learned that I thoroughly enjoyed doing scientific research.

One chilly New England morning, I walked into the microbiology laboratory where I had spent much of my undergraduate time training. I was tasked to retrieve bacterial plates from an incubator (fancy science word for what resembles an oven) to check if the chemical compounds (in the form of a liquid), I had been working with for months, could inhibit bacterial growth. I was to measure this by observing what is known as a "zone of inhibition" (i.e., an area where bacteria cannot grow) – a test for antimicrobial activity, also known as the Kirby-Bauer Test (Brown 1975). I reached out and grabbed the door handle to the incubator expecting nothing, and was pleasantly surprised when I saw several zones of inhibition (i.e., indicating that the compounds I had been working with did indeed have antimicrobial activity). I realized that this could be a potential precursor to a novel antibiotic in the future. Through this experience, I started grasping that my interest in biology, and more generally scientific research, was not only inspired by the quest for knowledge but ultimately driven by the thought of applying new knowledge to something that could help other people.

GETTING CHALLENGED BY A STRANGER

I could smell the stuffiness of the jam-packed Northeast Regional Amtrak train chugging its way down the Connecticut coastline. I was finishing a laboratory report for one of my classes and heading towards New York City for some much-needed time off from examinations and pop-quizzes. "Is this seat taken?" An elegantly dressed lady asked me. I looked up, made eye contact, and with a slanted smile shook my head before I dove right back into my biology homework. The woman smiled and sat down next to me. I resurfaced after finishing my laboratory report and looked over at her. We started chatting. She had just been to an Ivy League college game in the area. I got the sense that she was an educator. Our conversation steadily steered towards my plans after graduation. She asked if I had ever considered applying to one of the top-level schools. I said no. She asked, "why?" I always figured that my life would take me interesting places, but I had never considered ending up in a prestigious academic setting. Top-level schools, Ivy League, and others were not even on my radar. I mistakenly thought of those opportunities as reserved for others. We got off the train at Penn Station and said our goodbyes. A couple of weeks later, I decided it would not hurt to try, so I started working on applications to some of the leading graduate schools.

I graduated from college and with my newly-acquired biology degree, left Connecticut and returned to Norway for a laboratory technician job at a hospital. It did not take too many months of working at the local hospital laboratory for me to realize that I missed learning and challenging myself more. I had almost forgotten about submitting my graduate school applications earlier that fall. One cold November day, however, a letter popped up in the mail. The letter was from Georgetown University, my top choice for graduate school. With a modest scholarship offer, their Department of Microbiology and Immunology welcomed me to start my Master's degree in biological threat agents and emerging infectious diseases that following spring.

I remain forever grateful to the woman I met on that Amtrak train. A complete stranger challenged me to avoid underestimating myself, and because of her, I took a chance that landed me in a program that opened the door to a career focused on safeguarding the public's health from infectious diseases.

My Work of Science and Heart

My parents never pressured me into achieving specific career goals. Instead, they strongly advocated that I commit all that I am and all that I have, to whatever I chose to do. At first, I thought this meant effort. I later understood that they also meant heart. While in school and through my early years of full-time employment after finishing my M.S. degree, I struggled to pinpoint my passion. Was it the bacteria that I was growing in the laboratory? Was it the way that the virus so quickly adapted and could circumvent the human body's defense mechanisms? Was it how we used health data or privacy-assuring technologies to better understand epidemics or disease trajectories over time (Ocampo et al.; 2015, Ocampo et al., 2016)? For years, I had no concrete answer. In terms of what I wanted to devote my career to, I felt that I was in the right neighborhood, but that I was wandering around trying to find the right street. I knew that I was acquiring the right skill set, but I did not know precisely why I was doing what I was doing. Interestingly, the answer popped up in a place far away from my classroom and office.

While I was still in college, my microbiology professor and mentor showed me a picture of an empty lot in his native Ghana. He told me that it was a photograph of the village where he grew up. He had been working for years to solve a problem related to access to higher education and public health: how to provide more opportunities in higher education and basic clinical training and services to people in rural villages who were not able to travel to the urban centers? The photograph showed where he was building his lifelong dream: a university college that would help keep educational opportunities in and provide some clinical training resources to the village and surrounding area. The dream he made a reality inspired me. And while it is always beautiful to see someone achieve their dream, I think it is extra special when someone's dream (like an educational institution) can help others achieve their dreams (e.g., prospective students). So, naturally, I started volunteering to help his cause.

Before one of my trips to Ghana, I reached out to a childhood friend of mine who like myself grew up in Europe. His parents had immigrated from Ghana. I told him that I was going to visit his native motherland, and he jokingly asked me if I was going there to save his people. I told him that I was not going there to save them, but that I was going so that they could save me. My volunteering helped me realize that what I was trying to achieve in my life, had nothing to do with whether it was a bacterium or a virus, or even public health data. I genuinely cared about the well-being of others, and I wanted to do what I could to help those in need, and I wanted to learn from them how I could become a better version of myself in doing so. Simply put, I was working to acquire a skill set that could help me better help others. Reflecting on my volunteering activities while in a rural village in West Africa, I realized what my parents meant: my professional goals would only carry significant weight if they genuinely stemmed from my heart.

This is Why I Lead so Well

The Philippines has long been a melting pot of cultures from the East and West, and because of this, Filipinos have become very good at cultural adaptation over time. It is fascinating for me to think that I call myself "Filipina" because of a prominent European, His Majesty King Felipe II of Spain. Even more interesting is realizing that I have two English first names, and two Spanish last names, but no names originating from the indigenous cultures of the Philippine Islands. I have seldom been told that I look like I am from the Philippines, rather people have suggested that I am from Japan, Hawaii, Korea, or China. But I am a hybrid, like many of the Filipinos that I know. My family tree branches out from the Philippines, through mainland Asia, and Spain (I think). In other words, the cultural intersection that I have felt between East and West growing up as a Norwegian-Filipina has also occurred numerous times throughout my family history.

The Philippines was under Spanish rule for almost 500 years and then American rule for nearly 50 years. As a result of this colonial period, a feeling of cultural inferiority has manifested itself in different ways among many Filipinos. While I was growing up, I observed this in Filipino communities that associated success in the Philippines to a person's ability to leave the Philippines. I also found that some ignored their Philippine heritage, including the Islands' history, traditions, and languages. So, I decided to open my eyes to both the strengths and weaknesses of my entire cultural heritage. I overcame the inferiority complex that I had been conditioned to follow, and chose to focus on raising my Filipino heritage to a level of cultural equality instead. I started to learn Tagalog as the language of my heart, and actively listened to my parents' stories about the Philippines. What quickly followed, was that I started seeing that the qualities that my Filipino parents had passed onto me, helped develop my leadership skills. Like my parents, I worked hard, I learned continuously, I remained humble, I led with my heart, I showed respect, I laughed a lot, and I loved like there is no tomorrow. In other words, I grew up, got educated, paved my career path, and found that my success can be attributed to me being Filipina.

In writing this chapter, I asked my friends to reflect on what they have learned from me throughout the years. Their responses affirmed what I view as inherited and nourished Filipino cultural tendencies:

> To be fearless,
> To keep it together no matter what,
> To never take things for granted,
> To make the best of the situation that you are in,
> That with hard work, anything is possible,
> That it is possible to be smart, ambitious, vulnerable, and funny,
> That balancing a hectic life gracefully makes hard work seem effortless,
> That I should never limit myself.

The population of the Philippines has in recent years exceeded 100 million, and the diaspora, of which I am a part, consists of about 10 million (The Commission on Filipinos Overseas, 2013). By comparison, the diaspora alone is twice the size of Norway's population. Receiving the "100 Most Influential Filipina Women in the World Award™" was therefore very special to me. Not only because it recognized me as an influential leader among Filipinos, but because it gave me my very own professional link to the Islands that I cherish so much. It provided me, the only grandchild who was not born in the Philippines with something that I never visibly had before; my own standing anchored in my cultural heritage from the Philippines.

About a 10-minute walk from where I grew up in Norway, there is a centuries-old pathway that has always intrigued me when I walk it. It makes me think about how many winters have come and gone since that road was built, and how deep the roots of modern Scandinavian culture run. The artifacts at Oslo's Viking Ship Museum make me ponder this too. While excavating the Gokstad ship from approximately 900 A.D., archeologists found peacock feathers (University of Oslo, 2018). Given that peacocks are endemic to areas in Asia and Africa (National Geographic, 2018), attests to the extensive global trade that the Vikings were engaged in; long before our modern interpretation of globalization. I look at my life now and think, I am just like the peacock feather that was found on a Viking ship; the East and West come together in me. And my academic and professional life, spanning several continents and cultures, embraces that. For me, it is a comfortable embrace; one that I find natural, perhaps since my cultural heritage has facilitated cross-cultural bonds throughout history?

I have long wondered about the Island culture prior to our modern interpretation of the Philippines. Compared to other cultures (e.g., Scandinavian), we do not have much documented cultural history about the Philippine Islands, especially prior to our 1500s Spanish/American chapters (National Commission for the Culture and the Arts. 2018). It is my understanding, however, that the four horsemen of the apocalypse (The New Testament of the Bible); disease, war, hunger, and death have been frequent visitors to these Islands over time. Moreover, I believe that with these challenges, evolved a people with an incredible knack for resilience, resourcefulness, and gratitude for love and life. I have observed these traits through several encounters with people of Philippine ancestry across different cities, borders, and continents. I have seen how talented Filipinos are in linguistics, arts, sciences, medicine, trade, logistics, and business. I have also witnessed how many Filipinos have an amazing ability to combine excellence across several disciplines, all the while taking care of their families. **I see my heritage, and it is beautiful.** In my life, I have been resilient, resourceful, understanding, and loving. I am part of the culture that I inherited from my parents, and it forms the foundation of why I have succeeded and led so well, especially across different cultures.

Failing an Interview. Acing Survival

I have a tiny scar on my face. You can barely see it tucked away underneath my lip, but it is there. And it serves as a good reminder of valuable life lessons for me. As a toddler, I was happily exploring my motor skill development. I had recently learned how to run, and so naturally then, I ran around a lot. One day, I decided that I did not want to put down my bottle while playing, so I kept drinking out of it while running around. I know should have finished off my bottled milk before I started running around, but I did not. So instead, I ended up falling flat on my face, with the bottle cracking the underside of my lip, causing a blood-filled scene, with worried parents rushing me, their young toddler to the Emergency Room. This particular experience taught me that just because you know how to do something, like how to run, does not mean that you should do it all the time.

I gave my parents plenty of reasons to visit the Emergency Room while growing up. Those doctor's visits often followed times where I would treat myself as an experiment to test semi-scientific hypotheses. I think I must have been around five years old when I concluded, after testing an aerodynamic hypothesis, by jumping off my bunk bed, that humans simply cannot fly. Failures like these have clearly taught me valuable life lessons.

Similarly, in my professional life, failures have often been a preceding step to successfully reaching significant milestones. I suggest that is true for most people. Several reasons might explain this, but I reckon that is because after experiencing failure we define success differently. I remember sitting in my car, crying my eyes out, and gasping for breath as I told my mom over the phone that I had failed to get adequate scores on an entrance exam to graduate school. During the test, my nerves got the best of me, and I accidentally exited one of three sections without putting down any answers. My score plunged into the deep end of the low score pool, way below the minimum requirement of the graduate program that I was applying for. After I got off the phone with my mom, all I could think of was: "there goes years of work down the drain just because I could not hack it, just because I could not handle the pressure of taking a standardized exam." I wiped the tears off my face, drove home, and reflected upon this failure. In this situation, I had defined success as getting a high score on a test, so that I could get into a graduate school of my choosing. After reflecting on my test performance, however, I started defining success differently. I began viewing successfully getting through this moment, as unrelated to the actual test score. Instead, I anchored the definition of success to my ability to move on from this poor test performance. I learned a valuable lesson: do not let your nerves get the best of you.

But, what is success? Is it just the flipside of failure? Are failures naturally preceding steps to success? Or are they both essential parts of a gray zone that without tension blurs the two together? After countless academic, professional, and personal rejections, you would think that I had gotten used to the feeling of failure. In the process of writing this book chapter, I, for example, got distracted by the rejection of a prestigious scholarship. I felt I had failed. While handling these types of situations has undoubtedly made me emotionally stronger, I can tell you that none of these moments have ever left me feeling good about myself. But adding some perspective surely helps you to process these emotions. Following a few days of sulking about my scholarship application not making the final cut, a balanced perspective finally dawned on me. Here, I was huffing and puffing about a failed scholarship application, while at the same time, in my late 20s, I was invited to write a chapter for a leadership book by women of Filipina descent. Like my co-authors, my task was to write a chapter depicting parts of my own story to inspire others who are paving their pathways to success. Embracing my newly found perspective, I realized that this rejected scholarship application was not a failure, but that the opportunity was not meant for me. Such acceptance has the power to flip a previously perceived failure and turn it into a success. For I had indeed successfully submitted a strong application packet regardless of the outcome. Defining success and failure is a dynamic process that depends on context, timing, and perspective. Nothing illustrated this more strongly to me than losing a very dear friend.

First, I must admit that I used to dislike hugs. In fact, there were times where I actively tried to avoid them. One day in graduate school, while I was waiting for the next class to start, another girl came in and sat down next to me. I had seen her in other classes, but I had not spoken to her much. We started chatting and quickly bonded over several commonalities: us wanting to help others through a career in health and science, how much we cherished our families, especially our amazingly strong moms, and how much we both loved cooking. After days, weeks, months, and soon years of study sessions, recipe-exchanges, baking/cooking sessions, happy hours, coffees, basking in the Washington, D.C. sun, and museum visits, we formed a unique friendship that I will forever cherish.

I will always remember the first time she gave me a long hug. Midway through it, I told her that I was not a big fan of them. She proceeded with squeezing me even tighter, and said: "Well! Then I am just going to have to teach you how to start loving them. I am a very huggable person, you know?" And she did. And eventually, I started loving hugs. Especially hers.

A couple of years ago, she graciously helped me prepare for some Ph.D. interviews. She reviewed my scientific background materials, and affectionately calmed my nerves in the weeks leading up to my interviews. I texted her on my way to the first interview, but left my phone untouched while going through intense hours of interviewing with individual faculty members. I noticed some text messages randomly popping up on my phone, but I did not have time to read or process them. That evening, I was at a faculty dinner. After not having looked at my phone for hours, I could not ignore the weird composition of people who had left missed calls on my phone. Several text messages prompted me to call them up as soon as possible. Frustrated at my friends for distracting me from this faculty dinner that is an important social part of the interview weekend, I stepped outside to return their calls. I made the first call and was asked if I had heard anything from my friend from graduate school. I said no. I took a deep breath realizing that she never returned my text. I made the second call and was bluntly told that she had passed away. The music and people talking in the background melted into an emotional blur. No words can describe how tough it was to get through that evening and the rest of the interview weekend. I also did not get accepted into that Ph.D. program and felt like a professional failure. I grieved for months over the loss of one of my closest friends, who had taught me how to become a better me. One who I had dreamt of "saving the world" with. One who I saw myself in. One who taught me how to love hugs.

After losing her, I decided to take a break from all life-altering decisions. Coping with her loss was a wave-like grieving process that made me realize that I needed more time with my family and friends who I had been away from for several years while pursuing my academic and professional goals. So, I started looking for job opportunities closer to my childhood home, and a few years later I was back in Oslo. Seeing it all in retrospective, it is crystal clear to me now that it was a blessing in disguise to not enter any Ph.D. program at that point in my life. I first had to process the significant loss of a dear friend who I will cherish forever. I see now that there was no failure here, and that I did the best that I could, considering what was going on in my life. School could wait. I was busy succeeding in surviving life.

Our Future Starts Today, So Decorate Now

As a world traveler, I have spent years on the move, devoting minimal time and effort to decorating my temporary homes. I figured, since I was likely to move again soon, what was the point of investing in making the physical space around me look nice? Besides, I was trying to save up for my future home – one that I would truly invest time and energy into making my own. One day, a very good friend shared his perspective on this topic. Within financial reason, he wondered, why we would wait to decorate our current homes? "We are living our lives right now, so holding off on enjoying our homes for some future notion that may or may not come to fruition makes minimal sense." I agreed, and soon paintings, photographs, flowers, and other mementos were quickly going up in my apartment. Our future starts today. Therefore, I strive my best to avoid putting things off. All things. While it makes financial sense to save for retirement, we should not save everything for retirement. If something interests you now, you should find a way to incorporate it into your life today. As another beloved friend put it, devoting as little as five minutes a day to something that you care about, can, in fact, become something quite substantial over time. Similarly, if you see a golden opportunity now, go for it, as you never know if or when you are likely to run into it again.

My vocal coach once told me that our vocal cords could get over and under-toned very easily, meaning that when you spend most of your days speaking in a low bass voice, as in scientific presentations, then those notes become over-toned, while the other parts of your voice remain under-toned. Life is one hardcore balancing act, so we must strive to exercise all elements in order to make us the best and most balanced versions of ourselves. In my case, this means devoting time and effort to my physical, psychological, and spiritual health, to a meaningful career, to guide my activities by heart, to practice integrity in all that I do, and to spend loving time with my family and friends. That is how I succeed in living the life that I truly want to live, and that is how I define and achieve my version of success.

Lastly, I want to share that I am grateful for the spiritual guidance that has given me my strength throughout my life. I would like to thank my mom, dad, and brother who continuously provide the stable base from which I can navigate life. I am grateful to my nieces and nephews for reminding me of what is truly important in life. I am thankful to all of my friends and family members who put up with my phone calls and text messages about everything from exploring distant coral reefs and dense tropical rain forests to reminiscing about the past and to planning for how to save our future. I acknowledge the important roles of my professors and mentors who have helped strengthen my professional and personal weaknesses. I look forward to sharing my life trajectory with those that I have known, those that I know, and those that I have yet to meet. Finally, thank you, *mamaneg*, my cherished grandmother, for telling me to never forget the Philippines.

RACHEL U. SALINEL

FREELANCE BROADCAST JOURNALIST FOR THE FILIPINO CHANNEL ABS-CBN
CO-FOUNDER AND MANAGING PARTNER OF FILIPINO EXCELLENCE IN THE MIDDLE EAST (FEME) CONNECT
GLOBAL FWN100™ 2016

Purpose, Passion, and Pass It On

I recently went through a difficult phase in my professional life, and it was quite unsettling. It came when I was included in the list of those no longer needed as news presenters by the station due to slow business. Weeks after, I received more bad news after the training office I had been managing in Dubai for 15 years was also closed due to slow business.

Both announcements came at the wrong time as I was preparing to submit this story about empowering women in the global environment. I found myself without the energy to write even a single word that could inspire others when I was feeling discouraged myself. That feeling of being dispirited went on for many weeks. The more I thought of the deadline for this paper, the more I was in despair and could not start writing.

MY PROFESSIONAL AND PERSONAL CRISIS

I found myself withdrawing from public service except for my voluntary community work with our Christian Catholic group, Couples for Christ-United Arab Emirates (CFC-UAE). I hoped that my involvement could help me recover. Instead of holding a pen to write, I held the rosary in my hands. Instead of facing the screen of my laptop, I found myself kneeling before our altar inside our bedroom or in front of the Chapel. I was hoping to draw strength and wisdom from above as I read and reread the bible verse in Isaiah 40:29 "He gives strength to the weary and increases the power of the weak."

I have been a broadcast journalist for 30 years, and I live to tell the wonderful stories of the many people I have met. Sharing my subjects' inspiring stories were easy for me, and I often heard other people say that hearing inspirational stories had changed their lives.

Yet, here I was struggling to write my story that was intended to inspire others. I became more frustrated because I was more focused on what I had lost and was too distressed to consider that I still had another freelancing job in media and a promising social enterprise to pursue. I kept on worrying about the lost income and was overcome by my anxiety as I faced the reality that it would be difficult to find a new job in the UAE job market given the competition including qualified and ambitious young people.

I kept on dwelling on my fears and my insecurities were intensified by my being in my early fifties and thinking that I would have to start over again. I was depressed by the thought that I would become dependent on my husband's salary once my savings and benefits were depleted after paying my monthly personal bills. It is the kind of story I have reported often especially after my subjects had lost their job and had been unemployed for many months or even years. Some faced legal problems because they could not pay their credit cards or bank loans. Some even escaped to the Philippines leaving behind their unpaid cars, flats, and loans. Some chose to spend months in prison to clear their debts rather than be harassed by bank collectors every day. Some chose to go hungry or even become homeless in Dubai.

Divine Purpose

My professional and personal crisis went on longer than I expected and the weeks that passed were filled with excuses, despair, frustration, and guilt as well as shame on not meeting my deadline for writing my narrative. I was a disappointment to myself because I was allowing it to happen.

I found refuge in my prayers, and I committed myself to surrendering everything to God and sought Mother Mary's intercession for help dealing with my despair. I repeated Psalm 91: 2 I: "He is my refuge and my fortress, my God, in whom I trust." Prayer has always served me well when I faced any challenge be it small or big. In prayer, I have known that someone up there is listening to what my heart and soul were saying. Prayer is where I can be embraced by divine peace and calmness that only His Holy presence can give. Prayer provided an inner strength to go on for another day. Prayer is a place where I know everything will come to pass and that tomorrow would be the best day of my life. Tomorrow will be a day when God's miracle can happen.

I was asking Him why these setbacks had happened and why now. Then, I recalled the *The Praying Life – Living Beyond Your Limits* (Dean, 1994) that I read years ago. The book is about praying and it reminded me that "the purpose of prayer is not to change God, but to allow Him to change us. It is to discover and do God's will, not to obligate Him to do ours. That the purpose of prayer is to reflect God's mind, not to change it." Another reminder was by Hallesby (1994) "That prayer is simply opening our lives to God, acknowledging our total dependence on Him," and that "To pray is to let Jesus glorify His name in the midst of our needs." I have acknowledged that in prayers I could indeed receive God's mercy to bring about solutions to whatever problems I face given what the Bible says in Jeremiah 29:11: "For I know the plans I have for you,' declared the Lord, 'plans to prosper you and not to harm you, plans to give you hope and a future." This verse has comforted me and made me excited about what He will reveal to me in His own time.

THE REASON FOR LIVING

Then one day I received an email from a cancer patient being treated in a Dubai Hospital. She was seeking help to appeal on TV for funds to help her continue living for her three young sons who were in the Philippines while she was all alone in Dubai. Her story is not extraordinary for an Overseas Filipino Worker. She is separated from her husband who is a tricycle driver, and she went to work in the United Arab Emirates (UAE) to support her sons. She has been working in Dubai for almost three years when she was diagnosed with Leukemia in January 2018. Her treatment went on for nearly five months and resulted in nearly half a million Dirhams (about US$136,054) bill.

During my interview with her, I could not help but admire her courage in fighting for her loved ones. She tried very hard to overcome her fears every day and remained hopeful that soon she could leave the hospital feeling better. She also hoped she would find financial help to pay her hospital bills, continue her treatment, and go back to her children in the Philippines. She said she had to live because she had promised her children a better life and a good future. I found myself remembering a promise I also made many years ago. And that is never to forget my purpose of being a broadcast journalist. I recall writing that "Living without purpose is not living. And living without passion is not living that purpose at all."

I have been a broadcast journalist for three decades. Half of those years I spent in the Philippines covering news in Southeast Asia and Micronesia for Nippon Television

Network Corporation, a Japanese TV network. The other half was reporting from the UAE about Overseas Filipinos (OFs) in the UAE for TV, radio, and online. Working in the Middle East led me to my purpose and that is to serve God using my talents to help, inspire, encourage, and empower OFs.

There are so many issues involving the almost 700,000 OFs in the UAE. These issues include indebtedness, immorality, intoxication, and abandoned children born out of wedlock or out of illicit relationships. Lately, there has been a new concern about the mental and emotional health of Filipino youth and adults in UAE. Some psychologists have linked these problems to the easy and excessive access to social media. Depression, incidents of self-harm, and suicide among Filipino youth who are exposed to online games have been blamed on social media[1].

In UAE it is easy to get a credit card and a bank loan when one has a regular job. Filipinos are lured to max out their credit cards because of the frequent special offerings, or to get loans for their families back in the Philippines, many of whom demanding many material things. Sending money is their way to make amends for their absence.

Immorality and intoxications are said to be caused by loneliness or the lack of self-control, both of which are influenced by the cosmopolitan environment of Dubai. Because of these two common problems in the Filipino community, I have received many requests for assistance in securing travel documents for children who were born out of wedlock or out of illicit affairs between *kababayans* or between a Filipina and a foreigner.

My Passion

News to me is a passion that became a mission. News is a serious business because it involves lives. It can give hope and, at the same time, can destroy a person's reputation. In my early years as a journalist, I was exposed to many military uprisings and natural disasters in the Philippines and nearby Southeast Asian countries. I covered stories where I had witnessed people losing their loved ones in an earthquake, a plane crash, a boat disaster, or through common crimes like murder and rape. I recall the numerous times the information I reported kept spouses, parents, children, and relatives alive and hopeful; while the news also provided direction on necessary future steps.

In the UAE, I had covered similar stories like that of the cancer patient. There was the salon worker who was being treated for meningitis. There were heart and kidney patients who were severely ill and needed to go home for treatment. There was the Filipino who had an accident in Fujairah while still under a visitor visa

---

[1] https://gulfnews.com/news/uae/crime/blue-whale-game-link-to-two-dubai-suicides-1.2212432

and whose brain injury made it impossible for him to work again and even needed a nurse to accompany him for his trip back to the Philippines. All these required a significant amount of money.

I also reported labor cases involving OFs who were victimized by their employers and who had not received their salaries for more than three months. By airing their stories and with constant follow up with the Philippine Consulate and Philippine Overseas Labor Office-Overseas Workers Welfare Administration (POLO-OWWA), they eventually received medical, legal, and financial aid.

These stories left a mark on me, professionally and personally. I felt grateful that God has used me and my work to help people. I vowed, and I am recommitting myself that I will continue reporting in order to uplift the lives of individuals even when I am facing crisis of my own. I refocused on the many issues of our *kababayans* in the UAE and less on my own as I am assured that God will take care of my concerns as He uses me to deal with the problems of the Filipinos in my stories.

My father who introduced me at a young age to leadership used to tell my three siblings and me that a real leader thinks beyond his own concerns and does not lead his people by walking in front or at the back but by walking beside them. My father said: "Do not to hesitate to hold the hands of someone who is feeling lost in order to provide strength even if you as the leader has fears in your heart."

Beyond the News Deadline

The cancer patient's plea for help reminded me to remember why I embraced my job decades ago. It made me realized that my situation was nothing compared to hers. Her request for help made me more aware that aside from my freelancing job with The Filipino Channel I had yet to develop my social enterprise and advocacy effort called Filipino Excellence in the Middle East (FEME) Connect Directory. I see FEME as a gift from God and therefore something be treasured. Being grateful is a virtue a good leader needs to master.

It was my exposure at the Ateneo School of Government's Leadership and Social Entrepreneurship (LSE) program in Dubai in 2015 that opened the possibility of being a broadcast journalist and having a second vocation in social entrepreneurship. After I graduated from the program, I co-founded the FEME Connect directory of Filipino professionals and entrepreneurs in the UAE.

Advertisers funded the printing of the directory to allow for free distribution. FEME's objectives are to highlight the excellence of OFs and recognize their contributions to the UAE's success while they work as engineers, educators, medical practitioners, world-class entertainers, and in many other professions, in addition to being respected nannies for locals and expatriates.

I imagined that having a comprehensive directory of Filipino Expats in the UAE would provide more opportunities for professional growth, economic gain, and most importantly, validation as excellent individuals. Other than connecting Filipino entrepreneurs with each other, it would be a way to inform the Filipino expats about the contact details of the Philippine government offices, such as the embassy, consulate, and emergency numbers of the UAE police, hospitals, and schools, among others.

Weeks after the directory's formal launched, I was left to pursue the business plan on my own as my three partners had to leave the project due to health and employment problems. Alone in this endeavor and facing a new world, I continued the project armed with the purpose of using the directory to uplift the lives of OFs and backed by my passion for connecting them with other Filipino professionals and entrepreneurs. I had help from my husband, good friends, and several companies who believed in me.

The directory was published and distributed in the 2016 Philippine Independence Day celebrations as well as in the Diplomatic Reception in Dubai. A portion of the earnings was used to buy one-way air tickets for two distressed OFs.

The directory has brought me honors, from being named one of the Global FWN100™ in August 2016 in Cebu to being named one of the '50 GCC's Women Leaders' during the CMO Asia in Dubai and World Brand Congress in September 2016 in Dubai. I gave thanks to God for blessing me with these recognitions.

I used the directory to connect Filipinos who had lost their jobs. I organized free seminars led by Filipino Human Resources (HR) practitioners to teach unemployed *Kababayans* how to make better resumes and to prepare them for job interviews that led to employment. After I had lost two jobs in the past months, I know the pains and anxieties of the unemployed and it felt right for me to create a Facebook site called CFC SocDev UAE Available Job[2] where I posted job openings provided by my contacts from the HR group and Filipinos working in recruitment companies in Dubai and Abu Dhabi.

It was also this directory that I used in gathering the Psychological Society of the Philippines Dubai and Abu Dhabi Chapters to provide a free session for adults and parents on how to deal with depression and suicide prevention. We will connect Filipino lawyers in the country with the increasing number of Filipinos facing legal cases due to unpaid credit cards and bank loans after they lost their jobs. Inputs from the lawyers will help guide our *Kababayans* in addressing their cases.

The Facebook CFC SocDev UAE Available Job account is a validation that God wanted me to experience losing a job so I would use my resources and be creative to helping others. They can then Praise and Glorify Him as well as and help others. *Bayanihan* is indeed very much alive in the UAE.

---

[2] https://www.facebook.com/groups/1152725614784484/

Difficult Roads Often Lead to Beautiful Destination
(Unknown Author)

Being a successful woman or a leader does not free one from experiencing insecurities, rock bottom moments, and discouragements. In fact, going through this phase makes her stronger while overcoming challenges leads her to embrace her values and learn to appreciate more her real friends. I acknowledge that without faith in myself and trust in God I can do nothing.

Successful women or leaders are not Wonder Women with superpowers to solve everything, but they are women who are given opportunities to deal with their own crises and to be able to help others. Successful women first look inside themselves so they can be stronger.

During the time that I was going through my lowest moment, I recalled the interview I had with a priest who composes church songs. He reported that one of his reasons for composing was to protect people's ears from listening to wrong messages. I found myself doing the same thing and had to force myself to stop listening to my "bad self" who was putting myself down and to stop comparing myself with others. I had to stop listening to that voice of discouragement.

Aristotle Onassis once said: "It is during our darkest moments that we must focus to see the light." I have to remind myself to always say 'No' to anything that will not help me be grateful for the life that I have. To say 'No' to everything that will separate me from my passion and purpose to be a woman of God for others. To remember that passion needs to be fed with consistency and determination. To remember that the goal is to focus on the divine purpose.

Leadership Lessons in My Story

I am sharing this story to encourage others to have courage to face the unknown and to have the humility to seek help from others. There are people more than willing to support a cause especially if it uplifts the lives of OFs.

Be a brave leader willing to make a come-back, to believe in prayers, and to trust God and believe in His wisdom and provisions. To be a grateful leader for all the opportunities to live a meaningful life even if this means facing many challenges. Not to give up, instead to pursue one's passion in life as even during the hardest moments.

Do not use fear of failing as an excuse for not entering a new and unfamiliar world. Be willing to leave any situation that will not honor the life given us by our Maker.

As an FWN honoree, I have learned that to continue one's legacy it must be shared with others: one must live her purpose, passion, and pass it on.

As I finished writing this, I had spent my weekend in Abu Dhabi mentoring new correspondents of The Filipino Chanel's (TFC) Balitang Global and KWorld programs. The goal was to assist them to understand our mission of being a correspondent. I reminded them, a I have reminded myself that doing news should be done with public service in our hearts rather than with a goal to be a public figure, or to be famous. My goal was to show them how to be servant leaders. My hope is to see more Filipinos in the UAE be grateful for their being and their God. I have the same hope for Filipinos who practice Islam since the "purpose of life in Islam is to be a good trustee on earth by doing what is good to oneself and to others in worship of God" (Branine & Pollard, 2010, p8).

I Am Grateful

I want to thank my mentor Dr. Maria Beebe for not giving up on me. I am grateful that her patience carried me through as I faced my professional and personal challenges. She also provided guidance on refocusing my story to include my calling and mission as a broadcast journalist.

As I pray for the cancer patient from Dubai who is now in the Philippines preparing for a bone marrow transplant, made possible by donations following the airing of her story, I thank her for being God's instrument to remind me of my purpose and passion. Her determination, love for others, and fighting spirit will stay with me forever.

I would like to thank all those who helped me publish the FEME Connect Directory, my beloved husband Art Los Baños and son Eldrick Yuji for their untiring support and unconditional love; to my late father Jose Salinel who first introduced me how to being a leader and to my mother Lydia who is always there to pray and remind me to take care of myself; to my FWN sister Cristina Calaguian as well as her sister Paz Mejia for being my business partners; and to numerous private sector firms who believed in my business plan and the concept of raising the bar for Filipino Excellence in the Middle East. Thank you to my brethren in Couples for Christ-UAE. Thank you, too, to former Philippine Ambassador to the UAE Constancio Vingno, Jr and Consul General to Dubai and Northern Emirates Paul Raymund Cortes for their encouragement and support. Thank you to my colleagues in FWN. Mary Jane Alvero. Irene Corpuz. Arlene Pulido. Karen Graciles-Remo. Wafa Qasimieh. Lou Parroco. Lilian Bautista. Roxanne Martin.

I am a woman leader. My purpose and passion are clear. And now I am called to pass it on.

EDITHA TIJAMO WINTERHALTER, Ed.D.

Director, Administrative Services and Risk Management & Insurance
California State University, Northridge
GLOBAL FWN100™ 2017

Sangandaan

Mine is not a series of unfortunate events, nor was there a singular, catastrophic failure that turned my life around. Rather, mine is mostly an idyllic existence; a middle-of-the-road journey towards the American Dream. Curiously, it was so idyllic that were it not for three themes that kept resurfacing in my life, I could have easily lost myself along the way: Forks in the road, learning goalposts, and travel companions. Each in one way or another contributed to who I am today.

Taking the Fork in the Road

I am a late bloomer professionally because life seemed to enjoy changing my itinerary. Yogi Berra once said, "When life gives you a fork in the road, take it." The first of these turning points happened in early 1988, just before summer break in the Philippines. I was in the last stretches of my junior year of college at Far Eastern University-Nicanor Reyes Medical Foundation, majoring in medical technology. I was accepted as an intern at the Polymedic General Hospital. It was a well-trodden path: complete my internship, receive my bachelor's degree, continue to medical school, and become a doctor. Life was running along the course I had charted with confidence.

A couple of months prior to my acceptance, my father was granted his U.S. citizenship based on his military experience during World War II. My father was a member of the Philippine guerilla and Philippine Scouts that joined other resistance movements against the Japanese invasion to form the U.S. Army Forces Far East under General Douglas MacArthur. His U.S. citizenship presented a chance for the rest of the family to migrate to the United States and improve our family's financial situation. However, since it had taken nearly 40 years for my father to get his citizenship, I surmised that the immigration process for us would take equally long. To my surprise, he came home to the Philippines soon after receiving his citizenship and promptly began processing our immigration papers.

My first fork in the road dilemma was whether I should leave immediately for the States, or stay in the Philippines for a year until I finish my internship and graduate from college. The predicament was that I would turn 21 the following year and would no longer be considered a "child" under U.S. Citizenship and Immigration Services laws; I would not be considered an "immediate relative" eligible to migrate to the U.S. immediately. Instead, once I turned 21, I would fall under the category of "first preference" and would have to wait several years for my immigration to be considered. Even though I had a one-month window between graduation date and my 21st birthday, my parents worried that we would be cutting it close and did not want to chance my fate. So they decided for me to migrate without finishing college. Also, it was unthinkable for my parents to leave behind an unmarried daughter without parental presence; and my upbringing precluded me from voicing an opposing view. And to be honest, I did not mind leaving immediately. My imagination of America promised greener pastures. I reasoned I could finish college there. Thus, my life diverged from what I thought it would be.

As almost everyone eventually finds out, life is not always that easy in the United States. My parents, a younger brother, and I were the first in my immediate family who migrated, and so we needed all of our combined income to survive. That took going to college immediately out of the picture.

My very first job was at a fast food chain restaurant in Echo Park, California. Working was a major change for me. Prior to this, even though we were poor, I still led a relatively cosseted life in the Philippines. I never worked for a living while in the Philippines and, outside of my daily route of home-school-home, I was chaperoned everywhere I went. Therefore, to be earning a living, albeit at a wage of US$4.25 per hour, and being allowed to wander pretty much anywhere on my own, that is, anywhere the Rapid Transit District buses can take me within a two-hour ride was exhilarating. For these reasons, I did not mind not resuming my college studies immediately.

Learning Along the Way

Despite not going to college right away, the second recurring theme in my life is learning goalposts. Whatever I am doing, regardless of whether it is inside or outside a classroom, or whatever circumstance I find myself in, I always find something to learn. Some lessons may be more profound than others, but even those that seem insignificant provide a learning experience.

Systems Thinking

I learned most of my foundational work ethics and skills while working at that fast food restaurant. Based on ergonomics or human factors (International Ergonomics Association, 2018), I was trained to always factor in the layout of our workstation, the duration of specific processes, and my interaction with these different elements to produce maximal output with minimal movement. By doing so, I gained the ability to organize my work or projects efficiently and effectively, analyze processes, and apply a systems-way of thinking in all the jobs I held and of informing my doctoral dissertation. For my doctoral dissertation, I examined the impact of physical learning spaces on the learning experience of college students with attention deficit hyperactivity disorder, or ADHD (Winterhalter, 2016).

Respect Diversity

Most importantly, however, I learned how to work with different kinds of people. We were a very diverse crew, not only by nationality but also by age, economic status, and gender preferences. Some of my co-workers were students, some were working parents, and some were retirees. It was the first time that I truly interacted with people from different backgrounds, and it was interesting to explore the differences, and even more exciting to discover similarities. For example, it was exhilarating to recognize some Tagalog words (or very close to them) spoken in Malaysian language by a co-worker, which opened up opportunities for us to share our stories with one another. At a deeper level, I learned that once you peeled away the differences in our mother tongues, the different religions we believed in, or the different customs we followed, we shared similar values and aspirations. Despite our differences and different starting points, each of us wanted to improve our lives and help our families.

I also learned that different people have different approaches to life, and that is totally acceptable. For example, two of my co-workers were given a chance to train as managers of the restaurant: one was in her mid-thirties and a single mother, while the other was in her early twenties and close to finishing vocational school.

The former excitedly welcomed the opportunity because it meant promotion and increased wages for her family while the latter declined because it meant taking time away from her studies. Thus, I learned then that it is extremely essential to listen to other's viewpoints so one can better understand their actions.

I think working in such a diverse environment so early in my working life helped me develop a deep respect for people's differences. As a core value, this helped me as I moved up in my career. The biggest lesson for me was never to let the opportunity for a new experience pass you by because chances are, it is a lesson that will be helpful later on in life.

Continuing Education

While working at that fast food restaurant, I took night classes at a vocational school, working towards a medical assisting certification. I could not take classes at a state university because I had not yet been living in California for more than a year, the requirement for establishing California residency in order to qualify for the lower resident tuition fee rates. At that time, the next logical step for improving my situation in life was to aim for enrollment at a state university.

After finishing vocational school, I worked as a medical assistant in a doctor's office in Beverly Hills, my first office job or a "real job." I felt like Tess McGill from the hit movie, *Working Girl*. I was finally earning more than the minimum wage, driving my own car, and was experiencing a vastly different culture than I had seen so far while living and working in downtown Los Angeles. Not necessarily better or worse, just different.

Now around that time, technology was starting to permeate even small offices like ours. It began with fax machines that could deliver results in a matter of minutes instead of days. And people were talking about personal computers, Lotus 1-2-3, WordPerfect. Automated billing, digital bookkeeping, and databases of patients and vendors. I had to retool myself. I went back to school, this time at a computer vocational school.

Be Ready for More Forks in the Road

While in the computer vocational school, I met my future husband in one of my classes. That was the next major fork on the road, one that I happily took, and he became my best traveling companion. We got married while still in vocational school, and within a couple of years, we decided to start a family. Life was good. We had our first son, secure jobs, a home, and happy marriage. It was a very comfortable life, and I felt that I was living the American dream. I could have stayed in that space and would have been fine. However, even though my life had many twists and turns, what I want to emphasize is that I made sure I was never off the road. I made an active effort to ensure that I was still on my life journey. I was pursuing a general goal at that time of my life: to finish college and get a career started. It was not a straight road, and I took many stops along the way, but I did not let my fuel for learning run out.

Dealing with Bumps. Potholes. Detours.

I was twenty-seven years old when I decided that it was time to finish my college education, many years later than I had originally planned. Paradoxically, it was the first step that proved to be the biggest hurdle: applying to the university. For some reason, seeing the application form, with pages and pages of information to fill in, was daunting for me. The gathering of my high school and college transcripts from the Philippines and having those evaluated for American college course equivalency, taking the Test of English as a Foreign Language (TOEFL), and sitting for the English and Math placement tests seemed a monumental task to me then. In retrospect, it was probably fear of the unknown, tinged with a feeling of inadequacy, which held me back. Self-doubt crept in. Previously, I had taken a few classes at community colleges in California, but I was not sure if I was ready for an American four-year university. Was this the right decision? Was I selfish for wanting to pursue college and take time away from my family? Compounding the issue was discovering that for all those three years of college in the Philippines, only a few classes, such as physical education and Spanish, would count towards my college general education requirements. I was starting over.

Nevertheless, this twenty-seven-year-old-mother attended her first four-year university in America, alongside the eighteen- and nineteen-year-olds. Needless to say, I felt old and out of place. I feared that I would not be able to fit in the college culture. In addition, being a mom of a young active child and working full-time was incredibly tiring. Taking classes at night added physical and mental struggle. In hindsight, now that I am older, starting college at twenty-seven is not that old. Much to my surprise, however, I found that going back to school was exhilarating. I felt a renewal of energy, an excitement that at last, I was on the main road again and driving towards my goal. Besides, I discovered that as I learned from the classes, my classmates learned from me because I had my lived experience to share. The lesson for me was not to be intimidated by the unknown.

I wish I could say that it was smooth sailing after I enrolled in the university. The reality was that it was hard work taking classes at night, working full-time, and maintaining a family life. I missed playing with my toddler before putting him to bed at night. There were weekends when I could not attend his athletic games because I had to finish schoolwork. Of course, it did not help that I had a vision of what my family life would be, which I was not willing to give up. I knew I wanted to have three kids eventually. I wanted to have my family the way I envisioned it, but also have a career. There were moments when I thought I would need to choose between staying in college and pursuing my vision of a family. Each time these questioning moments occurred, my family and I made adjustments to accommodate both choices. For example, after I gave birth to my second son, I quit my job and took a lower level position at the university to be closer to home. The move also allowed me to take classes both during the day and immediately after work, reducing the time I had to spend in the Los Angeles traffic, and giving me more time with my family. The decision was made easier by enrolling in the Program for Adult College Education (PACE), a collaborative initiative between the Los Angeles Community College District (LACCD) and California State University, Northridge (CSUN) that let adult students the opportunity to take full-load units while working full-time. The program allowed me to complete my lower-level GE course requirements in less time than in a traditional semester enrollment. The lesson I took from this experience was that sometimes, it is okay to make compromises and take chances. I needed to take a step back and keep my goals reasonable as there may be better things in store for me. I learned that I should look far ahead to the finish line and strategize plans that are sustainable regarding life balance.

Reshaping My Road

When I was about one year away from graduation from college with a major in accountancy, I got pregnant for the third time as planned. What was not planned was that I would be having twin boys. Remember those forks on the road? Well, I reshaped the road. I did not want to have another excuse to halt my academic progress, as I was that close to my goal. Instead of taking time off my studies, I determined that I would stay on the path and finish. I kept working full time, continued taking full-load classes outside of the PACE program, carried the twins to full-term, gave birth in the summer, enrolled for courses in the fall, resumed working full-time again, and graduated the following spring at the age of thirty-five.

I was also very lucky that I was working in an environment that fosters growth, not only among our students but also in staff and faculty. Lucky because I had so many mentors along the way who advised me that getting a bachelor's degree and landing a nice job in a university was not the end of my academic journey. Because, again, I could have stayed in that space and be fine. But I did have a need to know more. And I recognized that I do have a lot to offer at our institution, given a seat at the table. To enable that, in addition to the skills and experience that I bring to my work, I knew that I needed to add to my academic credentials and learn more about how higher education works, the administration of a large, public university, and the issues and challenges facing higher education.

A few years after receiving my bachelor's degree, I went back to school and worked on my master's degree in higher education administration, and graduated in Spring 2010. Then in Spring 2016, I received my Doctorate in Education. Although it had taken me over twenty years to get a doctorate, I did it. Despite the forks in the road that I had taken, I succeeded in having a happy balance between my personal and professional lives. I feel blessed that I did not have to choose between career and having a family. I was able to accomplish both, because of the support and encouragement of everyone around me.

Learning from Travel Companions

The third recurring theme in my life, and one most important to me: my life and travel companions, the people who have helped me in the pursuit of my goals. They all helped me get to where I am today by giving me encouragement, support, and space to grow. That includes my parents, my husband, my kids, siblings, friends, and the people who worked with me. I do not think I could have worked full time, taken full load classes, carried my twins to full-term, and worked again full-time without the support of everyone around me. For example, my father would come daily to our house to take care of the twin babies while I was working during the day, and my husband would take over their care when he came home at night after work. Our oldest son learned to change the babies' diapers and gave them baths. Our second son became our do-it-yourself (DIY) kid, fixing things around the house. My *Ate* Tess provided transportation, picking up and dropping off our kids to and from school. The people I worked with were my cheerleaders. I had a support team at home and at work. They all understood my need to learn, my instinct to take action, and desire to keep moving forward. They mentored me, offered practical help, and became my sounding board. They became my gauge on whether to slow down, gas it, or take a turn.

I would like to say that my drive in life to make something for myself is one hundred percent from my inner fire, but that would not be exactly true, and would completely ignore the influence of the seven people in my life, who were my either my loudest backseat drivers or most precious passengers. Those are my mother, my older sister Tess, my husband, and my four kids.

Character Lessons: Strength and Pragmatism from My Mother

I got my strength and pragmatism from my mother. We had several serious setbacks as a family when I was growing up, but her willpower weathered any storm, and her capacity for creative solutions was formidable. I know we were poor in the Philippines, but I honestly did not know how poor we were, because Mama always seemed to manage to come through when most needed: when my father could not work because of surgery, when my brother got hospitalized for a length of time due to lung complications, or when the rate of inflation exceeded our income. She somehow made it exciting for us to eat just rice and *bagoong* with *calamansi* for dinner. Or rice and fish *chicharron* because we did not have enough money. And when I thought a circumstance would finally break her will and strength, she would sway slightly, but invariably bounce back. When my sister passed away to cancer in 2013, I was afraid of what this might do to Mama. But after fully giving in to her heartbreak, she looked around in the hospital room and rose again as the matriarch of the family, to take care of our emotional well-being. Whenever I face a difficulty, I draw on Mama's strength and think that if she could shoulder any of what she went through, I can certainly handle any of mine.

Moreover, Mama encouraged us to be aware and involved, not with her words, but through her actions. I think it was a given that she rallied for us to excel academically, but more importantly, she encouraged and supported us in our many extracurricular activities. She would stay up with me through the night while I finished projects, helped me prepare for periodical exams by reviewing with me and quizzing me, acted as my audience and critic for declamation pieces that I would be performing for school, or took me to the national library whenever I needed more than the reference books at school. She would open up our home to be the meeting place of our youth organization, helped us organize our very own volleyball league, or got us involved in our village's various activities that she led with my father in their capacity as officers of our homeowner's association. She would always say, "*Paano ka matututo kung hindi mo gagawin?*" [How would you learn if you don't do it?], and that, has always been my driving force to try new things and take action.

Leadership Lesson: My Ate Tess As My Role Model

My *Ate* Tess [Ate is honorific for elder sister] was always my model of a leader. She approached life with so much zest that she could not help but lead our youth club, our children's PTA, the many church organizations where she belonged, community support groups, etc. Whenever she saw a need, she would rise to fulfill it. And she would do it with so much excitement and enthusiasm that others could not help but join her. But most of all, she would care for everyone in her sphere to make sure that their needs were met first. Hers was the ear that would always listen, the shoulder one could always lean on, the epitome of Trevor Greenleaf's servant leader for me. And even though she is no longer with us, her words "*Kaya mo yan, sige lang.*" [You can do it, just go on.] would continue to carry me through, because I know I could not fail her belief in me.

Life Lessons: My Husband, My Compass

Perhaps the best backseat driver I could ask for is my husband, who is literally and metaphorically my compass. His excellent sense of direction guides me while driving on land, diving underwater, and most importantly, journeying through life. His sense of justice and fundamental instinct to do what is right has served as my moral compass. Whenever I face ethical situations, I would always ask, "What would John do?" And act accordingly. His voice, added to mine, has truly served me well throughout my career. But most importantly, by working with me in pursuing my goals, he helps veer me back to the main road whenever I take life's many forks. He would strategize with me on how we can balance the demands of work, school, and family. His oft-repeated phrase, "right, let's get this done" never fails to assure me that whatever it is, we will get it done.

Grit, Passion, and Self-fulfilment: My Legacy to My Boys

And finally, the major reasons I have to keep driving forward: my four boys Kurt, Sean, Otto, and Fox. I know in my heart of hearts that I would never be able to ask them to pursue their dreams to the best of their abilities if I, myself, did not do just that. I would feel such an impostor if I were to tell my kids to do what I did not have the courage to do myself. I wanted them to see first-hand how grit and passion could take them to self-fulfillment. Of course, I would never deny that I wish fortune, wealth, and security for all of them. That is a given. But most of all, I want them to be able to look back in their lives and say, "I did what I wanted to do," because the one thing that I would never be able to do is to give them back time and life gone by. I wanted to have the means of providing for all their needs so they can pursue their dreams freely and seize their moments so they, in turn, can provide a positive and lasting impact on future generations.

My Expanded Road Map

My road trip has taught me several lessons. A key lesson is that it is absolutely okay to ask for help and to receive it. As long as YOU, yourself, are helping YOU to succeed, people will recognize that and will help willingly. As human beings, we are meant to be in a community. So be part of that community.

More importantly, however, I want to impart that I did not just ask for help. Even though I did not know Kotter (1998) then, I may have unknowingly followed his steps to organizational change. That is, I communicated my need to finish college soon (establishing a sense of urgency), discussed each major decision with everyone in my life that was going to be affected (forming a powerful guiding coalition), and planned our actions together (empowering others). For example, I explained to my family why I wanted to go back to college, and we discussed childcare options. As Filipinos, family helping each other is a given. But a family conversation ahead of time made planning and executing those decisions easier. Thus, developing my team, and open channels of communication, were keys to my success in this endeavor.

I chose to stay in higher education because I felt that this was a space where I could truly make an impact because I love what I am doing. When you love what you are doing, chances are you will actually be good at it. And when you are really good at it, chances are you will be successful. I would like to add that when you are very good at what you do, chances are you will start to lead, and start making an impact. As an administrator, I like to think that I lead from behind, by ensuring that faculty and staff have the tools and resources they need so they, in turn, can ensure that our students succeed. Besides, I try to emulate my *Ate* Tess in listening to those I mentor, so I can best address their professional growth needs, understand what motivates people, or figure out what workplace values they celebrate.

In 2011, I met one of the previous FWN awardees, Susan Afan, at a leadership conference. She then introduced me to the International Society of Filipinos in Finance and Accounting (ISFFA). The introduction to ISFFA was very opportune because I was ready to give back for all the mentorship and support that people had given me along the way. ISFFA is about helping Filipino students, young professionals, and immigrants who wish to enter the fields of finance and accounting and provides them mentorship, leadership, and scholarship. I saw that this was another space where I could make a positive impact. Working with ISFFA was very fulfilling, seeing students grow into professionals and young people gain confidence. Thus, when I was voted to chair the national executive board of ISFFA in 2016, I gladly accepted. The enthusiasm and passion of the ISFFA members in helping not only one another but also those in need in the community is very inspiring. I considered it an honor to be tasked with supporting the continuance of its mission.

I have not yet reached the end of my trip. Indeed, I am just in the earlier leg of my life's itinerary. There are many more forks in the road to discover, more learning goalposts to heed, and more traveling companions to meet. I intend to keep paying forward for all the help that I received along the way. **I know that learning is best experienced when you take others along with you.**

MYRNA P. YOUNG, MSN, RN, CNOR

Nursing Education Specialist, Robert Wood Johnson University Hospital
GLOBAL FWN100™ 2017

Big Dreams, Broken Glass

When I think back to when I was young, I am amazed by how far I have come. I say it without humility because then I was naive, and like every young girl from the Philippines, I had BIG dreams. But I also had this passionate feeling that I wanted to make a difference. I did not know how I was going to do it, I just knew what I wanted. I wanted to leave a legacy of my impact on other people's lives based on my contribution to their success, happiness, and well-being.

Somewhere along the way, the many failures in my story became my successes in leadership. It is because of this story that I can bravely say, "I am amazed by how far I have come." Now, I hope that my leadership legacy becomes a part of yours.

Breaking the Glass Ceiling

> Life lesson: We all face challenges and obstacles in life.
> The difference is how we overcome them.
> - **Myrna P. Young**

Growing up in the Philippines, I was repeatedly told that for business in America, there is a glass ceiling for minority women, especially for females of Asian descent! What was this 'ceiling' and how could it keep in someone? How could it keep in young Asian females?

I thought. "It's glass. Let's break it."

And so began the journey toward one of many big dreams. Rather than be discouraged by myths of the unattainable, I went out into the world to find that glass ceiling and see what it would take to break through. Along the way, the *very* long way, I faced challenges. So I got braver. I faced racial discrimination. So I got resilient. And by the time I faced gender harassment, I was downright secure in myself and my power. It is here, in this place of power, that we crack the glass until it breaks.

How did I get here from there? I believe that true leaders recognize and seize the opportunity to motivate, thrive and grow. If you are strong enough to reward, promote and recognize those around you, leadership blossoms. When those around you on a team follow your lead, you know you have a collaborative team that can support each other. And that's when the magic happens! Collaboration. Synergy. Productiveness. The fuel to power any Leader.

I get ahead of myself. My story of humble beginnings starts long before I knew anything about business, or failure, or leadership.

Sacred Secrets

> Myrna's mentorship gave me the confidence to accomplish more than what I ever thought I could do. Myrna encouraged me to accept any and all tasks offered because our leadership would not ask us to do it if they did not think we could handle it. I have learned, under Myrna, that leaders can be present and exert influence in any position, whether as a manager or as a bedside nurse.
> - **Laura Sharlow RN, BSN**; Comment about Myrna Young

It was my parents' greatest dream to have all their children earn a college education. Having completed only six years of grade school, they were both hard-working and driven but had very few possessions. What they had in bountiful supply was the strength and tenacity to keep reaching for their dream of giving each of their children the gift of education.

Nevertheless, the expectations they had of me, as the eldest child in the family, often felt excessive and unreasonable. They put the responsibility and expectation on my shoulders at a very tender age. If I did not finish school, the rest of my siblings would follow my footsteps and would not have good lives. They said that I was the key role model for my siblings and that if I fail, they fail. This was a tall order for a 14 year-old girl!

In fact, because I was often social, energetic, boisterous, and always seeking fun; many in my community predicted I would be the one who would NOT finish school. Despite that prediction, I did finish, with honors. In freshman year of nursing school, I was one of the Top Ten (specifically 8th out of 165) students in my class. Believe it or not, my father was not too happy with that! He told me, "Only top three counts." Then, in senior year, when I was in the top five, it still did not matter because only first and second place "count" according to Dad.

The early road toward my professional career had not been easy either. It was difficult and often not fun. At 23, when I came to the United States to be a nurse to make a difference, there were many days and nights that I found myself assuming additional responsibilities for those around me. I assumed responsibilities for tasks my peers would avoid, when they suggested, 'that's not my job.' I was even called stupid, a push-over, a butt-kisser, and a sucker by co-workers who saw me put in extra efforts.

Hard as it was, I welcomed the challenges that made me stronger. I sought out those opportunities that others missed and began promoting my own growth. Eventually, I was given more formal responsibility and given recognition for my work. To be chosen to assume a leadership role in a hospital setting, back then, was an accomplishment made all the sweeter since it was given to me, the newest and youngest nurse in the department. In the 70's it was rare to see a young, female, foreign Filipina graduate rise to the position of managing an operating room. I did not stop there. I continued on to other administrative roles and these fostered more thirst for personal expansion and for sharing knowledge. Women in the workplace have come a long way, but there is more work to be done.

Failure or Challenges

> Myrna has won multiple awards locally, nationally and internationally. She has initiated numerous programs to benefit her colleagues in their endeavor to achieve higher ranks in the Professional Advancement System. She actively participates in various community outreach projects and multiple hospital-wide educational activities and is a well-known educational enthusiast. She is divinely inspired. Myrna is a gift to me and the world.
> - **Veronica F. Barcelona, BSN, RNC-LRN, RNC-NIC, CCRN-NIC**; Comments about Myrna Young

Can it be that failures lead to success? Absolutely. If you do not forget how to learn from failures. Walking away with your lesson(s) is not enough. We must take the lessons and share them with others, and then turn back into the failure, as if you have forgotten that you have failed before, and that you are ready try it again but differently. Expect a different outcome until you see it come alive.

I went through many different difficult times; a lot of financial investment losses, family and health challenges, and failures. So many failures. I dabbled in various ways to make money: business ventures, selling life insurance, mortgage, real estate, aggressive stocks investing, managerial per diem roles, legal expert consulting. I even started a business with some colleagues from the day-job and ended up in bankruptcy court.

One of the most difficult challenges that I faced was when I transitioned from the Operating Room (OR) where I had spent most of my career to a different specialty where I had very limited experience. I was highly respected and valued as I made an impact that brought the clinical practice to excellent standards and high level of performance in the OR. I was told that my OR colleagues regarded the 1:1 mentorship I had provided that helped them achieved their career goals. I remember the kind words of Kathleen Evanovich Zavotsky: "Myrna is a true transformational leader in every sense of the word. She has an amazing talent for motivating...she shares her talents with everyone she meets...a sign of a true leader."

I went through tough times when I transitioned. Sailing on unchartered water was devastating. However, Nicole, a colleague always reminded me that "things happen for a reason, something bigger and better will come and not to worry."

I kept my faith in God, but there were times that I questioned Him. Those were my weakest moments. Eventually, and thankfully, my nursing career advanced, and I encountered new challenges that included life and death situations, handling difficult and demanding doctors, juggling too many balls in the air while maintaining an efficient and effective department, to name just a few.

But none of these experiences helped alleviate the pain I felt from discrimination and harassment that I was subjected to along the way. I was addressed as that "Asian woman" instead of saying my name and subjected to harassing comments such as "how's your sex life", "don't you get tired of eating the same dish?" or "would you consider having an affair?" Even "you look great in that outfit" may have been benign without the leering eyes checking me out from head to toe. These micro-aggressions caused me heartache but not a derailment. I persevered and kept going. There was no option, I was not going to fail or my brothers and sisters would fail too!

Mentors and Mentees

> Myrna embodies "Transformational Leadership." As my mentor, she has provided me resources to better myself personally and professionally. She is the reason why I gained courage, determination, and confidence to look for opportunities. It's not all about herself but about her genuine intentions to help colleagues reach professional goals.
> - Victoria A. Pangilinan MSN, RN, CCRN; Comments about Myrna Young

I really never had an official mentor in my youth and my early career. I was always alone during my early career years and on my way to leadership. Because I missed out on mentorship, I made it my goal to make a difference for others through mentoring. Mentoring felt good and made me want to reach as many people as I can.

Later in my career, my path eventually led me to Robert Wood Johnson (RWJ) University Hospital in New Brunswick, New Jersey, where I received an abundance of opportunities to spread my wings and advance my career. The nursing division afforded me the opportunity to get involved in numerous endeavors including participating in research and delivering presentations at regional, national, and international conferences. I also had the pleasure of serving as a liaison and coordinator for RWJ's International Magnet Mentorship program with St. Luke's Medical Center in the Philippines. Based on all my contributions to the organization, I have been featured in various professional nursing journals and in system-wide projects in our RWJ Barnabas Health System.

I am well aware that not every strong and powerful female professional has been fortunate enough to have an RWJ in their professional corner. My advice would be to seek out professional mentors, even if your search takes you outside of your employment circle. Mentors can appear in your life in many different forms; trainings, conferences, associations, networking groups, online communities, videos and books, and the list goes on. As long as you have curiosity, drive, passion, and compassion; you will spend only a short time being alone. Learning from my nursing colleagues was not the only way my life and career has been enriched. Mentoring nurses to reach their personal best has added richness and depth to my life. Being there to relate, to inform, and to guide others that seek mentorship has become a passion for me.

BEING GRATEFUL MATTERS

> Myrna has an intrinsic ability to motivate others and help them realize their potential. If we did not cross paths, I would not have a graduate degree right now. Quite frankly, she is the sole reason I enrolled in school and I am grateful for it.
> - **Rafal Polinski, MSN, RN**; Comments about Myrna Young

I have no illusions that I could have become who I am without an incredible support system. It is clear that I have had my share of hardships, and I welcome the responsibility of sharing the lessons I have learned.

Ultimately, my humble beginnings, my culture, and the lessons my parents and community taught me, are the foundations that have given me my core strength. I still get the shivers when I think of the irony of being grateful for hardship.

As a female and a Filipina, I have often felt that I needed to work harder than most who were not like me, but I also embrace that I have much to be grateful for. In fact, my journey has not always been entirely up-hill and I am convinced that being grateful for all the experiences that have contributed to my success. Our words, our thoughts, and our actions should always come from a place of being grateful, as this is an incredibly infectious emotion. Eventually, those around you have no choice but to join you in being grateful.

I cannot speak of being grateful without giving my family great praise. In addition to the depth of character and foundation that my parents provided me, my super supportive husband Renato and my children Chris, Michael, Caitlin, and my beautiful grandson Cameron play a major role in my achievements as well. Their support and confidence have given me the inspiration to reach my goal of making a difference not only to my career but also to make differences for people who are less fortunate than I, those that do not have the means to meet the basic needs of their families or those who were afflicted by natural disasters. I feel that doing what I do gives me a sense of purpose, and God's way of recognizing my contributions to humanity is through the awards and recognitions that I receive.

That's A Wrap!

> Myrna Young is an energetic and passionate leader whose vision for excellence in the delivery of care is actualized through her tireless efforts to transform nursing practice, reaching our intercontinental partners using new knowledge and innovation. This work made Myrna the perfect nominee for the International Nurses Award.
> - **Lori Colineri DNP, RN, NEA-BC**, Senior Vice President and Chief Nursing Officer, Southern Region, Robert Wood Johnson Barnabas Health Visiting Professor, Rutgers School of Nursing, Rutgers, The State University of New Jersey; Comments about Myrna Young

In a recent interview, I was asked, "How do you want to be remembered as a leader?"

The first thing that comes to my mind is the ideal of Filipino culture, family, and education. What I hope to be remembered for beyond that is the passion with which I have chosen to act every day. If I am to leave a legacy, it would start at home, with my sons whom I made a point to teach and learn from, year after year as they grew. While they are both adults now, I still lavish them with 'I love you' texts, 'You got this!' emails, kissy face emojis, and other meaningful touchpoints. I want them to have the security of feeling my support in a way that I myself was seeking for so long. I would like to think that all of those hardships, failures, and do-overs in my past have resulted in my strong skillsets, tenacity, and good old-fashioned gumption.

What I most would like to be remembered is that I found my life's joy in activities that had nothing to do with work! It was my family that created that lovely connection between angst and relaxation. Spending time with my children and grandchild is the ultimate balance for the stresses or strains that come with a successful professional career. Aside from all holidays, birthdays, vacations, and dinners once or twice a month, I also enjoy the company and conversation that comes from an extended family circle. The bigger the better, with all aunts, uncles, cousins, nieces, and nephews!

Lest you believe that my joys come only from family, I assure you that is not the case. I love participating in various activities with both friends and family. I enjoy ballroom dancing, Broadway shows, slot machines, and movies. Shopping, celebrations, and "Words with Friends."

I have always been a believer in the power of love and gratitude. I have found that the more grateful I am for the love that grows my inner circle, the easier it gets to find peace and balance between the successes and the failures of a busy, skillful and educated superwoman, career leader, and engaged mom and grandmother.

I leave you with this parting thought: the more recognition, accolades, and celebrations one receives, the more important it becomes to remain humble. After all, the world is a better place with all of us in it. That is your legacy.

GERI ALUMIT ZELDES, Ph.D.

Professor, Michigan State University, School of Journalism
GLOBAL FWN100™ 2017

Was It Murder?
Leadership in My Quest for Truth

In July and August 1975, dozens of patients (reports vary) at the Veterans Administration Hospital in Ann Arbor, Michigan experienced sudden respiratory failure, and ten died. After an intense FBI investigation, two Filipina nurses, Filipina Narciso and Leonora Perez, were charged with murdering two patients and attempting to kill seven others by injecting a muscle relaxant drug called Pavulon into their intravenous tubes. FBI Investigators had two other suspects, Dr. Michael McLeod, an African American physician, and an African American nurse, according to FBI reports; news stories did not cover this information although Dr. McLeod confirms in the film he was on the suspect list. The Nurse Manager Betty Jakim, who was Caucasian, admitted before committing suicide on February 3, 1977 to her psychiatrist she had poisoned the patients. In the letter, she wrote Narciso and Perez were innocent. However, the letter was not considered credible.

On July 14, 1977, a jury in a federal court in Detroit convicted Narciso and Perez for poisoning five patients and conspiracy to poison others. The trial lasted 13 weeks and the jury spent 13 days deliberating, both time periods setting records. After Narciso and Perez spent about five months in federal prison, a judge, citing prosecutorial misconduct ordered a new trial, requested by the defense attorneys. Prosecutors, however, declined the offer of a new trial, because they knew Narciso and Perez would not testify in the new trial. Jurors in the original trial indicated that it was their testimony that caused them to think the nurses were guilty, indicating culpability. Narciso and Perez appeared nervous as the prosecutor grilled them with questions.

In 2011, some 30 years later, I, a Filipina-American professor and filmmaker at Michigan State University, learned about the case for the first time. I decided to pursue the question: Was it Murder? My film, "*That Strange Summer*," finished in January 2016, is an hour-long documentary that explores this complicated story. In answer to the question, yes, it was murder, but then it became as one of the sources said, like the board game *Clue*, a quest for the person or persons responsible for the crime. The film uses interviews with FBI investigators and former VA employees, thousands of pages of FBI documents obtained via the Freedom of Information Act, and archival TV and newspaper stories. The documentary examines coverage of the case in the local press as well as national TV coverage.

I examine stereotypes and perceptions that may have influenced the outcome of the investigation and trial, re-construct the investigation and trial of the Filipina nurses, and consider the movement that sought to prove the nurses' innocence.

My efforts to create a documentary about the case made me confront assumptions I made about the Filipino community, live through tensions in covering this group as a Filipino American, and recognize the legacies of this case on the collective consciousness of a generation of Filipinos. The hurt experienced by the participants in this study makes this a case for historical trauma, defined as the mental wounding of individuals and generations caused by a disturbing event. Using the theoretical framework of historical trauma, I will unpack instances of cumulative emotional distress I encountered in making this documentary film and describe my sense-making of how this project represents who I am, including my leadership as a documentarian. Even though I failed at interviewing the nurses involved in this case, I believe the work can contribute to a national conversation on racism. It also provides a voice for Narciso and Perez.

HISTORICAL TRAUMA RESEARCH

Clinical psychotherapists use the concept of "historical trauma" for the communal suffering across generations by individuals and groups united by an event or identity (Brave Heart & DeBryn, 1998; Crawford, 2013; Evans-Campbell, 2008; Gone, 2013). In the 1970s, research on historical trauma was critiqued because of the lack of controls (Kellerman, 2001a). In the 1980s, research compared clinical and non-clinical populations, and in the 1990s, as studies on historical trauma lessened, a major focus of research was designed to synthesize previous research on the psychopathology in children of Holocaust survivors.

Once thought preposterous, the concept of transferring trauma from parent to child is now studied as a vital component of trauma experiences such as war, political unrest, abuse, violence, natural disasters, and other tragic events. Historical trauma has been recognized in individuals and groups who faced oppression, victimization, or a traumatic event including colonized indigenous groups. In recent years, scholars have examined historical trauma as an explanation of health disparities in racial and ethnic minority populations.

Filipina Narciso and Leonora Perez endured trauma when they were accused of homicide of the patients at the hospital where they worked. The high levels of emotional stress they experienced extended to their families, their co-workers, and the Filipino American community in Ann Arbor, in the U.S. and elsewhere. Jay Gonzalez, a professor of politics at the University of San Francisco, noted that this case made Filipinos fear that if the U.S. government could convict the nurses based on circumstantial evidence, then the government could accuse anyone of wrongdoing.

The effects of this tragic event understood as premised historical trauma can be expected to impact the next generation. The impact has been less than might have been expected because, for most of the generations who grew up in the 1970s and 1980s and beyond, the event is largely unknown.

My Leadership Building Blocks

In 1973, my family immigrated from Baguio City, Philippines to Flint, Michigan. My mother was a nephrologist, schooled at the University of Santo Tomas. My father, an accountant in the Philippines, became a maintenance man at a nursing home, a job that gave him the flexibility to drive my mom from hospital to hospital. My two sisters, brother, and I attended Catholic Schools in Flint.

In 1992, I graduated from the University of Michigan in Ann Arbor with a bachelor's degree in English Literature and Communication. In 1994, I earned a master's degree in journalism at Indiana University. As I worked at a local TV station as a videographer and reporter, I pursued a Ph.D. in mass communication at Michigan State University, a degree I received in 2000. After several years as an adjunct professor and freelance journalist, I started in 2004 as a tenure-track assistant professor at MSU. In 2011, I was promoted to associate professor with tenure, and in 2017, promoted to full professor.

Learning to be a Documentarian

In 2007, I applied for a humanities grant to produce a film titled "Arabs, Jews & the News." This film demonstrated how the emotions of the Israeli-Palestinian crisis spilled over to the streets of the suburbs of Detroit. Bob Albers, a Professor of Practice in my college, directed the film. I became the producer and his all-purpose apprentice in filmmaking.

Finding My Passion

Creating stories with longer shelf lives than TV news stories gave me a sense of exhilaration, encouraging me to re-brand as a documentary maker. I had experience using content analysis to examine the influence of the race and gender of reporters on the race and gender of the sources they used. I went from a quantitative social scientist to a qualitative one. I, in my heart and on my Curriculum Vita, became a storyteller who used interviews and archival research to conjure long-form stories.

I have created 13 documentary films, two radio documentary series, and a comic book. *"That Strange Summer"* is my longest film at 56 minutes, my only feature-length film, and took the longest time to create, some five years from conception to completion. The making of *"That Strange Summer"* overlapped with the making of other films, but it was a constant. The film continued to haunt and delight and provided the opportunity to dive deeper into history, including the history of me.

Producing a Unicorn

Interviewed about winning an award for *"That Strange Summer,"* I was asked, "Do you think you won the award because *you* directed the film or because of the story?" To which I replied: "The film received recognition, not because of its production qualities. My camera work could have been better and the re-construction of events more professional. My audio could be better if I paid attention to extraneous sounds as I filmed."

By January 2016 I was tired of working on the film but still wanted to see it on the local Public Broadcasting Station (PBS). The local PBS initially said no because of the poor audio quality. Then, I got lucky. In 2017, a manager at the station corrected audio in the opening sequence and toward the end so the film could meet PBS standards.

I believe the story won the Indie Producer Award in March 2018 as well as other accolades because it is a unicorn. On April 8, 2018, the film received in Las Vegas an Award of Excellence from the Broadcast Education Association's Media Arts Festival.

I still believe though it could have been better if I had interviewed Filipina Narciso and Leonora Perez.

Even decades later, literature about the deaths of patients at the Veterans Hospital in Ann Arbor is sparse. As of 2010, only one book covered the investigation, *The*

Mysterious Deaths at Ann Arbor by Robert K. Wilcox. The book, published in 1977, recounted the investigation, not the trial. In 2016, Elizabeth Zibby Oneal, a freelance writer who lives in Ann Arbor, and Dr. S. Martin Lindenauer, Professor Emeritus of Surgery at the University of Michigan, who served as Chief of Staff at the Ann Arbor V.A. Hospital 1974–1981 at the time of the events detailed in this book, published in 2016 *Paralyzing Summer: The True Story of the Ann Arbor V.A. Hospital Poisonings and Deaths.*

Learning about the Case

In the summer of 2011, I was discussing with one of my colleagues at Michigan State University (MSU) plans for the International Conference of the Philippines scheduled for the following fall. I shared with him I had finished in December 2010 a short film called "The Death of an Imam" in which FBI agents shot and killed in 2009 Imam Luqman Ameen Abdullah. It was the first killing of a Muslim religious leader by an agent of the U.S. government. The film explored allegations of terrorism, conspiracy, the use of FBI informants, and the role of Muslims in the mainstream media. I also mentioned to my colleague that I had recently released a documentary called "The Kings of Flint" about Karate Masters Jacky and Dora King in Flint who taught their students how to defend themselves when attacked. My colleague suggested my next project be a documentary film about Filipina nurses imprisoned for killing veterans at a hospital in Ann Arbor. My response? Filipina nurses did what?

That evening, I Googled "Filipina nurses Ann Arbor" and the first result was a Wikipedia entry that began: "The Ann Arbor Hospital Murders were the murders of 10 patients by an unauthorized administration in their IV of a curare drug Pavulon in an Ann Arbor, Michigan, Veterans Administration (VA) Hospital during 1975." I shared the link with my sisters and brother with the message: "Have you heard about this case?" They responded "No." My jaw dropped.

How could we, who grew up in Flint, Michigan located 54.8 miles from Ann Arbor, not hear of this case? Granted, my sisters and I were ages, 5, 4 and 3 that summer and my brother was not even born. But, our mother was a physician, and half a dozen of my aunts who immigrated in the 1970s and the 1980s to Flint were nurses. Underscore this with the fact that we all attended the University of Michigan-Ann Arbor and had not heard about Filipina Narciso and Leonora Perez either in passing, through our history books and during conversations with friends. Moreover, my older sister was a physician, a nephrologist or kidney specialist, who joined my mom's medical practice in Flint, and my brother, Greg, was an attorney. Certainly, he must have bumped into this case in law school. Alas, no. My siblings, despite their involvement with medicine and the law and geographic proximity to the VA Hospital in Ann Arbor indicated they had never heard of the case.

The Wikipedia entry led me to Catherine Choy's (2003) *Empire of Care: Nursing and Migration in Filipino-American History* that devoted part of a chapter "Trial and Error: Crime and Punishment in America's 'Wound Culture'" to the Narciso and Perez case. The search also directed me to another resource published on June 14, 1977, in *The Washington Post* by Kirk Cheyfitz, who I interviewed for *"That Strange Summer"* that opened with:

> Two registered nurses were found guilty today of using paralyzing drug injections to poison five of their patients at the Veterans Administration Hospital in Ann Arbor, Mich. Filipina Narciso, 31, was found innocent of the only murder charge in the case and was acquitted of one poisoning charge. Leonora Perez, 33, was found guilty of all three poisoning charges against her. Both women also were convicted of conspiring to poison hospitalized veterans.

I emailed other Filipinos who grew up in the Flint area, but no one had heard about the case. No one, even my friends in the medical field. Obsessed. Frustrated. I woke up in the middle of the night thinking about these young women in their early 30s, younger than I. I read Perez was pregnant as she started serving her sentence at a prison in West Virginia. When researching the case, I had an eight-year-old girl, a seven-year-old boy, and a two-year-old boy.

These nurses experienced a series of traumatic events that scarred them. Badgered and intimidated by FBI agents during intense interviews the nurses would endure two years of stress and anxiety. Gene Ward, the FBI agent stationed in Ann Arbor, who was the first to arrive at the VA Hospital in response to sudden respiratory arrests, to this day believes the nurses are guilty. Ward, in the film *"That Strange Summer,"* characterized the polygraph exam of Leonora Perez, one of the Filipina nurses accused, as one of the most interesting polygraphs he had ever seen.

> During the test, she (Perez) had worn her hair in a ponytail. I remember distinctly the ponytail bouncing with the pulse rate monitor. So, it was if it was a pulse rate and a ponytail at the same time. The reason that happens is, the blood in the arteries – I hope my biology's right – the blood in the arteries have to go back to the veins, right, and they go through capillaries, and the capillaries in the head are in the back of the skull and that's why you see people under tension ... because in her case the ponytail was bouncing up with the blood pressure monitor.

He suggested that the bouncing of Perez's ponytail in unison with the monitor implied guilt.

The FBI interviewed more than 300 hospital staff workers and patients, talking to some sources two or more times, accounting for more than 750 interviews. Even after this process and examining the work schedules of hospital staff, FBI agents circled back to Perez and Narciso, who the prosecutors claim were the only ones present at the time of the respiratory arrests. Kirk Cheyfitz, a *Detroit Free Press* reporter who covered the investigation and trial also for *The Washington Post*, said he looked at the evidence that showed Narciso and Perez weren't the only ones at the arrests. Cheyfitz described the story as one of horror and fascination, "It was like a train wreck, you couldn't keep your eyes off of it."

The trauma the nurses experienced galvanized the community not only in the Ann Arbor-Detroit region but also in Los Angeles, Chicago, and the Philippines where rallies were held. The Philippine American community and others sent Judge Phillip Pratt, the federal judge in the case, thousands of letters, insisting on the nurses' innocence. After media coverage had extended globally, the case was quickly forgotten.

I asked my mom if she had heard of the case. She said, "yes." And, then I asked her "why didn't you and my aunties talk about it?" She said, she didn't want to. "It was a scary time," and she never dwelled on information that made her or other Filipinos look bad. "Why re-open a wound?," my mom added. I would think back to this conversation after attempts at interviewing the nurses failed. Her response explains in part why I had not heard about this case even though it involved Filipinos, and even though it occurred in Ann Arbor, a city close to my hometown of Flint, and the location of the University of Michigan where I earned my undergraduate degree.

Assembling a Diverse Team

With the International Conference of the Philippines (ICOPHIL) in 2012 as my deadline, I assembled in fall 2011 a documentary film team consisting of a student who had worked on the film "Arabs, Jews & the News" and who was interested in sharpening her editing skills. I employed a professorial assistant; a young woman enrolled in my introductory honors college course, a Filipino American student, and a man of Asian descent. I would later employ others, including a master's student in journalism who had a law degree.

This film about racism had a diverse crew. The diversity of my crew helped gain the trust of sources interviewed as well as helped to define concepts like Filipino culture. The inter-generational nature of film creators also led to unpacking the political-economic issues discussed during the 1970s in comparison to the present. The group worked inclusively and each member of the crew was made to feel welcome and respected.

Shortly after I had decided to pursue the film I made contact with someone who knew Filipina and who contacted Filipina on my behalf. The response from Filipina was that she would talk with me, and I should contact her lawyer.

The evening before an interview with her lawyers, I called him to confirm. Tom O'Brien told me Filipina Narciso had just called him, asking him not to give me an interview. She also told him she did not want to give me an interview either, saying she was retiring soon and wanted to spend her retirement writing a book about the investigation.

By the fall of 2011, I had contacted numerous sources who refused to speak to me for various reasons. I was able though to locate and interview several sources who would be key to re-constructing the case. These sources included Reporter Kirk Cheyfitz and Dr. Michael McLeod, who was a general surgery resident at the University of Michigan that staffed the VA Hospital. Dr. McLeod had been one of four original suspects in the case. What was interesting was that Dr. McLeod ended up as a general surgeon at Sparrow Hospital in Lansing, Michigan and a professor of surgery at MSU, my place of employment. We only had to drive a few miles from campus to interview him at his medical office.

By the spring of 2012, one of my students found an article titled "The Murders at Ann Arbor's Veterans Hospital: What Went Right and What Ultimately Went Wrong in the Case," written in 2011 on Ticklethewire.com by Greg Stejskal, a retired FBI agent in the Detroit bureau. Greg contacted Eugene "Gene" Ward, another former FBI agent, who investigated the case and encouraged him to give us an interview. Students working on the film said they were surprised that the agents seemed like nice guys contrary to their earlier opinion about FBI agents.

The Debut of the Documentary

At the ICOHPHIL on MSU's campus in October 2012, I debuted the half-hour rough cut of the film called "U.S. v. Narciso, Perez and the Press" to an audience of scholars from around the world. One of the attendees and presenters was Jason Magabo Perez, a doctoral student in communication and ethnic studies at the University of California–San Diego and the son of Leonora Perez. Initially, Jason agreed to give me an interview during the conference. After seeing the film, Jason indicated he was angry that I had interviewed the FBI agents who had cast doubt on the innocence of his mom.

I watched Jason's presentation that followed mine. It was an experimental performance sprinkled with expletives. Fux# The FBI! I understood. I had made a film about his mother and the case that devastated his family. What was playing out in front of me in Jason's performance was the summative impact of anger toward the government and especially the FBI agents responsible for tormenting his mother and his family. His mother was pregnant when she served time in the federal prison in West Virginia. Jason was the baby in her belly. Narciso was his Godmother. When we attempted to talk with Jason, he cried. Visibly upset, he said he no longer wanted to be interviewed for our film. He asked for a hug that I gave him.

We spent the next several months re-editing and adding material from the ICOPHIL conference.

My students asked why I, along with others, kept saying the Filipina nurses could not have committed the crimes because it clearly was not Filipino-like. "What is this magical Filipino culture?" one student asked. Our work then began to respond to this question. They learned through me and those who we interviewed about the caregiver culture that encouraged Filipinos to become nurses, and the dream of immigration to the U.S. The hope of immigrants was that they could make money to send to their families in the Philippines and maybe one day be able to sponsor family members so they, too, could come to the U.S. They would not want to jeopardize their income and the chance to bring their families to America.

The plan was to submit our documentary to film awards competitions. The following year, 2013, the documentary won the first-place Mark of Excellence Award in the News Special/Documentary category of the Society of Professional Journalists–Detroit chapter and a Regional Emmy® in the Documentary Cultural Category. The work also won national recognition: A Bronze Telly Award and Radio Television Digital News Association Unity Award. That October, I screened at the Philippine Cultural Center in Southfield, Michigan. The moderator before the screening read a statement from Jason that he had not given me permission to create the film, and that I had not given him a copy. In 2014, the work made it into the inaugural issue of the *Journal of Video Ethnography*, the world's first peer-reviewed journal of ethnographic movies.

That Strange Summer

In March 2015, I debuted the hour-long film "That Strange Summer," the new name for the documentary, at the Detroit Institute of Art (DIA) as part of the Detroit Free Press' Freep Film Festival. An MSU grant that supports humanities project funded an extension of the project. After the screening, a Q&A followed featuring me and Greg Stejskal, one of the retired FBI agents interviewed in the film. After the event, he said how disappointing it was to hear people in the audience accuse him of using the nurses as scapegoats as all he wanted to do was protect people. He endured some hard questions. Looking back, I wish I would have had my mom, siblings and children attend. Showing a film at one of the most iconic buildings in Michigan made me do the happy dance.

Closing Thoughts

Ultimately, the documentary helped me with my academic career in which I tenaciously argued the legitimacy of documentary film as an academic exercise, earning me tenure, promotion to associate then to full professor.

As a Filipina, I navigated the story between my identity as Filipino American and my identity as a journalist. "*That Strange Summer*" is an important film as it documents how an all-white jury convicted two Filipina women with no prior criminal records. This work fills knowledge gaps in American history and Asian American Studies as individuals have lost sight of the case. The story also highlights how grassroots activism played a role in releasing Narciso and Perez. Citing prosecutorial misconduct and the thousands of letters on Narciso and Perez's behalf, the federal court judge in the case ordered a new trial that never occurred, thereby freeing the nurses.

I resuscitated a 40-year-old court case that convicted two Filipina American women working as nurses. The give back is impact. Hundreds have seen this film at film festivals and screenings, making this group more aware of Filipino culture and the discrimination related to brown-ness. Reviews have characterized the film as riveting and heartbreaking, leaving those who experience the story angry, empathetic, and perplexed.

Finally, making the documentary helped me recognize that what I do is an expression of leadership. I was able to educate my crew, but more importantly, I was able to help others see issues through a lens of discrimination and racial prejudice. In trendy dialogues that espouse color blindness, what results is a denial that bigotry exists because of outward appearances. What this film exposes is that ethnic bias against Filipinos in this case in the 1970s was a factor in this federal investigation, the judicial process and in reportage. Bringing this film to fruition to a larger audience was my compass through the trenches of creating this documentary. Disappointed, yet undeterred by those who refused to speak with me, it made me even more persistent. I tell my students, something long-time *CBS News* Anchor Dan Rather said when he spoke to a group when he visited MSU years ago: "Persistence out trumps smarts and other skills." I also tell students to go after stories that keep you up at night and make you think: "Did this happen in America?" I led by acting fearless in telling this story. I believed at the heart of the Narciso and Perez case is "Other-izing," objectifying individuals based on skin color and other physical attributes. Narciso and Perez went through an American nightmare of prosecution for a crime built on circumstantial evidence in part because they were Filipina. My goal was: I wanted Filipinos and Americans to know this happened in America. I realize that there is still much to be done that requires my leadership.

The End of this Chapter and the End of *"That Strange Summer"*

The film explored views on race. It includes perspectives from Filipinos who supported the nurses and FBI agents who worked on the case, as well as journalists who covered the case. The varied interviews lead viewers through the investigation and allow viewers to make judgments of their own about the nurses' guilt and the roles of the press and the FBI. Jim Graham, a reporter who covered the trial for *The Detroit News*, begins the string of interviews that end the film and offers reflection about reportage on race:

> I think at the time, for reasons I can't really recall, and really don't want to remember I suppose, we were very, we were much too focused on the nationality of those women. I know they (press) always identified them as Filipino nurses, Filipino nurses, and I don't think we'd do that today.

Kirk Cheyfitz of the Detroit Free Press continues to ask why the FBI agents focused on these two Filipino women:

> The bureau has answers. They claim the evidence pointed toward the women, but I looked at the evidence, and it didn't. They (Narciso and Perez) were always two among several and who were known to be in the area, and God knows among how many who weren't known to be in the area. That's my problem.

Dr. Michael McLeod is the last interview in the film and provided the muse for the film's title:

> You know. Evidence was against the nurses. I don't know the details of it other than circumstantial. But everyone was trying to figure out a very bizarre chain of events. Nobody had a handle on what was going on. If there was a perpetrator, he or she knows I suppose. I don't think we'll ever know what happened in Ann Arbor that very *strange summer*.

Building Leadership Legacy

JOJI ILAGAN BIAN

Founder and President, Joji Ilagan International Schools
GLOBAL FWN100™ 2017

Dreaming Big, Giving the Best

At the age of 18, I knew I was going to build my own school. I was still a sophomore at the University of the Philippines in Diliman when I confided to my Mom my deepest wish of having my own school. Early on, it became obvious to me that it was not a pipe dream that I had, nor was it a plan borne of childish caprice. I knew exactly that I wanted my school to be small and exclusive; and distinct from the prominent universities and colleges.

The other thing I was sure of was that I loved to teach and could teach very well. Every time I went home for summer break, instead of staying home and wasting my time, I found fulfillment by teaching young girls poise and personality. Using the skills I learned at the Manila-based Karilagan Finishing School, I would hold classes in our house teaching teens, and young ladies poise and personality development, social etiquette, and grace. Soon enough, mothers came with their daughters in tow, asking me to work magic on their daughters during their awkward stage. That gave me not only extra income during the summer, but it made me realize what I wanted to do, what I wanted my legacy to be. What I did NOT know at that point was exactly how I was going to do it and when it would come true.

Wishing to Be a Star

My mom, who was also my best friend and number one fan, told me, "you are a headstrong woman and so confident of yourself. One day, you will be a star!" I held this close to my heart and never worried about the challenges ahead. As long as I knew what I wanted, I would make it happen.

Growing up in a close, middle-class family, the value of education was impressed on my siblings and me from the time we were little. My parents believed that education was the most precious legacy they could give us. My father, Jose Ilagan was a lawyer from Batangas who served as prosecutors in Davao while my mother, Ma. Celina Javellana, who came from Iloilo in Panay Island, was a housewife who devoted her time to organize the Divine Mercy Devotion movement in Mindanao. Our upbringing was a wonderful complement of discipline and gentle nurturing. As a result of this, my siblings and I stand as testaments to our parent's love, care, and belief in education. My brother, Jose Edgar followed my father's footsteps as a lawyer; my other brother Brian is an established pediatric surgeon; while my sisters, Marie and Bella are both successfully running their pastry businesses in Cebu.

When I finished my Hotel and Restaurant Management Course at the University of the Philippines, I got a job teaching at the Philippine Women's College. I taught for four years before I became Dean of the Hotel and Restaurant Management Department. Although I had already established a career as an educator and administrator in a prestigious school, I still kept my eyes very focused on the school I was to build. After all, the financial resources that were needed to build a school would be substantial. I did not have enough money to establish a school, and neither did my parents. Still, the dream stuck; it just would not fade. I never lost hope that it would happen one day.

And it did.

Realizing the Dream

My journey as an educator began at a time when no one believed that a technical-vocational school would flourish or be a good business for that matter. I took the risk. My vision was to establish a technical vocational school whose primary goal would be to train young people who could not afford a college education to get a career and be financially independent as soon as possible. Part of their training was in personality and communication skills, my core competence, and to inculcate in them the positive values that would give them a competitive advantage over graduates of other schools.

In June 1988 with minimal financial resources but with an abundance of faith and passion for giving life to my dream, I opened my first school in a building along Anda street that was then one of the busiest commercial streets in Davao city. Another risk that I took was that I gave the school my name; the Joji Ilagan Career Center. Others would think of a saint or a famous hero or landmark to name a school, but

I chose my name. I believed that one day I was going to make this name a byword in the hospitality education in our city.

Innovation in the 80s was not really the buzzword that it is today. Davao City, located in the southern part of the Philippines, was just coming out of a very difficult economic and political situation and this created a favorable space for small struggling businesses to grow. There was this prevailing perception at that time that those who enrolled at technical vocational schools those who did not have the mental ability needed to survive in higher education or were too poor to go to college. For some, technical-vocational was akin to being thrown into a life of manual labor. I thought otherwise. I wanted to raise the level of dignity and respect for technical-vocational graduates because there was a lack of skilled human resources necessary to support the growing business community. That was the start of the road I chose to travel, and since then, I never looked back.

That was it. Once the dream came to life, there was no stopping it from growing and thriving. What started with one small classroom in an old beat up building, became six government accredited international schools that offer senior high school education to tertiary level degrees, diploma courses, and national competency level skills certificates. Three decades later these became the Joji Ilagan International schools network composed of five (5) international schools. I was the first one to bring to Davao a true international school with global partners and offering transnational education; thus providing opportunities for young Dabawenyos to get excellent education right in our hometown.

In spite of the growth in the network, I have remained true to my original dream: keeping the schools small, exclusive, and learner-centered so that we can focus on giving our students the values they need to be successful. The combination of skills, personality, and values has become attributes our graduates are known for, and they are sought after in the industry even before they graduate. This recognition spurs me further because it validates that my brand of education and training is positively changing lives. Looking back at the road I have traveled, I realize that this is what keeps me going. I find it immensely fulfilling to be part of the lives of our students, to be able to play a role in the realization of their full potential.

Rising to Be a Star

A few years into the business, I became increasingly involved in the business sector. There I met other business leaders with shared passion and dedication to fulfill Davao City's potential as the gateway to Brunei, Indonesia, Malaysia, and the Philippines East ASEAN Growth Area established under the administration of then President Fidel V. Ramos. The robust economic climate of the time allowed our businesses to flourish.

It was during this period of economic optimism that I became the first woman president of the Davao City Chamber of Commerce and Industry. This part of my journey would test me to my limits.

In 1992, the Filipino and Chinese groups in the Chamber of Commerce were at odds, so they had to elect a president who was acceptable to both. When I ran for the position, the issues raised against me were not about whether I had the skills to manage the organization but how I would adapt to this well-entrenched "old boys" club.

Some whispers referred to "what happens after 5 o'clock" which was allegedly when the more critical networking and maneuvering happens. Coffee shops were unheard of then, for the men the options were either singing at Karaoke or drinking in bars.

"What will she do if we have a business delegation and the guys would like to go to a Karaoke, will she go with them? What will she do in the bar, will she drink with the men?" The whispers came short of actually saying, "She's a woman, what will she do?"

I eventually got the seat and soon addressed the "it's a boys club" issue and the "5 o'clock dilemma" in the most diplomatic way I knew. I told them, "I don't think negotiations and networking can happen in a Karaoke where you can barely hear each other. Of course, you can have fun, but I do not think this is the vision of the chamber. I think I can negotiate and talk with you in the boardroom. After 5 o'clock you can go on your own, I do not think I will go with you since you would not find it in good taste if I joined you." I convinced them that serious business matters have to happen in the conference room. Looking back, I think it was to my advantage that my business is in education, so I did not need to lobby as aggressively as those in other business sectors, like manufacturing and agriculture.

From that rocky start, it was a surprise that I became president for two terms, even moving up to become chair of the Mindanao Business Council . It was also during that year when the Davao City government gave me its highest recognition, the Datu Bago Award for Business and Education.

I felt invigorated to be breaking one glass ceiling after another. I think every woman wants to do that. Women want to blaze a trail for other women, and I felt great about being able to do that. I was the first woman to sit on the Board of the Philippine Chamber where I stayed for six years. Various recognitions were given to me; including those coming from two Philippine Presidents: Pres Joseph Estrada's Kabalikat Award for my Scholarship programs for out of school youth and for my leadership in the Technical Vocational; and from Pres. Gloria Macapagal Arroyo's

Presidential Service Medal of Merit for my membership in the Consultative Commission that reviewed and recommended revisions in the 1987 Phil Constitution.

Surviving the traditional biases of the time felt like a wonderful triumph for me. The learning that I got from my experiences would further mold my leadership for the challenges that would come.

Standing against the Flow

As a female business leader; one of my advocacies was for women to take an active role in affecting change in the business and social landscape. In all my involvements and leadership roles and engagements, I am able to voice out the perspectives of women and bring them to a national and international sphere of attention. As the former Vice Chairperson of the Mindanao Commission of Women, I advocated for the positioning of women to be key decision makers and beneficiaries for peace and development in Mindanao and make them active movers in the achievement of multicultural peace, dynamism, and harmony. As the Charter President of Women in Travel and founder of *Anak Pinay* Women's Group, I continue to organize and move women to be active nation builders by unlocking potentials and opportunities for advancement, particularly in entrepreneurship.

As a woman business leader I have transcended gender discrimination and have stood firm in my belief that women leaders are strong; straightforward and are results oriented. And I want each and every woman to have this strength of character at all times.

Having a close relationship with all kinds of women from all walks of life had subjected me to certain conditions that really put my leadership, values, and principles to test. During the late 80's; violence against women in all forms and in all circumstances had seemed to be an accepted norm in a society which was '*macho*' and granted men special statutory rights when it comes to women.

Unreported rape and sexual violence are prevalent in our Philippine society as it is in other parts of the world. The typical pattern is to undermine abuse charges, blame the victim, and condone the behavior of the perpetrator. CNN Philippines reports that in 2017 one woman is raped every hour in the Philippines. And 75.5% of these remains unreported according to a 2013 report from the Philippine National Police Women and Children Protection Center.

A friend of mine named 'Jane ' called me one early morning and told me she was sexually violated . It is a very sensitive issue for someone like me to get involved with. But I believed her and respected her decision. It is hard to stand against what is popular, what is easy. It is more convenient and safe to go with the status quo than abide with your principles and to be reproached for it. There were times I felt alone, very alone. I made a choice based on my principles and desire to do the right thing. I think Jane did not do it for herself only but for other women who shared her sorrow but who feared to stand up for their rights. Women should not keep quiet. Women should stand and be heard. In a way, her speaking out would prevent recurrence of such abuse, especially by men who hold higher positions. It was fighting power up there, and it was a long, arduous battle. As a leader, I felt it was the right course of action. I was, in a way, willing to sacrifice my friendships and business relationships. It was a business risk since in the business world, networks are very important. Those who were on the other side were people I needed to grow my business. Siding with Jane would not benefit me in any way as a leader, as a business person, or my networks and other associations. Still, I felt that she was important to me because she represented what could go wrong in a patriarchal and *macho* society.

If I had to do it all again, I would not change a thing. That experience made me stronger as a leader, and it cemented my resolve to stand by what I believe in, even if that makes me unpopular. That was one of the lessons I learned. It took four years before things quieted down but through it all, I persevered.

Foiled Political Plans

In 2001, I decided to run for a congressional seat. I wanted to reach out to more people and influence the way government serves the people. I believed that my experience in the academe and industry provided me with the intellectual capacity, networking, and public relations I would need to win. My rallies and meetings overflowed with people from all walks of life; I saw that people wanted change. They were tired of traditional politicians. I did not mind that I was fighting a political giant whose family had dominated politics for more than a decade. A public servant requires a caring heart and a passion for serving more than entrenched political interests. I thought that care and passion were all that I needed to win. Perhaps some would call that idealistic, but I truly believed that my sincerity would carry me through. Of course, this was not the case. I found that politics is an arena where there is a confluence of many factors that make up the winning equation. I do not regret my foray into the political arena. The experience I gained there became life lessons.

My dream of helping people did not stop even though I did not win a congressional seat. I have been helping people even before I ran for Congress and have continued to do so even to this day. I am able to influence lives, influence policy, influence the way people live, touch their lives not as a politician but in other ways. I took stock of what I learned from my experiences.

What I learned is that in politics, if you are a woman your heart is different. Meeting people who are living on the fringes of society brings out the natural instinct of women to nurture and take care of people. When you see people in grim places where they are poverty-stricken, and they need so much help, you want to change things. Some people choose to change things from their seat in politics while others, like me, change things through education.

Leading with Faith and Intuition

I love to watch movies with my grandchildren. One movie character I like is Dory, the blue Tang with memory loss in "Finding Nemo." She finds her way through life by sheer faith and intuition. We can have all the intellect and logic in the world and yet there are things that we can only navigate with faith and intuition. Faith and intuition play a large part in my life. So does listening and dreaming big.

I met one young man who was a call center agent in one of my companies, and he told me that he chose to apply at my call center because his mom was my student in college. He told me that his mom would quote me as saying "You do what you need to do, and do not ever be discouraged. Always dream and when you do, dream big." Encounters like that are very precious to me. It is a validation of what I consider to be my life's work. It is not the size of the brain that is the most important, what is most important is the size of your faith in yourself, how much you believe in yourself, and how big you dream. If you dream small, you achieve small. If you dream big, then you will achieve big. Everything starts with a dream. Not having a dream puts you in limbo, with no direction, no purpose. So it is really about having a dream. Everything starts there.

Another thing that has always helped me is realizing the value of listening with an open heart and mind. No matter where you are, no matter how much you have achieved, listening will always be your best asset. The more successful you become, the better listener you have to be. Listen to your people, listen to your colleagues, and listen to your networks. Listening gives you not just awareness or knowledge. More importantly, it gives you understanding and insight.

Listen. After that, you can decide on what to do with the information you have. Whether you choose to discard the information and say I do not need this or look at it very carefully, analyze, and evaluate, and eventually use it is up to you. People ask me where I get insight. My answer is I talk to people, and I listen to them. I have learned to listen very well.

In all the years that I have been leading people, I have learned that if you want to succeed in something, it's all or nothing. There were no half-measures for me. That has been the basis for whatever success I have reached. Think in terms of what is possible. I always get people to work for me knowing that nothing is impossible. There is always a way of doing things if you believe in it. So for me, there is never a NO. In business, even if it looks impossible at first glance, I know it can always be done. It is only a matter of finding ways overcoming obstacles by remaining focused and believing you are on the right track. That is why I do not like people who say "That's not possible." If you have not started, if you have not even moved a muscle, how can you say it is not possible? That is when you are really stuck.

I believe everything could be done even when I first started as a teacher and even when I started as a new business owner. I believe that to this day.

It also helps if we know how to be creative in the use of time. Women are very good at multi-tasking. We instinctively know how to juggle multiple tasks, and we are able to find a way of harmonizing them. How did I juggle all the facets of my life? I prioritized. I had to be creative in the use of my time. I think this is where I say that we women have a way of multi-tasking and having a 'fish eye' compared to a 'tunnel eye.' We have a way of doing everything at the same time. All women leaders would agree with me. We need to manage our home, we need to care for our children, and, if we own a business, we need to manage our business. Managing the home is a top priority for all businesswomen. As a business leader, I also had to provide leadership to my business and to all the business organizations that I work with. I never accept a leadership position if I could not deliver my best.

Well of Inspiration

When people ask me what inspires me, I tell them that my inspiration comes from my story of self-awareness, self-actualization, and self-transcendence. I have experienced social, political, and economic changes in my country that have had a formative effect on my development as a Filipino citizen, educator, and entrepreneur. Not to fail to mention my Roman Catholic faith which had my beloved parents instilling in me the valuable lesson on the Golden Rule and to always be humble, sincere, and authentic. When I look back at my failures, I balance that with what I have accomplished so far. These have helped me define my direction in earning a decent and honest living while being passionate about issues of social justice, corporate governance, community development, and poverty alleviation at the same time. I often assure myself that if I have surpassed the challenges which confronted me in the past, I would still persevere to travel in the same path in the present. Indeed, hindsight is the perfect vision.

I want to be remembered as a leader who listens with an open heart and is capable of empathizing. I want to be remembered as the woman who has touched many lives, especially that of the youth, and helped transform her community for the better. If I talk to you and left you a nugget of wisdom, I would feel fulfilled as a leader who has influenced the lives of people with the nugget of wisdom that I have imparted to them. I have met and known many people from all walks of life in my work and in the associations I have joined. I have worked hard to add value, when I can, to other people's lives. I believe that what distinguishes me as a leader and as a consummate businesswoman is my sincerity. My guiding principle in life is to do what is right. Only then can I be a blessing to others and truly enjoy my God's blessings in return. My integrity is non-negotiable.

I stay true to my commitment to providing accessible, quality, and relevant education to Filipino youth, both male and female. As the Chinese proverb says, "If you want happiness for a lifetime, help the next generation." All of my schools are focused on building the confidence and self-esteem side by side with the career choices of our students. I want to help the aspiring young entrepreneurs to start building their dreams for a better life they so deserve with the right commitment, hard work, passion, and dedication. Our course offerings in hotel management, tourism, and the culinary arts, teach our students how to become sustainable and financially independent. What we do goes beyond the classroom and provides real-life experiences in the field they have chosen. While still in school we ask them to do business plans and make viable product concepts which have to be unique. Aside from getting them ready for the usual employment after college or help them prepare to leave the country to find work elsewhere, I always encourage them to be entrepreneurial. There is a big emphasis on innovation which requires students to be creative and to learn as much outside the four walls of the classroom. They have to have open minds and see the world for what it is. This is the kind of mindset I leave to my students. I always believe that Filipinos are hardworking, and the quality of service that a Filipino offers is incomparable and undoubtedly of international standards.

I want to continue using my business ventures to provide economic empowerment to women and the youth to alleviate poverty. We need to change the way we address poverty. Addressing poverty requires more than just giving charity or livelihood. My mission is to promote sustainable livelihood or career placements with the corresponding financial support. I am networking with micro-financing companies to be able to provide the much-needed funding. Our program objectives include the need to diversify and adapt to global trends. I have training centers in welding, salon management, and other service skills for our scholars. I bring the training to their community so we can have more participants who do not have the money even for transportation.

I am a firm believer that a rock-solid foundation in education is a way for reducing poverty, and a means for changing lives for one's future and the future of one's family. And I would like to believe that I am performing my duty with such passion and purpose that I can be truly proud of as an empowered Filipina.

Passionately Grateful

I have a beautiful family; despite my enormous responsibilities as a business person and as a civic leader; together with my very supportive husband, we raised children who embrace the social entrepreneurial spirit. My daughter Dyan owns a very successful early childhood school in Canada. My son Mikee established his Call center and Business processing office in Davao City and has grown his workforce to 2000 in only six years making it one of the largest and most successful locally owned BPOs. My youngest daughter Nicole is my heir apparent for all of my schools. She is now the VP Education of the school, and everyone calls her the "mini JIB."

My downtime is usually spent at home with my family. It is a no-tech weekend for me; I turn off my phones or do not check my email so I can have time to devote to my family. I do not want to be a slave to technology.

It has been 30 years since the first day I stood in front of my class, in my own school. My journey has been fraught with good and not so good times, but just like Dory, my faith, intuition, and experience led me to greater heights.

My success is marked by humble beginnings, built with love and conviction, infectious passion, and leadership that only an empowered woman can provide.

My life is a tapestry of different weaves and colors, symbolizing the very diverse experiences that have given me a more comprehensive perspective and understanding of the complexities of life. I have walked the halls of power, as well as dined with the poorest of the poor, and from these experiences, I have learned that it is what we share with others that matters most.

Looking back, I know now what my mom meant when she said I would be a star. Perhaps she saw it first, with the intuition that all mothers have. She saw the path that I was going to take before I even started. I understand now what she meant by a star. She did not mean a Hollywood star, but like the North Star in a clear night sky, constantly guiding, giving light, and helping people find their way in the dark.

Leadership Lessons I Learned From My Mother
by **Nicole Ilagan Hao Bian**, Daughter of Joji Ilagan Bian

The saying "Mother knows best" is not just a cliché to me. In my heart, I know and believe my mother knows best. While many people spend their entire lives looking for a role model, I have had the good fortune of being raised and nurtured by mine.

My earliest memories are of tagging along with my Mom as she went about teaching and running her school. She would walk around her school, acknowledge the staff and students, ask them about their lives and their families. She would stop and listen to them regardless of who they were. The manager and the janitor both got the same attention, the same sincere concern, the same good wishes, and the same caring smile. She talks to them, and when she says goodbye, they seemed happier than they were just before she stopped to say hello. Whenever I see the effect my mother has on people, I feel an immense sense of pride. I want to have that impact on people too. I want to be someone who positively touches people's lives even if its just for the little things. My mother's belief in people is infectious. She believes that company loyalty is a product of leader's care and concern for people.

Watching my mother juggle her various roles has both amazed and challenged me. She is the kind of woman I want to be; tenacious, driven, tough but nurturing, kind, and warm. A woman who is well-centered and grounded at the same time. I think young women like me should look up to strong role model women like my mom.

While some say you cannot have it all, my mom would say "You can have it all, you just need to work harder, smarter, and be more focused." She would also say "Dream big, aim high because you can do it."

There are so many lessons on leadership I have learned from my mom. She is always quick to point to other strong women worth emulating. She continues to learn and grow. I try to follow suit. My mother has encouraged me to get my priorities straight, find a path, and stay the course. Throughout my upbringing, it has been instilled in me that my family is, and always will be, the top and non-negotiable priority. The family is the reason and motivation for all the work. The family gives everything meaning. Another thing I have learned from my mother is going after opportunities even if it means having to step out of my comfort zone. It has been my experience that opportunities remain just opportunities until they are acted upon. They do not stay available for very long. My parents, especially my mom have not sheltered me from learning the hard lessons. She would say that choices are not always clear-cut, not always black and white, and sometimes require making choices that I do not necessarily want to make but are necessary for the greater good.

People ask me why I want to follow in my mother's footsteps. Why wouldn't I want to? She is worth emulating. More than that I want to continue her legacy and blaze a trail of my own as well. I am her daughter after all.

❊

REBECCA MURRY

United Nations International School, Junior School Math Coach
GLOBAL FWN100™ 2017

Redefining Pathways

Beginnings...

All things depend on all other things for their existence. Take, for example this leaf...Earth, water, heat, sea, tree, clouds, sun, time, space – all these elements have enabled this leaf to come to existence. If just one of these elements was missing, the leaf could not exist. All beings rely on the law of dependent co-arising. The source of one thing is all things.
-**Thich Nhat Hanh**, 1991

How would we go about life if there were no failures and successes? Taoist philosophy advocates the practice of pure simplicity and the allowance of natural events in order to achieve harmony in life. It further emphasizes the belief that we do not grow from our successes alone; rather we learn from first permitting failures to happen, then reflecting upon these experiences, which help build resilience and courage. It is critical that we reflect on our choices and decisions; they are all part of a web of life. Sidney Poitier (2000) once said that "all of us live our lives, either book-learned, experience-gathered, or inheritors of our own ancestral history." In a way, we are a combination of the elements that Poitier mentioned. We must allow our natural tendency to develop and learn from our failures. What is challenging is building the capacity and stamina to persevere. Success is an outcome of failure. I could reflect and learn from the many trials and tribulations I have experienced. I continue to reflect on those childhood experiences as well as those that I have experienced as an adult. They help me navigate through my current life as an educator in the United States. I have learned to live my life with wonder, curiosity, and appreciation for whatever I may encounter.

Resiliency

From seven to thirteen years old I had significant enough interesting experiences to teach me lessons for a lifetime. During that period, I survived two car accidents that challenged my ability to stay mentally strong while undergoing rehabilitation. Re-learning how to walk at 7-years-old and undergoing mouth reconstruction at thirteen were painful, trying experiences that taught me resilience, courage, and a positive mindset. I was fearless at an early age. If it were not for a supportive family and friends, I would not have learned the importance of keeping a sense of humor, being self-aware, and avoiding feeling sorry for myself. As Margaret Wheatley (2006) observed, "life can either be in chaos or in unpredictable order...nothing functions in silos in the physical world."

Surviving that period left me with much to reflect on. I asked myself if this would ever happen again, how much adversity would I be able to handle? Not knowing the meaning of the word "resilience" I knew at that young age, I needed to recover from such adversities. My mother was tough and would always say, "So what if you have a problem? You solve it, you learn from it, and move on!" She instilled in me the importance and virtue of resisting self-pity. At a young age, this concept was hard for me to grasp because I still needed to be nurtured and cuddled. But my mother, who was widowed in her late 30's, had to make sure that her only girl would be strong enough to withstand conditions similar to what she had experienced during World War II.

Diversity and Equity

Wasting no time and embracing this mindset, as an 18-year-old, I left for Michigan to study architecture at an engineering school. My boyfriend, whom I ended up marrying, came from an expatriate family who lived in the Philippines, supported my new adventure and ambitious plans. His father was an American and his mother was half Burmese and half British. I grew up in a diverse community of expatriate families. Leaving Manila for college was simply an extension of my life and not foreign at all. This diverse lifestyle was akin to my identity and hence, I took for granted the supposed non-existence of equity and access to opportunity that unbeknownst to me already existed. Nor was I fully aware of the extent of colonial mentality within the Filipino culture. According to *Pinay Power*, edited by de Jesus, many Filipinos still regard their own cultural identity as inferior to that of Americans which in turn, encourages Filipino anonymity and continued invisibility.

My freshman year in architecture school challenged my deeper understanding about human equity and diversity. Michigan was a time of self-discovery, along with a new environment, people, and culture. During that time, the mid-west had an influx of engineering students from Iran and Iraq. In late 1979, fifty-two American diplomats were held hostage for 444 days in Teheran. A group of Iranian Student Followers of the Imam supported the Iranian Revolution and took over the U.S. Embassy in Tehran. I was blind-sided by how my life in Michigan would be impacted by this incident. My Iranian roommate was beautiful, kind, and loving. She treated me like a younger sister. A perfect match for me as I never had an older sister and I enjoyed learning from her about cooking, Iranian culture, and life in general.

Self-Discovery in Michigan

Eight months into our architecture studies, the US Immigration Services decided to gather all Iranian students as a result of the American hostage situation. Since I was living with an Iranian, I was included in the "round-up" of foreign students and obediently reported to the Immigrations Office. With the exception of myself, all other Iranian students were handcuffed while I was sitting quietly waiting for my turn to be interviewed. During my interview with the Immigrations Officer, I was challenged with accusatory questions about my intentions to study in the United States. The Officer asked me why I lived with an Iranian. I told him that we were all students of Architecture and Engineering and were assigned our roommates. Offended by his discriminatory questions, I told him that before they accused any of us of any wrong doing, he should check all our transcripts and background to verify our integrity. As he stamped my passport, he told me that I needed to return to the Philippines and reapply for a student visa. Devastated by this decision, I thought about how relevant my mother's advice was about being strong and resilient. My mother scheduled my flight back home to the Philippines immediately. I packed everything I could and threw away architectural models of projects I cherished. Numb and disoriented, I went to the airport trying to figure out what had just happened. While on the plane home, I wondered whether this was something I had caused. I pondered about how the hostage crisis had impacted my life and naively, swore never again to be in a situation such as this. With intense emotions of anger and humiliation, I realized that what I had just experienced was a form of racism. Nobody is ever prepared for the level of mental pain and invasion when confronted by racism. I never realized my color was different from others. Once I arrived back in the Philippines, I was able to secure a new student visa and returned to Michigan. In my absence, the school awarded me the Most Outstanding Freshman Architecture award. Still reeling with anger and unresolved emotions, I decided, despite this award recognition, to leave Michigan and return back to the Philippines. I was accepted as a transfer student into the University of the Philippines Architecture School. To some extent, I felt I had overcome this humiliation by getting into the best architecture school in the country. Like my mother always said, "you get up, dust yourself from a fall, and move on."

Gaining My Own Version of Clarity

We each start with a clear understanding of our own individuality within our own initial environment consisting of family and friends.
- **Margaret Wheatley**, 2006

Learning to lead with conviction and passion became an objective that evolved throughout my architectural studies. Believing in following your "true North" required focus and hard work. Three years into my studies, the political situation under the Marcos Dictatorship became intense and was beset with the unknown. Ninoy Aquino was assassinated on August 21, 1983, the same day I had to finish the submission of a school project application. The next day, classes were cancelled indefinitely, and people began to protest. My long-time boyfriend decided to move to the United States to be with his brothers after graduating from college. The Dean of Architecture advised me to leave and finish my studies abroad. With my mother's support, I left the Philippines and planned to continue my architecture studies in Spain. Part of this plan was to first visit my boyfriend in Louisiana in the United States. Life has a way of creating detours: my boyfriend called my mother to ask for permission to marry me. In a quick span of three months, I found myself settled in Louisiana where my husband's brothers lived. Determined to practice architecture, I immediately worked in an engineering firm in Louisiana.

Eight Months in Louisiana

At that time, Louisiana was not used to an influx of immigrants from various countries with the exception of Vietnamese refugees. Part of my job was to survey for water valves in various counties. Eugene, Louisiana was a particularly southern white community where people had guns. That morning, as I was walking and inspecting a particular water valve in front of an old house, I found myself confronted by a white middle-aged man in suspenders with a rifle pointed at me. He was accusing me of trespassing. Strangely enough, it never occurred to him that I was wearing a hat with the logo Louisiana Water Company and a t-shirt with our engineering company name on it. We also had the truck with a huge sticker label of our engineering company's name. This man was more fixated on my color than what my supervisor and I were doing. My boss, Ray, spoke Creole and came out of the truck to clarify the situation. The man told us to leave. As we were driving out of the area, Ray looked at me smirking and said he would not have hired me if I were Vietnamese. I was shocked at the blatant xenophobia. Once again, like my experience in Michigan, I was in a situation that was beyond my control. When I shared this with my husband, he realized how serious racism and gender inequity issues were in Louisiana. Naively, it never occurred to me that racism could be so overt in a country that had acknowledged Martin Luther King's fight for equality. For the second time in my life, I was a victim of racism no matter how qualified I was for my job. The only thing separating me from "them" was the color of my skin and my ethnicity. I was convinced that in order to increase an awareness of inequity and work towards its elimination, I need to take a lead in this effort. I thought I could use architecture as a vehicle for working to ensure equity and fairness for all.

I believe that nothing in life happens in isolation. Events are somehow interconnected within an open system that could be in a state of chaos or order. As explained by Wheatley (2006), "one and one makes two" requires understanding "one," understanding "two," and understanding the meaning of "and." For me, "and" means working towards integration in order to change minds about racial inequality. As defined in the Merriam-Webster dictionary, integration is the incorporation of varying equals into a society of individuals of differing groups, such as races. Working towards integration means changing minds about racial inequality. As a leader, one must never forget the roadblocks to equity by those who are marginalized in the context we live in. Yet, I must admit, having grown up in a time when colonial mentality was the norm and being fair-skinned was celebrated, I felt the only way to fight for this cause was to do so quietly and indirectly.

After eight months in Louisiana, my husband and I concluded that the environment there was not supportive of a mixed-race marriage. In 1984, we decided to move to New York City which we assumed would be more open to a multi-racial family.

Moving to New York

Without delay in October 1984, I applied as a transfer student to the architecture school. The advice of my Dean in the Philippines was that as a woman and a minority, I was better off with a U.S. degree in a field that was not only elitist historically but also dominated by white men. I applied and was admitted to Pratt Institute. Pratt is a highly regarded architectural school with a reputation for providing opportunity for both men and women in the fields of engineering and architecture integrated into the fine arts. Historically, Pratt offered a variety of courses that supported women. Despite this reputation, I was confronted at Pratt by another form of bias. My senior thesis mentor, a famous Italian architect, advised that I would be better off as a saleswoman at Bloomingdale's since I would not survive as a woman architect. Notwithstanding his advice, I worked harder. In the end, he acknowledged his mistake and apologized. In 1986, I graduated with honors and secured a job at an engineering firm in New York City. Soon after, I was recruited to work at an architecture firm and was assigned to design the concession stores at the base of the Statue of Liberty. As a first project for an immigrant, a woman, and a minority, I considered this as an accomplishment. Ten years later, I was still opening one new door after another to corridors historically reserved for white men. My hard work paid off as I achieved leadership roles in the field.

After a decade in the industry, and now in a leadership capacity, I continued to experience the relentlessness of discrimination. As a woman leader, I felt isolated and vulnerable all the time. I would be greeted at a construction meeting with snide comments about my own background as an Asian and a woman. This did not deter me from my desire to be an architect. Sometimes feelings of failure crept in. But the moral support of my husband and my mother, who had decided to live with us in New York, kept me focused on my goal to succeed. Without hesitation, every morning at construction site meetings, while being the only woman surrounded by men, I developed an inner strength to ignore the discriminatory behavior. Eventually, I gathered enough courage to address their attitude towards women. I became the Program Director of a $2.8 billion capital design and construction program for new courthouses and juvenile detention centers. Though I continued to experience both racial and gender biases, I was able to overcome the everyday battles of inequality in a leadership capacity. Women electricians and plumbers looked forward to my construction site visits and thanked me for my policy to remove the calendars with nude women. I also required that contractors hire a cleaner for the toilets that women used. Despite these small achievements, I felt beaten and morally exhausted. According to Linda Pierce, denial of one's internalized oppression helps sustain the colonial complex (De Jesus, 2005). She further stated that imperial whitewashing is systemic and occurs globally, making it hard to deconstruct the discriminatory biases.

My mother always told me that I should persevere and stay resilient. She told me to never show my vulnerability to what anyone would say or how I was treated during meetings. Despite my misgivings I did not give up. I became stronger and tougher through the years.

Failing Work-Life Balance

In the middle of my architectural career, I became a mother to a beautiful daughter. Thinking I could do it all, I decided to take that short three-month maternity leave and then returned to work. I was so blinded by ambition, that I did not realize the demands of motherhood. Seven years too late, I discovered I had failed to achieve a work-life balance so integral to the success of a career woman. One day, on my way home from an exhausting negotiation, I broke down into tears and realized that I had not been a good mother. I had left all the child-rearing to my mother, and I had become a part-time wife. I was a failure in my personal life. Even after two decades into a successful architectural career leading a billion-dollar capital construction program, overseeing a staff of 20 project architects, 13 resident engineers, and managing multiple construction projects in New York, I felt like a complete failure. I felt lost and desperate for clarity in my life.

This cross road led me to take a two-year sabbatical. Focusing on renewing my own role as a mother was a priority. Fortunately, both my husband and mother remained supportive of my search for meaning. During this time, I enjoyed being a full-time mom and still found myself questioning my need to repair the inequities in my field. Thus, I enrolled at Columbia University's International Affairs program and majored in Infrastructure Policy Development. What I was starting to realize was that motherhood was a once-in-a-lifetime opportunity, a chance to take care of a beautiful human being, this was the validation I was seeking. When my daughter turned 10 years old, I left Columbia University and decided I needed to redefine a new pathway for myself.

A Search for Meaning

> Failure provokes a change in one's course of direction. It forces not only a change in thinking, it unpacks misconceptions.
> - **Margaret Wheatley**, 2006

Ongoing moments of failure are relentless but with resolve and conviction, one can persevere to break boundaries, deconstruct the traditional mold, and be prepared for disruption. The best advice I ever received was from my mother, Rebecca Verzosa Santos, the first international stewardess of Philippine Airlines, who served on the epic first Trans-Pacific flight of PAL to fly home American soldiers after World War II. She identified three important lessons. The need for love for family and friends, for grit and courage, and for getting up, dusting yourself off, and moving on after failure.

She was an icon in the airline industry. She knew how to reinvent herself in the midst of generational changes and challenges. She became a single working parent after she was widowed at the age of 38. She never judged me, yet she always held a high standard, which was at times hard to achieve. She taught me five competencies that I use to guide my leadership to this day. In order of relevance, these are:

- A strong work ethic requires patience
- Failure is a moment to grow
- Purposeful collaboration helps clarify ideas and encourages agency
- Intentional and effective learning eliminates unnecessary complications, and
- Reflective practice allows thinking beyond the box.

Making Choices

> In any moment of decision, the best thing you can do is the right thing. The worst thing you can do is nothing.
> - **Theodore Roosevelt**

During my sabbatical, I discovered teaching as a profession. My daughter was close to graduating from middle school. I immediately enrolled in graduate school and focused on both General and Special Education, with the goal of learning how to help children cope with learning differences and multiple intelligences. Having interacted with children in the playground revealed children's many layers of learning and how one could optimize learning through all kinds of physical environments and cognitive opportunities. The playground was a gold mine for developing identity. Not only did I have more time with my daughter, I also discovered a new passion for teaching children. I graduated with a Masters of Science General and Special Education from Bank Street Graduate School of Education. Redefining my pathway for still another time was quite humbling yet was the best thing I had ever done. I was hired by the United Nations International School. Teaching children for the next seven years was inspiring, energizing, and continues to be a life-long learning experience.

When I reached my eighth year of teaching, I was asked to join the math curriculum committee. Seeing that I had the reputation with parents of an engaging math teacher, the administration got me into analyzing math content material used for teaching. Soon after, my responsibility expanded to coordinating the math curriculum for the entire elementary school. I later worked with the middle and high school faculty to ensure there was a smooth transition from one grade to the next. I enjoyed this work because it was like design and construction.

Leadership in Math

As a new math leader, this pathway was not simple. In 2010, I became a full-time math coach. Without hesitation, I finished the necessary professional training and continue to function as a math coach for two campuses at the United Nations International School. To do this job, I had to redefine my understanding of leadership. As math coach, I am both a peer and teacher mentor. As an architect, I was a collaborator and a catalyst. Every building was a symbol for change and innovation. Teaching is a much more gradual and gentle profession. Though collaboration is key, teacher development requires a participatory role by the coach to partner in the teaching and learning of children. Ensuring that every teaching moment is intentional, purposeful, and reflective in mathematics is not easy. I believe that children should not be told what to think. They should be given the opportunities to explore, develop how to conjecture, and experience what it means to be wrong and to fail. Making generalizations requires understanding what works and what does not. This differentiated approach to teaching and learning adds a complexity to coaching traditionalist educators. Moreover, research findings prove that math content and instructional methods in urban schools tend to be biased by both gender and race. Once again, I am confronted by issues of inequality in education; the same ones I faced as an architect.

As math coach, I am also a servant leader to teachers helping them retain their voice and agency in how they teach children. As servant leader, I prefer to operate behind-the-scenes, indirectly guiding and facilitating a learning environment that is student-centered and equitable. Witnessing the growth of teachers through self-discovery and collaborative partnership is one of the joys of being a coach. Good leadership means having an open mind, a belief in nurturing growth, constant humility, and the ability to foster a sense of connectedness toward others. Servant leadership in math coaching means providing a safe environment for trial and error while providing immediate constructive feedback.

Self-imposed Change

> Change is prompted only when an organism decides that changing is the only way to maintain itself.
> - **Margaret Wheatley**, 2006

With nations around the globe electing nationalist and populist governments, the current political climate directly impacts and weakens our high standards for children's education. According to Howard Gardner (2001), strong character is difficult to achieve particularly at a time when religious, communal, and family traditions and values are weak, and the principal messages conveyed by the media are irrelevant at best (p.246). It is a challenge to maintain high ethical standards when the government does not support educational ideals. Instilling a sense of realism, along with an appreciation for math is important if we are to meet the demands of the 21st century. Mathematics can help with the struggles for emancipation (Nasir, et al, 2007). According to bell hooks (1994), "despite the contemporary focus on multiculturalism in our society, particularly in education, there is not nearly enough practical discussion of ways classroom settings can be transformed so that learning experience is inclusive (p.35)." She further stated that a consequence of this lack of understanding of diversity is teachers who are uncomfortable with equitable multicultural education.

This need to improve access and equity is most obvious in the teaching of mathematics. Textbooks are designed for a specific sector in society: most problems are focused on a white audience. As a math coach, I have an opportunity to expand this by working internationally. In the last five years, I have coached a racially diverse educator audience from six different countries across four continents. I am determined to work towards eliminating this racial and gender inequality towards learning mathematics. Advocating for the implementation of innovative best practices is one way to improve access to the teaching and learning of mathematics. If we are to prepare children for careers that currently do not exist, we, as educators need to face the challenges presented by traditionalist thinking. Continuing to be mindful of mathematical pedagogy is critical as well. Disrupting this mindset is imperative if we are to educate for the future, much less for the present day.

Recently, I co-authored a book about linear measurement aimed at providing girls with the opportunity to find mathematical solutions about topics that are commonly thought of as masculine tasks like building with construction tools. I present at math conferences to explore areas in mathematics that need to be disrupted.

There is no way of knowing how what I am doing today as a math educator is related to my decision to shift careers from architecture to education. I credit this change of focus to my mother. I am also quite fortunate that my husband has always been an anchor and has made sure that I maintained a reasonable balance. He has always given me the mental space to recycle my failures and use them to achieve new aspirations. He constantly reminds me to be open-minded, flexible, and fearless. Lastly, I am thankful to my daughter, who despite having a mother whose blind ambition was a constant distraction continues to keep me sane and lets me know that I was not the failed parent I feared I was. In her mid-twenties, she has grown into a beautiful person. Her work as an artist, writer, and a future journalist is focused on social justice and civil rights. I am fortunate be to be surrounded by all these thought-provoking and intelligent people!

Fritjof Capra (2014), a scientist, educator, and activist, coined the term "Autopoeisis" to describe a very different universe where all organisms, including human beings, are capable of creating a "self" through engagement with all others within what he calls a web of life. He stated that we live in a world that is rich in processes that support growth and coherence through paradoxes that need to be contemplated. This implies a reflective practice that even leaders should adapt.

Ilya Prigogne, a physical chemist and Nobel laureate noted for his work on dissipative structures, explores paradoxical truths in the sciences. He stated that disorder and chaos can be a source of a new order. A lesson I have learned after all these years is that as we get older, we stumble upon unexpected experiences, face curve balls and distractions, and have new relationships that provoke us into thinking differently. We then adjust and correct our preconceived beliefs and evolve into who we become. Yet because the web-like networks of events we experience cause constant disruption, we change our planned course of direction. These interconnections and disconnections keep us in a dynamic evolution. Being aware, reflective, and maintaining our humility is a stabilizing disposition for survival. Surrounding ourselves with those we love and trust and being persistent about keeping them close is of utmost importance. Finally, we should never forget the intricate pathways we experience through our life. These are important signposts that allow a person to stay grounded. Taoist thinking reminds us that permitting adversities and failures will only ensure the gates to open for success. Whether you are already a leader or just about to start your path to leadership, remain open, think outside the box, and have courage in redefining your own pathway.

Reflecting on Mom's Story
by **Alex Murry**, daughter of Rebecca Murry

There is nothing more revolutionary than knowledge, and if there's one thing my mother embodies, it is the pursuit of knowledge. She is the ultimate student and, in that way, the best kind of teacher. I have spent my entire life watching her grow. Since I was young, my mother has continuously transformed herself, following her ambitions and passions as they took her from industry to industry. My mom masters every skill she takes on; a quality that is at once unnerving and awe-inspiring. Her natural capacity is based on dedication; she genuinely cares and that's what makes her different from most people.

I know many people say this about their moms, but in my case, it's true. My mom is the most selfless person you will meet. She is the center of our family; our rock, caring for each and every one of us and stronger than all of us combined. People flock to her. When I was eight years old, and she worked as a recess chaperone, I fumed at how my classmates sought refuge in her hugs. It was a constant struggle between *get away from my Mommy!* And *UGH Mom STOP*. She inherited this charisma from my grandmother, who had the exact same effect on people. They both emanate a sort of strength and vibrancy that immediately puts anyone around them at ease. Others feel they are in good hands when they are in her presence.

Only a few years after my mom moved to the United States, she moved her own mother as well. Watching my mom take care of my *lola* [grandmother] will always be one of the most powerful and impactful experiences of my life. By the time I came into the picture, the power balance in their relationship was shifting. My mother went from the cared for to the caretaker, and my grandmother vice versa. With this came necessary growth. While one had to learn to make the executive decisions, the other had to become comfortable with allowing the choices made by the other. Both women have always been extremely headstrong, so this was a constant challenge. But they adapted as they always do. They built a new life in a distinct environment. They were my whole world. And as my grandmother moved through the hurdles of aging, my mom never missed a beat. She designed our apartment to be handicap-friendly, always sought out the newest and most advanced therapies, created a herculean medical schedule, the complexity of which was beyond everyone but herself. My mom was there for my grandmother, providing what she does best: providing structure.

In her chapter, my mother writes about diversity and equity; and her belief that to care and understand is to uplift human dignity. My mother observed that you do not have to know the fact of an atrocity to imagine the person who committed it and that we display our capacity for empathy in our everyday behaviors. Reading my mom's chapter, I was surprised by a lot of the experiences. She had not told me about many of them but I can certainly imagine them. I will admit I did not realize how central social justice was to her pedagogy. But I saw her practice it every day I was growing up, and I see it still in her efforts to do her very best work. Perhaps most of all, though, I see her dedication to equity in the way she interacts with everyone around her. She respects humanity and practices empathy.

These are her qualities that I most aspire to. The persistently high standard which she sets both for herself and the world around her, and the acute thoughtfulness that she gives to every challenge she takes on. In her chapter, you will come to know my mom's fearlessness; reading her describe this in words was humbling for me as a daughter. Watching her move through life has always been inspiring. Reading her reflect on her life is a true privilege. I hope you will enjoy the following pages as much as I have. Remember, as my mom always says, be resilient.

DINA DELA PAZ STALDER

President and CEO, Stalder Group of Companies
GLOBAL FWN100™ 2017

Blow. Fall. Bounce.

In June 2017, I was chosen as one of the honorees for *Istorya ng Pag-asa* [Story of Hope], a travelling photo gallery project of the Office of the Vice President, Leni Robredo. The project aims to unify and empower the nation through different stories of hope of Filipinos; also, to inspire less privileged youth not to give up on their dreams. Coming from humble beginnings in San Pablo, Laguna, my voyage was hard but inspired by the aspiration to develop expertise in aesthetics and the ambition of opening my own laboratory and clinic in the Philippines. Now, our products have started crossing borders and have brand name recognition in Asia, the United States, and Europe. The Stalder Group of Companies was established as a private corporation. I am proud that it earned a blue-ribbon award from the Laguna Lake Development Authority, as an environmentally responsible business. In addition to employment, the company provides housing for employees.

Retrospection

My parents were farmers. I grew up in the sleepy little barrio in San Pablo, Laguna, a place distant from any school. I am the youngest of eight. Growing up, I helped my parents plant crops and raise livestock. We planted corn, beans, pineapple, papaya, and a lot more. I made charcoal from coconut shells to sell. When it was raining hard, and the weather was stormy, I prayed improvements in the weather. I never wanted to be absent from school, and I was afraid of waking up and finding all the trees had fallen on our house built in the middle of the coconut plantation where my father was the caretaker.

My former classmates, colleagues, and clients would probably describe the story of my life as a rags-to-riches story. What they do not know is that there is much more to it. In truth, life has dealt me some tough blows: knock-down blows that made me fall. Falls were temporary setbacks. And the harder I fell, the quicker I would bounce back.

Hard Blow, Fall, Bounce: The Cycle of My Past Life

Of the many hard blows in my life, several stand out. These blows gave me so much anguish and so much pain and left me with a sense of betrayal so sharp and intense that it cut through the core of my being. Family members caused the blows.

#metoo

At the young age of seven, I experienced the trauma of being molested by one of my extended family in-laws. My father helped me keep this secret to keep the family intact. I clenched my teeth. I had to endure the pain and disgrace, as though it was my fault. Because of this, my father did not encourage me to marry a Filipino. Looking back, I now realize that my younger self coped with that devastating experience by immersing myself in schooling. Almost obsessed, every day I would walk 45 minutes to school; balancing myself on the *pilapil* [rice paddies], crossing the raging river, and walking barefoot to save my slippers from wear and tear. I often fell, stood up, and continued forward again. I kept my resolve.

Grit

In school, I would spend all my time studying hard and participating in curricular and extra-curricular activities. Since we do not have electricity, my father used gas lamps to tutor me at night. And when the morning came, we still found a way to laugh because our nostrils were blackened with soot due to the smoke of the gas lamps. In the afternoons and during weekends, I would work alongside my parents and siblings tilling the land. Nothing mattered to me more than studying hard in school and working hard at home. After years of hard work and determination, I finished my elementary years with top honors and my high school years with honors. Courage and resolve, also called grit, would become the cornerstone of my character and existence.

During my college years from 1980-1985, I was a bed-spacer. I had to work as a weekend maid for my aunt who lived in Manila and who gave me a weekly pay of fifty pesos and a kilo of *galunggong* [the poor man's fish]. I had to make the fish last for all my meals for a week. My aunt was quite finicky about her bathrooms. They had to be scrubbed spotless and cleaned thoroughly not only once during the weekend, but several times. And she had forbidden the use of cleaning gloves. The low pay and no-glove rule, I bore in silence. When I was in my second year of college, she told me to work for her full time and stop studying because there was no hope I would get a job since no employer would want to hire a girl with my looks and my height. I felt the pain cutting through me, the intense sense of betrayal overwhelming me. I swallowed my pride and continued working for her. Right then and there, I vowed I would prove her wrong. I would work harder on my studies, find a job that paid well, and show her that even without looks and height, I could be a success in my chosen career. I graduated college in 1985 with a Bachelor of Science in Medical Technology from Centro Escolar University.

After a year working as a medical representative first, and later, as a supervisor for a well-known Dermatological Company, in 1986 I had the opportunity to open a drugstore. One of the pharmacists from the company, who would then become my cousin-in-law became my business partner. We had great hopes for the partnership. She was the pharmacist, and I was the industrial partner handling our connections and speaking with most of my doctor friends whom I had met when I was a medical representative. I was good in retail and very good in building reciprocal relationships with our customers who treated me with kindness and respect.

Grit as an Overseas Filipina in the UK

I noticed that my partner might have experienced what I call 'professional jealousy' as our customers recognized and respected me. To avoid the hostility, I decided to go to England to try my luck and entrust our small business to my partner. I trained my nieces and nephews in the business so that they could take over some of the responsibilities while I was away.

From August 1988 to April 1989, I worked as a domestic helper, babysitter, and inventory clerk in the UK. On a happy note, I managed to enroll in short-term courses in aesthetics cosmetic formulations through a correspondence program while I was working there.

More Grit Back in the Philippines

Deciding that Lady Luck was not going to favor me in England, I came home to the Philippines to find that my cousin-in-law had all but dissolved our partnership and started her own business. The pain of betrayal, again! I never did understand why she did what she did. The drugstore was doing so well. She left only an empty cabinet and a *Santo Niño*. Nothing else. Gritting my teeth, I decided to let go of the drugstore and in July 1989 opened Beauchamps Pharmacy as the first of the several companies in the Stalder Group of Companies. I had to start all over, but this time, I began Beauchamps as a single proprietorship. I was the medical representative of my own company. I had to buy the raw materials, do the packaging and labeling, take care of delivery, and collect payments for invoices. Over time, I took the same set of nieces to help me and soon, the pharmacy started earning a profit. Former clients during my medical representative days moved their accounts to Beauchamps and remained loyal.

Life was looking good until my father fell ill. I had to leave the pharmacy in the care of my nieces to care for my father. In a year's time, things started to go wrong. Soon, I discovered that my nieces had all but absconded with all my products and formulations. They were my nieces! I had trained them. I fully trusted them. And they betrayed me. They were once my allies who became my rivals, and they were the children of the in-law who had molested me when I was seven. I only helped them because my father asked me, regardless of the wrong done by their father to me. Here, I would like to say that the apple does not fall far from the tree. Rotten apples fall from a rotten tree. I could not bear the pain, but I had to. I squared my shoulders, and I set out to recoup my losses, recover my clientele, and regain my business reputation. I worked harder than ever, and within a year, Beauchamps was on its feet again! Life was once again looking good. And then I got married.

My Unbalanced Life

I was in love with another man, and I was sure that this man loved me for who I was. But, life is complicated. I married the man whose last name is Stalder because my father approved of him and because I had always been a dutiful daughter. I honestly thought he was going to be a good husband. For many years, I was a good and devoted wife. I bore him three beautiful children.

In 1995, I decided to return to the United Kingdom for further studies about the skincare trends and procedures. I earned a certificate in aesthetics. Upon my return to the Philippines, I established Dermaline Facial Care Center.

My husband turned out not to be a good husband and a compassionate father to our children. He was abusive. He was insensitive. He cared only for himself. Beginning in the first year of our marriage, I discovered that my husband was having an affair; but I kept it from my children because I did not want a broken family. I bore all these patiently, until one day, I decided that enough was enough. I stood up to him, and the fights began.

But Dermaline flourished with the care and attention I poured into it despite the stormy home front. The fights became worse.

He started being physical. I did not flinch. I stood my ground. My thought has always been to protect the children.

In 1999, I established Stalder Laboratories, Inc. and BCP Dermatological Corporation as its marketing arm; I could not keep up with the volume of orders we received.

My husband continued womanizing. Oh, what an overwhelming sense of betrayal again. But I worked harder while trying to give my children as normal a life as possible. When my children were safe at school, I would focus all my energy making the business flourish. Too many people depended on the companies; not just my children and relatives, but also the employees, their families, and our clientele. My children and the businesses became my paramount concern; not my marriage nor the man I married.

Resolve. Action. Reward

I worked hard for my immediate family, including my husband and my children, and for my extended family including my parents, my siblings, my nieces, and nephews. Sharing my financial success, I have been able to give my parents a comfortable life and to help my siblings and their children. I employed hundreds of people and developed thousands of entrepreneurs in and out of the country. I felt the need to give back. So, I decided to start a housing development for the employees and livelihood programs for the community. For the environment, I established a zero-waste management, and programs for materials recovery facility (MRF), wastewater treatment, composting, and organic farming. Also, to keep alive something from our culture amidst the prevalence of modern technology, social media, and video games, we built *bahay kubos* with space for native games like *sipa*, *piko*, *patintero*, *tumbang preso*, *luksong tinik*, and, *sungka*. For those more inclined to western games, we built a covered multipurpose court for basketball and table tennis. To complete the housing development, we paved the pathways with a combination of sand and ground bits of plastic from the micro-business I have helped set up. I have provided my employees with profit sharing, retirement, travel, and health benefits. These projects have been established with sustainability in mind. Thus, for a few years now, they have continued to operate well, making people's lives more comfortable, and making my need to give back, a reality.

I still vaguely recall when I was six years old, I would usually request my father to make me a small nipa hut that I would pretend was a store, and I was the retailer. I would always role play as the owner of the store. My playmates would be my customers, paying me leaves as money. I loved to make different concoctions out of leaves that turn out to be gel and flowers that could become soap. I did not realize that the simple mixtures that I had made would become the stepping stone to what I do today. And the businesses continued to expand and grow. And the industry acknowledged me as one of its movers and shakers. I was featured in a local business public service program entitled '*My Puhunan*' [my capital] where I was able to help a struggling sidewalk vendor start her own business in 2013.

Almost Losing Hope

Just when I thought that things could not get any worse on the home front, my husband was stricken with herpes in September 2013. What hurts the most was that I knew the type of herpes he had was human herpesvirus 2. Due to this infection, he was ordered to be in an isolation room until he got better. I could not even tell my children what it was all about. His beddings had to be changed every day, every single piece of clothing had to be ironed, and everything he had to eat had to be sterilized. The burden fell on me. I could not let anyone else do this for him because of the shame I felt. My only consolation was that his illness did not infect me since we had stopped sleeping in the same room before his illness. I had to swallow my pride again because I thought we had to stay together for the children.

In 2014, my son ran away from home; and announced he hated me and blamed me for the failure in our family life. This was the most heart-rending pain ever! My son with whom, I thought, I had a special relationship, whom I loved unequivocally ran away because he hated me. What was worse, was that my husband knew my son's whereabouts for almost a year. I found out that he was helping, aiding, and abetting, our son. My husband would bring a few of his belongings every time he went out. When I started to suspect what was happening, I knew I had to take action. I traced my son's location through my husband's sim card billing statement that revealed my son's address. My son was on the brink of insanity when my husband returned him to me on February 23, 2015. My son had to go through psychological treatments for a year and seven months. According to the doctor, the interviews showed my son had a bipolar disorder and antisocial personality disorder (APD). During the same meetings, my husband was diagnosed with bipolar disorder, antisocial personality disorder, and narcissism; tendencies that my son might have inherited from him.

But I did not give in to despair. I did not give up hope. My son needed me. My daughters needed me. My employees needed their jobs. And so, the hard work continued. The businesses continued to flourish.

Today, my son is back in our lives, and his father is out of our lives. My son decided to begin again, and he started by going back to school. He studied short courses in automotive services. He has used his new knowledge and skills in helping our business for he now does the necessary maintenance of all the vehicles of Stalder Group of Companies. Because of this, he was inspired and motivated to continue his studies from where he stopped before. My alma mater has been very kind as to accept my son as a returning student. He is now in his fourth year in college taking up Computer Engineering as his course and is excelling in all his subjects. My youngest daughter is academically inclined and at the same time is active in extra-curricular activities. She is grounded in values, motivated in her studies, and living a well-balanced life. In spite of having no father, I would say that my children have become strong. Very slowly, a sense of normalcy has descended upon our family. I continue to work hard. The businesses continue to grow.

I have been sharing the knowledge I have gained through the years to those who I believe are in great need. And who would have thought that my story was featured in another local TV drama anthology series hosted by Marian Rivera in May 2017. It showcased my life in the United Kingdom and the experiences I had there. On June 28, 2017, as noted in the introduction, I was one of the champions of the Vice President of the Philippines, Leni Robredo's, '*Istorya ng Pag-asa*' project. We provided stories of hope for other Filipinos. In the year 2018, I received the 'EVE Award' or Escolarian Vision Exemplar during the alumni homecoming of my beloved alma mater, Centro Escolar University. I lived up to the values that my school had bestowed upon me when I was also awarded as one of the most outstanding alumni of Centro Escolar University in 2007. Thanking God for all of this recognition, I always look back with no regrets for the hardships I have experienced. I feel honored that I had to go through all those challenges that made me the person I am today. I am a risk taker. My fighting spirit and gut-feel drive me to fulfill my dream. I have achieved so much in life, now that I am free from the burdens of my past. I have fallen and bounced back. I am now rising up and looking forward to the future.

Introspection

As I think of my journey, I cannot help but wonder how the path we choose can bring us to distant destinations. The way may be rough, the distance seemingly impossible to cover, but, in the end, the course can bring us through valleys and to the mountaintop, offering us a vista of life, a perspective that becomes genuinely and uniquely our own.

Life is all about making decisions, and the decisions we make quite early impact our lives and those of the people surrounding us. A confluence of factors comes into play when we make decisions. These factors can be of the heart or of the mind. Feelings and thoughts are constantly in a state of flux as we are called upon to make decisions. Should feelings prevail over thoughts? Should thoughts prevail over our feelings? Or should they be in consonance with one another? My feelings and thoughts were not always in a sense of equilibrium. But I tried.

We are what we are now because of the decisions we have made, the choices we have taken. Every decision made has far-reaching consequences, not felt at the moment, but felt at some time yet to come. Our present is the totality of past experiences so to make the present work for us; we need to make peace with our past.

Experience has taught me there are really no hard and fast rules to follow in life's journey. There is only context. And determination. And hard work. And maybe, the rewards will come.

Accepting My Mother's Legacy
by **Diana Stalder**, daughter of Dina Dela Paz Stalder

Our legacy is created from the choices and decisions we make in life. How we live and love and how we touch others through our lives creates a legacy of respect. My mom always tells me her story of how she persevered and strived to attain her success. She has always been this great example that I believe most people should look up to. Her 'rags to riches' story may serve as a kind of motivation for those who lack faith in themselves; my mom is a woman of strength and courage.

One of the best values of my mom is her unconditional love for us. Giving birth to us is already a sacrifice that only a mother can give because she gave us life and took care of us. I cannot compare my mom to anyone else because she is both mother and father to us, her children. She may be a strict disciplinarian, but all she wants was to give us the best, and she loves me for who I am.

My mother believed in education. She has always said that being well educated is one of the most significant achievements one could attain and that no one can take away. With her as my inspiration, I graduated college in 2015 with my Bachelor of Science in Pharmacy as my chosen course and studied for six months in the UK for aesthetic procedures specializing in laser treatments. This education has expanded my knowledge and helped me in managing our dermatological corporation.

I would say that I am lucky to have her as my mom because she instilled in me her values and principles that have made me the person I am today. I was given the opportunity to join different organizations like the Junior Chamber International Philippines in 2016 in which I was the Director for Internationalism in 2017, and a Local Training Director in 2018. These associations helped me become a woman of purpose and gain confidence just like my mother.

Not only did she teach me what is right, wrong, and everything in-between I needed to know to succeed, but she also shared with me her expertise and experiences in our family business. She trained me as she took me to her meetings and events. She introduced me as her successor. We participated in a local public service program on April 2, 2018, entitled 'Mission Possible' where we helped a blind person with his massage therapy business. It was such a great experience to be able to share and give back despite the humble beginnings of my mom.

It takes a lot of trust and responsibility to be someone's legacy. However, I will do my best to live up to it. How we live our life and how we touch others' will be our legacy but for me, those are also based on the seeds sown by my mother; seeds that will soon bear fruit that shall be reaped not only by me but by future generations.

MILA EUSTAQUIO-SYME

Justice of the Peace, Ontario, CA
GLOBAL FWN100™ 2017

with

MA. VICTORIA E. AÑONUEVO

Chairman and President, Mejora Ferro Corporation
GLOBAL FWN100™ 2014

Success Amidst Adversities

My younger sister Marivic was five years younger than my twin sister Lourdes and I. She was the 10-year old child who curiously watched her two 15-year old sisters playing *piko* [hopscotch] in our backyard, swooning over Elvis Presley's music, and attempting to learn the latest steps in the boogie dance. Marivic would eavesdrop when Lourdes and I would talk about our crushes on various NCAA basketball players. We also knew that sometimes she would be peeping through the window when we had our visits from boys. But wonderfully, Marivic caught up to us. She questioned us, debated our interpretation of facts, gave us more recent information, and suggested innovative solutions to various situations. She confirmed that she was no longer the baby sister.

Our father who became the top bureaucrat in the legislative assembly as Secretary of the Philippine Senate wanted all of us to be physicians, with each of us with a different specialty. But alas, not one of us met his dreams. My twin and I were horrified by the thought of having to touch dead bodies, or cutting through live skin, or seeing blood profusely flowing down our hands, or smelling the stench of various chemicals. Marivic, considered the obedient daughter, attempted to meet this dream by enrolling in a Pre-Med course, only to give up as it was not her calling. Thankfully, my father accepted our decisions as we followed our separate pathways outside the field of medicine. Our mother began her career as a grade school teacher and then moved on to a government position as an auditor assigned to the Central Bank of the Philippines. She accomplished this while successfully balancing a career and raising a family. Her contemporaries who were housewives were puzzled as to why she pursued a career when my father, who was a lawyer, earned enough for the family. Our mother impressed upon us that having a career of her own provided her with financial and psychological independence.

Marivic received her GLOBAL FWN100™ award in 2015 and I received mine in 2017. Although we were both recognized as influential, we both faced adversities. Mine was to live alone in a strange foreign country, Canada with no close relatives for moral encouragement, no dear friends for immediate and trusted feedback, and no ready resources for instantaneous financial support. Hers was to raise three young children in the Philippines as a single mother after her husband sadly succumbed to cancer at the young age of 40. The narrative that follows relates how we achieved success in our chosen careers despite these challenges.

HER WORSHIP MILAGROS EUSTAQUIO-SYME

I will relate what led me to Canada, what factors led me to grow in my career, my journey to participation and leadership in associations, and how I managed to get to where I am. The journey includes failures and the zig-zags in my life that led to success. I came to view failures as mere chapters in the road of life.

I never planned to migrate. I enjoyed my job as a Manager for Philippine Airlines and later, as the Director of the Orient Airlines Association. Both positions gave me the opportunity to travel for business and for pleasure. However, in September 1972, then President Ferdinand Marcos imposed martial law that included a travel ban. Under this ban, only business travel and immigrants were allowed to leave the country. I felt this ban deprived me of my benefits. When I learned that Canada was accepting immigrants, I rationalized that I could enjoy my travel benefits once I had a Canadian immigrant visa while staying in the Philippines. I got my Canadian visa and enjoyed my travel. However, when a Canadian Visa Officer found out I was not a "real" immigrant, he threatened to cancel my Canadian visa. This left me with a dilemma: should I now become a "real" Canadian immigrant or should I continue to live in the Philippines and give up my Canadian visa. Realizing how difficult it was to obtain a Canadian immigrant visa, I decided to try living and working in Canada.

I then discovered the trials and tribulations of being an immigrant: the stereotype that individuals who were educated and had employment experiences in a third world country had inferior education and experience. My Master's degree in Statistics and my experience as a Director of an international airline association were considered the equivalent of Grade 13.

I determined that I would meet this challenge by starting from the bottom and proving my worth. I removed my master's degree education and executive position experience from my resume. Instead of applying for a mid-management position, I applied for a Statistician's position. After two long months, I found employment. The realization that for me to move up in the organization spurred me to get a Canadian education and experience. While working during the day, I took my MBA at York University, now called the Schulich School of Business in Toronto. Lucky for me, I was then single, and there was no family dependent on me for food, housing, and education.

The Lord has been good to me, and I reached a good position as Director of Planning for a major corporation. It was during one of the trips for the company that I met my husband who was then flying as well on a business trip.

Changing Policy to Improve the Status of Filipina Women in Canada

When I first moved to Canada, many of the Filipino women were domestic workers. A good friend of mine who made it as a successful professional and who lived in an upscale neighborhood in Toronto related to me how, during one of her early walks in the area, she admired the garden of one of her neighbors and told her so. The neighbor then replied: "Oh, thank you. I am sure your master's garden must be just as nice!!"

In the early 70's, the Canadian government opened categories for new types of immigrant women, including live-in caregivers and mail-order brides. I realized that these new immigrants who were mostly Filipino women were treated differently from other immigrants. The live-in-caregivers were allowed to work only on a temporary basis for a maximum of five years and often worked 24/7 without days off or vacation leave. Only after two years of proving themselves as good citizens could they apply as immigrants to Canada.

The other group of Filipino women who came to Canada was the mail-order brides. Many of these marriages had succeeded, but some failed. If subjected to domestic violence, they had no choice but to suffer and bear it because if they reported the abuse to the police or filed for divorce or separation, the Canadian Immigration officers would very likely deem their marriage to have been a fake and deport them back to the Philippines. Sometimes a violent husband, in retaliation for the wife wanting a separation, could claim that their marriage was fake.

In the early 70's, women from developing countries were not given full credit for their education and experience. This was my situation as I indicated earlier.

To work on improving the status of Filipina women in Canada, I decided to work on immigration policy advocacy. Along with other Filipina women, we formed the Network of Filipino Women in Canada. At the same time, I was appointed the First Chair of the Women's committee of the Canadian Ethnocultural Council, the umbrella group of about 50 ethnic groups in Canada. We realized that other ethnic women shared the problems of Filipina women. Thus, the Network of Filipino Women, along with other immigrant groups, undertook studies on these issues. We presented the results to the provincial and federal government ministers, and advocated for better living conditions for live-in-caregivers, for special consideration for mail order brides who became victims of domestic violence, and for measures to recognize the degrees and experience obtained from developing or third world countries. Among the legislation, the groups were successful in advocating was the Employment Equity Act. This act included affirmative action for immigrants, visible minorities, Aboriginal people, the disabled, and women.

In 1994, I was appointed an Immigration Judge for the Federal Government. As a judge, I made determinations on refugee claims. One of my decisions (R. v. Fernando Enrique Rivera, May 2004) made the headlines of the Canadian national newspaper *The Globe and Mail*, and this decision was quoted in several subsequent cases.

In 2005, I was appointed a Justice of the Peace for the Province of Ontario, where I make decisions relating to the federal Criminal Code of Canada. I preside in Bail Courts; issue search warrants, arrest warrants, child protection warrants, and make decisions, among other things, on convictions under the Highway Traffic Act, the Environment Act, Fisheries Act, and Municipal offenses, including breach of bylaws and parking violations.

Becoming Her Worship

The Immigration and Refugee Board of Canada (IRB) is an administrative tribunal responsible for making decisions on refugee applications of individuals claiming asylum in Canada. As in the United Kingdom, IRB Board Members (or IRB "Judges") do not have to be lawyers. All one has to prove is that he/she is fair and capable of good judgment. A non-law degree can prove to be an asset as non-lawyers can analyze, decipher facts, and weigh evidence from a human perspective. My mathematics major and Masters in Business Administration, along with my experience of working with Filipino associations and intercultural councils, were deemed sufficient to meet the eligibility requirements. Similarly, Justices of the Peace in both Canada and the U.K. do not have to be lawyers. In both cases, Board Members and Justices of the Peace are given extensive training and orientation before they can begin hearing cases. This training includes a strong emphasis on professional, fair, and ethical conduct.

Expectations for IRB Members can be found on their website[1]. IRB members are expected to:

- Act honestly and in good faith, in a professional and ethical manner.

- Conduct hearings in a courteous and respectful manner while ensuring that the proceedings are fair, orderly, and efficient.

- Conduct themselves with integrity and avoid impropriety.

- Demonstrate a commitment to the values of honesty, good faith, fairness, accountability, dignity, respect, transparency, openness, discretion, cultural sensitivity, and loyalty.

When I was appointed Justice of the Peace, I was assigned to Brampton/Mississauga. I was one of seven justices appointed in 2005. There were about 7,000 applicants for the position. Among the previous Filipinos appointed Justice of the Peace are Delano Europa and Ric Mananquil. For information concerning the appointment process, including qualifications, see the Justices of the Peace Act[2]. The appointment comes with the title "Her Worship." I am the first Filipina woman to earn the title "Her Worship."

Dare to Prove That Stereotypes Against Filipino Women Can Be Wrong

As I look at the 40 years that I have lived in Canada, I am grateful that I have been blessed and given the opportunity to effect changes for the benefit of other immigrants through my leadership in associations. I would like the next generation of Filipina women to remember that while stereotyping may still exist in other people's minds, they must go beyond these and prove to others that a Filipina woman can succeed just like native-born Canadians.

---

[1] http://www.irb-cisr.gc.ca/Eng/BoaCom/Pages/MemCom1.aspx
[2] https://www.ontario.ca/laws/statute/90j04

Maria Victoria Eustaquio-Añonuevo

I took on a different path altogether than my elder sister. I stayed in the Philippines.

Challenges as the Middle Child

I was the middle child, and as experienced by most middle children have gone through, I had to make myself visible. I was sandwiched between the twins, Milagros and Lourdes, who were objects of curiosity and delight as they looked so much alike and even dressed alike and the youngest, who was the fairest and cutest of the lot. This was probably the reason why I had to become self-confident and an over-achiever. Early on, I had to be the sister who excelled in both academics and extracurricular activities. I served as president of the class and student organizations from grade school to college.

Challenges as a Single Mother

A life-changing event encouraged me on to succeed despite being a female and that is, the early demise of my husband at the age of 40. He left me with three kids ranging from 15 years to 9 years. I was all they had, and I had promised myself that just being a solo parent would never prevent me from sending them to the best schools, giving them a comfortable life, and providing them opportunities to experience the best things in life like traveling.

Accomplishments in Spite of the Challenges

I successfully moved up the ladder from Assistant Manager to Senior Vice President, President, and Chairman of various Ayala Land subsidiaries. In 2011, I was appointed Philippine Managing Director and Chief Executive Officer of the Millennium Challenge Account-Philippines (MCA-P), a U.S.-based funding agency akin to the United States Agency for International Development (USAID) for poverty alleviation. Together with these successes, there were setbacks and disappointments, sometimes reflecting gender bias because as I discovered a female had to work twice as hard as her counterparts to be recognized. Sadly, this is prevalent in the private sector as well as the public sector.

While at MCA-Philippines, I had many occasions to discuss the strides women had made as a result of the emphasis placed on gender equality in MCA-P funded programs. I explained how women have taken leadership positions in their communities and gained new skills for better employment. I shared stories of women who felt empowered because MCA-P gave them training and gave them opportunities and a voice in leading their communities. Several specific examples were hiring women in construction and giving gender incentives for non-traditional employment, including welding, plumbing, etc.

What I am most proud of is that I helped more than 1.5 million Filipinos in 42 provinces who had lived below the poverty line, improve their lives through projects. Help was provided by projects like 1,500 km of highway and farm-to-market roads, health facilities, bridges, school buildings, irrigation, and other infrastructure projects. In my work with MCA-P, I had overseen the disbursement of US $434m in grant funds for poverty alleviation. We funded projects worth P20 b in these communities that were implemented without a hint of corruption at any level in my organization, starting from the top of the leadership all the way to the bottom of the organization. We were the recipient of various accolades from the administration of the U.S. funding agency, Millennium Challenge Corporation and we were named as the best-managed and accountable among their country programs. We proved Filipinos could, with a Filipina at the helm, administer a program with excellent performance and with no hint of corruption.

Lessons Learned for Leadership and the Next generation

Four things I can pass on to the next generation:

First, while men are seen as superior competitors sometimes, and women are viewed as inferior sometimes, men can also be your best allies as you move through various roles in life; as a daughter, spouse, subordinate, colleague, or the opposition, sitting across the negotiating table. I was lucky that there were so many supportive men in my life who prodded me on and gave me nuggets of wisdom. These men included my father Atty. Regino Eustaquio, my husband Roy Nilo Añonuevo, my former bosses, and my sons. They have guided me and opened doors for me to maximize my potential. They reminded me that being a woman is not a barrier to achieving my goals.

Second, never linger on a failure or disappointment. Get up, move on, and reinvent yourself if you must. You will soon discover that the feelings of disappointment you experience today will be gone in a week's time.

Third, nobody is there for you forever except yourself. You create your own destiny with 99% sweat and only 1% fate. Everything you do today no matter how insignificant you think it is, it contributes to what you will be tomorrow.

Fourth, let me end with a quote from me about "Women Breaking Barriers: Finding 'Gabriela' Within Us All" on the Millennium Challenge Corporation website in 2013:

> The Philippine Revolution was dotted with women heroines. One of them is Gabriela Silang, who is usually depicted riding a horse and leading a charge of rebels against the Spanish soldiers. In the late 18th century, Gabriela's husband was a rebel leader killed in battle; she took over as the leader when she saw the troops were losing heart. She symbolizes the courage of the Filipina—even now, a leading feminist movement in the Philippines is named after her. I would like to think that I too am a Gabriela, and for that matter, every Filipina can be a Gabriela when circumstances call for her to be such.

CATHERINE TEH, M.D.

Vice President, Philippine Association of HPB Surgeons
GLOBAL FWN100™ 2017

Turning Struggles into Strengths

Surgery has long been considered as a man's world. Surgery's demands for long hours of operation, irregular hours of work, and high levels of stress were considered not to be compatible with family life. Challenges of hepatobiliary pancreatic (HPB) surgery are similar to that of other surgery, with the difference being that HPB is one of the latest medical frontiers to have been developed and is still evolving. There are fewer women in this field of surgery compared with that of pediatric, gynecologic, plastic, neurosurgery, orthopedic or general surgery. HPB is challenging because of its ongoing evolution and the need to keep up with changes. It also takes a long time to advance in this profession.

Preparation to be a surgeon is focused on the human body and patient care. There was little consideration of other things. When we become doctors and surgeons, we become leaders but focused on providing care. In my narrative, I will share disruptions in my medical education and initial medical practice that strengthened my leadership first as a surgeon and then as a successful medical community leader.

From when I was a child, I always knew what I wanted. I set the goal for myself and worked towards that goal. Everything seemed to work as planned. Excellence was the name of my game. Deviation was not included in my vocabulary, and failure was not an option. Everything progressed in life as if it was God's plan. I was born and raised in a traditional Filipino-Chinese family. I learned and lived the values of hard work, courage, strength, resilience, perseverance, and patience from my parents. My tiger mom run our lives impeccably. My father did not receive a higher education, but, he was the most successful person I know. He was my model and my inspiration to strive for success.

I have wanted to be a doctor since I was three. I never wavered. My dream never changed. I was able to pursue my dream of becoming a physician. After medical school, the next hurdle was to get into a surgical program, since surgery was part of my medical dream. Getting into a surgery program was not easy. Women surgeons were not common at the time. However, I still applied for the program and scored high in the assessment examination. Then came the interview. I was the only female to be interviewed at that time, along with 20 other male applicants. My interview consisted of being asked the question of why I wanted to be a surgeon. During that same interview, the panel of distinguished surgeons told me that surgery is not for women, advised me to consider obstetrics and gynecology, dermatology, cosmetic surgery or some other medical field more appropriate for a woman, and reminded me that working hours are long and the demands of surgery are high. The competition was tough against the male applicants, many of whom also made use of their political connections. I did my best and soared above the rest. From then on, surgical residency became the focus of my hospital work and my life. I reached my goal; I became a surgeon after five years of perseverance and grit.

So today, here I am. Yes, I am a surgeon, I cut people up.

Disruption # 1

Be steadfast. Know what you really want in life, find your goal, aim towards it and go for it!

I braved 1,825 days of sleep-deprived, weekend-less, residency training as a general surgeon. This meant taking written, oral, and practical exams while looking after patient after patient. Patient care included staying at their bedside and providing the support and comfort they needed when all else had failed. There was the formidable task of defending your actions when something went wrong with a patient, data to analyze and research papers to write, administrative duties in the hospital as well. It was not the amount of hard work that was challenging. Matters concerning inter-collegiality were far more heartbreaking. Once I was nominated as the most outstanding resident in training in the country. The recognition was almost in the bag. However, as politics was rife, and even when all I want to do was learn and hone my skills well by being diligent, reliable and responsible, pushing myself to do more and more than what is expected of me, people misinterpreted and made my perseverance an issue. Some doctors in the hospital tarnished my name to the judges while I was abroad in a conference. I lost this recognition to another candidate from a different hospital who perhaps deserved it too. However, I sobbed in despair and carried much angst in my heart because I knew the process was unfair. Not only did I lose the recognition, but the hospital also lost its opportunity to shine as well. However, after a while, I let it go. My father once said to me, it is better to be an underdog but sleep peacefully at night rather than be evil and unjust. I learned to forgive them but not really forget, after all, I am just human. I continued to strive for excellence. Although I finished as the chief resident and was respected by my mentors, colleagues, and hospital staff, I was also accused by the hospital director of being arrogant when I stood by my principle and sanctioned a junior resident for his failure to perform his duties promptly that caused the demise of a patient. This resident belonged to the affluent class, and according to the hospital director's norms, I had no right to "dishonor" him. Because of that, I was unceremoniously terminated, thrown out of the hospital. I was in despair for a moment, but I knew that what I did was right.

Disruption # 2

Do what is right, stand by your principles and values. You cannot please everyone.

As I spend most of my time with the sick, my heart gravitated towards cancer patients. I wanted to give them a new lease on life in my capacity as a physician. I left the country for further studies and training to become a breast cancer surgeon. It did not happen as planned. The breast cancer positions were taken, and the only specialization that was available and seemed to want to do was hepatobiliary pancreatic (HBP) surgery. HBP deals with the liver, the gallbladder, bile ducts, and pancreas. I was the first fellow who took that specialization. It is a valuable leadership lesson to remember that even if HPB was not my choice, I took the opportunity and made the best of it. It was not my choice. I never thought of HPB, and HPB was never in my mind. Despite this, I persisted for another three years of intense work on a specialty I hardly knew about when I started. Getting into the HPB program turned out to be a life-changing experience, it was challenging but gratifying in the end. I was the first trainee they accepted that they eventually employed based on their satisfaction with my performance. I had an exceptional and brilliant mentor. I can never thank him enough for sharing without reservations his expertise with me. I turned from an apprehensive and indecisive trainee to a happy and confident HPB surgeon ready to conquer the world of liver, biliary, and pancreatic cancer. Unfortunately, a severe infection I was exposed to in the hospital called SARS almost took my life. I saw my colleagues die, I was isolated for 21 long days, and survived. My parents called me back home to the Philippines for fear of losing me to SARS. To my parents' relief, I returned home reluctantly because I thought I had already found my happy place abroad. Once again, my plans were shattered, and my ambition put on pause.

Disruption # 3

Make plans for your life but keep in mind that sometimes, life has other plans for you. What does not kill you will only make you stronger.

Upon my return, the senior surgeon whom I looked up to asked me: "Why did you come back? Many more colleagues welcomed me home with signs of skepticism. Physicians and friends questioned my specialization. This was in 2004. HPB was not well-regarded in the Philippines, highly advanced procedures on liver resections, pancreatic surgeries including laparoscopic approach were not usually done back then. Doctors sent me general surgery cases, including wound debridement, excisions of breast masses, and other minor and medium general surgery cases. I began to teach medical courses at my alma mater. However, I was not happy with what I was doing. I was not doing HPB; I was not teaching HPB. I resigned. I left my university in search of an institution where I would be able to do what I wanted to do.

I was seen as an aggressive female surgeon who posed a threat to the men in the surgical world. I worked twice or even thrice as hard to achieve good outcomes. I left again, this time for France under the tutelage of world-renowned pioneer liver surgeons in search of more knowledge. I continued to hone my skills for highly advanced approaches to conquer liver and pancreatic cancer as every day I saw an increase in the number of Filipinos suffering from these diseases, but they were not being treated appropriately. I wanted to give my patients the kind of medical and surgical care that the west was providing. There were many barriers. Instruments and types of equipment were severely lacking even until this day. Hospitals were reluctant to purchase them for HPB as they saw no return on investments. Patients were in dire need of finances. I began to use what I have learned coupled with some creativity to offer relief to our unfortunate patients who needed the surgeries and care. They needed the surgery to live longer and to enjoy their lives with their loved ones even if just for a few more months or years. I aimed to make my patients smile and to keep their families happy. That was all I wanted. Years later, here I am, still trying to find innovative ways to extend their lives, sometimes, challenging the standard. I have received several accolades for my achievements, but in reality, the best awards are the love and trust of my patients. Today, those who initially criticized me, send their patients to me and ask for my help. These moments are priceless.

Disruption # 4

Be resilient. Don't let other people dim your light. Dare to be different! Keep your desires pure and genuine. You will be appreciated one fine day.

I once told myself that when people talk about liver cancer and pancreatic cancer, I wanted them to be talking about Catherine Teh. After years of hard work and perseverance, I have received numerous acknowledgments of my work. I feel that I have achieved my goal and that I can enjoy my success. The question now is how to deal with possessions, power, and prestige. Currently, I am receiving many invitations to speak, to lecture, to do surgeries and I am garnering awards and recognition. Every day, I start with a prayer and thank God for my beating heart. I ask the Lord to guide my hands so I may follow His way for the glory of God. As much as possible, I attend mass at seven in the morning before I begin my work. At the end of the day, whatever happened, no matter how tired I was, I would reflect on what I had done, and again thank God for all His blessings, for sharing His wisdom with me, and for making me His instrument to heal. This has given me serenity. I resist letting my ambition be all about me and focus on the needs of others. Having to a great extent conquered the world of medicine, I have again achieved what I have desired. My daily prayer to Christ is to allow me to be His servant as His instrument in healing as I pray to God, to give me wisdom, to strengthen my heart, and to guide my hands as I treat each patient, as I balance my life, and as I wear a thousand and one hats each day.

Day and night, as a specialist surgeon, I face life and death. One may assume that death is a regular event at the hospital and that perhaps death does not really affect physicians. That is not the case. One day, there was a 38-year old energetic gentleman who came to me as a last resort after being rejected by four surgeons. He had a 32cm liver tumor that was bigger than a watermelon. His waist was gradually increasing corresponding with the pain. He waited for four hours at my clinic for his turn. A patient who had had almost the same experience told him to cheer up and encouraged him by joking: *"pag tinanggihan ka ni Dra Teh, magpakamatay ka na!"* [If Dr. Teh rejects you, go ahead and kill yourself.] His turn came, I studied his case and told him that I would have to deliberate more and he should wait for further results. Meanwhile, I gave him instructions to prepare for possible surgery.

I thank God for answering my prayers even when He gives me difficult cases. I try my best to save their lives from cancer. This was a tough case. I prepared the patient carefully knowing that this was an extreme case. The surgery went well, and I excised the tumor. However, the patient's blood pressure plunged to zero. I was upset with my anesthesiologist and blamed him for not anticipating what happened. We tried every possible way to revive the patient. After twenty minutes, it was clear we had lost the patient. I felt the pain as though I had lost a battle. An on-table death is the worst experience that can happen to a surgeon. I took it personally. The family despaired. I grieved.

I grieved because I had lost my patient. I grieved because I broke my promise to the patient that I would save him from his suffering. I grieved because I felt that I did not do my best! I grieved because I asked God to be with me but I felt that I was abandoned. That moment of self-doubt made me ask: "Why do you my Lord Jesus give me all these challenges, make me spend all my time working for people I don't even know? I am trying my best to save lives, and yet I hardly have the time to spend with my child. While trying to save this patient, I again missed my daughter's school activity." I felt alone and defeated. This was a moment of profound agony.

I had dared to question God, and I knew I would not find an answer to my question on Google nor in any liturgical book, I had to search within me. The answers came from what I learned from this gentleman when he expressed his fears, and I tried to console him. When I was trying to comfort him, I saw a little ray of hope in his troubled eyes. I glimpse a reluctant smile from his anxiety-laden face as I told him that day that I was willing to take his case and try to relieve his pain. Now, I understood why he thanked me profusely because I listened to him, I discussed his situation with him, I answered his queries scientifically, I disclosed all possibilities including death without withholding information, and I gave him as much time as he needed. However, I am only human and cannot save every patient. Now I realize that my God had not abandoned me when my patient's family continued to extend their gratitude. In that moment of acceptance, his family and I found love and peace; his family amidst the anguish and pain of losing their loved one and me for my frustration and disappointment in losing a patient.

Perhaps that was the true and deeper meaning of God's challenge for me. To cure sometimes; to heal and comfort always.

Disruption # 5

Be grateful. Put God in the middle of everything you do. Reflect and ground yourself as you go up higher and higher the ranks. Although created in the likeness and image of God, we are not perfect, but we should strive to be the best versions of ourselves.

> The greatness in humanity is not in being human but in being humane.
> - **Mahatma Gandhi**

My ambition is to build a community of HPB surgeons in the Philippines who can address liver cancer that is now the third highest cause of cancer-related deaths in the Philippines. Pancreatic cancer is catching up to liver cancer. These are challenging cancers that are difficult to treat. It is important to share one's knowledge and skills, especially to the next generation. It is our duty and obligation to teach and empower the next generation of surgeons. There is a need for surgeons who will treat patients not only with their hands but also with their hearts and the minds. That way, we will be better physicians.

It was when I went abroad and learned from the best in the world that I realized how far behind we were in the Philippines. It is sad that our culture in the Philippines seems to be "that of a dead man's shoe," wherein people cannot make progress in their careers until someone senior to them retires or dies. In contrast to the west, our young professionals are not given the opportunity to develop and become experts in their field of expertise. We are expected to assist the seniors in their pursuit. I experienced this when I came back from my training abroad. Because of this, I have vowed to change the professional hierarchy. I spend as much time as I can with my trainees and associates. It is my goal to train them, nurture them, empower them, and push them to be the best persons they can be. It is also important to note that we must not underestimate the ability of the younger generation in that we can learn from them too. Thus, I created a foundation to help indigent patients and also to assist young surgeons in training.

Disruption # 6

The secret to success is not in any surgical bible. It must be found in one's heart and brought to one's hands. Be a giver. Share and impart knowledge and skills. Collaborate and work together. That is the best way to achieve since one cannot do everything by oneself. There is an African saying that goes: to go fast, go yourself. To go far, go together. Most importantly, give back to the community.

I found myself a place to hone my skills and practice my craft in HPB surgery. For more than 11 years, I served this institution to treat patients with liver cirrhosis and cancer, biliary and pancreatic tumors, trained residents and turned a department that was almost non-existent to one that was functional, with increasing surgical volume and started a unique residency training program. For many years, I committed all my time in this department including the creation of a liver center in an institution I called home. With the hope of helping Filipino patients with liver diseases, my goal was to gather and empower a team of doctors specialized in the treatment of liver cirrhosis, creating the liver transplant team. A team that collaborated and worked together in making institutional protocol on liver transplantation, a team that started from ground zero and made liver transplantation successful with financial support gathered from the Philippine Charitable Sweepstakes Organization (PCSO) for indigent patients. It was almost a dream come true until one fine day after a change in leadership in the institution, my genuine aspirations for the institution, for the patients, and all the hard work were shattered. While operating on a cirrhotic patient who needed a new liver, I was told to give up my role as the surgeon at that time and allow another surgeon favored by the medical director to continue my surgery. This surgeon was not even affiliated with the institution. Without prior notice, without proper endorsement, this scenario happened. I can never understand the reason behind this sudden decision, nor could I accept this unprofessional act. However, for the safety of the patient, I stepped down because I was full of anger and frustration that my hands trembled and my mind perturbed. The moral injury inflicted was so immense that it had affected my performance. No amount of work tires me out, and anything that I can do for the good of the patients can only be tireless for me. What happened clearly was a violation of basic human respect, and there was no professionalism observed. It was indeed a depressing moment. Politics and personal agenda got in the way. After some downtime, I conditioned myself and moved on. Instead of fighting and stooping down to her level, I gathered my strength and shifted my energy and continued to pursue my goals elsewhere.

Disruption #7

Sometimes, no matter how much we give our best and commit to our duties and obligations, our efforts and intent may not be valued. Look far and beyond in crisis like this. Instead of wasting your energy in hatred and discord, shift your energy to acceptance and renewal. It also means letting go of our attachment of being right, letting go of our pride in keeping the values we practice. However, it does not mean that we let go of doing the right things, it does not mean letting go of values that we are made of. Instead, it is letting go of what you cannot change, and letting go of the past. I urge you to see the opportunities right in front of you, move on and start anew, for, after the rain, the sun will always shine brighter and stronger.

To me, life is work and work is life. Because of all that I do, my success had cast a disaster for my well-being. I often neglect my own health, I do not have enough sleep, I do not eat properly, and I have no "me time." Even when I was sick, I still went to work and operated on patients even while I had an IV drip in my arm. I have neglected my family and friends, people who are dearest to me, and people who matter the most to me. I do not pay attention to their desire to spend time with me because I reason they will always be there for me. My dad jokingly once said to his friend that, "He had to make an appointment just to see me." My daughter at the age of 5, told my mother: "I only see my Mom early in the morning when she sends me to school and at night in my dreams." I am often an absent mother, one who was never visible at school activities and in the PTAs. My justification has been that I have a responsibility to my patients. It is my responsibility to honor my commitments to the medical societies and communities that I represent. People look up to me, and I must deliver what they expect of me. There is a price to pay in meeting these responsibilities. Everything has a price in life, but the challenge is recognizing what the price is. Sometimes we are not aware of the price until it is too late. Looking back to when I decided to return to the Philippines in 2003 after the SARS near-death experience, I realized that was when my perspective on life changed. I knew at that time, nothing else mattered to me, no glory nor fame will ever make my life complete, without my loved ones. I try to fulfill my multiple duties as a physician, mentor, friend, daughter, and mother. Many years after, being a SARS survivor, I make it a point to go home to my parents' house often. I bring my daughter to meetings, workshops, the hospitals, and even in the operating room. I know that the time I can give them is not enough since my life continues to be hectic, but I think, whatever time I can spare from my hectic everyday schedule will be good enough. I strive to bring my daughter to school every morning; it is a precious time I cherish where we can communicate in the car on the way to school. I try to go home to my parent's house every night after work to have dinner with them, it may not mean so much to others, but to me, it's my way of saying I am here for you. I thank my loved ones all the time and let them feel loved. I try to spend as much quality time with them.

Disruption #8

No matter how much work is calling, take good care of yourself, for you will not be able to be your best when you are not well enough. Always thank your family and tell them how much you love them for you do not want to miss that chance. People we neglect are the most important people in our lives.

Prescriptions for Leadership in Surgery

What makes a great surgeon is generally equated with technical ability, knowledge, and diagnostic acumen. The nontechnical abilities, including community health leadership skills, translate into enhanced patient safety, experience, and outcomes.

Leadership includes those beliefs, values, ethics, and character are learned from family, from school, from mentors, from peers, and from patients. Here are a few prescriptions that are foremost in my mind.

- Believe in yourself. It is better to have traveled than to have arrived. What seemed to be unachievable yesterday will become a routine tomorrow with much perseverance and resilience.

- Go chase your dreams, own it for no one else will see your dream except yourself.

- Be fearless in the pursuit of what sets your soul on fire!

- No one is perfect, we all have our shortcomings. However, by knowing our limitations and learning from our mistakes, we can be better persons. It is only by recognizing our imperfection that we can get closer to perfection. Perfectionism is not achievable for only God is perfect. It is our shortcomings and limitations that bring us together. We need to call on each other for support.

- We must get beyond just talking about women's empowerment, getting women to own their power, and making our stand as women for who we are. We know that the voices of women have been suppressed and undervalued. It is time to walk the talk.

- To achieve gender equality, the first step is to value the place of women in the world. We must empower our girl children and help them realize that there are opportunities everywhere and that security does not come only as wives and mothers. It is what we can offer to the world that matters. It is how we work together, both men and women, that will make a difference.

- Dare to be great. GREAT is a reminder of the ingredients to greatness:
  G. Gratitude. Appreciate. Acknowledge.
  R. Resilience. Adapt. Adjust.
  E. Explore. Dare to be different. Pave your own road.
  A. Achieve. Put words into action.
  T. Trusting. Integrity

REFLECTIONS
Joie Emelline Teh (age 12), daughter of Catherine Teh, M.D.

My mother is a wonderful mom and surgeon. She is always very busy yet she somehow makes time for me. She is an extraordinary liver and pancreas surgeon. She has studied in numerous countries, and given lectures and talks in many others. Although it is hard being a single mom, she has given it her best shot. I often complain about how much she works and travels to other countries. What I often fail to realize, is that countless patients need her help daily and many young doctors learn from her. Also that everything she does is for me. You do not know how blessed I am to have a mother like her. Mama is always going to other countries to teach and to learn from others. On exceptionally long trips during vacation, or short trips during the weekends, she brings me along. Because of this, we often travel to various countries. I now realize how blessed I was to have been to so many places at a young age.

I often marveled at how mama balanced her job as a mother and her job as a surgeon. Mama sometimes let me accompany her to the operating room. The second or third time I accompanied her I was eight. I had forgotten the previous times because I was a still a toddler then. I was bored. I was scared of the blood, so I did not enter the operating room. I merely stayed outside in the hall, facing the open door where Mama was working inside. I was reading *How to Kill a Mockingbird* but I had gotten bored waiting and waiting. As I found my courage, and walked into the operating room, I lost all fear. As mama was operating, she explained to me everything she was doing. She had done this since I was two. Although, I did not understand it then, it had been funny when I had diagnosed one of her patients with liver cirrhosis and turned out to be correct. I was proud to know that my mother still found time to think of me while doing a complex surgery. After all, it is hard to explain things to younger children while doing something complex.

My mama's narrative taught me seven lessons:

1. *Be steadfast. Know what you really want in life, find your goal, aim towards it and go for it!*

    When I was younger, I did not really know what I wanted in life. Unlike my mama, I had goals that I would give up after a short time. Now that I am bigger, I know the importance of knowing what you really want in life and staying on the path towards it. Because when you're older, you might feel sorry about not following through.

I'm sure that all of us have a goal. It may be big, or it may be small. What matters is that the goal is what you really want in life. You must have passion and motivation to go for it. Work towards your goal and do not give up. When others say that you cannot do it, prove them wrong! Keep on the path to your goal; there will be naysayers trying to push you off that path. Ignore them and show them that they are wrong. You can do this!

2. *Do what is right, stand by your principles and values. You cannot please everyone.*

While we work towards our goals, we must always do what is right. In life, we have to make mny decisions. Millions, maybe billions, of decisions. There are always some that are harder than the other, where one decision might mean hurting somebody or disappointing another. We must listen to our conscience, and think before acting. Sometimes, the best course of action is not a perfect one.

3. *Make plans for your life but keep in mind that sometimes, life has other plans for you. What doesn't kill you will only make you stronger.*

We all have setbacks. But we must learn from our mistakes and try again. Or maybe, go in a different direction. The path to happiness is not always smooth. Sometimes, life will drag you back and you will lose hope. But remember, an arrow has to be pulled back before it can fly and hit the target. We must let our setbacks propel us to our goal. All we need do is aim for the bull's eye. Every cloud has a silver lining and you need to find it on cloudy days.

4. *Be resilient. Don't let other people dim your light. Dare to be different! Keep your desires pure and genuine. You will be appreciated one fine day.*

I have always been proud of my mom, seeing that she was usually the only female surgeon in pictures or lectures. And even if there were other females, they usually were not in HPB surgery. I felt happy knowing that my mom was unique. So, when I heard her story, I thought of what a great revenge story of sorts it was. Before, when she was still in training, lots of people thought she could not become a successful HPB surgeon. But look at her now! She is very successful and has won many awards.

5. *Be grateful. Put God in the middle of everything you do. Reflect and ground yourself as you go up higher and higher in the ranks. Although created in the likeness and*

image of God, we are not perfect, but we should strive to be the best versions of ourselves. The greatness in humanity is not in being human but in being humane. (Mahatma Gandhi)

I always thank God for giving me Mama. Or maybe for giving Mama me?

She always teaches me lessons that I will never forget. Mama is always patient with me and she always tells me to never forget God. She always told me not to be mediocre. She always told me to do my best, not to be the best. After all, there will always be someone better than you. Or at least, 98 percent of the time there will be. ;-p

Mama used to compare me to superior people all the time. I would always ask her why she didn't compare me with inferior people. She would say that if I compared myself with inferior people, then I would be bringing down my standard. By comparing me to superior people, I would bring up my standards. She said that my competition is me, myself, and I. I must be better than I was in the past. That way, in the future, I would be the best version of myself.

6. *The secret to success is not in any surgical bible. It must be found in one's heart and brought to one's hands. Be a giver. Share and impart knowledge and skills. Collaborate and work together. That is the best way to achieve since one cannot do everything by oneself. There is an African saying that says: to go fast, go yourself. To go far, go together. Most importantly, give back to the community.* Whenever we do a group project in school, there are two things that often happen.

- Arguing and discord, leaving our project undone until the last minute or poorly done.

- One or two people in the group do the group project themselves while the others pretend to help.

We do shoddy work, or a couple of group members work extra hard while the rest slack off. But when we collaborate, and try not to argue too much, we accomplish great things. I am not saying that we should just nod along and agree. No. We should offer all sorts of different ideas, and work together to decide on one, or maybe use a little bit of everything. What was important was that we would have teamwork. Not discord. What I have found is that when all the work is up to another friend or me, we would be able to work faster because there were fewer opinions to take into account. But what we failed to realize was that with fewer opinions, there were fewer opportunities to make the project better. With all our group members, all of us doing our best, our project would become the best version of itself.

7. *Sometimes, no matter how much we give our best and commit to our duties and obligations, our efforts and intent may not be valued. Look far and beyond in crisis like this. Instead of wasting your energy in hatred and discord, shift your energy to acceptance and renewal. It also means letting go of our attachment of being right, letting go of our pride in keeping the values we practice.*

While she was removing the liver of a patient another surgeon was disrespectful to her and forced my mom to leave the operating room she was disrupted and forced to leave the operating room. When I learned about it, I was angry, wanted revenge on that doctor. After a long deliberation, mama resigned from her post as chairwoman of the department of surgery. I was urging mama to reclaim her position as chairwoman and get her revenge. But instead, she took advantage of the opportunities offered and decided to enroll in a Harvard program, and focus on her clinical practice and what she could offer to other hospitals, such as Makati Med and Saint Luke's Medical Center. I remember mama rushing home because she did not want to miss another 9:00 pm online study session. She would stay in the office in her pajamas, with the air-con on and a blanket around her. I would lay out a sleeping bag on the floor and stay with her. After all, it was a miracle that we were together at home, in our pajamas, at 9:00 p.m. on a school night. Sometimes, she would eat dinner while studying, and I admired her dedication. Surgeon by day, student by night. In the end, she got even. After 12 months of late-night studying at the end of a long day and scrambling to balance work, me, mentoring her trainees, she graduated as the top-student of the Harvard program. I was extremely proud of mama! She was also awarded as one of the most influential Filipina in healthcare. At the hospital she had left, they stopped doing liver transplants after my Mama left. I would have rubbed this in their face, but Mama has excellent self-restraint, and by some miracle of God, she did not brag. I bragged and would say that I was more proud of her than she was of herself. I was so proud of my Mama, and when she was depressed I wanted her to know that I supported her. Fortunately, mama holds her emotions well, she is a very strong woman. She takes advantage of opportunities and does not waste her time on the past. Remember, there is always a storm before a rainbow. Even though I so wanted her to take vengeance right away, I learned that revenge is best served cold.

8. *No matter how much work is calling, take good care of yourself, for you will not be able to be your best when you are not well enough. Always thank your family and tell them how much you love them for you do not want to miss that chance. People we neglect are often the most important people in our lives.*

You must always do your best. But how can you if you are not well? Trying to work while ill will not help you recover faster. Listen to your loved ones when they tell you to rest. Children grow up so fast. To them, it seems long, but to adults, it is just like a blink of an eye. Spend time with your parents and if you have a child or children spend time with them. You will never regret spending time with the most important people in your life.

PS:

To all the women out there: Don't give up on your passion. No matter how many people put you down, or say that you are not capable enough because you are a female, JUST KEEP GOING. Strive for the best, work hard to get there, and never despair. Failure is an option, learning from your mistakes makes you better. Don't let other people's opinions weigh you down. You are more than capable of achieving your goal. Just aim high, work hard, and stay steadfast. You can do it!

Leadership and Entrepreneurship

MYLENE ROMUALDEZ ABIVA

President/CEO, FELTA Multi Media Inc., Philippines
GLOBAL FWN100™ 2016

Filipina Champion of the Geeks

'One of the challenges of being a woman and an entrepreneur is that many men in the high-tech industry of Educational Multimedia and Technology try to put you in your place by testing you, trying to see if you really know what you're talking about. Men traditionally dominate the technical niche.'
- **Mylene Abiva** (2018).

'First in Educational Learning Trends Always' (FELTA) Booksales, now FELTA Multi-Media Inc. was the brainchild of my parents, Felicito and Teresita Abiva in 1966. What began as a business of importing visual aids, books, and other simple educational materials, FELTA is now 53 years old and a robust company engaged in the international trade and manufacture of educational courseware, licensing educational software, laboratory equipment, educational computer laptop and tablets, and LEGO Robotics for the Filipino children. FELTA sets the standards for providing top quality educational and training materials.

My journey to lead FELTA Multi-Media Inc. was not easy. It was not a walk in the park. I believe my leadership of FELTA is a result of resilience, hard work, ingenuity, passion, and Divine Intervention.

Let me share with you how I made the "I am possible" into a reality.

Becoming a Bonafide Over-Achiever

I came from a large family with five sisters and a brother. Since there are several children in the family, there was a constant struggle to get our parent's attention. Our parents were involved in the family business, FELTA, and they were constantly busy running the everyday business operations and finances. However, they made sure we went to the best schools of our choice. I suffered the "Middle Child Syndrome," as the third daughter. I was born when my parents were yearning for a boy. My grandmother, Asuncion Abiva wanted to adopt me and raise me to be her own child. I would spend summer vacations with my grandmother, but eventually, my father declined her offer to adopt me. My older sisters were school leaders with good academic performance until they finished college. I then grew up always striving to be the best in everything that I do. I was in the Honor's Section in High School at St. Paul College Quezon City. In college, I was a consistent Dean's Lister, student leader, and college athlete. I even won the *Binibining* [Miss] La Salle title at De La Salle University (DLSU). I wanted my parents to be proud of me, and thus I became a bonafide over-achiever. At one point, the Student Council President who happened to be male even told me "Mylene, You're too pretty and too intelligent. Boys are intimidated by you." I said "I don't care. God gave me so many blessings and boys should accept me for who I am." I have no regrets about the response I gave.

Show Resilience. Gain Respect.

I graduated from college during challenging and uncertain times in the Philippines. There was political uncertainty brought about by 1985 EDSA people power revolution and the subsequent change in government. From 1983 to 1985, I was the President of the Association Internationale de Estudiante Sciences, Economique et Commercial (AIESEC) at DLSU. AIESEC is an international organization for business students. When I was offered a scholarship from AIESEC, I accepted, and I was given the opportunity to work at AIN Plastics of Michigan, a Detroit based firm that manufactures plastic parts for the car industry. There I was, this little Filipina woman, working with mostly men, who from the start, were hostile. I was a threat to them. I was a Woman, an Asian, and more highly educated than they were. I held a marketing position with a fancy job title International Trade Relations Officer. It was a blue-collar work environment. I was harassed! I came to the parking lot after work one day to find my car rammed and dented. One time, I found my tires slashed in the parking lot, in the dead of winter. If one of my kinder co-workers had not been there to give me a hand, I would have frozen to death! There was also name-calling. But I learned to hold my ground. One day, when I had had enough from the name-calling by my immediate supervisor (My bad self remembers him as a fat, lazy, and an old man.), I barked back "Why would you call me that? You have no right to call me that. I'm just doing my job, and you better do your job because if you don't, you'll be sacked, and then I'll be doing it for you!" Sure enough, over the next few years, they all did get sacked. I outlasted them! I proved that I was not only brilliant in what I did, but I was also resilient, and I could not be pushed around. I finally got the respect for the work I was doing. And it was good training for my work at FELTA.

Building a Sustainable Family Business

When I returned to the Philippines in 1989, my father offered me a position in FELTA. Up for a new challenge, I agreed. I brought to FELTA the structured professionalization that I learned in the United States. While the business was doing very well at the time, FELTA was still run like a small family business. I began with cost accounting because I knew that for a business to do well, you need a good bottom line. I brought to FELTA financial documentation, commission structures, and marketing plans. I introduced mechanisms to help the family firm draw boundaries between the family and the business. I enhanced the quality of strategic decision making, introduced a system of checks and balances, and developed competencies needed to compete in a changing marketplace. Most of all I developed a roadmap for FELTA, implemented it, and led it to become the top firm in school technology in the Philippines.

I am now the President/CEO of FELTA Multi Media Inc. I became President/CEO because of my leadership skills, global management experience, competence in strategic marketing, brand building for FELTA product mix, and passion for quality education in the Philippines.

Form Strategic Partnerships

In 1999, LEGO Education was looking for an exclusive distributor in the Philippines. After meeting with the top LEGO officials and after they had completed due diligence of FELTA operations in the Philippines, we were approved to begin promotions and training for LEGO Robotics. I had my trepidation on how to proceed. My initial years of introducing LEGO Robotics to teachers was an uphill climb. When I asked teachers if they knew what Robotics was all about, they would exclaim "Robotics? Isn't that Voltes V and Transformer?" They thought only about Robotics in the movies. I began training teachers how to use LEGO Robotics as part of a classroom strategy and a tool for learning Science and Technology. We began with eight brave schools as pioneers and now have over one thousand schools in the Philippine Robotics Olympiad Program. The moral of the story is you should be fearless and innovative as a leader.

I introduced LEGO Robotics before schools in the Philippines had discovered Inquiry-Based Science Education (IBSE). IBSE was designed to motivate students to use critical thinking and experimentation fully. Now, hundreds of thousands of students have a positive attitude concerning learning Science, Technology, Engineering, and Mathematics (STEM). My dream and vision continue to be to have more Filipina women engineers, scientists, and inventors in the Philippines.

Consistent with our efforts to bring world-class School Technology to Philippine schools, INTEL Education appointed FELTA Multi-Media Inc. as the manufacturer of INTEL devices. These devices included school-centric computer laptops and tablets that were shock-proof, water-resistant and included interactive lessons and a classroom management system. FELTA focused on training ICT heads, school principals, teachers and Department of Education school division superintendents to use their computers for education as opposed to using computers as glamourized typewriters. FELTA and INTEL Education conducted ICT Planning and Management workshops throughout the Philippines. Workshops included helping each participant prepare a plan of action on how they can fully utilize technology for Education. In 2013, after the onslaught of Super Typhoon Haiyan, known as Typhoon Yolanda, the INTEL devices manufactured by FELTA were used in the "learning spaces" of evacuation sites for children of the survivors. When placed in plastic box containers, the sturdy and rugged devices served as a digital learning tool while classrooms and schools were being reconstructed.

I went to the reconstructed schools to ensure the proper use and deployment, along with the corresponding training, of the INTEL devices. The INTEL devices were also used in non-grid schools or schools without electricity where solar power powered them. Our showcase was Marilog Elementary School, Marilog, Davao where numerous indigenous people live. Since the introduction of technology through the INTEL devices, the school has achieved higher National Aptitude scores. The indigenous people have increased their self-confidence and have integrated better in their community. A leader must have compassion and be ready to take action.

Achieve Work/Life Balance by Compartmentalizing

I believe the secret to success, especially for women is compartmentalization. Women are natural multi-taskers. We are always doing everything at once. The key to having a healthy mind and spirit is finding work, life, and love balance. I have learned to separate different aspects of my life so I can give each aspect the attention it needs. I make time for my family, tell my office not to call or text when I am home, except for emergencies. I make time for my business, I make time for myself, and I make time to be with my partner. I also make time for my advocacies, one of which is the Go Negosyo Movement. As a pioneer Angelpreneur or An Angel Mentor, I have mentored and spoken to thousands of aspiring entrepreneurs since 2005. I have given talks on marketing essentials for entrepreneurs. As an Angelpreneur, I provide the technical know-how and mentoring for aspiring entrepreneurs to succeed. One day, as I was giving a talk to the Department of Trade and Industry (DTI) in Zamboanga, I was pleasantly surprised that the woman I had mentored eight years earlier was now a mentor herself and had even established the Zamboanga Jeweler Association. It gives me joy and fulfillment to see others succeed. A true leader multiples success and shares her wisdom.

It only takes four seconds to create a first impression. I try to be physically fit, energetic, stylish, and youthful. I smile a lot and never lose my sense of humor. While smiling reduces wrinkles, it also makes it easier to establish friendships with clients and suppliers alike. Even as I have gotten older, I signed a contract to be the muse of international designer, Ica Serafica, the first Filipina in-house designer for Marks and Spencer, Debenhams, and Wallis. "Women of Substance, Style, Passion, and Purpose" is our *peg* [something used as an inspiration]. Ica gives me "work to cocktail" outfits that I wear, and once photographed, are used for social media promotions. I am an avid mountain climber, rock climber with several mountainous conquests in the Philippines, and abroad. To name a few, Mt. Tarak (Mariveles, Bataan), Mt. Batur (Bali, Indonesia), Mt. Pulag (Benguet), Blue Mountains (Australia), Mt. Hapunang Banoi (Rodriguez, Rizal), and Mt. Fuji (Japan). I plan to climb more mountains in the future. I showcase the beautiful natural ecological sites in the Philippines that keep me fit. A Filipina woman leader stays fabulous (*fab*) at any age.

Commitment to Excellence

In LEGO Education culture, they say "Only the best is good enough." This has served as my mantra for both my work and my personal life. I demonstrate excellence in all aspects of life. I was recently commissioned by the Intramuros Administration and Royal Danish Embassy Manila to reuse and revitalize a 16th-century building at Fort Santiago. The project is called iMake History Fortress, a LEGO Architecture, Art, History and Technology Gallery and Learning Center. It is a blend of the old and the new, with historical cathedrals and buildings rebuilt using LEGO architecture bricks, a LEGO Philippine Eagle Robot, LEGO Jeepney, and LEGO Tourist sites. Top Architecture colleges and universities in the Philippines participated in the iMake History Fortress Architecture competition. Philippine Fauna is part of the exhibition. The iMake History Fortress was my first effort as a Curator. In just a few months, I have created a new attraction in Fort Santiago that will draw both local and international tourists and is a legacy for the Filipino people. A woman leader is patriotic and committed to excellence.

Pray

Throughout my journey from childhood to becoming one of the 100 Most Influential Filipina Women (FWN) in the World 2016, I have recognized our Lord's divine strength. Having a prayerful life will pull us through during challenging times. I have been successful in sustaining a business established over five decades ago. I knelt down during times of despair and joy for our successes. These are blessings to strengthen our soul and our faith. A leader must know how to pray for Divine Strength.

Have a Succession Plan

FELTA Multi Media Inc. celebrated 50 years in 2016. I know few family-owned companies in the Philippines that survive this long. Sustainability and maintaining a good business reputation is a remarkable feat. The sense of ownership can get diluted as later generations inherit the business and do not have the same sense of responsibility the original owners had. Usually a business flourishes during the second generation, then is squandered by the third, and is gone by the fourth. Having a succession plan provides a guideline for the people who are qualified to run the business as opposed to family connections. Putting a relative in a sensitive position just because of family connections can bring down your entire company. True leadership is about having the integrity to do the right thing.

Be a Value Innovator

As I have gone around the Philippines since 2005 to speak to aspiring entrepreneurs for the Go Negosyo Movement, I emphasize that "Change is the only thing constant in business." FELTA Multi Media Inc. began as a book importer, a manufacturer of colored slides and transparencies, and science equipment. It eventually transformed to LEGO Robotics, software development, and manufactured school-centric computer laptops and tablets. FELTA has transformed itself from an education trade company to a manufacturer and distributor of major IT global brands, such as Intel Education, LEGO Education, ADOBE Education, and Microsoft Education, among others. I established the iCreate Café Manila, an on-demand LEGO Education Creativity Learning Center located in a mall setting and includes a LEGO-themed snack bar to give access to the general public to learn about robotics, renewable energy, animation, and digital publishing using the LEGO Education platform and software. Soon iCreate Café Manila will be available for franchise. My advice to technology entrepreneurs: Make your product different from the rest. Be a value innovator.

Multiply Leadership

I travel at least once a month both internationally and within the Philippines. My travel is mostly with the Philippine Robotics Team when they are competing in international Robotics competitions. Making sure that FELTA Multi Media Inc. operations and activities run smoothly despite my being at a distant location and in a different time zone is important. Therefore, the FELTA team left behind in the Philippines have to manage and be the "leaders" themselves. The FELTA team has a strong sense of ownership in the company. They work together to make sure the company succeeds. The FELTA team represents the whole image and reputation of the company.

As an entrepreneur, you must learn how to empower your team and create opportunities for leadership while giving power to their people. A leader must have strong character and multiple leadership to her people.

I aim to pave the way to for an even brighter future for FELTA Multi Media Inc. My father once told me "Life is short. Make your mark on this earth but also build your castle in heaven." All you have to do is to know yourself. And, believe in yourself.

CRISTINA CALAGUIAN

Owner/Managing Director,
Dagaz HR Consultancy and Recruitment Company
GLOBAL FWN100™ 2017

The Road to My *Ikigai*

I am the founder and Managing Director of Dagaz HR Consultancy and Recruitment Company, a company based in Dubai, UAE since 2011. My career started in the Philippines where for 11 years I was a licensed stockbroker. This was followed by nine years of experience in Dubai as a financial consultant, immigration consultant for Canada, and a business development executive in an advertising company. After more than 20 years focused primarily on generating revenues and profits, I gradually evolved into a Social Entrepreneur and this is where I found my *ikigai* [a reason for being]. In my early years, I dreamed of owning a company. I dreamed of building my own corporate headquarters. But I never thought about being a social entrepreneur. Not until 2012 when my perspective about business changed.

Learning about social entrepreneurship inspired me to develop Dagaz as a social enterprise. In addition to providing revenue-generating regular human resources and recruitment services, the purpose of Dagaz became empowering and helping people with disabilities and other challenges to find work. This purpose supported the Dubai Government's initiative and campaign to be named as "Disable-Friendly" by 2020.

To help individuals identify their best career paths I use the Harrison Assessment Tools (HATs). I went through this assessment to help me validate and improve on my personal development and leadership skills. The Harrison Assessments System provides a comprehensive assessment of the behavioral competencies required for specific roles and accurately predicts success factors and potential obstacles. Integrated selection tools include performance-based interviewing questions, ways to attract potential candidates for a job position, and the ability to calculate eligibility, suitability, and interview ratings for a composite ranking of individuals being considered. It helps assess individuals' decision making, communications, motivation, flexibility, conflict management, and innovation skills and traits.

I will share the factors that made a big impact on my decision making and paved the way for my *ikigai*. The Japanese people believe that everyone has an *ikigai*, a reason to jump out of bed each morning! The *ikigai* model, as shown in Figure 1 is from Winn (2014)[1]. In the model, Winn (2014) asked if you have found your *ikigai* by doing that which you love, that which the world needs, that which you are good at, and that which you can be paid for.

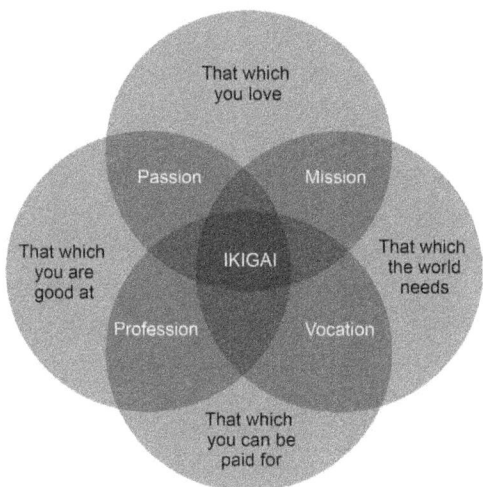

Figure 1: 2014 Winn's Ikigai Model

START OF MY JOURNEY: A CROSSROADS

Two roads diverged in a wood, And I – I took the one less traveled by, and that has made all the difference.
- **Robert Frost**

There are times in our lives that we will stand at crossroads. I wanted to do something that would give meaning to my life, and I thought of setting up a business. I was so excited on the morning of July 28, 2011, the day that Dagaz HR Consultancy

[1] http://theviewinside.me/what-is-your-ikigai/

and Recruitment Company was established. My longtime friend Jay Fernando, the Vice President of Magsaysay Global, convinced me to set up a recruitment business. I had no idea how to start a business, far less how to run one. I was on my own in the United Arab Emirates (UAE), a country (UAE) still somewhat alien to me. Dagaz was a one-woman shop. Having recognized my deeper desires, I had resigned from my secure salaried job and left my comfort zone. It felt very liberating, but my euphoria of freedom did not last long. I realized that my 17-year-old son Paulo was about to start his first year of college at De La Salle University. Kaya, my daughter, was ten years old and we would soon need to put her in high school. I was concerned that I had not realized the risk. There would be no fixed income every month. As a single mother, I was all by myself. I was tired of being an employee; I just wanted to do something different. Recruitment was a totally different field for me. I became so excited just getting my trade license, but in my excitement, I forgot that I did not have any company branding. I was paying my office rent but not yet fully operational; I had no business card or website. After all those years working for established companies, I was used to corporate branding and marketing materials as a given. I was ready to go to meet potential clients. With a little persuasion my brother Jay quickly created a logo and associated branding. Then I worked on my website with the help of my friends. It took me months and months to finish the website. My bank account was being depleted paying my daily expenses and sending money to the Philippines for my children with nothing coming in. I attended summits and seminars about start-ups to keep on moving and focus on what I wanted to achieve. I went to workshops to listen to peoples' stories of how they had started their businesses with only pennies in their pockets. Every day I listened to podcasts, read books, watched YouTube, listened to audiobooks, including my favorites, *7 Habits of Highly Effective People* by Stephen Covey, *Think and Grow Rich* by Napoleon Hill, *Eat that Frog* by Brian Tracy, and *The Success Principle* by Jack Canfield. I was inspired by "*The Secret*" by Rhonda Byrne. I attended classes on presentation skills to overcome my fear of public speaking, to improve my knowledge of human resources (HR), to develop my leadership capabilities, and to understand UAE labor law. I had to use all my business and personal connections to attend conferences for free or get a discount. I thought having my own business would be fun because I would be mistress of my own time but that was a myth. Setting up a business can be quite easy, but sustaining it is difficult. I was working 24/7. I wore all the hats: I did the accounting, administration, the sales. and made the coffee. It was a real struggle, second only to my experience of being a single mother. I had to fuel my optimism and my belief that in every situation there are good things that will result. I learned a lot about myself and my real strengths. I learned how to conduct HR audits, develop HR manuals and procedures, and improve HR management. I gradually built my team. The first administrative assistant I hired worked online because I could not afford to pay a salary and sponsor a visa at that time. Kathleen was very helpful, and she knew her job well and was an excellent virtual assistant. My preference was to be out of the office and to meet clients since that is the best use of my time.

DETOURS

> I alone cannot change the world, but I can cast a stone across the waters to create many ripples.
> - **Mother Teresa**

Overtime, I started to feel isolated and lonely, facing the many challenges, especially financial challenges. I was a Filipina business owner in the United Arab Emirates, a very male-dominated business community. It was difficult to approach potential clients most of whom were men and most of whom were not Filipinos. I recognized that I needed to develop an excellent marketing strategy and reposition the way I would be viewed by prospective clients even before they had met me. I changed my title to "Managing Director" to improve my branding and image. I decided to hire Pakistani and Indian recruiters to avoid being labeled as leading an entirely Filipino company. One client once asked me how I reacted to my competitors. I answered that I just look forward and focus on my mission. If I focused on my competitors, I would have been scared and questioned my own capabilities. I remained focus on my mission of empowering people to develop their skills. I experienced a somewhat painful insight as I realized that, despite my belief in my mission and my personal drive to succeed, Dagaz was just like any other recruitment companies and I was just like other company managers. I needed to outshine my competition. Cristina and Dagaz needed to be better than, and different from, the competition.

In November 2012, I enrolled in the Leadership and Social Entrepreneurship (ALSE) program at the Ateneo School of Government. The program is designed to inspire and train Overseas Contract Workers (OFW) to be new business leaders. When I first started Dagaz HR Consultancy and Recruitment Company, I was just thinking of family security and financial satisfaction, but after completing the ALSE course, my perspective changed. I was inspired to recognize and accept a passion that goes beyond the functional processes of recruitment. I found my passion in social entrepreneurship, empowering those within a marginalized sector of the community, people with disability.

Being a Social Entrepreneur

I learned that social entrepreneurship was first defined in 1980 by Bill Drayton, founder of ASHOKA. He has built the most extensive network of social entrepreneurs. Drayton defined a social entrepreneur as someone who works in an entrepreneurial manner, but for the public and social benefit, rather than just to make more personal money. (See Table 1 below.) I embraced this path and found my mission of enhancing the quality of life for the marginalized people, especially people with disability and the distressed Filipina workers who were victims of abusive employers.

Table 1: Social Enterprise vs. Traditional Business (ALSE – SE1)

Primary Stakeholders and Objective: Traditional Business	Primary Stakeholders and Objective: Social Enterprise
Stakeholders: Stockholders, Individuals, and Families	Stakeholders: A sector, community or group, usually involving the marginalized sectors of society who may or may not own or control the enterprise
Bottom line: Profit	Bottom line: Financial sustainability; growth; improvement of the quality of life for marginalized sectors; environmental sustainability

As I developed myself as a social entrepreneur, I was inspired to do more volunteer work. I found the volunteer work more satisfying and enjoyed doing something for others and not expecting anything tangible in return. I found my real passion in helping people, especially those with special physical and mental challenges and in helping them to achieve their full potential. The ALSE program made a significant difference in my perspective on life and awakened authentic, deeper values. It inspired me to be a servant leader and to give back to my community. I realized that I wanted and needed a business with a heart so I researched people whose life story and business histories provided inspiration. I gradually changed my business model from a "just-for-profit business" to a "more meaningful-for-me social enterprise." My social mission is "To empower people with disability to be equals in the community." I still needed to generate cash flow and profit and pay the bills, but this was now with the purpose of achieving my social mission of contributing to a positive change in society. Gradually I realized that my understanding had changed from viewing money as a measure of my personal achievement to recognizing that only a limited amount of money was necessary for secure living. My objective became building a reputable organization and the focus was less on making profit. Moving forward in my mission, I partnered with Tamkeen, a UAE government organization that operates under the umbrella of the Knowledge and Human Development Authority in Dubai. Tamkeen provides services for people with visual impairments and offers training programs aimed at upgrading their skills necessary for employment consistent with their abilities. I volunteered to give talks on career management for visually impaired individuals including how to produce resumes and develop interview skills. By participating in a national exhibition and making new friends who are visually impaired I have learned about their special talents. Soon I became more involved in volunteer work. I volunteer with the Philippines Labor Office in Dubai where I give regular talks to motivate Filipina household workers, and providing coping skills to women in distress who had been victims of violence and unfair treatment of labor, and victims of rape and human trafficking. I cover personal development, goal setting, building confidence, overcoming obstacles in life, and conflict management. I also conduct the Post Arrival Orientation Seminar (PAOS) on Middle Eastern cultural awareness, as part of helping Filipino new hires understand the culture and social environment of their new host country and understand the UAE Labor Law under which they will work.

As a leader in my company and in my community, I serve as President of the Alumni Association of Ateneo Leadership and Social Entrepreneurship (AAALSE) in UAE as of 2017 had 300 members. In this role, and as a member of the Board of Trustees, I can implement change not with talk but by acting as an agent of change. The mission of the AAALSE is to empower Overseas Filipino Workers (OFW) to be servant leaders in their communities and help them develop their appreciation of, and commitment to establishing, socially valuable enterprises when they return to the Philippines. Since the AAALSE is still developing to meet the changing needs of the organization, I have to implement many new processes and procedures. I authored the "Code of Ethics for Volunteers," designed a new organizational structure, conducted workshops on "Values Formation" and "Team Building," and planned a schedule of events for the members. I participated in the formation and became a founding member of the Leaders and Social Entrepreneurs Cooperative to help alumni of Ateneo Leadership Social Entrepreneurship (ALSE) fund new social enterprises. For two consecutive years, I mentored multiple groups of students of ALSE in social enterprise business plan development. I am proud to say that several of these groups have become recipients of awards at graduation.

Overcoming Roadblocks

You got to go down a lot of wrong roads to find the right one.
- Bob Parsons

Since 2015, lower oil prices have resulted in economic difficulties across the Gulf region. Throughout the oil-rich Gulf, the slump in crude prices is forcing governments to slash spending and delay projects, while private companies shed staff and, in many cases, have shut down. Recruitment of staff has declined as hotel projects and construction have been delayed or even canceled. Redundancy and terminations are occurring and even large, long-established companies have had to let go of staff. Payment of salaries is in some cases delayed for many months. We never thought that those of us who chose to work in the UAE would experience the economic downturn. As an economist, I, and others like me, should perhaps have seen this coming. The saying in the stock market "what goes up must come down" means a bubble will burst. Thousands of Filipino workers have lost their jobs and tens of thousands of family members back home have lost their remittances. If big companies were affected, then small and medium enterprises have been equally affected. Small business, including mine have to find a way to weather the crisis. Filipinos have become unemployed in the Gulf region in all industries and I cannot find new work for them if companies are not hiring. Still, I needed to find a way to assist and guide my people seeking jobs in difficult times. By chance, one day I attended an event on an approach to HR called "Harrison Assessment." I was introduced to a new way of addressing the economic downturn.

In December 2016, Dagaz HR Consultancy and Recruitment Company became an Authorized Solution Provider of Harrison Assessment Tools. We are the only recruitment company in UAE who are using this advanced assessment tool. The Harrison Assessment predicts job performance by analyzing an individual's behavioral tendencies. When behavioral competencies are measured, such as emotional intelligence, personality, and work preferences, a high degree of accuracy is attained in predicting performance.

The Harrison Assessment is based on the Enjoyment Performance Theory (See Figure 2). Enjoyment Performance Theory states that an individual will perform more effectively in a job if they enjoy tasks required by that job, have interests that relate to the position, and have work environment preferences that correspond to the new workplace.[2]

---

[2] http://harrisonassessmentsna.com/theories/

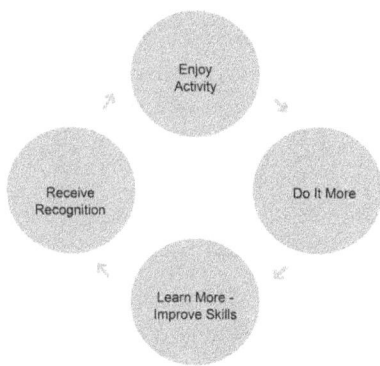

Figure 2: The Enjoyment Performance Theory Cycle

If you enjoy an activity, you tend to do it more often and more intensively. By doing it more, you tend to learn and improve the related skills. As a result, you tend to gain recognition (including self-recognition) which helps you enjoy the activity more.
- **Dr. Dan Harrison, Ph.D.** CEO of Harrison Assessments

The Harrison Assessment also predicts stress behavior and provides a framework for understanding of self and direction for self-development. The results of my Harrison assessment revealed I have deeply rooted insights that influence my high-performance and that are related to my current position as Managing Director of Dagaz. It specified my work preferences and behavioral competencies and pinpointed career planning needed to achieve personal satisfaction and improve my job or business performance.

The Harrison Assessment predicts how an individual communicates, influences, and leads. It also predicts how an individual will handle autonomy, take personal initiative, resist or facilitate change, handle conflict, seek to learn, grow, and excel, and plan and organize. The tool helps individuals identify their greatest strengths and passion, their values, preferences, interests, and career options. For the individuals I work with, the Harrison Assessments are used for talent management since they predict an individual's likelihood of success at multiple levels within an organization and allow managers to create a developmental plan to accelerate employee progress. The tool helps identify high potential individuals, predict multi-level capabilities, identify alternate career paths, leverage the talent pool, and increase retention. It can also reveal team dynamics in a way that has never before been possible, enabling individual team members to quickly identify how their own behaviors contribute to, or obstruct team objectives. It also provides a step-by-step plan in which each team member can make adjustments to facilitate optimal team performance. I can say that by using the Harrison Assessment I can measure "happiness in work and job satisfaction."

The Road Ahead

Forget the failures. Keep the lessons.
- **Dalai Lama**

While having dinner with a college friend, who has run his own business for more than 20 years, I asked him "when will the struggle stop?" He answered me with a hearty laugh and said, "it will never stop. As long as you are running a business, your struggles will never stop." His answer did not surprise me.

I know I am in a lifetime roller coaster-ride and that whether I choose to enjoy or get scared of the ride is up to me. I have had my share of ups and downs in my life, but that does not stop me from pursuing my mission. My big or small struggles will continue and failures or at least setbacks will always be there. I no longer fear failure. If I fail, I know I can find the opportunity to grow and become a stronger person.

I would like to change the words "setback" and "failure" to "challenges." Challenges are an adventure, without challenges my life could be boring. I think that naturally successful people subconsciously choose their particular obstacles to benefit from the challenges they encounter and overcome. Launching myself into new challenges when I first encountered them are no longer intimidating. Everyone is haunted to some extent by fear. Some people fear a new life. Some people fear new challenges and some will find them exciting. Sometimes what we think of as "fear" is just excitement and a perfectly natural and healthy apprehension before entering the unknown.

I am incredibly proud to be a Filipina, but sometimes we must set aside national identification. I recognized that from a very young age I had been blessed with self-assurance and confidence in inverse proportion to my height. I wish that more of my *kabayans* [fellow country people] would develop the confidence they need to achieve their full potential and succeed.

I believe that the success that I have achieved have come about primarily because I started with the belief that I will succeed. It is not merely our abilities that define us, but it is our choices in life and attitudes. I may have forgotten some of my failures because I never dwell on negative situations. The pains of wrong decisions are buried in preparation of facing new beginnings. The challenges of wrong decisions are temporary, and I let them go. I use the lessons to keep moving on. It is the "now" that I can control, not the past and not the future.

As I move on to the next challenging phase of my life and career, I am proud of my personal achievements and will continue striving to develop my true passions, and set my sights high for the future.

To Walk as A Leader

As my journey continues as a leader, I believe in:

- **Servant Leadership.** While servant leadership is a timeless concept, the phrase servant leadership was coined by Robert Greenleaf in "The Servant as Leader," an essay that he first published in 1970. According to Greenleaf, "The servant-leader is servant first…. It begins with the natural feeling that one wants to serve, to serve first. Then conscious choice brings one to aspire to lead. That person is sharply different from one who is a leader first, perhaps because of the need to assuage an unusual power drive or to acquire material professions." Greenleaf made a distinction between the "leader-first" and the "servant-first" and suggested that "between them, there are the shadings and blends that are part of the infinite variety of human nature." Servant leadership encompasses the values of humility and integrity.

- **Commitment.** I give my full commitment to everything that I do, especially with helping with the growth of others. By helping people grow and develop they become better in what they do while also growing their confidence and developing as people. As we develop our people, we develop a better community and organization. This is aligned to being a servant-leader with a primary focus on the growth and well-being of people and the communities to which they belong.

- **Trust.** A leader must cultivate a culture of trust. This is very crucial for leaders, so that they are able to serve their community and their team. It is important that they know and trust their leader and believe that their leader truly trusts them.

- **Continuous learning.** A leader must have the passion for learning and developing. I am always looking for opportunities to learn even during setbacks. I learn from others and from my experiences.

- **Develop other leaders.** And lastly, a leader must develop other leaders. By serving others, other leaders will begin to emerge for the future.

Finally, I would like to recognize and thank some special people who have supported, advised, and encouraged me as I have progressed along my journey of discovering my *ikigai*. I apologize to anyone I may have missed. I am blessed with loving and supportive parents, brothers, sister, and my children Paulo and Kaya. I also extend my gratitude to my generous partner Ian Hyndman, my best friend Marivic De Guzman who never stopped believing in me, Rachel Salinel who opened the doors for many opportunities, Zenaida Requizo for her support, Dr. Maria Beebe for her patience and guidance, and my mentors Labor Attaché Atty. Delmer Cruz, Madam Ofelia Bautista Domingo. My thanks to Marc Winn for allowing me to use his *ikigai* model.

JANETTE NELLIE GO-CHIU

President of GCH Holdings, Inc., Philippines
GLOBAL FWN100™ 2016

Innovator By Happenstance

I was born the second of three children during the Year of the Monkey and baptized as "Janette Nellie Go." According to the Chinese zodiac, those born in this year are independent, honest, cordial, positive, and possess foresight and acute intuition. Their strong curiosity causes them to try boldly everything interesting. Those born in the Year of the Monkey are believed to be accommodating individuals who always do their best to help others. They possess an upbeat attitude that influences them and the people around them.

I turned out to have these qualities, not because the Chinese zodiac said so but because my parents, who raised my siblings and me in a low-key and conservative environment, emphasized the values of discipline, hard work, filial piety, and trust as the keys to success especially in dealing with people.

Being the middle child gave me the unique opportunity to be my family's keeper. As a keeper, I literally kept everyone's records and documents. I made sure things were planned out before anyone could think about them.

I may have been born as the middle child, but I did not have middle child issues of feeling "left out." My level-headed and perceptive father gave me challenging tasks because he found a kindred spirit in me who shared his passion for diligence, creativity, and versatility. Even as a child, my insatiable curiosity about the world around me and my love of nature had impressed and "provoked" my parents to assign to me the more challenging tasks. Being a middle child enhanced my resilience and sharpened my response to life's challenges. I became my Dad's little helper in fixing the car when it did not start and assisted him in rewiring or fixing appliances and other machineries. I also became my mother's all-around secretary. I was in-charge of running various errands including the tasks of preparing the helpers' payroll, keeping an inventory of my mother's gifts to friends and family members, and even wrapping and delivering them to her special friends. I wrote notes and special messages for them. Whenever I would ask why she wanted me to do these tasks, my mother always said "because your handwriting is more legible" or "because you can wrap the gifts nicely" or "because you will come back quickly with the job accomplished."

I did not ask for these tasks to be given to me. I was simply trusted to accomplish them, and I responded with a willing mind and an open heart to do what I was asked to do.

I grew up to become neither the fiercest nor the most fearless woman of my generation. But it was these life experiences that built my skills to be a smart decision maker alongside being a compassionate mentor and mediator. I learned to become an innovator in the midst of circumstances and challenges, mostly not by choice, but by happenstance.

Role Models

I was a dutiful daughter born into a Filipino-Chinese family with parents who served as role models and who showed me that the values of honesty, hard work, and perseverance can actually translate into productive results in business and in social development work. My parents both lost their fathers at the young age of 12 and 13. Life was difficult for them as they had to work hard to earn money for their families to survive. Through their examples, my parents became my role models.

My father, Go Ching Hai, had a deeply inquiring mind, and was a creative inventor and a visionary. His tireless efforts and strong desire to improve the economic and social conditions in the country earned him the Perlas Award in 2002 for his efforts as a civic leader and a catalyst for economic innovations. He was given the Dr. Jose Rizal Award in 2005 in recognition of his excellent inventions.

My mother, Martina or more popularly known as "Beling" is a woman of action. She organized FORWARD (Federated Organization of Women Active and Responsive to Development) in 1990 that became a prime-mover of numerous development projects in Cebu City. We call her the "Iron Lady" because of her determination and fortitude. When she sets out on a mission, you can be sure that she will pursue it to the very end. Her enthusiasm is so contagious that it takes very little effort to convince friends to join her quests. We have her to thank for making us more conscious of the many challenges our world continues to face.

One of the important lessons I learned from my parents is to take care of your name, your integrity.

I worked for a bank right after graduating with a degree in Business Administration from the University of San Carlos. It was one of those days when I accepted from clients bundles of money for deposit. One client left a bundle of money to deposit that day. The total amount was Philippine P1,000 short of the amount he wrote on his deposit slip. I was shocked when I saw this because my salary at that time was only Philippine P300 per month and I would have to pay for every shortage.

I called the client to inform him of the "missing" Philippine P1,000. He did not believe me. He rushed to the bank to see my manager to complain. Cebu is a small city where everyone knows everybody. But when the client learned that my father was Go Ching Hai, the look on his face changed. He said, "If she is Go Ching Hai's daughter then perhaps, I made the mistake."

That moment defined integrity to me. My father's integrity rubbed off on me. I felt that I had the inherent responsibility to be a living example that integrity matters at work and in all our dealings.

Later, in my quest to establish new business ventures, I put up a "*tela* per kilo" business called "Tex'Styles." To expand my sources, I went to Manila to look for additional suppliers. My cousin Victor introduced me to a wholesaler, who upon learning that I was from Cebu and starting a new business, extended a 90-day of credit to me saying, "We are in the same industry. Let us support each other." That was an eye-opener for me. How many people would actually extend that kind of help to a budding entrepreneur? How many individuals would trust you with their hard-earned money so that you can start a business?

These two experiences proved to me that integrity is not just a buzzword. Integrity transcends people and generations. It is not only hard work that helps you succeed. Success is also defined by an honest reputation and the commitment to fulfill your promises.

My Dad summed it up in this famous Chinese proverb: "When a tiger dies, he leaves his fur. But when a man dies, he leaves his name."

Business Values

I learned about how to start businesses from scratch and from there worked for success. In running businesses, I learned the values of patience, perseverance, and passion.

I embraced the value of patience when I started out my dried mango business. It was my first business venture and served as my training ground in handling operations and human resources. I had to wake up at 4 a.m. to be the first in line to buy fresh mangoes by the bushels. At times we would work from midnight to dawn to quickly process those mangoes especially when filling a big export order with a tight deadline. The scarcity of mango was always the limiting factor, and prices were erratic. Sometimes the vendors would deceive buyers by putting large mangoes over small mangoes to demand higher prices. So I worked out a simple system to be fair to both parties by buying them by the kilo. Since then, I can proudly say that I started the concept of paying for all kinds of fruits by the kilo.

From dried mangoes, I went on to develop other fruit preserves such as guyabano, papaya, pineapple, and star fruit that had a high demand abroad. I also supplied processed fruits, such as jackfruit, banana, and papaya for ice cream manufacturers.

Being my own boss and in-charge of the 20 ladies working for me also meant waking up as early as 3 a.m. twice a week to buy fish at the Pasil Market, where the freshest catch was sold. In doing business, it matters that you treat your employees well. They are the real assets and do the work for us. When we truly care for them, they will go the extra mile to help.

The value of patience and determination gave me the capacity to tolerate delays, face trouble, or accept work pressures without getting upset. This is very true in running the dried fruits business. Being versatile and resourceful are essential to staying competitive. Meeting deadlines and sudden increase in the size of orders; honoring commitments to clients while being fair to my suppliers and workers are all part of the challenges in building the business.

Perseverance is another value that helped me in my business dealings and in my personal life.

My marriage to Antonio in 1985 shifted my attention to raising a family and focusing on another new business. I assisted my in-laws in raising prawns and milkfish in their 20-hectare fish pond in what was then the municipality of Carcar, located about 42 kilometers from Cebu City.

Those were exciting years of learning about aqua farming. We started from the ground up in building dikes and fishponds. I was unfamiliar with the nuances of aqua farming, but I was diligent and curious. I persevered in learning the business even though it was new to me.

Addressing the vagaries of nature was always a test of perseverance and foresight. From prawns and milkfish, I went on to buy *Lapu-Lapu* fingerlings and grew them to the weight of one-kilo fish within four months. I was among the first entrepreneurs to supply restaurants with live fish and prawns using aerators and oxygenated plastic bags. The financial and personal success derived from this business required hard work and dedication. Running an aqua farm meant going to the area at 2 a.m. to supervise proper harvesting of the prawns in time to supply the fresh market and fulfill export processing demands during the rest of the morning. In addition, I had to take special care of my health as I was pregnant with our first child, Janice and later, our second child, Jillian. Our family further grew with the birth of our son, Jason.

I believe that an entrepreneur succeeds because she is passionate about what she does. Passion pushes a person to do more and be more. This is exactly the case with Meat Magic, a venture that my father started but one where I was called to manage and grow.

My father did not only invest money when starting and growing his business; he poured his heart out to make the business work and give people jobs and sources of income for their families. A family conflict threatened the legacy that my father had built. I was passionate about continuing what my father started. But my father feared that because I am a woman, I may not be able to manage all the intricacies of the business.

But I did not stop to think about his fear and instead poured my passion into setting up different departments and defining their responsibilities. I took on several roles: human resource officer, accountant, sales and marketing manager, purchaser, food developer, and innovator.

Our flagship business, that we were most proud of, was the manufacture of a soy-based, healthy meat alternative called "Meat Magic." We developed it in 1991 when meat alternatives were not popular with most people. When I came back to help the business in 1996, sales figures were just in the range of five to six digits. Selling it was almost like selling sand to the Arabs or ice to the Eskimos. At times, it seemed that our efforts did not do justice to a very functional and beneficial product.

Although meat alternatives have been known for many years, my challenge was to develop the marketable acceptance of a healthy and affordable meat alternative made from soy. My role was to use creative positioning to gain market acceptability and provide a healthy but inexpensive food for the consumers. The biggest challenge was to make consumers appreciate its health and cost benefits regardless of the tedious preparation involved. I had to inspire my sales and marketing staff to be passionate about the product in order to convince customers of its health benefits.

My mission was to transform negative customer's views through training, creating consumer demand for a healthy alternative with less fat and cholesterol, and to convince them they could eat less meat without sacrificing the taste and flavor of real meat. We created new variations to suit customer's needs. We became a reliable supplier and food ingredient developer for the meat alternative with on-time delivery and quality assurance. Passion pushed me to do all these and more.

Meat Magic won several awards, one of which was given by the Department of Science and Technology (DOST) as the "Most Innovative Healthy Food Ingredient." At a DOST National Invention Contest in 2005, it was recognized as the only textured vegetable protein manufactured locally.

Over the last 25 years, we worked with people to bring positive change in their lives especially those who started businesses in their homes. Meat Magic is widely used by commissaries, canneries, fast food chains, and for many other food preparations. Meat Magic has made their products more affordable and healthier. To make the product more versatile, we diversified into many variants and grades in addition to the standard flake and cutlet forms we created when the product was first made available to the market. Through Meat Magic, we were able to provide families with an affordable and healthy alternative, making it possible for families to stretch their hard-earned pesos and at the same time, keep the family healthy, fit, and strong.

Our vision in growing Meat Magic remains true to this very day: "A healthy and strong family makes a healthy and strong community for a healthy and strong nation."

Today, the GCH Group of Companies is a proud umbrella of five active business manufacturing and service companies and two foundations.

Patience, perseverance, and passion combined with the values of hard-work, creativity, and resourceful made me an innovator and a leader. These values powered my resolve throughout the years to succeed in many areas of business.

Woman Leadership

Unconsciously, by focusing on fulfilling my tasks, I have earned my father's trust and confidence that a woman can run a business. I was able to prove that being a woman is not a liability. Instead, a woman in business can be a valuable asset.

This has become my leadership philosophy. Leadership, to me, is the ability to steer people into action by example. In my case, I was able to show them that a woman leader is resilient and sensitive to the changing times. I was able to show that being more sensitive to the needs of people around us is not bad for business.

Women can work harmoniously with men to create success in our organizations. These successes are created out of our ability to adapt to changes and provide immediate solutions to pressing issues and demands.

I was raised in a time when women were viewed as plain homemakers. I was not on a mission to disprove that women are limited to their homes. I just focused my attention on working and helping my father. In the process, I proved to my father and the people surrounding me that a woman at the helm can steer the ship to safe harbor through the rough seas.

Focusing on Women and Children

A woman can be the successful and powerful captain of a ship. This is why I am passionate about my membership of the Zonta Club of Cebu 1. I joined the group in

2007 as a way to develop programs in professional and community development by focusing on women and children.

In the past years, Zonta 1 conducted yearly Cancer Prevention and Screening activities in different *barangays* and inside the prisons. The Club has supported day care centers in *barangays* Ermita and Budlaan and expanded our help to schools, such as the Tulay National High School in the town of Minglanilla.

During my terms as Club Secretary in 2012-2014 and later as president from 2014 to 2016, we created new ways to strengthen our service and advocacy. We organized the first Fun Run for the "Zonta Says No to Violence Against Women and Children" to raise funds for our Violence Against Women (VAW) Center. We had then Cebu City Mayor Michael Rama and Philippine Senator Pia Cayetano as participants of the event.

I spearheaded a Community and Livelihood Program to empower women's ability to earn additional income for their families. The program promoted entrepreneurship at weekend livelihood markets and opened avenues for them to participate in exhibits and bazaars.

We also joined the 2013 Enterprise Performance in Asia Conference initiated by the University of San Carlos after the 7.2-magnitude earthquake hit Bohol and super typhoon Yolanda (international name: Haiyan) ravaged Tacloban, Leyte, and neighboring Visayan cities and towns in October and November 2013. Everyone was involved with relief operations, and we were able to solicit donations from as far away as the U.S. and Japan. Zonta 1 also partnered with GCH Foundation in combining feeding program and livelihood projects.

Because Zonta 1 advocates for preventing violence against women, we held campus awareness campaigns at Benedicto College and University of Cebu Banilad Campus. We amplified Zonta's voice by conducting symposia on the issue. We identified women who are survivors of domestic violence and helped transform their lives through empowerment, courage, and determination.

To strengthen our campaign of "Voices Against Violence," we implemented a two-year program of giving seminars and lectures on laws affecting and protecting women's rights and providing redress for their violation in five *barangays*: Kamagayan (which is known as Cebu's red light district), Zapatera, Talamban, Banilad, and Lorega. We also had nutrition workshops to help promote proper nutrition and disease prevention in these *barangays*.

We earned the Cebu City's Outstanding Institution Award in 2016 that commended us for "steering the city towards a better and brighter future" and our continuous community service to the underprivileged through our numerous programs and projects. I feel that we are privileged to be living blessed lives; it should be natural for us to give back.

In this organization, I saw what I can do and what I cannot do. I also realized that I could do only so much in solving problems. At times, it is frustrating to see a woman coming to a center complaining about an abusive husband but then return to the same husband because she could not move forward with her life without his financial support. But a story like this is not enough to stop me from pushing for the end of violence against women. It only strengthens my resolve to do more and carry out more awareness and livelihood projects to empower women to stand up and speak up.

Environment and Community

Stopping violence against women and children is not the only issue that I feel strongly about.

Because I was raised by parents who love nature, I grew up to be an animal lover and a staunch advocate of environmental stewardship.

I learned that man is a part of nature and as stewards of God's creation, we should help ensure the well-being of wildlife, especially those tagged as endangered.

On November 2000, I established the Crocolandia Foundation Inc. that resulted in a conservation education facility called Crocolandia Nature Park in Barangay Biasong, Talisay City. The goal was two-fold: to preserve and conserve dwindling Philippine wildlife and to encourage children to love and protect our environment. My three children practically grew up in this environment doing science school projects with their schoolmates. Club activities, such as camping and nature exploration were conducted there.

The 10,000-square meter home of Crocolandia was once a turtle farm. The farm later became the dwelling place of "Magellan," a saltwater crocodile which my family raised in our backyard. To date, they have more than 40 offsprings, born and raised on the farm. They have been joined by more than 68 animal species, many endemic to the Philippines, including birds, lizards, turtles, wild cats, deer, pythons, and fish.

Last January 2018, we marked Crocolandia's 17th anniversary with our annual inter-school competitions, including Treasure Hunt, Spoken Word, and I Am… I Matter. The Spoken Word contest had high school students from schools in Cebu, Minglanilla, and Talisay delivering their presentations on man's responsibility in taking care of the environment.

These competitions aim to awaken the consciousness of the youth concerning the environment and wildlife conservation, to be stewards of the environment, and to be one of the earth's warriors to conserve and sustain life. It is inspiring that for 17 years we have made an impact on these children. It is our quest to continue our advocacy.

Every Sunday afternoon, we have an animal encounter at the park. Guests are given the opportunity to be up close and personal with these animals and to experience first-hand the toughness of the skin of the lizard or crocodile or feel the scales of the snake. These encounters help allay fear towards these creatures.

Being nature lovers and staunch supporters of activities like tree planting and other clean-and-green projects, we celebrated my Mother's 84th birthday by planting only native Philippine trees and giving talks on why we need to plant them.

With the closure of the Cebu City Zoo, Crocolandia is now the only facility in Cebu where children can visit and get up-close and personal with animals. I am passing on this advocacy to my children so that we can give future generations a place to learn about wildlife and learn about how they can help protect and conserve them.

My father never indulged in any luxury for himself even in his old age, while instilling in us honesty, hard work, loyalty, and integrity. We benefited from the help and support of the community where we live. He believed that proper nutrition is essential for a child's brain development especially during the formative years. We established the GCH Foundation in 2000 to address the issue of malnutrition at the *barangay* level.

We searched for *barangays* with the highest number of malnourished children and adopted these for a 90-day feeding program. Later, we implemented a 120-day feeding program among the malnourished children from ages one to five years old. Specially formulated meals were fed to the children, while monitoring increases in their weight, appetite, and activity.

We also conducted talks on nutrition education and sanitation to the mothers so they could continue providing their children with proper nutrition and hygiene. By the end of the feeding program, it was gratifying to see improved mental alertness in the children, who have since become more sociable with other children and more responsive to the classroom and school activities. I have come to realize that my sense of fulfillment does not come from knowing that I have succeeded in business as it actually comes from knowing we have made a difference in the lives of other people.

It is true when they say that when you love what you do, you never work a single day in your life. I always wake up in the morning with the challenge of making today better than yesterday.

Innovation and Devotion

Innovation is commonly associated with breakthrough, change, upheaval, and transformation. It is turning an idea into solutions that are of value to the people around us. In this world of radical business disruption, we must remain steadfast and highly focused to become successful innovators.

I never thought that I would become an innovator. My brand of innovation does not happen in state-of-the-art laboratories or sophisticated office setting. My innovations were based on passion and finding better ways to help improve lives, going the extra mile, and not counting on how much I could gain from every instance.

I learned that one could not reap success without hard work. The difficulties I encountered in life may not be the same as others. But these difficulties were strong forces that at times almost pushed me to give up.

But what kind of innovator would I be if I did not think of ways to overcome those challenges? I keep in mind that no one is shielded from problems. Trials and conflicts are perennial parts of everyday life. They are inevitable. We thrive in life when we tackle these issues. I live with that thought and this is why I endured whatever the challenges that were thrown at me. I firmly believe that these difficulties are life's lessons to make us better and stronger.

Disruptions in our lives are parts of the package. They come in various forms, shapes, and people. They will disappoint, frustrate, and dishearten the strongest among us. My hope is that my story inspires and encourages women to be determined, creative and innovative in performing their tasks and pursuing their dreams despite any disruptions. Being successful invites competition and even envy, and this is why I keep updating myself with what is new and provides productive solutions. I had to be stronger than my fears. I came out scarred from some of these trials and challenges. But I was never broken. It is true what someone said about a diamond needing to go under pressure in order to sparkle.

My life's narrative, counting more than 60 years is a testament of how a woman can choose to never be afraid in standing up for what is right. In my life's journey, there were many forces which threatened to destroy or push me down. But giving up or walking away was never my option. Despite the challenges, I remained strong in protecting my name and my integrity.

I am now working on my lifelong dream of becoming a farmer. In contrast to my previous work on aqua farming, I am now spending time in the mountains of Barangay Sirao in Cebu City cultivating gourmet varieties of tomatoes, vegetables, and herbs; and special varieties of roses, gerberas year-round, and poinsettias for Christmas. Farming has become my passion and I look forward to spending more time on the farm as I help experiment with new farming techniques and plant interesting varieties and crops for Cebu's growing needs.

At this stage of my earthly existence, the question of whether or not I have succeeded in life is a question that always pops in my head. I am comforted by the words of Mahatma Gandhi who once said: "The best way to find yourself is to lose yourself in the service of others."

My greatest blessings are my husband Antonio and my children Janice, Jillian, and Jason. We help each other, pray together, eat dinner together, and support each other during the most trying of times. I am happy that my children have finished their studies and are now helping us run the businesses. Childhood discipline and diligence have paid off. They have diversified our pet food business by putting up a one-stop shop for every pet's needs. They have turned their hobbies into businesses, raising dogs that became entries in dog shows to promoting our products and developing networks. With my children's participation in the business, we have been able to expand our manufacturing business to packaging solutions using the latest technology and state of-the-art machinery to manufacture laminated woven plastic sacks.

To this day, I continue to love what I do. I teach my children to strive hard to succeed but to always remain humble, honest, and fair in work and personal dealings. "To reach your dream, stay focused, be determined, believe in yourself, be creative and be innovative. God gave all of us talents, and it is for us to discover and develop those talents." These are my constant reminders to my children.

My alma mater, the University of San Carlos, lives by the motto of *Scientia, Virtus, Devotio*.

"*Scientia*" is the Latin word for Knowledge or Learning, both as a process and a product. "*Virtus*" means Virtue or Moral Character. "*Devotio*" means dedication or faithfulness to a person, task, or duty because of a vow formally or informally taken.

I faithfully dedicate my life to service. I vow to become the kind of leader who fosters more leaders. I commit to fulfilling my duties as a citizen, wife, mother, leader, and steward of my God-given skills and abilities. Living the "Devotio Spirit" can only mean living a life of fulfillment through service, goodness, dedication, and generosity.

Fr. Antonio Pernia once reminded us to be the "salt and light for others." I can do this by being a faithful herald of God's boundless love for humanity. I believe that the blessings you give to others will come back to you a hundred folds. Trust me on this. You will never lose when you give; instead, you will receive more. This is my way of sharing the bountiful wealth of the earth.

SANDY SANCHEZ MONTANO

FOUNDER, COMMUNITY HEALTH EDUCATION EMERGENCY RESCUE SERVICES (CHEERS)
GLOBAL FWN100™ 2016

Intensity 7

In 2006, our dream, like the dream of many nurses in the Philippines was to work in the United States (U.S.) where possibilities were endless and opportunities for professional growth were boundless. They said America was where dreams come true. So, my husband and I braved the challenge. We flew to the U.S. and hit the ground running. We attended seminars and conventions, updated our knowledge on hospital care, discovered the latest and newest guidelines on life-saving. We were intent on finding our place under the sun and were on our last leg in completing hospital orientation for what we believed was every nurse's dream job. We thought we would be starting a new chapter in our lives. We were a young family with two kids, and with both husband and wife in the medical field. Everything was set.

As we put our plans into motion, news from back home arrived. There were calamities, disasters, death, and destruction. My *kababayan* [countrymen] were suffering. I felt pain for them. It brought me back to that awful day in 1990 during the Great Quake.

In 2007, we received a call from my father-in-law. "It is the Philippines who nurtured you, educated you, made you strong. Now that you are strong, you serve other people. Please consider coming back and serving your countrymen." This resulted in many discussions between my husband and me.

We questioned our plans, our dreams, and the plans for our kids.

We had questions about our livelihood.

To which, my father-in-law, astute as he is, countered our questions with his own: "How much money do you want in the bank? How many houses do you want to build? How many cars do you want to drive? How much is enough for you to really say you are happy and contented?"

It was all in the form of questions. But it actually provided me with the clarity to find the answers I needed. It was a lightbulb moment for me. We were on our path to a deeper purpose that my husband and I happily found together. We faced challenges, bouts of short-lived hopelessness, surprises, gifts, joys, and lots and lots of hard work.

Prelude to Social Entrepreneurship

Before we left for the U.S., I already had ten years of experience, as an instructor for first aid and basic life support in the Philippines. It was, therefore, a rude awakening to find out that I still needed to undergo training at the beginner's level. I was told that whatever knowledge I had was not at par with international standards in the field of emergency cardiovascular care.

Through Mr. Ahed Al Najjar EMS International Consultant, we found out about the American Heart Association (AHA), American Safety Health Institute (ASHI), and other organizations like NREMT, AREMT, PHTLS, and OSHA. We promptly went through the process and eventually acquired our certificates as providers and instructors.

Coming Home

It was mixed feelings that we finally decided to go back home in the Philippines. It meant literally starting over with nothing. As we started to settle in, we realized we were in for a lot of work. A lot. We needed a strategy and to run a very tight ship. Decisions, most of them tough decisions, needed to be made. Fortunately, our families were very supportive. Aside from the fact that they were happy because we now were in the same time zone, they believed in our budding advocacy, maybe even more than we did.

The Five Stages of Social Entrepreneurship

Tanabe's (2016) framework on the five stages of entrepreneurship influenced me and help explain my style of leadership. The five stages are: (1) defining the systemic problem; (2) starting a social enterprise; (3) organizing partnerships; (4) broadening the Support for CHEERS; and (5) achieving Systemic Change.

My primary social entrepreneur motivations are health social issues. Therefore, I needed to develop a structure that could solve the social issue of health education, and emergency medical services, while generating economic value.

Defining the Systemic Problem

Records show that the impact of disasters in the Philippines have been increasing year after year. In 2011, the National Disaster Risk Reduction Management Council reported that during the period 1990-2006, annual direct damages caused by disasters was roughly 0.5% of the Gross Domestic Product (GDP). This translated to about PhP 20 Billion a year. In 2009, I experienced firsthand the damage from the relentless savagery of storms Ondoy and Peping. My Apong [grandfather] Ben and Uncle Bening drowned while my Apong [grandmother] Sidra was saved from the floodwaters. However, she suffered from hypothermia and eventually died. Loss of life and property due to these two storms took 2.7% of the country's GDP.

Given a disaster-prone environment, with a Philippine population in 2018 estimated at 110 million, the need for professionally trained and internationally certified Emergency Medical Service (EMS) was glaring.

Starting a Social Enterprise

There was a lack of experts in the different categories for emergency medical technicians, including paramedics, which comprise the Emergency Medical Services (EMS). EMS is a system that provides emergency medical care for people with critical health needs, such as serious illness or injury that may be life-threatening. It was shocking that as recent as 2008, there were no registered paramedics in the Philippines.

Recognizing the existing meager resources and the need to increase the number of skilled professionals involved in disaster planning, preparedness, and response, my husband, Alvin and I founded CHEERS Foundation. The initial focus of CHEERS was to conduct medical missions, feeding programs, and search rescue and responses. But as we immersed ourselves in the community, we met plenty of passionate people who wanted to help but did not have the skills and knowledge, and some with training lacked certifications. Others have been in the pre-hospital industry and needed updating and continuing professional education. A majority of them were currently employed in health and medical positions and wanted to upgrade their health and medical careers. This situation ignited our resolve to set up the CHEERS Academy.

We developed a range of training and certification programs for Basic EMT, Advanced EMT, and Basic Safety training for Safety Officer.

Organizing Partnerships

Disaster-preparedness, mitigation, recovery, and rehabilitation are elements that are equally essential in preventing human, property, and economic loss. CHEERS developed a Global Disaster Preparedness Program (GDPP) and Risk Reduction Resiliency Emergency in Disasters (Code RED) program that can be customized to train virtually anyone, including the youth within the K-12 program. The youth are a formidable force with energy, strength, and time on their side. If a majority of the young ones are trained and given skills this will not only help them in times of emergency but also help their loved ones and the community.

To ensure the successful roll-out of GDPP, CHEERS partnered with the Department of Education. CHEERS submitted a program portfolio for Interfacing Curriculum for K12, Emergency Medical Services, EMS Kids for the Elementary Level, GDPP for High School, and Adopt-A-School programs. CHEERS also became an official partner of the American Heart Association to provide training and certifications for Basic Life Support (BLS) and Advanced Life Support.

Venturing even further into the grassroots level of the Philippine Community, CHEERS also reached out to various Local Government Units (LGU). Bacoor City was the first LGU to recognize the importance of EMT Training and enrolled city personnel in the course. All the participants successfully completed the program and received certifications, including the Mayor.

Broadening the Support for CHEERS

Disaster spares no one. Given this reality, I initiated mutual support agreements for CHEERS with numerous public private partnerships. By engaging multiple stakeholders, CHEERS was able to start solving a systemic problem through a collective process with a multiplier effect. CHEERS' efforts to transfer knowledge and skills on community health emergency rescue services have evolved. CHEERS' expertise on pre-hospital care provided by EMS and occupational safety will now be shared with various government institutions nationwide.

As a pilot project, CHEERS is proud to announce its capability to address three of the six strategies identified for Metro Manila for earthquake preparedness. Should a strong tremor hit the metropolis, loss of life and property could be catastrophic.

The three strategies which CHEERS is ready for are:

1. Strengthening disaster management and response through the Metro Manila Development Authority (MMDA) Metro Manila Emergency Volunteer Corps (MMEVC) where CHEERS is a Co-Founder.

2. Ensuring access to critical information before, during, and after disasters through the First Responder application.

3. Enhancing disaster management capacity through self-reliance and mutual risk-management assistance, including disaster awareness through education using the CHEERS Online learning management system.

Achieving Systemic Change

The initial aim of CHEERS was to train Filipinos to become globally certified providers of emergency cardiovascular care, as well as to provide training in first aid science, paramedics studies, and more generally to give them the knowledge, skills, and confidence to save lives.

To date, CHEERS has trained 47,000 healthcare students and professionals, disaster front-line responders, and ordinary citizens. Those trained are now equipped with up-to-date, internationally recognized skills to respond to emergencies. Of those trained, some are working for the government, active in volunteer groups, or some have ventured abroad.

CHEERS has also expanded its emergency-related services by investing in the production of emergency food reserve slated as part of a Go-Bag, a bag packed with survival-essential items. The Go-Bag is prepared, and ready if there is a need to evacuate one's home. Addressing the need for emergency rations stems from my belief in the Hippocrates' mantra that states: "Let thy food be thy medicine and thy medicine be thy food."

CHEERS partnered with Industrial Technology Development Institute (ITDI) under Department of Science and Technology (DOST) and started technology transfer training programs to organize disaster-stricken communities to use resources found within their area. Survivors are encouraged to plant climate-resilient crops, such as cassava, sweet potato, mung bean, and moringa. These crops can be dried, pulverized, and processed into flour, as part of a recovery effort. Continuous research and development led to the development of recipes for Chocolate Energy Bar, healthy *polvoron*, and a nutritious porridge with moringa that could be part of a feeding program for combating hunger and malnutrition. The organic, gluten-free flour products are substitutes for protein-rich food essential for health, wellness, and recovery. Although this program was targeted to communities recovering from a disaster, other poor communities have requested the same training focused on livelihood.

Uphill Climb

It was not easy though. Far from it.

Despite commitment, challenges would come. The decision to go home to the Philippines and start over meant doing several things simultaneously, including re-orienting ourselves, taking care of a young but growing family, generating the necessary funds to sustain the social enterprises, rebuilding and strengthening new dreams, and creating new plans. During our sixth year back home, we almost closed shop, packed our bags, and left for the U.S.

It just seemed too hard and sacrifices were too great. It was almost an impossible dream.

And just as hope and confidence were about to run out, the heavens decided to step in to tell us otherwise.

Our efforts were acknowledged when CHEERS received the ASEAN Most Admired ASEAN Enterprise award. At the same time, I was recognized as the First ASEAN Woman Leader. It was like a mother giving birth. After the pain of labor, came the joy of the gift of a child.

Amidst the joy and the celebration, there was disbelief. Our baby, CHEERS, has been acknowledged not only in the Philippines but also by our ASEAN neighbors. I, Sandy Sanchez Montano, who came from a small farming town north of Luzon, was honored as the First ASEAN Woman Leader.

To think that I died in 1990.

My Intensity 7 Story

I was eighteen years old and studying nursing in Baguio City. I was a typical young Filipina with simple ideas of life but with noble intentions.

Going to Baguio to study was the most significant and riskiest decision I had ever made. I was raised in the traditional Filipina-Ilokana way. There was mischief and there was discipline. Our lifestyle was a modest farming household where food was as plentiful as the fresh air around us. There were tasks and there were rewards. There were dreams to pursue. Life was very good.

On July 16, 1990, I was in class when a 7.7 strong quake struck.

Our professor, shaken and unsure of what to do, instructed us to go home. And so we did. Back at the boarding house, things were a blur. The shock of the strong tremor and the lack of information rendered us almost as headless chickens, running around with no direction. And then, there were aftershocks. Strong, scary aftershocks.

Then, the unthinkable happened.

The building collapsed.

I was pinned under heavy rubble.

Moments later, I found that there were three of us, helpless, injured, and scared to death. The quake struck a little past four in the afternoon. The building collapsed a couple of hours later.

We estimated that we were buried for three nights. There was absolute darkness. For three days, there was no food, no water, and no warmth. There was no relief of any form. We could feel one aftershock after another that seemed almost as strong as the initial quake. We felt the oxygen running out. We could not move. We feared the rubble would collapse further and finally kill us all. Hope was running out. We had no identifiable way to tell the actual amount of time that had lapsed, but it seemed like forever. We were cut off from the land of the living. We had no idea what was going on in the world above us, beyond the rubble. We did not know how devastating the earthquake had been. We were confined in a world of total darkness, without food or water, unable to move, and running out of air and hope.

On the third day, I was forced to accept the strong possibility that this was my end. I did not pray anymore to be saved. Instead, I prayed that my body could be found so that my family could lay me to rest and have closure. So, they could move on and live their lives without me.

After that prayer, I felt light as if I was floating. Then I saw people frantically searching and digging. Dogs were sniffing through piles of wood and cement and then the dogs started barking furiously. This got the attention of the people who were searching.

That was when they found me or rather they found my body.

I was not breathing. I had no pulse. I was declared dead. Fatalities were being brought to the open area of Burnham Park. My body was among them, lined up for identification. I was dead to the rescuers.

There were not enough cadaver bags. Even the Department of Health was not prepared for the magnitude of this disaster. Bodies, including mine, were covered with whatever material was available. That night, there were heavy rains. The cold climate of Baguio City plus the cold rainwater were the miracles that God sent. My exposed body, soaked to the bone, revived my heart. There was a heartbeat. My lungs gulped for air. My brain started to work. It told my muscles to move.

I WAS ALIVE!

I found myself with the others, like zombies, and on survival mode. We were all tired, weary, and starving. We were rummaging for food. Out of desperation, we were able to eat what others would call unpalatable food, like sardines with raw egg.

We had to survive.

There were more trapped survivors under the rubble. They were banging blocks of cement to bang and trying to create loud noise. After a few days, there was only silence. It was eerie. The stench of rotting bodies started to fill the air. We stayed in the open space that Burnham Park offered for fear of other structures collapsing. We shared that space with covered cadavers. Later, when we found the courage to identify the bodies of our friends through a familiar set of shoes, or jeans, or a wristwatch. It was all so surreal. It was grim and macabre.

I later learned that the 7.7 quake took more than 1,600 lives.

Baguio remained isolated. No vehicle could pass through any of the roads leading in and out of Baguio due to massive landslides and collapsed roads. Communication was down. Electricity was out. Water supply was damaged. Emergency rescuers and responders from the local government were hindered because they were victims themselves.

When we could not bear the stench any longer, a few other survivors and I decided to brave the perilously slippery Naguilian Road leading to Bauang, La Union. The road was roughly 51 kilometers to La Union. From La Union, there is a road leading to my home province of Pangasinan. Another 87 kilometers. A total of 138 or so kilometers, about 85 miles. We made this journey on foot except for a jeepney ride for the final leg.

I arrived at home to find my family in sorrowful prayer. In front of them was my picture adorned with lovely flowers and with a huge offering of food in front of it.

They believed I was dead.

I called out to my parents, and when they first heard my voice, there was mournful wailing because they sincerely thought it was my spirit, visiting them for a final goodbye. When I reassured them that I was still alive, I received the warmest, tightest, and most loving hugs and kisses. They could not believe I was alive. My Papang Panie already sent my brother Noel to Baguio to search, identify and bring my body home.

But I was home, and I was alive.

Only God can do this.

And He had a plan.

My Path Was Carved: Through Rubble

Weeks after, I struggled to sleep. I would be terrified of the slightest movement or noise. Doors closing or even creaking would make me break into a cold sweat. Voices under the rubble were calling and begging for help. Those were the flashbacks I saw as I closed my eyes to sleep. They said I had Post Traumatic Stress Disorder (PTSD). Overcoming PTSD was almost as hard as surviving what had caused it in the first place. It was a slow, arduous, and sometimes, painful process.

I had to relearn to value myself. I had to come out of the shell I created to protect myself. I had to stop hiding from people and start socializing again. It was like coming out of the rubble that was inside my head.

Throughout, my biggest strength was from God. Even then I already knew He had a plan for me and that was why I had survived. This gave me strength to find out what that plan was.

I continued my nursing studies in Manila.

I devoted my time to various community outreach activities, medical missions, volunteer teaching, and rescue training. I was the Red Cross Youth President of the United Doctors Medical Center (UDMC), and I rallied all the nursing students to be members of the organization. Later for ten years, I became one of Red Cross' leading volunteer instructor for ten years.

When there was extra time, I participated in blood donation drives and first aid safety service and cardiopulmonary resuscitation (CPR) training for different schools and companies. I was part of the first responder team for disasters and calamities for the Red Cross in Quezon City

I was so intent in all these activities that my parents started to get alarmed. They feared it was taking too much of my time away from my studies. They talked to me on how I should focus first on my nursing studies but they could not discourage me.

They decided to withhold my allowance. They believed the lack of monetary support would stop me from participating in Red Cross activities, especially if the activities involved traveling.

I had to find a way to support myself. I found a job working for Jollibee, a local fast-food chain. I started as a window cleaner and was promoted to cashier. They saw my child-friendly demeanor, and I became the Kiddie Party Host. This provided me with enough money to sustain my volunteer activities. My parents were amazed but proud of me. They never said it out loud but I felt it. This emboldened me even more.

In 1994, my dedication to the Red Cross earned me a Diploma in Service, and I was chosen to represent the Philippines in the *Hajime No Ippo* [First Big Step] in Japan. This was a month-long student exchange program. It was a choice between going to Japan or attending my college graduation. I chose Japan. I made the right decision.

Path to Leadership

The Japanese exchange program was fundamental for me recognizing my leadership potential. It was my first exposure in the international arena of medical services and disaster preparedness. It taught me the principle of *Ikigai*, the Japanese secret to health and happiness. I realized that the Japanese managed to stay calm amidst earthquakes due to one fundamental principle, first aid is one of their life skills.

My leadership skills came naturally as I led a team composed of participants from other countries. I learned that leadership requires: First, participate and learn; Second, lead; Third, develop other leaders and share; and Fourth, lead by continuously learning.

Participating in Community Health Education

Upon my return to the Philippines, I was revitalized. I was excited to educate people in saving lives. More than 100,000 benefitted from these activities. My work in community health education came to the attention of the Rotarians. In 2000, among hundreds of applicants, I was chosen to become a Rotary International Foundation Scholar in the Group Exchange Study (GSE) Program in Minas Gerais, Brazil. Together with four other Filipinos, we served as ambassadors with responsibility for fostering goodwill and friendship. This exchange program included cross-cultural country orientation and living with Brazilian host families. We were given a chance to do industry-related immersion. My profession as a nurse brought me to the rural areas of Brazil's developing clinics, their homes for the elderly, and their childcare centers. I learned how they took care of their persons with disabilities (PWD). The highest causes of death in Brazil were vehicular accidents, cardiac arrest, heart attack, and stroke. From Minas Gerais, we proceeded to São Paulo and then to Rio de Janeiro. These travels exposed me further to the humanitarian efforts in South America. After the official GSE trip, the whole team flew to New York City, where we had reunions with our families in the U.S. and had meetings with more Rotarians. The group visited more clinics, childcare, nursing home facilities, hospitals, and social welfare facilities for the homeless. We received countless offers to work as nurses and caregivers. It seemed like years of immersion and exposure to health systems in Brazil and Japan had given me perspectives and ideas to take back to the Philippines.

Back home to show my gratitude I took on the responsibility of coordinating the Matching Grants for ten Rotary Districts in the Philippines. This program required a $1,000 donation from a Rotary Club Member that was matched by a foreign Rotary Club counterpart and the Rotary International Foundation. We secured the local contribution from donations of medicine and from fundraising campaigns aimed at parents and students. These program activities were *Hahaba Ang Buhay Kung Atay Ay Matibay* (Hepatitis B Vaccination for elementary students), *Bata Ay Sisigla Kung Bulate Ay Mawawala* (Deworming program for elementary students), Tuberculosis six-months medication, and *Tinimbang ka ngunit Kulang*, a feeding program for undernourished and stunted children. These programs were implemented in ten Rotary districts and resulted in total service of 100,000 public school children. As an add-on, most of the programs included a free seminar on first aid and hands-on CPR.

Spreading My Wings and Flying

All the things I have narrated seemed to be a precursor of bigger things to come as part of God's Plan. My commitment expanded to include women and their mostly untapped capacity to do wonderful things. But to awaken this latent power, I had to be one of the first to venture out. To speak, I had to first find a voice and a podium.

This voice was given to me when my efforts were noted. First in 2014 at the ASEAN Business Summit in Naypi Taw, Myanmar I was recognized as the first ASEAN Woman Leader, and where they said I "transitioned from a killer earthquake victim to a lifesaver." The 2015 ASEAN Women Entrepreneur Network (AWEN) recognized my efforts in sustainable livelihood when they chose me as an Outstanding ASEAN Woman Entrepreneur. The 2016 "100 Most Influential Women in the World" lauded my contributions in the micro-small-medium enterprises sector, in mobilizing highly skilled talents as part of APEC's global value chain, and in my performance in pre-hospital care. In 2016 at the ASEAN-Japan Women Entrepreneurs' Linkage Program (AJWELP) in Osaka, Japan I was invited to be a co-presenter and organizer. At this forum, I was able to highlight my significant role as a Filipina who survived, lost, and found herself, overcame all the obstacles life had to offer, found her voice, and made it loud enough to be heard above the loud voices of the males who dominate the environment. AJWELP was an excellent venue for helping Asian women find recognition for the hardships we overcome.

Through this, CHEERS flourished with me.

At the APEC Summit, CHEERS was featured as one of the success stories. CHEERS also became the first international training center in the Philippines of the American Heart Association (AHA). In partnering with APEC economies in nation-building, CHEERS continuous to develop a disaster recovery network based on resilience planning and community assistance in preparing for tomorrow's uncertainties.

Leadership as a Social Entrepreneur

I am giving back what God has given me. LIFE.

From that fateful day in 1990 where the cold rain revived me, to the day I take my last breath, every second is a bonus, a new lease on life. It was only through the Grace of God that I am still here.

I have decided to make my life count.

My goal is to help save lives by addressing the lack of knowledge and skills for disaster preparedness, response, and recovery. Looking back decades ago to the aftermath of the earthquake, I realize that much could have been done, had the knowledge and skills been available.

As a social entrepreneur, I have shared the vision, the knowledge, and the life skills to survive, not just devastating disasters and calamities, but the biggest plague of our time, poverty. I believe there is more room for gain in this, rather than in pursuing wealth.

A true survivor can overcome any tragedy. A true survivor can overcome the trauma after the disaster. A true survivor can rise up and rebuild. A true survivor can learn from the past and make herself stronger and more resilient. A true survivor refuses to be a victim forever and refuses to let others be helpless victims as well. A true survivor shares her story to inspire and strengthen others. A true survivor feels the sorrow and the sadness of others because she was once one of them. A true survivor is the best teacher.

I firmly believe I am living out God's plan for me.

I know my life's purpose.

I am happy.

And I cannot wait to share my happiness with others who are searching for it, just like I was searching.

It is so good to be alive.

❊

ANNE QUINTOS

Managing Partner, PageJump Media
Global FWN100™ 2016

Butterflies in the Gut:
Leading Outside Comfort Zones

'This generation needs to sacrifice and to stay.' As I wrote these words, ink from my pen blotched the yellow pad, front to back. Most of my classmates, who took the same comprehensive exams at St. Scholastica's College just before we graduated, were wide-eyed about what the future had in store for us. Many had set their sights on leaving the country for better-paying jobs. It did not matter that overseas jobs often advertise the need for a minimum of two years of work experience. Fine-print like that are ignored when dreams are at stake. Most of us were dreamers, wanting nothing short of the world. But not me.

I was a dreamer of another sort. I stubbornly believed that I would rather struggle as a creative in my own country than be a salaried employee in a first-world corporation. "Impact and personal worth are how truly you know you've made it," I told my dad during one of our existential talks that extended past midnight. I considered leaving the Philippines to earn dollars a form of disloyalty. "I would rather have my soul with me when I'm old and gray, thank you."

The Idealist: Sticking to Guiding Principles

I sensed my dad's proud smirk when I began speaking like him: cynical yet hopeful, stubborn but a bit gullible. I was not very coy about my juvenile rants and larger-than-life ideas when I was with him. He threw in two Ayn Rand books and a handful of Teddy Benigno's *Philippine Star* columns for me to read, digest, and regurgitate with him after his work hours. It must have felt awesome for him to see me grow up as a headstrong feminist and a rhetorical activist.

On the other hand, my mom had subtle ways of molding her four daughters. Our childhood was filled with memories of preparing packs of *polvoron* for Christmas parties of out-of-school youth, assembling laced *abaniko* souvenirs for attendees of Christian life seminars, and making bright pink *gulaman* trays for the neighborhood fiesta. Our car rides to and from school became my mom's opportunity to teach us about life from her perspective. She repeatedly told stories; almost in the same manner, with her usual hand gestures, and even verbatim, about strength of character and love for the less fortunate. It probably was an effective technique for helping us remember her lessons without us even thinking much about it. Her voice pretty much became the sound of my conscience.

But if there was one thing louder than the voice of my mom in my head, it was the personality of my grandmother. Lola Chayong would not leave any battle unfinished. As the matriarch of our household during her golden years, I witnessed her staying strong while taking care of my grandfather, who was bedridden for ten years due to a stroke. Despite this predicament, Lola was unflinching and even patriotic. The books she read were about Philippine politics, and she avidly cut out noteworthy articles from newspapers for her personal compilation. During times of turmoil in national government, she was first among us to march in rallies.

During her spare time, she scoured Divisoria, usually with one of us grandchildren in tow, to buy in bulk cheaper items for her sari-sari store. Divisoria and the Sta. Cruz area were the places I dreaded going because of the maddening crowd, but it also served as the fertile ground that strengthened my belief that to be a Filipino is to be part of the struggle. To me, back then, it was the kind of struggle that can easily be won if only my generation would stay in the Philippines, shun greener pastures, and apply our talents to the land that most needed us.

The Desperate: Breaking Through

I learned about sacrifice shortly after college graduation. So that I could start standing on my own feet as an adult, my mom cut my allowance and set my monthly contribution to our household budget. My parents never needed my measly contributions, but they knew it would teach me something important about finances. I learned how to budget my paycheck, save for my master's degree, and start a personal investment. I was responsible for paying taxes and wondering where my taxes went, since the rainy days meant I had to trudge along the flooded pot-holed streets of Makati.

I was now part of the labor force, I reminded myself. I began to understand how clockwork behavior became unbearable at the office, during commute, and while you wait for the next day to end and for the next day to begin again *ad nauseam*. I did not look forward to this 8-to-5 madness. My dream was to become a film director, and it became nearly impossible to chase this aspiration even on the side once I landed a job in the tech industry, where days could be hectic. However, I deeply enjoyed my work as a tech writer, no matter how different it was from what I imagined myself doing after I graduated. I was immersed in the world of software and gadgetry, indeed, my fascination with cinema took a backseat in favor of the computer screen. At 21 years old, I went on my first business trip to Taipei, where I got to interact with developers, project managers, and customer support specialists who worked behind the products I wrote about.

Despite my conscious attempt to still cling to my interests in the arts and cultural issues, things started to turn corporate for me. Soon enough, I was reading reference books by Malcolm Gladwell, Jim Collins, and Robert Kiyosaki rather than fiction by John Grisham, Mario Puzzo, and James Clavel, authors that my dad endorsed. That handsome red book called *Good to Great* (Collins, 2001) became my date during my lunch hours. In a fastfood restaurant, I remembered earmarking what Collins (2001, p. 164) described as the flywheel effect:

> Picture a huge, heavy flywheel—a massive metal disk mounted horizontally on an axle, about 30 feet in diameter, 2 feet thick, and weighing about 5,000 pounds. Now imagine that your task is to get the flywheel rotating on the axle as fast and long as possible. Pushing with great effort, you get the flywheel to inch forward, moving almost imperceptibly at first. You keep pushing and, after two or three hours of persistent effort, you get the flywheel to complete one entire turn.

Of course, Collins was not talking about a persistent protagonist in a fantastic story. The flywheel anecdote was to picture how great corporations made breakthroughs and stayed on top of the game. I was hooked as if I was reading a plot-driven novel.

> Then, at some point—breakthrough! The momentum of the thing kicks in your favor, hurling the flywheel forward, turn after turn … whoosh! … its own heavy weight working for you. You're pushing no harder than during the first rotation, but the flywheel goes faster and faster. Each turn of the flywheel builds upon work done earlier, compounding your investment of effort. A thousand times faster, then ten thousand, then a hundred thousand. The huge heavy disk flies forward, with almost unstoppable momentum. Now suppose someone came along and asked, 'What was the one big push that caused this thing to go so fast?'

I, too, cannot pin an exact point or time when I transitioned from being a free spirit to a corporate yuppie. My dad's favorite fiction novels would have taught me a thing or two about life but I was set to embrace my reality. I was not afraid of leaping forward on this new path.

Even without a background in engineering or the hard sciences, my newfound passion for tech motivated me to enroll in a Master's in Technology Management at the University of the Philippines (UP). The program suited my interests well since it focused on research and development for different technology products. It helped me grasp concepts I usually encountered at work, such as product lifecycles, OEM/ODM processes, and project management. It did not matter that the commute from my workplace to UP Diliman was unbearable and how a significant chunk of my salary was funneled to my tuition fee. I was learning new things, and that was all that mattered.

After two years on my first job, I accepted an opportunity with an international enterprise software company. This shift led to a deeper understanding of the industry-standard tools, content management best practices, and data models used in technical communication. The scope of work also became bigger: I was working with colleagues not only based in the Philippines, but in Sweden and the United States as well.

Even though I was happy at work, I kept my doors open like other ambitious young people. I was still on the lookout for something that would challenge me. My former employer Ms. Jay contacted me one day to ask if I was interested in a position based in Taiwan. Since leaving the country was not an option for me then, I respectfully declined.

A year after taking my second job, I got a job offer for a managerial position in a tech startup. Without evaluating it carefully, I accepted the job. Two weeks after my onboard date, I resigned. I did not realize at that point that while working for a startup looked appealing on TV ala Silicon Valley; it was not for everybody. The constant changes and the general ambiguity were not for me. Before long, I was in the job market again. But it was at the worst possible time: the global financial crisis in 2009 hit the Business Process Outsourcing (BPO) industry in the Philippines pretty big, leading to job cuts and hiring freeze. I found myself jobless for months.

"Thank you for taking time to evaluate my credentials." I nervously typed these words on my computer. "I deeply appreciate your interest in my application for the technical writer position in Taiwan."

The Misfit: Cross-cultural Adjustment

My boyfriend, Raymond gave me the cold shoulder after hearing that I was seriously considering the possibility of living and working in a foreign land. Making the decision did not come easy but I knew I needed a shake-up. I have been in limbo for a longer time than my pride could handle. I never wanted to depend on anyone, especially when we have our eyes set on starting our own family. "If I have to do it," I told Raymond, "I have to do it now." Getting married seemed like the end of an era for me. I wanted to try living on my own even when things were quite uncertain about my career.

Moving to Taiwan was a very gutsy move. While I have experience working with Taiwanese, I did not speak Mandarin. Thankfully, among the managers were two Chinese-Filipinos, and they gracefully answered all my questions and concerns. It was also my first time to be away from my family for an extended period. Coming from a tight-knit family, the decision that I thought would make me stronger made me quite vulnerable to homesickness and depression. My first nights in Taiwan were as blank as I can remember. The room that my employer provided was almost barren, even the bedsheets a plain white. My stuff was all in my luggage with no definite date on when I would want to unpack. I curled up in a fetal position on the edge of the bed as if taking up the smallest space would somehow make me feel warmer inside.

My mom regularly called me and motivated me to shrug off the negativity. She understood exactly why I needed to leave the Philippines. "Fire is the test of gold," her motherly tone calmed my nerves. "Adversity is the test of a strong man." I added, "Or woman." Yes, I belong to a family of strong women. From my mom to my Lola Chayong and to Lola's mother, the women were not satisfied just to keep their men happy. Women in our family, even though they chose to give up their careers, proved their independence by establishing their own businesses and personal endeavors. So, my mom perfectly understood me when I told them that I needed to teach myself to stand on my own before I decide to settle down. Raymond also respected this decision, and to be with me, he patiently searched for job opportunities in Taiwan.

To survive, I needed to start doing what I was good at: learning new things. While I was an introvert, I did not pass up the opportunity to connect with my co-workers about life in Taiwan. I carefully observed how they dealt with others even if they mostly spoke in Mandarin. I asked them friendly questions, curious about the culture at work and life outside it. Slowly, I was no longer just reacting but adapting to their work styles, their personal boundaries, and their sense of responsibility. I was no longer the girl who was late arriving at meetings. I mastered how to use my soft skills to collaborate with my teammates. I enjoyed their gentle and kind-hearted laughter during our team gatherings. I only had one problem; I was a bit stubborn.

Generally speaking, East Asian culture rewards you by how well you follow your superiors, not by how often you voice out your contradicting opinions. For some reason, I was unable not to speak what was on my mind. The butterflies in my gut violently reacted when I do not get to say my piece, no matter how stupid I may sound. At first, I felt that eyes rolled as I kept on asking questions and voicing out comments. A few months later, I became the girl in our department who has an answer to an impromptu question "what's your idea on this?"

My first year in Taiwan quickly went by. Raymond followed me from the Manila to Taipei, and we got married after a year apart. We began building our lives and dreams together. We were certain that we had our lives figured out. Well, that only lasted until I got pregnant with our first child.

The Rebel with a Cause

Everything the movies taught girls about motherhood was completely the opposite of my experience. It was not all bright, pink, and dreamy. I was sensitive, antisocial, and depressed. Day in and out after work, I ended up sulking in the bed with a face mask stuck to my nose. I could not bear strong scents, and threw up again and again until close to my due date.

Pregnancy in Taiwan was a pleasant experience, though. The government subsidized medical expenses. Doctors and nurses follow strict protocol and hospital procedures. We were also able to find a Catholic hospital near our place. What we had to worry about was childcare. Getting a nanny was very expensive. Taiwan also has tighter requirements for foreigners hiring domestic helpers from other countries. Even bringing in a family member for an extended period can be a very long process, if not nearly impossible. I was faced with the possibility that I might have to give up my work to take care of my baby.

I have learned that every mother is different. While most are happy to be stay-at-home moms, I was at my wit's end just thinking about it. I began to feel inadequate as a mother, as a woman, and as a person. At the same time, I knew that the welfare of my baby was not something to be bargained with. So, while pregnant, I prepared myself that I might have to quit my job soon after I give birth. I began thinking about other ways of keeping myself busy. Creative writing again became my refuge. By the time I gave birth, I was able to complete the manuscript of my first book, *Abroad Me: 22 Success Strategies for Young Overseas Filipinos*.

Writing about overseas living was my way of tying up loose ends from my youth. In my heart, I still believed that choosing to stay in our homeland was a very noble thing to do. Overseas experience, in so many ways, opened me up to bigger possibilities and wider horizons. It taught me a lot about my limitations as well as my strengths, and my faith in God. The problem I realized as a Filipino in Taiwan was that many of us only see our overseas experience as a springboard to earning dollars or a better life. Many spent a decade or two working and sending money back to the Philippines until they are hit by the reality that their lives had already passed by. In my book, I was very clear in my message that *Abroad Me* is not about flying out. It is about spreading our wings to get a broader perspective of the world for our success, monetary and otherwise, and for our collective progress as Filipinos.

After completing my manuscript, the butterflies in my gut vehemently kicked in again or maybe that was just the baby in my womb! I told my husband, Raymond that I need to get this book published.

And I did it. With my husband's help. I gave birth to both a baby and a book concept. While I was on maternity leave, I was laying out the pages, and he was editing the content. During breastfeeding nights, I had a newborn in one hand, and printed drafts in the other hand. Back in Manila, my sister Corinne helped me push it out to market, and she did such a great job that National Bookstore and Fully Booked accepted the book for consignment. Our next challenge was forming a legitimate company, complete with legal documents and receipts, so we would be able to sell the book. Raymond was swift in deciding to activate our early plans of starting a business in the Philippines. On our fifth month as parents, we took our daughter back to the Philippines for her baptism, and we also dealt with the paperwork for our new business: PageJump.

In Taiwan, though it was a difficult decision but things eventually panned out when we found a daycare center for our daughter. It was not ideal, so Raymond and I worked very hard on alternative paths for our growing family. A few months later, we have launched *Abroad Me* in Fully Booked, Metro Manila's largest bookstore. From this single book that already saw a reprint, along with an upcoming student edition, PageJump grew to publish nine more titles in three years, collaborating with award-winning authors and artists. I was in charge of the creative aspect of PageJump, while Raymond focused on its business side. We found ourselves juggling our day jobs, our Manila-based business, and our roles as mom and dad. To make it more exciting, we found ourselves another big surprise: I was pregnant with baby number two!

"Must we stop?" I asked my husband one night when we were unsure of what we were doing. And I answered myself: "Probably not. In a way, this is really my best take at resistance." I was resisting against the general expectations that moms would be tied only to the home. I was resisting against succumbing to the vicious cycle for overseas Filipinos; that we only work and build our lives abroad and forget about the responsibilities we have for our beloved country.

And in my resistance, I was slowly owning my voice and realizing there was only one thing left to be done: we needed to go back home and take care of what we had started. Full-blast.

The Crazy One: Building Legacy

So now we are home. Our two girls are fast growing up; while our business is starting to take flight after we formally opened an office/media studio. Through it all, we learned the ropes as we proceeded. We have our eyes set not on financial gains but on leaving a legacy. We have published books closely aligned to the different advocacies we support: social protection of overseas Filipinos and their families, support for creative talent and entrepreneurs, financial literacy and entrepreneurship, and even gender equality.

Our business was not meant to follow a linear growth path, but we have had early successes along the way. As of this writing, several of our titles have been recognized as winners: *Toto O.* by Charmaine Lasar won the Grand Prize (Nobela) for the young adult novel category in the 65th Palanca awards; *Cyberpreneur Philippines*, co-edited by Raymond, my husband is a finalist in the prestigious National Book Awards; and *Ang Pag-ikot ng Salapi sa Panahon ni JLC* by Andrian Legaspi won the Palanca Awards for Literature. We have ventured into producing short films and online videos as well as developing apps to support our media brands and partners. On the events front, we have designed a learning series for college students and young professionals, and even hosted "strictly adult" coloring sessions as a platform for sex and gender discourse. We will continue publishing and exploring creative pathways in different formats and platforms. While our traditional counterparts may call us crazy in our endeavors, pushing boundaries is how we learn, fail, and move forward.

All of these efforts have been overwhelming for my young family and I have made bold moves. But that is how the journey goes, with its crazy twists and turns. And here we are, back in the Philippines. You can even say I am wide-eyed and hopeful like my young self after college graduation. We are starting our married lives over again, working on something we have built from the ground up. We do not know if we will be able to make it fully happen as we have envisioned. But my youthful past taught me that, no matter how much I hate ambiguity and uncertainty, I should rise up to the challenge for the love of learning, for the fear of giving in, and for the trust we have in ourselves. For that, I thank the butterflies in my gut.

ROWENA ROMULO

Owner of Romulo Café London, U.K.

GLOBAL FWN100™ 2017

Nothing is Impossible:
From Banker to Restaurateur

I grew up in a compound that was called *Kasiyahan*. I lived with my parents, grandparents, my uncles and aunts, and my first cousins. The Romulo family was a very closely-knit family. We had one main kitchen and dining room, and so we usually ate all our meals together. Lola's chicken *relleno*, Tito Greg's *kare-kare*, and The General's chicken and pork *adobo* were my comfort food.

Little did I know that 35 years later, I would have the chance to share with others the dishes that my sister, cousins, and I enjoyed while growing up in that magical family home called *Kasiyahan*. Growing up, successful role models surrounded me. I was lucky to have witnessed the many achievements of my grandfather, Carlos P. Romulo. He left us with an extraordinary legacy and even if nobody said so, I knew I had the responsibility to do well.

In the late 80's, I left the Philippines to pursue career opportunities in banking. I fancied traveling and learning more about the world. I wanted to be more independent, stand on my own two feet, and to make a difference.

I was lucky in my choice of a banking career, but I did work hard. In a career spanning thirty-two years, I worked for two major American banks. I was posted to New York, Milan, and London. I climbed the corporate ladder on merit and became a managing director at forty-one, responsible for a global business.

My success was built on managing businesses, expanding into new markets, motivating a diverse team of professionals from around the globe, leading start-up projects, and handling complex transactions. I traveled the world, wore expensive suits, and stayed in the best hotels. It was the typical corporate lifestyle of the accomplished senior banker. It was the life I lived and breathed. And I was making a difference.

The best memories of my banking career were in Milan where I worked for twenty years. There I developed my leadership skills, rose to the challenges of relocating to a foreign land, and began to make a name for myself in a male-dominated industry. Milan is also significant because this is where my one and only lovely daughter, Giulia, was born and raised, and where she still lives.

Rising Star As an International Banker

My international banking career began in 1988. I was sent by Citibank in Manila to Milan for two months to market a remittance service called Citifast. Citifast was developed so Filipinos working abroad could send money safely and quickly. Marketing the Citifast product meant literally selling to Filipinos door-to-door, mainly during Thursday afternoons and Sundays when they had their day off from work. I would visit places where Filipinos congregated, including churches, public parks, the Duomo in Milan, and basketball games. My team would even crash weddings and parties, not how one typically did business in the banking world. I had fun and have fond memories of my early banking time in Milan.

I moved to Milan permanently in October 1989. Citibank had launched a new service and was busy winning new business. They needed someone who spoke fluent English to improve their operation and customer service unit to better support their international clients. Because I had established a great working relationship with my Italian colleagues while marketing Citifast, Citibank felt I would be a good fit and offered me the job. Although I knew it was not going to be easy, I felt the time was right for me to pursue this international assignment. Aside from an aunt who lived about an hour away, I did not know anyone else, and I did not speak Italian! I was nevertheless determined to make this move. My parents were supportive, as I had reassured them that the assignment was only for three years. Little did we all know that I would never again return to Manila to live.

Adjusting to an Expatriate Life

Integrating into a new culture has its challenges. Moving abroad brings multiple levels of stress, fears, and worries. I was fortunate that my Mom accompanied me to help me settle in. At first it was an exciting adventure as we were apartment hopping, buying appliances, and decorating my new flat. But when she eventually had to head back to Manila, a sense of loneliness, unfamiliarity, and feeling out of place began to creep in. Nevertheless, given that I had made the choice to move to Milan, I resolved to make the most of it. As such, one of the first things I did was to take Italian lessons. I enrolled in Berlitz Language School four days a week for nine months. This was a time when, apart from colleagues in the office, it was not easy to find people who spoke English. Except for CNN news, everything on TV was in Italian. Being able to speak the local language became an invaluable skill. It gave me confidence and allowed me to form strong connection with the locals. It definitely helped ease my day-to-day interaction with my staff and colleagues. I also wanted to make the most of my expat experience, and this meant breaking out of my comfortable little cocoon and taking the time to learn and embrace the culture and history of the place. As the saying goes, "when in Rome...." Italians love their *calcio* [football]. Football in Italy is more than just a sport: it is a way of life. It was a typical conversation topic on Monday mornings at work because Sundays were when the matches took place. I took an interest in *calcio* and I could follow and participate in conversations. I learned how to drink coffee like a true Italian by ordering using a single word: *caffè*, a strong shot of *espresso*. Italians had to have their coffee three to four times a day as a break from work. I picked up the habit of inviting people for coffee in order to get to know them on a personal level. I attribute a great part of my success during this time to my ability to adjust and adapt to the way things were done in my new environment and to "going native."

Understanding Customers

The 1990's were a time of great innovation in the Milan branch of the bank. We launched numerous new products and services. My mentor, Giulio Di Cerbo, who also became a very dear friend, not only advised and encouraged me but, most of all, he believed in me. He sadly passed away suddenly in 2014, but I will always remember this remarkable man who taught me the business. Giulio understood customer needs and what was required to deliver first-class service. These were lessons I took to heart and applied throughout my banking career, and later as a restaurateur.

Giulio was a workaholic who followed a 6-day work week -- passionate, vibrant, full of energy, and simply tireless! And so was I! My colleagues compared me to the Duracell Bunny, the anthropomorphic alkaline battery-operated pink rabbit in the famous ads. Unlike zinc-carbon batteries, alkaline can go on almost forever!

Working with Passion

I have been extremely passionate about what I do, and my optimism is often infectious. I believe that great leaders should not just focus on getting the group members to finish tasks; we need to have a genuine passion and enthusiasm for the projects we do. People are naturally attracted to you when you have a positive attitude. By being positive, I have learned to live a happier life and to be surrounded by other positive people. I have always tried to live every day with passion, enjoyment, and enthusiasm.

Fostering Gender Equality

In 2000, my career continued to flourish in the Milan branch. While I was raising my daughter, I was promoted to managing director (MD). My position covered two jobs: (1) as Country Head for Italy with responsibility for three main product lines and all aspects of the business, and (2) as branch management head responsible for a network of thirty-one branches in Europe, Middle East, and Africa (EMEA). I was the only female MD in the branch then. In the same year, I helped launch and co-chaired Citiwomen in Italy. Our objective was twofold: to foster gender equality and remove barriers to entry into the workforce for women, and to provide the necessary development and training so that women would be prepared to take on senior positions. On reflection, I was lucky to have had bosses and peers who recognized my abilities and coached me so I could achieve my potential. Otherwise, it would have been even more challenging to climb the corporate ladder in a male-dominated industry. For this, I will always be grateful.

Managing a Diverse Team

As my responsibilities grew and I was tasked with managing people from different countries and different work units, it became more difficult to know every detail of what they were doing or to understand all the rules and regulations of doing business in every country where we worked. I made an effort to understand all the aspects of the business and challenged my team members to ask the right questions. I attempted to provide the senior management with the correct information. I always believed that knowledge is power and that everyone needs to continue to improve themselves in every possible way. The person who thinks he or she is an expert has a lot to learn. To never stop learning has become one of my guiding principles.

As a result of all this experience, I became and continue to be a very hands-on manager. I liked being actively involved in the day-to-day operation of a business and being where the action was. Thus, I took the opportunity to visit each branch, sharing my vision, my mission, and my goals with the personnel in person. I thought that being present in person was a more effective way to improve the business and get the team's buy-in than mere conference calls.

Delegating as a Balancing Act

The flipside was that I repeatedly drew comments during my performance reviews about not delegating enough to others. I was told that without the ability to delegate effectively, it would be impossible for me to advance to higher positions of responsibility. I got too bogged down in the detail instead of focusing on the big picture. This was a real problem for me. It became unclear whether the objective was to get the job done, or to create a masterpiece. I bought into Napoleon's observation that, "If you want something done, do it yourself!" I slowly learned that doing everything myself was not scalable and no matter how much Duracell battery power I had in me, it would eventually run out. I would finally have to start believing that I was not the only one who could do the job properly.

Delegation will always remain one of my biggest challenges. I will continue to learn as I shift from banker to entrepreneur that the right level of delegation is a balancing act. It depends on a person or team's level of maturity and the relative impact of the decisions made.

ADJUSTING TO THE SHIFTING GLOBAL CONTEXT

The collapse of Lehman Brothers, a sprawling global bank, in September 2008 almost brought down the world's financial system. It took huge taxpayer-financed bail-outs to shore up the industry. The global financial crisis highlighted the inadequacy of both domestic and cross-border financial legislation. This led to consolidation in the banking industry, new regulatory reform of all types to ensure better corporate governance ensuring capital adequacy in the event of a significant financial crisis. As a result, the focus of the business shifted rapidly. It was not so much about growing the business or developing new products and services but rather, more about cost containment, effective controls, risk management, and compliance, among other issues. This was the course the financial services industry would take for many years to come.

Expanding My Global Reach: From Milan to London

In early 2010 I started interviewing for a global job with another bank. The Bank wanted to become more international and to diversify its revenues outside of the U.S. They were looking for a senior Product Executive to develop and execute the firm's international expansion plans. It was very similar to what I was doing at that time with the big difference that I had to build it from scratch practically. This seemed like the dream job for me, and after a lot of soul-searching, I accepted the new challenge. I would now be based in London.

It was difficult to leave Milan, a place I had considered my second home for 27 years. My bosses tried to convince me to stay, but I knew it was time to leave. It was kind of them to say that they would always welcome me back. I was feeling more confident in my abilities to lead businesses, and it was time to gain a new experience. In addition, the thought of being on "garden leave," a period where employees are restricted from working but still get paid for three months was truly heavenly!

The first two to three years on the new job was both exciting and challenging. I was a newcomer to the firm, with responsibilities for a start-up project that few people inside the firm knew anything about. I was given the opportunity to develop and execute a strategy, build a team of professionals, and establish a global operating model with a new technology platform.

I had the chance to form a cohesive and dynamic team of professionals from diverse cultures and backgrounds. I used my energy, drive, and commitment to bring a sense of community across locations. This helped to create a strong feeling of purpose that is fundamental when building a new business. Happily, every year I either met or exceeded the objectives that we set up for the activity. I learned the organization and how to navigate it, developed good relationships, and accomplished a great deal. My performance review at the end of 2011 read: "Rowena knows her business inside out, has a clear vision and is on track across a broad range of significant deliverables in building out the business for the firm. She has command of the details of her business, thinks commercially and strategically, and hires well. She adds energy and a sense of urgency to the culture, helping to drive the management team in a productive and constructive way and moving the culture in a positive direction. She is a pleasure to work with. Rowena needs, however, to make sure she does not allow herself to get too frustrated with the broader organization, even when the bureaucracy feels overwhelming."

However, the only thing constant in this organization was a change in leadership every twelve to eighteen months. Along with changes at the top came changes in strategy, priorities, focus, and overall direction of the business which meant having to explain the strategy of the business over and over again. An approved budget did not mean it was a final budget. Priorities of the overall business changed because of challenges the bank had to deal with. Budget, resource, and capacity constraints meant a delay in the implementation of projects, if they were not completely shelved. Despite my unwavering commitment to the business, frustration started to kick in. I found it difficult to watch the business I had built being drained of resources while being expected to make progress when management felt the time was right. I waited patiently and did what I was told. My team continued to maintain constant client focus while working through and balancing the needs of the firm. I also got more involved in other bank activities and was a member of the Bank's Mentoring Program, Analyst and Associate Development Program. I was also involved in the Recruitment and Summer Internship Program, Learning and Development Program, and the Diversity programs. If I could not accomplish what I was initially hired to do, at least I had the opportunity to engage in activities that were close to my heart.

By the fourth quarter of 2014, I felt my excitement and inspiration beginning to ebb. I felt that I was not being used to my full potential and that my talent was being wasted. I decided to look at opportunities outside the Bank and see where the industry was headed. The banks were hiring more legal and compliance specialists rather than business people.

The Beginning of an Idea: Be a Restaurateur

Around this time the idea and feasibility of opening a Romulo Café in London actually came about at a dinner. My partner Chris and I attended a fundraiser for victims of Typhoon Haiyan at The Savoy. When people found out that I was a Romulo, they asked, "Why don't you open a branch of Romulo Café in London?" I thought that sounded like an interesting idea. I did have some restaurant experience when together with my uncle and aunt we opened a Thai restaurant in Manila in 1986. I did not know where to start in London. I questioned why I would want to leave a high-paying job in banking.

Ignoring the Idea: Exploring an Idea

I approached my banking boss and told him that since my experience was not being used to the maximum, it was time for me to do something different. I advised him what role I was interested in and where I believed I could make an even more significant contribution. I assured him that for my current position my succession plan was in place and that I had identified team members who would be ready to replace me if a new role became available. He really seemed to like what I said. After all, it was not too often that someone actually raised her hand to say she wanted to do more.

After getting the buy-in from the rest of the management team, I defined a roadmap for my new responsibilities, created an organizational chart, revisited the operating model, and ensured it was aligned to client needs. I felt a renewed sense of energy and motivation. I was told that the announcement of the new re-organization of the business would be made by March 2015. In the meantime, we were to take on our new responsibilities and start organizing our teams around the new organization model. At first, I was happy to settle for this level of ambiguity because I wanted to move on to a new challenge. It was not, however, easy for our team members. At that same time, the bank was going through a firm-wide redundancy program. Everyone was feeling very uneasy, morale was low as people did not really know whether they would be part of the new structure or be terminated. No announcements were made as we were entering the end of the second quarter.

Given my highs and lows with the bank as I entered my fifth year, and the constant change in management and direction, the Duracell battery was wearing out. One of my philosophies in life is to do what I love. As Steve Jobs said: "You've got to find what you love... Your work is going to fill a large part of your life, and the only way to be truly satisfied is to do what you believe is great work. And the only way to do great work is to love what you do." It was inevitable that this chapter of my life would come to an end and it was time to move on. I recognized, of course, that businesses do change direction. Maybe I was so passionate about the business that I failed to see the bigger picture. My peers obviously had a different point of view. I still hear from ex-colleagues that my strategic plans for the business are being re-used and are gradually being put into place. At least I left a legacy behind.

Opening Romulo Café London

While all this uncertainty was happening at the bank, my partner and I continued to discuss the idea of opening Romulo Café in London. Given his background in restaurant operations and his understanding of adapting business models to the local market, this would be something he could do with me. I approached my family and cousins with the idea and they asked for a feasibility study. We decided to hire a UK consultant to help us put together an unbiased business plan. We knew that London was a city of 'foodies' and that there was an openness to new tastes, textures, and flavors. The question was whether Londoners were ready for Filipino cuisine.

By March 2015, the idea turned into a 63-page business plan that included market research, a 5-year financial projections, an analysis on Strengths, Weaknesses,

Opportunities, Threats (SWOT), and a comprehensive marketing plan. The moment had come to convince the family. I will never forget the initial reaction of my father. He said:

"Why don't you just invest your money in a MacDonald's franchise? It's less risky and less of a headache to run."

I replied: "Really, Dad? I would never invest money in something I didn't believe in!"

After much more prodding on my part, my family gave their blessing, subject to finding a suitable location and a Head Chef. It took us about six months to find the right location. When the Kensington site became available was the turning point. My gut feel told me that it was now or never. The maxim 'location, location, location' rings true for restaurants as well. The site felt right for the following reasons: (a) It was close to major Filipino hubs ; (b) It was associated with key British landmarks and parts of the British establishment; (c) It was accessible, possessing good transport links with a bus stop directly in front and equidistant to two train/tube stations); (d) It evoked a perception of quality and prestige; and (e) It was the first location of the Philippine Embassy when my maternal grandfather, Jose E. Romero, became the first Ambassador to the Court of St. James. My mother lived in this area in the late 1940's and early 1950's. The negotiations of the lease took about three months, and finally, on January 6, 2016, I was handed the keys.

The other critical factor was finding a Filipino Head Chef. Since there were no Filipino restaurants in London, we did not know where to begin. We were fortunate that a good friend, Charlene Ching, introduced us to a potential Head Chef. His name was Lorenzo Maderas. When we called Chef Lorenzo for an interview, he mentioned that his dream was to open a Filipino restaurant in the name of his father, Romulo. As luck would have it, the restaurant was to be called Romulo Café. Lorenzo flew to the Philippines for about two months to train in my sister's kitchen and learn the family recipes plus do a bit of touring with his family before the restaurant opened. I joined him in Manila and on my last night, he was tasked to cook a full meal for my family. I could see he was quite nervous, as my family is not easy to please. The dinner turned out to be a success, and I will never forget his rendition of pork adobo. He served it with sweet potato mash and glazed baby shallots. It was delicious! And today, this is one of our signature dishes in the restaurant.

In addition, to help in finding our Head Chef, Charlene introduced us to a Filipina interior decorator, Karen Soriano-Hristov. She transformed the elegant Georgian townhouse into a comfortable Filipino home. Her inspiration was my grandfather himself, Carlos P. Romulo, and what she imagined about his residence if had he lived in Kensington. The outcome was an appealing space that bridges Filipino culture with the locality, revealing a rich sense of personal and family history.

There were lots of hurdles to overcome with regard to the opening of the restaurant but I would say that the most difficult part was the renovation of the site and getting the restaurant ready for the soft opening on March 14, 2016. We had a very tight deadline of only weeks to get everything done because my family had already bought their tickets to London. At first, it was not easy to find a construction company that would take on the job given the timeline we outlined and the budget we set forth. There was so much work to do and so many moving parts. We ran into a lot of unexpected problems and there was a point when I did not think we would ever get it done! I still remember two specific incidences that almost gave me a heart attack! One was on the delivery of Carrara marble tops for the tables. I was not at the restaurant when the foreman accepted the delivery of the table tops. When I arrived at the restaurant that morning, I noticed that they were stacked one on top of the other in two big piles. Apparently, the driver specifically said not to stack them up and true enough, five of the marble table tops cracked because of the weight of the pile. The company told us that it would take 4-6 weeks to replace the cracked ones since they were coming from Italy but that they had white marble tops in their storeroom if we were willing to replace some of the black tops with white tops. There was not much choice and Karen was able to change the table seating plans so that the mix of white and black tables seemed to have been done on purpose. The second incident involved a custom-made private bar that was to be installed in the basement of the restaurant. A private dining area was to have its own private bar to resemble either a library or the den of a house. The builders did not consider that the doors were not very wide, the stairs to the basement was quite narrow, and the ceiling not very high. They delivered the bar in one single piece and it was impossible to get this into the basement. The only solution was to cut the it in half, bring the parts down, and re-assemble the bar without making it appear that it was actually two pieces instead of one. One of the builders finally agreed to do the job after a few days of consideration. We managed to have this beautiful bar in what we now call our CPR Library without anyone even noticing that it had been cut into pieces. In the end, everyone really pulled together to make the opening a reality!

Transferring My Banking Skills to Being a Restaurateur

It has been two years since the restaurant opened and I embarked on my new and exciting adventure as a restaurateur. At first, it was not a smooth transition, especially since I was used to a much more structured routine at the bank. Now I was outside my comfort zone. There were so many things that I felt I needed to learn about the business and at times this seemed daunting. But at the same time, the training, skill-set, and disciplines I had acquired during my banking career helped me manage the day-to-day operations of the restaurant. Having a financial background allowed me to manage the bookkeeping, accounts, and profit and loss of the company with ease. Having run a global business previously, I had experience in start-up projects, people management, and product development; all skills that I have been able to apply in the restaurant.

The restaurant business is tough and competitive. It requires long, long hours of sacrifice and personal time. Judging from my sister Sandie and brother-in-law Enzo's experience, I knew it would not be a walk in the park. Donnie Madia, one of Chicago's restaurateurs, once said: "As much as people would like to think that the restaurant industry is glamorous, it is more than anything a hardworking business. Beyond providing great food, wine, and service; your job is to make someone you don't even know happy!"

Opening Romulo Café was never about getting recognition but rather, the creation of a family restaurant and dining experience that could hold its own and compete in London, a gastronomic capital. It was also meant to be, in its own small way, a showcase for the Philippines, our food, history, culture, and people.

Until recently, it is fair to say that Filipino cuisine did not have much of a distinctive profile in London. In fact, one of our major challenges was working to familiarize food lovers and restaurant goers in London with Filipino food. Filipino food has been the quiet man (or woman) of gastronomy for the longest time. And yet in terms of tastes, flavors, and variety, it has so much to offer. We addressed this by trying to explain the food on our menus as simply and distinctly as possible. We did not hesitate to promote, via social media and other media channels including exhibitions and food festivals, that we existed as purveyors of 'a taste of the Philippines in the heart of Kensington.' What has been important is plating and presentation: we wanted to show off our dishes in ways that can be appreciated by sophisticated British and international foodies, and that instills a sense of pride in Filipinos. We have been determined to raise the bar regarding how Filipino food is presented in a good restaurant environment.

Another major challenge is competing in a crowded culinary marketplace. According to TripAdvisor, there are over 24,000 restaurants in London. We had to make sure our dishes taste good as well as look good because people dining in our area expect a certain standard. We have had to cater to the schedule of diners since eating out is no longer a treat for many in London; it is part of their lifestyle.

We have to make sure we are competitive with establishments in our style and price bracket. In just under two years, we won the Time Out 'Most Loved Restaurant in Kensington' in 2016, received a 5-star and top ratings from trendsetting lifestyle/food bibles like Time Out and Square Meal, and were included in Harden's and the

Tatler Restaurant Guide (the A-list of top restaurants in London and the UK). This recognition has helped us enormously. In fact, in 2018, we learned we'd won the Time Out 'Most Loved Local Restaurant in Kensington' as well as two other distinctions: Most Loved Local Coffee Place, and Most Loved Local Brunch Place in Kensington. To top it all, we were second Most Loved Local Restaurant in all of London!

Another task we have had to face was convincing Filipinos that we could offer a viable alternative to Filipino home-cooking or Mama's cooking. We never claimed that our food was the definitive Filipino dish; rather, that it is the family rendition of Filipino favorites or our Chef's innovative twist. I am pleased that we have also been able to convince a number of people that fine wine goes well with fine Filipino food. Our Philippine-inspired cocktails have also been popular, particularly one called Imelda's High heels, where the cocktail is sipped from a shoe.

My key takeaways from starting this venture are that you have to build a team that shares your commitment, energy, and passion for delivering first class service every day. Every day is a new day. I try to be at the restaurant every day, and I do my part because I find it is important to set an example for the team. I usually handle reservations and welcome guests, manage the Bar area, take orders, and walk the floor to make sure the guests are enjoying their dining experience. I know that I cannot do it alone and this is why I need a team that shares my passion.

The customer is always Queen! We listen and respond to our customer's feedback. I recognize that no matter how hard my team tries, we cannot please everyone all of the time! I personally respond to every review on Trip Advisor, Facebook, and other social media. Every negative review means failure to deliver a first-class dining experience. I take comments personally since it is our family name on the door. I use the feedback to help us improve and do better.

We know that innovation is key to our survival. We work to keep abreast of the latest trends in order to remain relevant in the industry.

If there is a valuable lesson that I have learned from this new experience, it is that at times, we need to take a risk, have the courage to venture into something new, and get out of our comfort zone. We are never too old nor is it ever too late to start over. I found a new passion as a Bartender. I learned how to make cocktails. I never realized that making coffee was an art and I am still perfecting my lattes and cappuccinos. I recently passed an exam to obtain my personal license to sell alcohol on the premises and took a Level 1 course in wines to gain the basic skills to describe wine accurately and make food and wine pairings. Knowledge is power.

People always ask me if I would ever go back to banking or if I miss that world. Honestly, the answer would have to be NO. This is my life now. I am not one who likes to live with regrets. Yes, I have made mistakes. I could have made better decisions, but I just treat this as part of the circle of life. I believe that everything that happens to us, happens for a reason. I move on, try to do better, and hopefully learn from my mistakes. And definitely, whatever mistakes or failures I had done in the past have made me a stronger person.

I would never have gotten this far without the support of my family, my cousins, friends, my daughter Giulia, and most especially my partner Chris. They believed in me and encouraged me to pursue this new adventure. My journey continues as we enter into our third year of operation. Numerous challenges await, but I am enthusiastic about some of the new things my team and I have in store for the year.

As I finish writing my chapter, my daughter Giulia is starting her own career. I hope that my story will inspire you to dream and to work hard to pursue those dreams. Dreams can and do come true. Nothing is impossible; the impossible only takes time.

NIKKI TANG

*CEO AND CHIEF BEAUTYPRENEUR DMARK BEAUTY
AND DERMASIA CORPORATION, PHILIPPINES
GLOBAL FWN100™ 2017*

No Way to Go but Up

Many people believe that a CEO must be flawless. That a person who is leading a big company must be perfect to a tee. I am here to say that business leaders face the same adversities and struggles as other people do. After all, we are all human and prone to the same vulnerabilities.

But it is not the failures that we should fear; it is not our mistakes or our missteps. We always tiptoe around these things as if they could push us off course, and it is true, they can. Inevitably, the lessons we learn from our mistakes push us to soar higher.

I have been a CEO for most of my life, but the road was not always perfect.

MY EARLY INFLUENCES

I grew up in a conservative Filipino-Chinese family, and I am the eldest of six children. Being the oldest, I always felt pressure to live up to my parents' expectations. We grew up in Chinatown in, one of the oldest and busiest Chinatowns in the world. It was the center of trade and commerce in Manila so even as a kid I had exposure to the front-end and back-end of the business world. I would work at our family's hardware shop in Binondo where we socialized during our school breaks and on the weekends. I was taught how to maintain the stocks and the inventory. I would wake up early to work at the store instead of hanging around watching TV like the other kids. At a very young age, my parents instilled in me the value of discipline and hard work, making me understand that it is not easy to run a business, and harder to ensure that the business earns money.

Strong Women Role Models

Firm and resolute female personalities raised me. My grandmother and my mother are very typical Asian women and very strong-willed. They also happen to be my greatest mentors. Each of them was able to balance the life of a mother, while also managing her business. Until today, they are still working and working.

The Value of Internships

In college, I finished a degree in Manufacturing Engineering and Management at De La Salle University in Manila. There, I learned how to be highly analytical, and to see problems as opportunities in disguise. I took an internship at a global beauty company that exposed me to the manufacturing side of the business. During that year, I was able to move around the different departments from quality control to production to systems. I was able to experience and understand that you have to have a system perspective and make sure that everything is in order, starting with production until the product goes to market.

Following My Entrepreneurial Spirit

After graduation, inspired by my family's entrepreneurial spirit, it was natural for me to start my own venture. In the 1990's, I started going into the dental care business; selling oral care to clinics and dentists. This was not easy and meant two years of struggle.

And then one day, while on a business trip abroad, a top dermatologist told my mom about a breakthrough anti-aging product. My mom helped sparked my interest and journey into the business that I do now.

When she told me about it, my first thought was excitement, and it dawned on me that this might be a better business opportunity than oral care. I knew that there was a need for anti-aging products. I realized that every woman in the Philippines would most likely want to know about this beauty secret. Every woman wants to feel beautiful, and if every Filipina could get her hands on this product, there would be a demand for it. Thus, the idea of engagement in the dermocosmetic market segment was born.

It hit me: there was room to disrupt the beauty industry. The prospect of breaking new ground challenged me. I felt that my mission was to make all Filipina women feel beautiful, confident, and empowered; similar to the feelings that made me feel good when I was "all dolled up."

A Significant Turning Point in My Life

My entire world crashed when my husband of ten years, who had been my first and only boyfriend, left me when my sons were just one and two years old. After having been in a relationship with him for so long, I was suddenly left behind to fend for myself as a single mom. Coming from a typical Chinese upbringing, I was afraid that I had let many people down because I failed to meet their expectations for me as a woman, as a mother, and as a wife. I knew I was expected to build a happy home and maintain it forever. I never knew there were so many words to express grief.

I felt abandoned.

I was a failure.

It was difficult dealing with the loss.

It broke my heart.

It shattered me.

I had two wonderful boys who needed me to care for them. I remember waking up and just wanting to stay in bed the whole day. I would cry. It was hard to get through the days, especially at a time when I was an aspiring entrepreneur. I needed to work, work, work!

I decided that I needed to break the cycle of despair. I needed a change in mindset. I told myself, "Everything is a choice." I talked myself out of my grief: "Do you want to be miserable forever, or do you want to pick yourself up and go back to doing something for yourself and your two boys?"

Rising from My Grief

Slowly, little by little, the process of healing began. I traveled, I went out with my friends, and I was able to spend more time with my kids. I found these things therapeutic. I finally had time to search for myself, meet new people, and allow myself to grow. My two boys became the source of my strength. Just by being there, they reminded me of what was most precious to me. They made me realize that I needed to move on.

I became even stronger because of the betrayal of a loved one. I pushed all the negative thoughts aside and redirected all my energy into building the business that

I envisioned. It was then that I decided to leave the dental industry behind and move forward with dermatological products and equipment.

Entering the beauty industry was a very different industry to tap, I was a newbie in an already thriving dermatology industry. I worked with just one assistant, and I was disrupting the existing behavior of dermatologists at that time. Skin doctors were already formulating their own products. I was approaching doctors and asking them to replace their prescriptions with the dermocosmetics I was offering. I was essentially their competitor, trying to sell them competing products by claiming that mine was better. It was a major challenge asking my potential clients to significantly shift from what they were used to, and what they knew. I had to get them to trust me, even if I was unknown and was perceived as just a girl playing in the so-called "big boys club."

As I was about to launch my first line of products, my staff suddenly resigned. I was left alone again, to ensure a successful launch by myself. I had to do almost everything on my own. I was determined, and I believed in my work. I found that I had grit and resilience and felt fiery, feisty, and strong. I believed that my products were outstanding and I had confidence that women would like them. They were the top-of-the-line products from world-renowned beauty brands. I had tested the products myself. I had faith in my marketing ability. I let go of my fears and built relationships with doctors one by one. I assembled a small team of sales representatives, and we showed up at major events. We did our homework We were innovative.

I became a catalyst in the dermatology industry by making doctors switch to my scientifically-tested products. My first product Neostrata was top-rated among the doctors and their women patients. It became popular because it was one of the first laboratory tested and FDA-approved anti-aging products in the market. It was a game-changing product for the entire beauty industry. I am glad that I took that leap of faith.

A Leap of Faith

Taking a chance led me to where I am today, the CEO of DMark Group of Companies, composed of DMark Beauty and DermAsia Corporations. I identify myself as a beautypreneur: an entrepreneur in the industry of beauty products and sciences that is always on the lookout for the latest innovations. As a beautypreneur, I focus not just on the business of aesthetics, but also on the business of empowerment. Women empowerment is one of my personal advocacies. I like to think that the beauty business is also a form of empowerment for women. By providing innovations, solutions, and technology that can enhance the beauty of women, women become less afraid and less self-conscious about themselves. They gain confidence. I have found that women tend to be their harshest critics, and sometimes a little help on the beauty-side goes a long way toward boosting self-confidence. As I have learned for myself, self-confidence is an essential tool in recognizing our worth as women and charting where we want to be in our life.

I see this as my calling as I deal with the challenges of being a woman. Today, DMark Beauty and DermAsia are considered as trusted sources of anti-aging skin care and minimally invasive skin rejuvenation treatments.

After the success of Neostrata, I followed my intuition. Intuition is a reaction to something your body is telling you. You must listen to it. So, when it comes to choosing products to bring to market, you need to rely on faith sometimes informed by research and sometimes by sheer instinct. That is why it is important to know what the market needs are, to understand what the trends are, and to keep up to date. It also helps to have a good network.

Hard Work, Good Communications, and Empathy

What I learned from my experience and from other people as well, is that being a good leader requires hard work and that communication is key to building work relationships. Communication skills are especially critical when one needs to impart his or her message, goals, and vision to other people you are about to work with internal and external to the company. If you are unable to communicate what the goal is, then it will leave people lost. I also learned that empathy is key to motivation that being a great leader means that you cannot do everything alone and that motivating people requires understanding their starting point and listening to them.

Open to Learning, Innovation, Adapting to Change, and Being Honest

I learned that leadership requires being open to constant learning, keeping abreast of innovation, and being able to adapt to change. In addition to this, leadership requires being honest with yourself.

All of my successes, I owe in part to my mother and my grandmother. Being around them and listening to them has provided me with much-needed guidance. They have incredible wisdom, and although they are quite traditional in their approach to life and business, they are also open to the modern world and the changes that come with it.

Why Beauty Matters

Some people think that beauty is superficial. In the past, beauty products were pitched to beautify a woman. But for me, beauty is more than "skin-deep." As I have indicated earlier, feeling beautiful helps to put our best face forward and adds to our self-confidence. The inward effects of beauty are just as incredible as its outward effects. An economist, Daniel Hamermesh, author of *Beauty Pays: Why Attractive People are More Successful* (2011), who examined data from several countries and cultures, found that beauty is absolutely connected with financial success. Dale Archer indicated in the *Psychology of Beauty* (2012):

> Beauty is an asset, just like physical prowess, charisma, brains or emotional intelligence. The key with any gift is in the way that you use it. It doesn't define you as a person. Rather, it's an asset to be used judiciously and with an understanding of how it is just a small part of who you are. Those that get this will do well; others that don't, not so much. Everybody has insecurities. We cannot really fully comprehend every person's burdens.

But what we can see is how beauty can change lives for the better. We need to see past the surface of the effects of beauty, to really see the potential power of women. DMark Beauty and Dermasia support the beauty and healthcare business, and this involves working with doctors, pharmacies, wellness centers, and customers to provide dermocosmetics and aesthetic devices that can improve the lives of people. If we could understand this, if we could all see beyond just the surface of beauty, then we could break down all these misconceptions about the effects of beauty.

Woman on Top

Over time, I became aware that to be an extraordinary leader, one has to plan, be organized, be focused, and to have grit. In my leadership journey, I have had to deal with the consequences of my decisions. Some decisions I made in the past led to failures, and these were often due to lack of relevant and timely information. I learned from my mistakes, pivoted, and made changes to establish strategies, processes, and controls for the success of my businesses. I have demonstrated perseverance and passion for long-term goals. I assume that every loss or failure is working toward a larger goal and that every setback is a learning experience.

I believe that a person's success means nothing if he or she does not advocate for things worth fighting for. And when you have something that is worth fighting for, and you are willing to do anything to fight for it; this is where grit comes from. You learn about grit by holding on, especially when you feel like giving up. Grit is that last sliver of strength inside you that keeps you from yielding, that keeps you fighting, and that keeps you going. Grit is the immense determination and perseverance to accomplish our goals and the passion for reaching for the stars despite the obstacles. I believe that grit lives inside each and every one of us, but unleashes itself in different ways, when we allow it to.

Principles I Live By

Through the years, I have developed a set of principles that I never forget and that I know are necessary for my business to survive and thrive.

- **Embrace Innovation.** Research and development should never stop. Just as in life, we must keep learning. Do not be afraid of innovation. Do not be afraid of change.

- **Be resourceful.** Think about strategies that allow the company to benefit in extravagant ways. I personally travel a few times a year outside the country to attend trade and business conferences in order to find new clinically proven products and machines to add to our offerings and make accessible for Filipinos.

- **Remain passionate.** Keep this passion burning within you. It will be the primary motivator of your work when things become difficult. Through the years, I have heard life-changing stories from my clients, and their stories drive me to continue to do the work that I do. I wake up every day with beauty in my mind. Seeing how it affects people's lives pushes me to go further even during the difficult times.

- **Personify the Effects.** When you are selling a product, it is not enough to talk about the product. You have to show people their magic. Use it and show them the results. I have personally tried the products we carry at DMark Beauty and Dermasia, and that is why I know they are effective. This is one of the reasons why our loyal customers trust us with their beauty needs.

- **Work with a Heart.** We believe that skin and aesthetics concerns are not shallow problems. Bringing beauty solutions to people means helping them regain their self-confidence and improve their quality of life.

I Am Reborn

Building two companies from scratch was not an easy task, nor did it happen overnight. It meant spending hours inventing and formulating products and testing devices that are safe and effective. It means convincing doctors to endorse these products and devices based on the experience of their patients.

My role as a chief executive in my companies, plus all the leadership roles that I have played in this industry, and in the charitable organizations I support, has allowed me to reflect on the positive impact I have made to empower women and to resolve to reach more women.

Preconceived notions that a specific gender must lead a particular business needs to be torn down. One of the hallmarks of a great leader is somebody who can lead with clarity in times of uncertainty. A ship needs a captain who can sail not only in the right conditions but also during the stormy conditions because it is only in times of adversity that one's mettle is truly tested. My people are always looking to me for guidance, and I make sure I am able to lead with a clear vision especially during tough times. This allows us to avoid hitting a plateau or start going backward. I also believe that especially when an idea is daring, bold, and game-changing, then things do indeed become harder, more complicated, and more difficult. But this builds a tenacity within us that makes for better leadership.

The most important thing that my mom taught me was always to have a vision. You must not walk blindly or aimlessly, and you should always find things that will challenge you and push you to be a better person. This can only be achieved when you have a vision. It is important to have a vision and to know where you want life to take you; but even more important is to do all the work that is required to make that vision come to life. No one else is going to make it happen for you. Only you can make it happen for yourself.

I recall my 20-year-old self when I talk about rising to almost the top of my game. The society so burdened the younger Nikki: pressured as the oldest daughter to pursue a business, as my parents had; pressured to maintain a picture-perfect marriage; and pressured to balance all of that with being the best mother and having the perfect family.

But through the years, and especially, through the hardships, I learned that the most important things and the most beautiful things happen when you have to fight for them. You do not need to have everything figured out down to the last detail when you are young, but you must at least have a plan and a direction. For me, the hardships awakened the pursuit of success and developed the grit to push harder in my career. Thanks to my Catholic foundation, I rose from the proverbial ashes and found myself on higher ground, soaring to my full capabilities. When you have a vision and you have a direction, and you are full of grit and passion, wonderful things happen. You know there is little that can stop you.

If I could go back and talk to my younger self, I would tell her to explore more and to see everything that life has to offer. I would say to her to always be open to new experiences and possibilities. I would remind her to try not to be overcome by fear or uncertainties. I would tell her to take care not only of her physical sustenance but also to care of her mental health. I would remind her that being happy and content with your life radiates externally, so staying positive amidst hardships and trials is a must.

Raising my children is also one of my most precious achievements. I am so proud to say that I have raised God-fearing, smart, and kindhearted boys. Our relationship is unique in that they have become a source of energy, wisdom, and motivation for me. They remind me to embrace challenges and turn them into opportunities. They are my treasures, my workforce, and my rock. They complete me by filling the void inside me. They continue to make me smile and fulfill me. They give life and the business more meaning because I am reminded that I am working here for something that is much bigger than just myself. I am now working not only for Nikki, but for my boys as well.

As I reflect on the work that I have done, I am happy to know that I made my mark and had created my legacy. I want to continue to revolutionize the beauty industry through constant innovation, research, and providing state-of-the-art technology and products that radiate health and beauty.

To be a real game changer, to be able to contribute something that people will remember, one needs to take risks. One needs to make small and massive steps, be open to the road bumps and be willing to fall down and get hurt sometimes. And this takes courage. It takes a certain chutzpah to be successful. There needs to be room for error, and even more room for rising from errors.

That is why a great leader is not someone who has the least mistakes but someone who, despite their setbacks, has moved upward and onward.

※

Being First and Foremost

CYNTHIA BARKER

Elected Councillor in the UK
GLOBAL FWN100™ 2017

Building My Political Backbone

'Sadness, Sacrifice, Success.' This was the headline in the *Philippine Panorama* (28 June 2015) for my story as the child of an Overseas Filipino Worker (OFW). This cycle of sadness, sacrifice, and success is familiar to many leaders and is especially applicable to those OFWs who have had to leave their country in order to provide for their family left behind. My mother who was an OFW from 1972 sacrificed to give me everything.

As I recall the struggles that have led to this point in my life, some clear patterns or themes have contributed to the building of my backbone, of my inner resilience. These include moving to the West with my Philippine cultural heritage, starting businesses in a different cultural environment, and being undermined by men. The most significant fight has been my battle as a woman in a leadership position and the opposition of powerful men. I have always been a very private person, and I have chosen to suffer in private. Few people know the hardships I have faced or the struggles I have endured even after entering the public arena as a politician. But I choose to be private because I refuse to speak power to the people that have tried to break my spirit.

Here are a few stories from my past that have contributed to my becoming the leader I am today. I hope I can connect with you the reader and inspire you to rise as a global Filipina.

Provincial Girl Moves to the Big City

In the nineteen seventies, I left the province to attend university in Manila. Attending university in the city was a pivotal moment in my life, one which shaped my progression from naïve provincial girl to ambitious urbanite. When my mother left us to work abroad, my four siblings and I had to assume a large amount of responsibility even though we were young. As the third eldest child and the eldest girl, some of the traditional roles of a Filipina mother fell on me. We held each other accountable for our actions. We learned how to be independent, how to maintain our household, how to manage our budget, and how to make major decisions for ourselves. We felt the physical absence of our mother, but she always made sure to send letters and gifts, which we eagerly awaited every month. Even though we had significant responsibilities, we had a simple and wonderful childhood in the province, filled with good memories and laughter.

During my teen years, however, I began wanting to leave the province and to move to the capital, so I could fulfill my dream of becoming an accountant. Because of my good grades at school, I was offered a government scholarship. But the scholarship was only for agricultural or engineering programs. This was my first real sacrifice. For the sake of a brighter future, I abandoned my dream of studying accounting and chose to study engineering at Adamson University on a scholarship.

Manila gave me my first real taste of adventure. The journey to the university, with the big city unfolding around me, thrilled me with a spine-tingling sense of possibility. Years later, arriving at London Heathrow airport, I would experience this same feeling. Coming from the province, I was innocent and naïve, about life in the city. I was lucky to have wonderful people in my boarding house. Our room had four bunk beds, with two people per bunk bed. Back in the province, my siblings and I used to share one big room, and we would sleep on the floor. It was not the way to sleep in beds. On that first night, I rolled out my mat on the floor. My roommates told me, "Cynthia, you don't have to sleep on the floor. Get on the bed!"

Thinking about that now, I chuckle at how naïve I was. I had been so sheltered that I did not know what to expect. Simple things like that marked my journey from being a rural girl to becoming a city girl. My female roommates looked after me, mentored me, and set the foundations for me to learn to become an assertive and independent woman. I am still in touch with those women. They were wonderful influences, and I am grateful to have known them.

A Quiet Kind of Power: Developing My Own Leadership Style

I aspire to the type of leadership described by Rachael Chong, Founder of Catchafire. "I believe in a quiet, strong and grounded leadership. I think some of the best leaders are those whose work is widely known and respected but who, themselves, are relatively unknown."

My leadership style is simple. I like to observe quietly, once I understand the operations of an organization or community, I then start to question and improve it. I also treat my teams as friends and family. Strong family values were instilled in me from birth and evolved throughout my childhood. My siblings and I relied on each other. I grew up caring for my younger siblings like I was a mother, because our mother, as I have noted earlier was overseas in England and working three jobs so that we could have good lives in the Philippines. My mother's sacrifice was in our bones that helped us support each other. If one of us was struggling, we all felt the struggle. If one of us was successful, we all felt successful.

Bayanihan

I had learned about *bayanihan* in the province. *Bayanihan* refers to the spirit of communal cooperation to achieve a shared objective. *Bayanihan* underpinned my first negotiation at university, where I sacrificed my grades to help a friend succeed. Studying engineering meant that my classes were male-dominated. My classmates in the program were sixteen men and four women. We became friends. It was examination time, and one of our male classmates was failing math. I excelled in mathematics. We loved our classmate dearly and did not want him to fail. His shame would be ours. So, I took the initiative to negotiate a deal with our professor. I asked our professor if I could donate some of my good grades to my classmate. It was a very unorthodox proposal, and definitely not the norm, but surprisingly, the professor agreed. I think the professor admired my boldness, and my wish for my classmate to pass. The final examination arrived. I had a very high grade, and my classmate had a low grade, but the professor gave him a passing mark and lowered my grade. My friend was able to graduate and go on to have a productive career. In this case, having the confidence to ask led to a change that made a difference.

Transformational Leadership

After graduating from university, I worked in Manila for several years as a production supervisor. This is when I began to develop my specific style of leadership, and when I grew passionate about enabling change in the workplace. I was hired by a factory that produced undergarments for export. The factory workers had been there for decades and were used to the structures. I had ideas and wanted to introduce change. From my first day, I realized that proposed changes were not going to be easy. Everyone was resistant, especially the senior ladies who had been there for decades. They questioned why I, an inexperienced young woman, was proposing changes in the way they operated.

Over time, I learned how to use a more transformational type of leadership based on engaging everyone. Emotional intelligence was needed to engage the existing team. I responded to their concerns with sensitivity and diplomacy, meanwhile observing what they did on a daily basis, and making notes on ways that operations could be improved. I started to implement time-studies. Based on the results of these studies, I concluded that if the workers were able to produce X number of undergarments a day, then we could be achieving X number of sales per month. Eventually, we were able to set and exceed these targets and streamline the production process.

Based on my experience, I concluded that when leading, you must bring your team with you. You navigate hardships and lead yourself, your work, and everyone else. The value of bringing your whole team with you, I continue to practice as part of my leadership today. When it comes to leadership, you have to rise above petty things and get the best deal for everyone.

I have volunteered to help various groups in the UK, including the Elstree and Borehamwood Museum, National Society for the Prevention of Cruelty to Children, the Sixty Plus Club, the Filipino Women's Association UK, and the Rotary Club. I have made it my goal to help with diplomacy and sensitivity. I am always conscious of first impressions and ensure that I present a relaxed and approachable demeanor.

Working in politics is even more challenging because there are more engagements with diverse people. I learned to be a non-linear leader: I engage upwards, downwards, sideways, and even backwards! Relationships between people and organizations can affect every move in politics. Yet one poor word choice or misconstrued sentence can ripple out and cause a chain-reaction. In politics, I have learned that if my personal beliefs and opinions are no longer the same as the group I represent, then it is time to step down. Integrity is critical in leadership. Strong leaders are not afraid to step down, to admit fault, or to enact change.

Whenever I am asked to consult with an existing organization, I am always highly sensitive and compassionate towards other team members. My leadership advice is: Before you can change something, you have to understand it. There is a need always to spend time getting to know the lay of the land and existing practices before proposing new rules or experimenting with new processes.

A Whole New World: Confronting Cultural Baggage

My personal life and professional career in the UK have taught me these things about my ethnicity and culture:

1. My cultural roots and background instilled in me a desire to achieve great things.

2. My race and physical appearance determine how people perceive me.

3. As a Filipino, I have carried, and continue to carry, cultural baggage, some of the results of colonization.

If I had never moved to the UK, I would not be who I am today. The move marked the beginning of my rise to where I am now. I still feel excited about the UK, and I will always view it fondly. Creating a new life in England was one of the greatest adventures I have ever taken. In the early nineteen-eighties, I got off the plane at London Heathrow airport full of dreams and excited to be with my mother again. I was ready for adventure. It was wintertime, and one of my very first memories was seeing crowds of tall, mysterious Englishmen walking around in their dark coats. To me, they were the epitome of western civilization. I immediately thought: "I want to be here. I want to stay here."

Fresh from the Philippines, where America was idolized, and white skin was revered, it felt amazing to be in the West. Everything seemed so clean. Everything seemed so modern. Everyone spoke English. It was a different world. From day one, it was love at first sight. I knew that unknown opportunities were waiting for me.

The main reason I had moved to the UK was for my mother. Falling in love with the country was a happy coincidence. Everyone I spoke to appeared civilized and respectful. They queued up, they were helpful and charitable, and there was an unspoken semblance of order. I suppose I was suffering from a dose of colonial mentality. I saw those in the West as superior and viewed myself and my cultural background as inferior. I was carrying cultural baggage, a symptom of the colonized.

I have spent my career working to undo that colonized mentality. My cultural background is both my greatest weakness and my greatest strength. I adore the Philippines and the community I come from. Repeatedly, I have been professionally victimized in the UK because of my cultural background. My cultural background also provided an opening for my fellow kababayans [countrymen] to take advantage of me.

When I first began making presentations around the UK, I could feel tension in the room. I realized that the typical white British customers were suspicious of me. Often I would get the sense that they were wary of my 'foreignness.' As soon as I brought in a white British male to assist me with marketing, he was closing orders within minutes of arriving. He was trusted, I was not. It was a matter of race. I have never harbored any resentment about this xenophobia because I considered it part of human nature to distrust someone unfamiliar. If anything, it made me work harder, and I learned how to present myself effectively so that people would trust me.

I still encounter some racism, although in more subtle ways. Race relations in the UK still have a long way to go. Prejudice and ignorance exist throughout daily life. When Muslim-born Sadiq Khan became Mayor of London, it was a milestone for ethnic minorities in politics. As change is brought about, I continue to receive genuine interest and warmth from organizations and political leaders who want to create a team that is diverse, fair, and reflective of British society. It is rewarding to know that I am an integral part of these changes.

Riding the Business Rollercoaster

I especially appreciate the statement of Arianna Huffington, Co-founder/Editor, Huffington Post that "We need to accept that we don't always make the right decisions, that we'll screw up royally sometimes – understanding that failure is not the opposite of success, it's part of success."

I have always been very career-driven. After getting married to Dave in the UK and giving birth to my beautiful daughter, Christine, I decided to become self-employed and run a small business. I first became a travel agent. My brother, Gene, taught me how to become a sub-agent and I was able to work from home. I felt cooped up in the house and wanted to go out. In the evening, just to get out of the house, I would start physically delivering the tickets to whoever had purchased them. Driving long distances and using petrol, I lost most of my markup. That was my first try at business. After a while, I started selling vacuum cleaners door to door with my daughter Christine in tow. I demonstrated the vacuum cleaner and sometimes, halfway through a cleaning demonstration, I had to excuse myself to change Christine's nappy before continuing with the demonstration. Earning a living was tough. I was enjoying myself. That is why I found my life in the UK to be one big adventure.

Spotting a New Business Opportunity

The vacuum cleaner business was not very lucrative, but one evening in the late nineteen nineties, I spotted an opportunity. There was a news segment on TV about a nursing shortage in the UK. I immediately remembered that we had a surplus of nurses in the Philippines. Excitedly, I called some recruitment agents and arranged a meeting. And then, at the very last minute, they called to cancel. They had already found agencies in the Philippines to work with. I felt devastated; my idea had been crushed within a single day. But then, I thought to myself: "Why not just start my own agency?"

I told my friend who owned a business center about my idea of starting an employment agency for expatriate nurses. Because of my lack of business experience, my friend said he would help. He offered me a corner table in his office and agreed to chaperone me to meetings outside the office. He set up our company legally and told me that we would split everything 50/50. In the next few weeks, I booked dozens of appointments. My friend could not accompany me everytime but I kept on going. This was twenty years ago, so business relationships were very different, and so was I. British employers only wanted to deal with British individuals and not with a foreign woman. I would initiate meetings, but, as mentioned previously, I could not close the deals.

I told another friend about my sales woes, and he referred me to a mutual friend, Charles, an English businessman who had a similar idea about creating a nursing recruitment agency. Charles could not commit to the business full time but wanted to give it a try. My first friend put Charles on the phone, and he immediately started closing deals. We booked so many appointments, and we went together to Moorfields Eye Hospital in Old Street. Within half an hour, he had all the agreements signed and the order forms completed. He closed very quickly in comparison to the long time it took me to present and close. After we left the hospital, I started whooping in excitement. Charles, always calm and collected, simply said, "Please stop screaming!"

Our business soon started expanding because we had so many requests for nurses from abroad. We employed another staff member. After a month, we told my first friend what was happening. He was very happy for us and offered to sell Charles his shares. They set up a private transaction between themselves. After that meeting, Charles announced that he owned the entire company; one hundred percent of the shares. I protested that fifty percent was supposed to be mine! Charles told me. "He didn't give you anything. He invested in the business, and you were the one making it successful." I was in shock, but Charles made sure I was given my rightful half of the company. Charles was fair to me, and soon he became my full-time business partner. We have worked together for over twenty years now, and we have split everything 50/50. That experience taught me the need to ensure that nobody experiences what I experienced and that everyone receives what is fairly owed to them.

When They Try to Undermine You

I agree with G.D. Anderson's statement about feminism. "Feminism is not about making women stronger. Women are already strong. It's about changing the way the world perceives that strength."

I have found myself in situations where men have attempted to undermine, control, or con me. These men took advantage of my kindness, business inexperience, and at that time, submissiveness. They charmed me and told me that they could move the earth. Even though my instincts told me something was wrong, it was tough to say no, especially if they were a fellow Filipino. Only after I began to focus on developing my leadership abilities, did I realize that these incidents taught me valuable lessons about how to conduct myself and who I should work with.

Setback Number 1: Beware of Charming Kababayans

The very first time I was hustled in business was by a man whom I will call Jose. This was before I started the nurse recruitment agency and I was working from home. Jose was very charming and confident and assured me that he could bring Filipino stars to the UK. I hired a small office and set him up because I believed in his vision and wanted to help him. Suddenly, all the money I had invested was disappearing. I was receiving telephone bills that were costing over £800 per month which, in the nineteen-nineties, was a lot of money. I asked Jose why the phone service was so expensive, and he said it was because he had to phone the Philippines. Later that week, I spotted an itemized telephone bill in his office. I scanned the numbers; they were all premium and pay-per-minute phone numbers charged to gay sex chat hotlines! Every night, Jose would call them and speak for hours. That caused me thousands of pounds, but the moral outrage was that he was married. I confronted Jose, and he got angry and aggressive. Then, he begged me not to tell his wife. I told his wife, but she did not believe me. She was an older woman, wholly charmed by him. He was a total bully.

Setback Number 2: Beware of Religious Hypocrites

Fast forward several years later, when our nurse recruitment agency was doing well. We needed to hire an extra marketing consultant. A friend referred his religious uncle whom I will call Mike and who was retired but still worked. She vouched for him, and I trusted her opinion. For three months, Mike was getting orders in from everywhere, but suddenly things slowed. The diary was full, and the company credit card we provided Mike for expenses was maxed out. I was so busy with administration and orders that I was not watching the money. Charles was suspicious and did an audit to check the sales. He saw that the diary was full, but there was no money coming in. We asked Mike to come immediately to the office. His response was, "I'm at Westminster Cathedral, praying." Charles decided to open Mike's briefcase that was company property. We found dozens of signed contracts and cheques made out to an unknown company! We realized that we were losing all our orders to someone else.

Setback Number 3: Beware of Friends Dressed in Sheepskin

Once again, we needed a marketing consultant. I was wrapped up in administrative tasks, and Charles was unable to commit full-time to the business. My friend whom I will call Randy was working in a bar as a waiter. Randy asked if I could train him in the recruitment business. He and his girlfriend were renting a house and had been given the notice to leave. They begged to stay at my house and ended up living there for several months. Randy, meanwhile, took up the tasks that Mike had left behind. Suddenly, he was doing all the marketing like Mike, closing deals, filling up the diary with meetings and suddenly, history repeated itself. Orders dried up. Money stopped coming in. I received an unexpected phone call from an employer. She accused me of being unethical. "You deliver the nurse, then the next month, you poach the nurse and move her elsewhere." I then realized that Randy must have been 'reselling' the nurses shortly after confirming the orders. I phoned Randy immediately. I was angry. I asked him whether he could have recruited nurses from somewhere else. Randy replied that I did not own the market and that he had set up his own business. I was angry and pained by the broken trust.

Due Diligence

From then on, I have been diligent about who I work with. I always surround myself with people with strong moral character and are willing to help me grow as a businessperson. I have stopped trying to help others who I sense only want to take advantage of me. I am now selective about who I conduct business with, and I make sure that the people in my team are either experienced managers and leaders or qualified business people. This is why I enjoy politics so much, because the typical people I deal with are mature, conduct themselves well, and tend to be transparent.

Finally, Success

I regrouped and started forming a new team. We decided to employ predominantly women. With a strong and trustworthy team in place, we diversified and expanded from recruitment into training and immigration. We branched out into immigration in 2002, even publishing a book to help educate foreigners on immigrating to the UK. Then in 2007, we founded a college that trained vocational healthcare workers. We were very successful. At our peak, we were valued at £5.5 million!

I recently read Richard Branson's autobiography, *The Virgin Way: Everything I Know About Leadership*. This quote particularly resonated with me, and my leadership style:

"It's all about finding and hiring people smarter than you. Getting them to join your business. And giving them good work. Then getting out of their way. And trusting them. You have to get out of the way so YOU can focus on the bigger vision. That's important. And here's the main thing... You must make them see their work as a MISSION."

In March 2013, we sold the company. I thought I would retire because I felt that in the past 20 years, I had worked the equivalent of 40 years. However, I remained active in my local community, volunteering, and leading the Rotary Club as President. Soon I was invited to join a political party. A new chapter of my life had begun.

A Natural Progression into Politics

Bill Gindlesperger observed that "All of us are neck deep in politics every day of our lives. Politics can be a good thing when we bring people to the table to sit down, work together, compromise and get things done for the common good."

The UK is a land of equal opportunity, where there are no bars to opening a business, buying property, and even entering into politics. At the time of writing this, we have a female Prime Minister, the Home Secretary is the son of a Pakistani bus driver, and the Mayor of London is the son of a Pakistani bus conductor. We are celebrating 100 years of women having the right to vote, and the first female statue was recently unveiled in Parliament Square to commemorate the work of Millicent Fawcett. She was a suffragette without whom we would not be able to vote, let alone run for office.

What I learned as a businesswoman, pushed me into politics. Politics is one facet of my professional career. I set aside political issues when I spend time with family, or else we would never get along as a family.

When our business was at the height of its success we had money but not much time. I started volunteering for charity for a few hours each week when I was not swamped with work. Mainly, I volunteered at the Rotary Club, which invited me along because I was managing a successful local business. While volunteering with Rotary, I learned about charity and giving. Joining Rotary made me a better person, and I grew more active in volunteering my time and skills as well as some money. In 2013, I was honored when they asked me to become President of the Rotary Club of Elstree and Borehamwood. I was the second female president of the club. It is noteworthy that in the eighties, Rotary did not accept women as members. I then became well known in the local community. That was when political leaders started inviting me to get involved in local politics, specifically the Conservative Party. They said they wanted to attract more members and especially more women from a diverse background. They admitted they did not know much about that demographic but wanted to learn more. I joined the Conservatives in 2014 and started helping with campaigns and events. Then, in the General Election 2015, they asked me to stand. By that point, my outer shell had been hardened by business, and I felt that I was ready for the challenge. It was my first time to run for a public office. I made history as the first Filipina woman to be elected as a Town Councillor and as a Borough Councillor. It is one of my proudest career moments.

Micro-aggressions

Since entering politics, I have experienced a considerable amount of hostility from other women. It is often difficult to pinpoint whether their hostility is due to territorial issues, or if they are responding to the 'threat' of my non-white ethnicity. The Filipina woman is often considered passive, meek, and subservient. I am diplomatic in my approach, but I am far from meek. If I disagree, I will let my opinion be known.

Around four years ago, the CEO of a social care company tried to bully me. She was at the top of her game, and there was no need for her behavior. When I was elected as the President of Rotary Club, she set out to create a miserable environment for me. If I were leading a prayer, she would shuffle papers to distract me. If I were speaking, she would do the same. I learned how to tune her out and block her negativity. She probably hoped I would give up when she tried to gather support to campaign against me while disparaging my leadership. I was determined to complete my presidential year successfully. I have since been nominated to be president of our club for the second time.

In November 2017, I was asked in writing to lay a wreath for Remembrance Day. It was an honor. That week, I kept asking around for the wreath so that I could prepare for the ceremony. A senior community leader, who had grown accustomed to leading events in her authoritarian way, had decided to keep the wreath in the trunk of her car. When I went to speak to her, she stopped walking and firmly cried out: "I don't want you to lay the wreath!" A fellow councillor witnessed the incident, and he shouted, "Give her the wreath!" I am glad he was there to witness the moment and stepped in.

During a community meeting, I had another run-in with a member of her team. I questioned the necessity of spending taxpayer's money on souvenir merchandise that I thought were unnecessary. The moment I finished asking my question, the community leader slapped my leg and said, "Don't ask questions!" Not only did she cross a physical boundary, but she undermined my position and openly belittled me in front of the community. I held my ground.

Last year, when I tried to report a personal assault by a highly-reputed member of the community, these same women mocked me. It saddens me that some women turn against other women. I respect any woman who has the strength and bravery to come forward and speak her truth against anyone when the odds are unfairly stacked against her. Today, I find the courage to seek justice in any circumstance, especially in a political one, even when others wish me not to speak and rock the boat.

Women around the world are now being listened to more than in the past. From pay wage gaps to exploitation in all forms, we, as women, are now empowered to come forward and report these abuses. As a Filipina woman, who has suffered under a patriarchal system and understands the non-confrontational nature of the culture, I urge anyone, of any gender, who feels that they are suffering in silence to speak up and create a support system.

I am grateful to the Conservative Party for giving me, a second generation Filipino migrant, the opportunity to stand as Councillor. I am also grateful to the United Kingdom for the opportunities it affords migrants like myself and my family to prosper here. Ultimately, getting involved in politics has provided different leadership challenges. I have learned to negotiate with people from diverse backgrounds. In my position as a councillor for two areas, I am responsible for funds and spending. I engage the community, fellow councillors, council officers, and party members, to find appropriate solutions to community problems. Running for public office has opened my eyes to the various facets of humanity and society. I have never regretted my decision to join the political arena. I know that I am working to bring value and positive change to a community I care about. See Sidebar 1 for a fuller description of what a councillor in the UK does.

Drawing Strength from Struggle
What Does Not Kill You Makes You Stronger

Eleanor Roosevelt is reported to have said: "A woman is like a tea bag; you never know how strong it is until it's in hot water."

Everything has evolved from navigating most of my childhood, and then early womanhood, without my mother being physically present. The foundations of my backbone were laid when Mum left our family in San Pablo, Laguna. She sacrificed not being with her children as they were growing up so that she could give them a better life. She passed away in January 1997. Not a day goes by where I do not think about her or the sacrifices she made for all of us. I take my inner strength from her.

The cultural barriers I faced at the beginning of my leadership journey, I learned to use to my advantage. By thinking before I speak, I can act assertively in times of conflict and respond, rather than react. Emotional intelligence is crucial in leadership, too. Reading people, learning to say 'no,' and being able to work with different people at any level as if you are one of them are skills I have developed. I view everyone as an equal partner.

I am now at a stage in my life where everything seems woven together. Having been a punching bag so often, there is nothing I feel that I cannot tackle. It is my courage, resilience, and strength that I bring to the leadership table as a Filipina Woman Rising.

Everything I did in the past has contributed to where I am now. I learned the skills, the system, and community engagement. I understand hardship, resilience, and diplomacy. People might mistake my cultural background as a weakness, but it is a strength. I thank my mother for all she taught me. I thank my siblings for being there for me. I thank the people in my life who have made me stronger. Business, politics, and life are made up of problems and solutions. Finding strength and perseverance is a daily work-in-progress. What does not kill me, strengthens me.

Sidebar 1: What A UK Councillor Does

Councillors in the UK are elected to the local council for a four-year term to represent the area and its residents as well as help make decisions about local issues. My term of office is from May 2015 to May 2019.

As a Councillor, I play a key role in our local democracy, whether it is through representing local residents, holding executive members and officials to account or campaigning for policy changes on issues affecting local residents. I have helped numerous residents and represented them in presenting their issues to the council. I chair the Member Development Panel for the councillors to ensure that they pay attention to their professional development and I arrange training programs for them.

How councils work depends on the type of council. There are several types of local councils in England, including, town or parish, district, borough, county, metropolitan, and unitary councils. Sometimes these are referred to as local authorities. All councils have in common the way they work and make decisions on behalf of local communities. They are all led by democratically elected councillors who set the vision and direction of the council. Most are run on a system similar to that of the central government, with an elected executive (or cabinet) to decide on policy and make decisions which other councillors then examine in detail. All councils except for town or parish councils are large organizations which play a significant part in the local economy and influence many aspects of the lives of the people who live or work there. A large proportion of the work councils do is determined by the central government. Local councils vary widely in terms of their style, political leadership, and approach to delivering these central government programmes, and it is here that local knowledge and commitment can make a significant difference.

Depending on the type of local authority, a council can be responsible for a range of services, such as education and lifelong learning; social services and health; housing and regeneration; waste collection; recycling; roads and street lighting; arts, sports and culture; community safety and crime reduction; environment; planning and regulation; addressing issues of disadvantage and building strong, stable communities; taxing and spending; and transportation. These activities are mainly funded through payments from central government and the collection of council tax, although council tax makes up only about a quarter of a council's income.

Sidebar 1: What A UK Councillor Does

I have volunteered for three Task and Finish Groups.

- First, the Review Committee ensures efficiency of all Departments. Four of us new councillors made recommendations to the council some of which were subsequently adopted and put in place.

- Second, the review of the council's Corporate Vision and help establish the council's Corporate Vision for the next four years.

- Third, the Market Review that was completed a year ago and is now being revisited to consider other recommendations.

There are 100,000 residents in my area of responsibility, of which 200 are Filipinos. There are a total 300,000 Filipinos in the UK.

Our Council's area of responsibility includes Elstree Film Studios with 100 years of film history and home of the iconic Star Wars movies.

MARIA ROSA 'BING' NIEVA CARRION, Ph.D.

Founder and CEO, My-Cord (Philippines)
GLOBAL FWN100™ 2016

What Makes an Effective Leader

Once upon a time, there lived this young, curious girl on the heart-shaped island of Marinduque in the center of the Philippines. She grew up in the company of her happy and nurturing family, with a tall, handsome and larger-than-life Castilian father, Ramon Saiz Carrion, a mining engineer who headed the iron ore mines as General Superintendent, and a beautiful, caring wonderfully strong woman who ran a warm, welcoming home. This wide-eyed energetic observant girl, one of eight siblings enjoyed the best of both worlds since she grew up with the copper mountains of Balanacan in Mogpog on one side, and the deep blue sea on the other side. She relished and enjoyed the beauty and bounty of nature, during magical moonlit evenings, the sweet smell of the delicate Sampaguita flowers hanging in the warm summer air and the multi-colored lights of the fireflies on the huge acacia trees surrounding their white house on top of the hill. These are strong images that remain etched in her mind to this day. Then she would look up at the skies and see the twinkling stars, and when she looked down to the Bay, she would see the single lights emanating from the fishermen 's *bancas* [small boats] illuminating the sea making it like a star-studded sky. This young girl reflected, "What an awesome, magical sight of God's wonderful creation."

Legacy: Generations of Strong Women

Together with her siblings, she enjoyed a charmed life, abundant with the luxuries of the good life provided by an indulgent, successful, and generous loving father. She thought this halcyon life would last forever. But at the young age of 9, her world was shattered as her father died of a stroke and her bereaved mother was left with eight children to care for, the youngest being two-year old twins.

They moved to the capital town of Boac where they lived in the hundred-year-old matriarchal home with her beautiful, strong-willed grandmother, Elvira Sarmiento Nieva, the widow of the first Governor of Marinduque, Juan Morente Nieva. In this old-world setting, she became deeply conscious of her rich roots as she heard stories about the Nieva Clan that included five generations of strong, powerful, influential, distinguished, religious, and principled ancestors who originated from this town, the capital of the province. The wide brown narra-paneled walls in the matriarchal home were very much part of her activity-filled childhood. This stately white-colored home right in the center of town, and only a hundred steps to the Catholic Church represented to her a legacy of family and history.

Widowed at the young age of 39, her mother Rosario, manifested her resilience and strength by bringing up her eight children singlehandedly. She was the quintessential Mother Earth and a woman of dignity, elegance, character, and gentility. It was from her mother that this young girl learned her leadership skills during her growing-up years.

Fortunately for her brood, this strong, brave and determined mother maintained her positive attitude towards life and ingrained in her little girl and the little girl's siblings a deep sense of spirituality, shown by example, through her habitual meditation. During prayer they all thanked the Almighty for His abiding grace as He cared for them from day-to-day, from school year to school year and from milestone to milestone.

A strong leadership trait her mother taught her and her brothers and sisters, was always to be grateful to those who had touched their lives. This is a virtue that this young girl would live by throughout her life.

As an educator, Rosario Nieva Carrion encouraged her children to study their lessons well and to be well-groomed from head to foot. She encouraged them to keep well-written journals of their school lessons written in beautiful penmanship. She emphasized the importance of strict adherence to good manners and right conduct. Her mother encouraged them to read good books, select magazines, and biographies. She would then discuss the value and lessons learned from each book as a way to improve their analytical and verbal skills. Of the eight children, it was this young girl who wholly immersed herself into the reading habit that in turn, developed her love for literature and honed her creative writing talent.

This little girl is me, the author of this chapter in this FWN *Disrupt 3.0. Filipina Women: Rising.*

I have emphasized the leadership traits I learned from generations of strong women. In the rest of the narrative, I will share a poem I wrote about who is a leader, the leadership rules I learned from winning the International Federation of Women's Travel Organizations (IFWTO) Convention, and the leadership lessons from my mother. Finally, I will highlight my contribution of strengthening women to be agents of change and my initial steps of establishing a Leadership Center for Excellence for Filipinos.

Who is a Woman Leader?

A leader is a strong woman.
She is brave and adventurous.
She is confident and self-assured.
Because she knows who she is.

A leader is a spiritual woman.
A reflective person, she inspires others
To be good and to do good
So that others may succeed.

A leader is a woman who is grateful
She is appreciative of life's blessings
She is humble and joyful of heart.
She is a servant for others.

A leader is a woman of character.
Focused in her mission to mentor other women to succeed.
Unrelenting in her true calling
She is possessed of a forgiving heart.

A leader is a woman who perseveres
No matter the difficulties.
She is an effective mediator
And creates a win-win solution for all.

A leader is a woman who is full of love.
Who shares her gift of giving
With everyone she meets.
Her sense of humor is palpable.

A leader is a woman who forgives.
As she knows human foibles
And weaknesses of the human spirit
And she is the better human being because of this.

Hail thee woman leader.
For you lead in these troubled times
To lift up the marginalized members of our fractured society
So that we may win in this war against poverty, ignorance, and hate.

Winning the IFWTO Convention

When I was the Marketing Director of the Peninsula Hotel Manila, I had to be active in travel industry organizations, because it was good for the hotel. One such organization was the International Federation of Women's Travel Organizations. I was able to use many of the leadership lessons I learned from my mother in my work with this 25-year old organization.

Between May 2 and 8, 1988, I chaired the Manila Convention of the International Federation of Women's Travel Organizations (IFWTO). More than over 400 delegates representing 66 countries attended this milestone event. I secured for the Philippines the right to host this international event.

Winning the bid to have Manila as the site of that year's convention was like passing through the eye of the needle. The international board members were seriously considering Australia as an alternative site for the 19th convention because of concerns about the peace and order situation in the Philippines at that time, including coup attempts. I had the critical responsibility as head of the Host Chapter of overseeing the planning of the Manila Convention.

I flew to Harare, Zimbabwe where the IFWTO was holding its 18th Federation Convention. At the IFWTO board meeting, I was deluged with questions on the Philippine peace situation. To the amazement of everyone present I showed a video of the then President Corazon Cojuangco Aquino inviting and assuring the international membership with this message: "We would like to welcome you all to experience our warm friendship and hospitality and to assure you of your safety and security during the week of your visit to Manila for the 19th International Convention."

There was complete silence in the boardroom after I presented that video. They were surprised with the personal message of the Philippine President Corazon C. Aquino. The board then passed a resolution confirming that the 19th international convention would remain in Manila as host country. Then one after the other extended their warm congratulations. They commented that the video tape was a great way to present the defense of keeping the Convention in Manila. Getting the Philippine President to assure delegates of their safety and extending the President's invitation to visit the Philippines was viewed as a winning argument.'

The convention in Manila succeeded. President Corazon C. Aquino addressed the over 400 delegates who then became strong spokeswomen for the Philippines based on their first-hand experiences of the warm friendship and famous Filipino brand of hospitality. President Aquino was the first head of state to address the all - women international federation in their 25-year existence.

Leadership Guiding Rules

What were the leadership rules that guided me during this crucial milestone event?

First, you must use originality and creativity to reverse a negative situation. I used my close relationship with a confidant of the President to enhance my successful marketing presentation to the IFWTO board.

Second, you must be focused on your purpose and be resolute in ensuring that all details of the presentation are perfect.

Third, you must use your network to ensure the success of the event, in this particular case: the Philippine Tourism Secretary and the Immigration Commissioner to ensure seamless arrival in the international airport, and the Manila Hotel General Manager who made sure that all delegates were cared for as VIPs.

Fourth, I needed to convince all the Officers and members of the Women in Travel Philippines to own the event and to assume responsibility for making the delegates feel at home, happy, and secure.

Fifth, explain to your family and relatives of the importance of the event, so they become your emotional support during this stressful time.

Sixth, ensure there is a dedicated and hardworking Secretariat to assure all details are covered, all speakers are confirmed, and each workshop is well attended.

Seventh, hire a good public relations agency so that the Convention message is communicated to the public via newspapers, radio and television and a daily newsletter. Use social media and avail of Facebook, Twitter, Instagram, etc.

Eight, ensure that you choose an ideal gift for each delegate that communicates who we are as a people.

Ninth, choose the best sponsors to support the event. You must ensure that the sponsors get the best mileage for their contributions.

Tenth, give thanks to the God Almighty for the guidance, the love and the abundance that ensured the success of the event.

My Mother's Leadership Lessons

The greatest influence in my life as a young leader was my awesome mother, Rosario Sarmiento Nieva vda. de Carrion.

She always told me that to be an effective leader one must be an effective communicator and to be an effective communicator one must speak well and think clearly and logically.

A very effective and well-respected educator, my mother instilled in me the need to listen to others with sensitivity. She often said listening opened lessons on life and a new awareness of ourselves as we continue to learn from others.

A deeply spiritual person, she taught me to have an abiding faith in the Almighty and to never tire in thanking Him for all of life's wondrous blessings.

She impressed on me a deep sense of value for who I am and pride in my roots that in turn developed my self-confidence and, enabled me to grow as a confident, self-assured, intelligent and successful adult. I developed strength of character believing that I could accomplish anything I dreamt of. I believed I could fulfill all the desires of my mind and heart because of my deep desire to succeed.

My remarkable journey as an individual has been reinforced by my mother's nature of teaching by example. She encouraged me to be an individual with choices, allowed me to bloom, and grow with a strong kind of spiritual and emotional freedom. She encouraged me to be true to myself in making decisions and choices, and standing by these decisions.

She always told me that a sense of humor and laughter were essential to enjoying life's blessings and experiences.

My mother often reminded me that living with integrity and joy, having fun, and learning when to relax and enjoy oneself were the secret to a long and fulfilling life.

She would tell me that I should always tell the truth, even when it hurts because it was the right thing to do.

She always shared with me that one must take risks and face challenges and solve them to the satisfaction of everyone involved. She always maintained a win-win solution to every problem.

She advised me to look for the best in everyone because all of us have unique gifts to offer.

My mother was a stickler for being on time for every occasion or appointment. She said that we must respect ourselves, and the person we are meeting as time is fleeting and once gone is gone for ever.

One advice of hers that I cannot forget is the need to make time for the essential moments in our lives because the time will never return and we shall never forgive ourselves if we miss out on family bonding moments and special occasions.

She also reminded me always to come prepared for any project or undertaking I commit to because it speaks of who I am as a person.

My mother said that a good leader must be a good follower. It does not matter the number of people you lead, but your success as a leader is judged by the number of people you serve sincerely and lovingly.

The principles I live by today as an empowered woman leader I learned and imbibed from my remarkable mother.

We may live in different continents and live separate lives but our collective desire to change the world are anchored in our belief that as human beings we are here to work together, to learn from each other, and to love one another.

My Legacy: Women as Agents for Change

As an executive coach, I always find it effective to understand the moods and listen to the language and the body language of each woman I mentor. It is not the words they speak but their body language and eye movements that reveal their stories.

I firmly believe that if we are going to be effective change agents and reach as many women as possible, we must build bridges of hope that they identify with. Build bridges of love to nourish their hearts, bridges of generosity to nourish their physical bodies, and, build bridges of spiritual growth so that they can heal.

There are sunrises that brighten our world. There are surprises that give hope to our aspirations. And, for us empowered women leaders, it is the challenge, as human beings, to witness the enormous changes and development happening in and around us. The time to act is now. Not tomorrow but today. This is the challenge I pose to all empowered women leaders.

Good leaders serve by endeavoring to think and to act for the benefit of all. They are sought after for their guidance and are always willing to mentor others to be empowered members of society. A good leader aspires and inspires. They have an open mind and an indomitable will in the face of challenges.

Good and effective leaders are transformational human beings. They elevate good deeds to a noble and higher purpose.

My objective for writing this chapter is to communicate that women leaders are human beings whose greatness comes from their humanity. I hope that young and aspiring women will be able to identify the qualities that make women leaders effective and eventually see in themselves the virtues and characteristics, their gifts, and their potential that are waiting to be tapped for making them a better person. The goal is women who contribute significantly towards creating a happier home, an environmentally sounder community, and a kinder world. It is when we have stretched our limits, broken through our glass ceiling, and grasped what we thought was beyond our reach, that we become avatars or the very embodiment of the causes, aspirations, and ideals we ultimately live for.

Let us, as involved, committed women leaders, be an inspiration to others.

As a successful author and publisher, social historian, poet, executive coach, branding consultant, and crisis management advisor, my biggest dream is to establish a sustainable Leadership Center of Excellence for Filipinos.

I believe that we are going to leave this Earth as nude as when we were born, and the only thing that will define our lives are the good deeds we do for the marginalized members of society.

Long after we are gone from this Earth, the power of the written word remains to impact those who read the words in my books and hopefully change us all for the better.

❋

JENNIFER MARIE B. JOSÉ, M.D.

Robotic Gynecologic Surgeon,
St Luke's Medical Center Global City and Makati Medical Center
GLOBAL FWN100™ 2017

The Woman's Room

Since my teenage years, I have struggled with progressive adenomyosis. I dreaded my monthly periods. I was dependent on strong painkillers and usually stayed in bed, incapacitated for days. This condition affected both my work and social life. I even turned down job assignments abroad for fear of living alone when the pain was at its worse. Since I had never had any major surgery, the postoperative pain was one of my greatest concerns. Before meeting Dr. Jennifer Jose', I was hesitant about robotic-assisted laparoscopic surgery. Although I had read online about Da Vinci robotic surgery, I had never met anyone who had undergone this procedure. This fear kept me from doing what I should have done years ago.

This statement from one of my patients is the reason I became a robotic gynecologic surgeon. My name is Dr. Jennifer Marie B. Jose. I became the First Filipino doctor to make it into the Surgeon's locator list of Intuitive Surgical, the maker of the Da Vinci Surgical System. I became first and foremost in this field by exceeding expectations, by sheer determination and hard work, by overcoming challenges, and by staying focused on my goal.

Early Influences

I am the second to the eldest of five siblings. We have one brother who is the middle child. Both my parents and grandparents raised me. I belonged to a very conservative family that was involved in the real estate business, had a toy factory, and road construction business in Lahad Datu, Malaysia. I grew up in a setting where my parents had to be in and out of the country for their international business while my grandparents took care of my siblings and me while my parents are in Malaysia. I lived a sheltered life. My parents gave me an idyllic childhood, sent me to good schools, was attended by *yayas* [nannies], and dressed in finery. I recall that my sisters and I were dressed like dolls and that I had many imported stuffed toys. I traveled a lot as a child. Whenever we received good grades, our grandparents would bring us to Tokyo, Japan for a month during summer break where we learned how to cook, wash the dishes, do the laundry, and make the bed.

However, things changed for the worse. I am not sure what happened, but the business in Malaysia failed. Life became different. I saw my father become stressed, but as a young girl, I did not comprehend what was happening. My father became sickly, and he passed away at the young age of 40. This was so traumatic for me. I could not understand why he passed away and that is the reason I wanted to be a doctor.

I remember that as a young girl I had a good business sense. I used to make cakes and sell them to the employees of my grandmother during *merienda* [snack] time. The cakes were tasty, and I enticed the employees to buy cakes every day.

We lived in a huge resort-like house in Maycauayan, Bulacan. I was not able to explore the entire house because it was so huge. The business problems changed our circumstances. When my father passed away, my grandfather prepared to give me to my aunt, my sisters to another aunt, and my brother to stay with my mother. My mother did not allow this to happen. Instead, she gathered all of her children and lived in Malate. The mother of my mom bought us a big house in Malate when my father passed away. Life was no longer like in a bed of roses.

Ensuring Best Education

My mother made sure that we still had the best of the basic necessities and the best education. My mother made our house a home. She socialized us in culture, arts, travel, and what I would call the good life. I am very proud to say that she is the best mother in the world. It was a financial struggle for her to send my eldest sister and me to medical school and my two younger sisters to dental school. It was the dream of my mother and father to see that my eldest sister, Geraldine would become a doctor. They dreamt of her wearing a white doctor's uniform while my father would wait outside the campus to pick her up after her class. As I recall, my mother always told me while we were at the dining room table that even though life was hard "I want to make sure you are ready for life, I want to make sure that you are ready for battle. You cannot be anything less than your sister!" She wanted me to finish medicine as a back-up since she said I could also do business even if I became a doctor.

Business or Medicine

I went to a Montessori school for my nursery and elementary studies and then attended the International School in Malaysia. I finished my high school in St. Paul's College in Pasig and my three-year college degree in BS Biology at De La Salle University. I was accelerated three times, and I was always the youngest among my batchmates. I entered medical school when I was at 18 years of age. After the first year in Medical School at the University of the East Ramon Magsaysay Memorial Medical Center (UERMMMC), I did very well in my studies, but I was unsure if I liked what I was doing. I took a year off. I helped my mother in the real estate business and took charge of renovating our house in Pampanga. I came to realize that my mother was right. I decided to go back to medical school and finished medicine at UERMMMC. I was in the top 20 of the graduates.

Choosing a Medical Specialty

There were so many fields in Medicine, and I did not know yet what field of specialization I would do. I thought that I wanted to be an expert in my chosen field and I wanted it to be both surgical and medical. I applied to the Makati Medical Center since I was hoping to practice there. As a child, my parents always told me that I was born in Makati Medical Center, that my mother had a complicated delivery, and that my parents were 'hats off' to the Makati Medical Center doctors because the birth complication was managed very well. My parents always pointed to the hospital building as we traveled on Ayala Avenue in Makati. I could see the happiness on their faces as they recalled their experience when I was born. Even then, they envisioned me as a doctor there. It was very tough getting into a residency program at the Makati Medical Center. We were nine applicants who were called for the interview. Eight were from the University of Santo Tomas, and I was the only one from the University of the East. I knew that their preference was for graduates of the University of Santo Tomas, but I still tried. I was chosen as one of the four residents. However, they chose me to be an adjunct resident which meant finishing an additional year without stipend. This was frustrating because other hospitals had offered me a straight residency appointment, but I did not accept their offer. Initially, I was not happy with my situation at the Makati Medical Center because I had good grades in medical school and I could not understand why the offer was for me to be an adjunct resident. One of the senior residents told me that I had been accepted because of my high grades and also because of my personality, that was I smiled a lot. I did my residency in Obstetrics and Gynecology at the Makati Medical Center where I graduated with honors. I received national awards for some of my papers. I participated in different conventions where I presented my winning papers. My mentors told me that what we lacked in Makati Medical Center and in the Philippines is a subspecialty in Urogynecology and Pelvic Reconstructive Surgery. Dr. Isidro Benitez, the chairman of the Obstetrics & Gynecology Department, advised me to find a good training program in Urogynecology and that upon my return to the Philippines, they would set up a Center for me.

Preparing to Excel in My Specialty

I knew that practicing in any subspecialty of Obstetrics and Gynecology would be very competitive. I prepared myself; I went to Chennai, India and, I trained in laparoscopy for a month under Dr. Kurian Joseph. I also studied Obstetrics and Gynecology Ultrasound at the Philippine General Hospital for four months. I applied to the St. Georges Hospital in London, UK; the Mount Sinai Hospital in Toronto, Canada; and the KK Women's and Children's Health in Singapore. Surprisingly, all three hospitals accepted me. I had three excellent options. I followed my passion; I chose to train in Mount Sinai Hospital, Toronto, Canada because it offered a three-year training program and I could do minimally invasive surgical treatments as well.

My choice of Mount Sinai proved to be a challenge. I knew it would be competitive to get an appointment there. I went to Canada for an interview during the SARS virus epidemic. Each of the panelists that interviewed me wore a mask. My competition for the slot consisted of Canadians and thirteen applicants from around the world. I felt that there was some cultural bias. The position was offered to me by the Urogynecology Unit headed by Dr. Harold Drutz. I would be under review for three months. I felt like I was being graded every day. I was tested about Urology which is different from Obstetrics and Gynecology the areas I trained for in residency training. At the end of the day, I studied books on Urology. Sometimes I would be crying when I got to the apartment because I was so tired and I was too cold. I felt like a sponge trying to absorb everything. I knew that whatever I was learning would be beneficial when I returned to the Philippines.

During my three months observation period, I tried to impress my professors. It was very difficult for some of them to believe that this Filipina was a doctor. Some of them appeared to think of Filipinas as their subordinates or stereotype them as nannies or caregivers. I worked to do my best, in terms of knowledge, attitude, desire for learning, and teamwork. I focused on achieving my goal. I prayed to Mother Mary to assist me to get the position. I passionately wanted the position, and I envisioned myself as a urogynecologist. I knew that there was no turning back. When I was under final consideration, I was asked during the meeting, "Who will support you?" I answered, my mother. I knew that my mother would do anything to help me achieve my dreams. They were all surprised. The Canadians and some others will not train without a stipend or funding. When I was selected, I already had decided that I would live simply. I had to remain focused on my goals. I developed a lot of friends who guided me and assisted me in my journey. I did well. I stayed focused and, learned everything that I could.

I was very frugal because my money came from my mother who wanted me to succeed. The Filipinos in Canada sent money back to the Philippines, and I received money from my mother from the Philippines. I planned my day to scrimp on food. A whole loaf of bread would be my breakfast for the week along with jam and coffee. I had a second cup of coffee and a muffin for lunch. My friends would invite me to dinner. I walked instead of taking the subway to the hospital every day to stretch my money. I spent weekends with friends. If I were alone, I would stay at the Chapters bookstore and read self-help. I always imagined that I would have an excellent practice when I returned to Manila. I was very focused on returning to Manila. I knew I belonged there. I knew Manila was where I wanted to practice medicine. Birthdays, Christmas, and holidays were lonely in Canada, and I longed to be with my Mom and my siblings. The homesickness became overwhelming, and my hands started to shake uncontrollably. I refused to go home for a visit since the airfare was expensive and I wanted to finish my fellowship training on time. Whatever extra money I had, I spent on Urogynecology books to take back to the Philippines.

Fighting Harassment, Not to be Derailed

Eight months before finishing my fellowship training, a Filipino-Canadian harassed me in my apartment when I was sick, cold, and with no voice. I fought him, and I took him to court. I won the case, and I requested a restraining order to prevent him from getting near me until I finished my fellowship training. This man tried several times to go to my apartment as seen on the CCTV. My mother and sisters wanted to take me from Canada because they were worried about me. However, I was steadfast in my decision to finish my fellowship training. I wanted to become a urogynecologist, and I did not want that harassment incident to stop me from my goal. I ignored the calls from Manila so that I could finish. Despite the trauma caused by the harasser, I succeeded in reaching my goal. When I finished my last surgical procedure, I sat in a flower box in front of Mount Sinai Hospital, and I cried my heart out from sheer exhaustion and sheer joy. Nurses whom I knew approached me and showed their concern by asking about why I was crying. I told them, I had finished my last requirements and I had accomplished my dream of completing my fellowship. This dream was one giant step towards my bigger dream.

I returned to the Philippines immediately. My mom and my brother picked me up; I did not know how to react, I held back my tears. I had not seen them for three years, and I really had not talked to them since I ignored their calls. I saw my mom had gray hair and she looked older. Silently, I diagnosed it as menopause, and in my heart, I knew I could help my mom regain her inner happiness.

Turning My Dream into a Success

On August 27, 2007, I showed up at the Makati Medical Center. I met my colleagues who have been earning money for three years, and I was just starting my medical practice. I applied to be a consultant at the Makati Medical Center. I was surprised at the volume of referrals; I had to do my initial consultation in a coffee shop across from the Makati Medical Center. I would examine patients in the delivery room at the Makati Medical Center. I had to take a loan to buy stocks in the hospital in order to get a clinic at the Makati Medical Center. Finally, Makati Medical Center, set up a Urogynecology and Incontinence Center that I have been heading for the last ten years.

I became one of the founding members of the Philippine Society of Urogynecology and Pelvic Reconstructive Surgery. Another challenge came when urologists and gynecologists held discussions about integrating the overlapping medical and health conditions that we treated. Shortly after those discussions, I was appointed to be the head of the Comprehensive Pelvic Floor Center of St. Luke's Medical Center Global City. At the same time, I was named the section Head of Urogynecology and Pelvic Reconstructive Surgery in both the Makati Medical Center and the St. Luke's Global City. I continued to conduct workshops for Urinary Incontinence and Urodynamics at the Makati Medical Center and at the KK Women's and Children's Health in Singapore. I also partnered with drug companies to do layfora on urinary incontinence, overactive bladder, and pelvic organ prolapse. I am fortunate that I am able to do a lot of laparoscopic surgery.

Eventually, I trained in Robotics Gynecologic Surgery with Dr. Arnold Advincula in Florida. I received a trailblazer award on March 17, 2016, from the Da Vinci Surgical System for the outstanding achievement of being the first surgeon in the Philippines to perform one hundred robotics surgeries. I earned the distinction of being the first Filipino doctor to be included in the Surgeons' locators list of Intuitive Surgical, the maker of the Da Vinci Surgical System[1]. Being on the list is an honor and recognition as one of the robotic surgeons from all over the world by the Intuitive Surgical for proficiency in robotic surgery. I received an award from St. Luke's Medical Center as an outstanding physician involved in innovation, treatment, and pioneering work.

I continue to teach robotic surgery in Hanoi, Vietnam to urologists and urogynecologists and laser gynecology in Ho Chi Minh City. I have done live surgeries in conventions and conferences. I also have been giving talks in Korea and Singapore. I wrote an article about robotic gynecologic surgery outcomes, a summary of which is attached as Sidebar 1.

My passion for improving women's health and improving the quality of life of patients had become stronger. I did further training in Aesthetic Gynecology in Istanbul, Turkey. I am presently doing laser vaginal rejuvenation, and I have treated close to 500 patients since last year. I have been active in forming the Aesthetic Gynecology Society in the Philippines which is now recognized by the Philippine Obstetrics & Gynecologic Society. Besides, I am presently the Vice-President of the Aesthetic Gynecologic Society of the Philippines and we are working on International affiliation. As busy as I am, I am happy. My passion is my career. My career is my passion.

Sidebar 1: Robotic Gynecologic Surgery Outcomes

Robotic-assisted laparoscopic surgery is the latest development in surgical technology. It combines the precision of robotic, the maneuverability and minimally invasiveness of laparoscopic surgery (surgery that accesses diseased organs through small incisions. Long instruments with small surgical instruments on the end are inserted through the small incisions), and the expertise and proficiency of the surgeon. All of these have allowed superior results in surgery.

Over the years, robotically-assisted surgery has continued to grow in the area of minimally invasive gynecologic surgery. This has immensely improved how gynecologic surgeons address the condition of female reproductive organs that need to be operated on.

The robot provides the surgeon with a high definition, three-dimensional view of the organ being operated on. The enhanced visuals and the greater access to organs located in small, tight spaces like the pelvis give surgeons an improved ability to identify normal and diseased tissues taking care not to damage blood vessels and nerves while performing the surgical procedure. It also contributes to the lessening of blood loss, less infections, less canes for complications, less pain, faster recovery, and return to normal activities.

With the robot, surgeons are able to perform surgeries with greater versatility and dexterity because the instrument has distal ends that mimic the intricate movements of the human hand. The 'wristed' instrumentation affords greater flexibility and provides seven degrees of freedom, similar to the human hand. This is a vast improvement from the movements in conventional laparoscopic instruments. Robotic technology allows surgeons to easily and simply perform complex laparoscopic maneuvers and do more sophisticated procedures that are otherwise difficult to do using conventional laparoscopic procedures.

Robotic surgery is used for procedures, including hysterectomy, myomectomy, tubal reanastomosis, lymph node dissection, and sacrocolpopexy.

JUSLYN C. MANALO

Mayor, Daly City, CA, USA
GLOBAL FWN100™ 2015

If at First You Don't Succeed

If you asked me years ago, what I wanted to do in life, my answer would have been to help people. It has always been my passion to serve others. I knew deep inside that this was my purpose. However, when asked by my college counselor, I did not know what field or discipline would give me the best chance to make a difference. Despite the uncertainty as to what career path to follow, I completed a Master in Public Administration at San Francisco State University's School of Public Affairs and Civic Engagement. I was elected to the Daly City Council in November 2016, and when I was sworn in as a first-time council member, I was also elected Vice-Mayor in December 2016. A year later, on December 11, 2017, the Daly City Council unanimously selected me as the Mayor.

My journey as a Filipina leader has been shaped by experience with community service, along with the attendant struggles, disappointments, and triumphs. It is true that you cannot feel the real highs in life if you do not have the very lows in life. My leadership identity was formed through community organizing during my student life, working in the nonprofit sector, advocacy, and working with government officials and departments.

Serving My Community Beginning in My College Years

When I was eight years old, my parents who immigrated from the Philippines moved from South of Market, San Francisco to Daly City, California. Being raised in the multi-ethnic city of Daly City has given me a sincere appreciation for diversity. I learned about the Filipino American struggle in my Asian American Studies classes and in undergrad this would become my college major because I was intrigued by the plight and progress of Asian communities establishing a new life in the U.S. I also learned about the issue of the Filipino World War II Veterans and the lack of recognition of their U.S. military service nearly 75 years ago. The last point pushed me to learn more, and I tried to find ways to advocate for our *lolos* [grandfathers] and *lolas* [grandmothers] and thus, began my service to the community. I started as a Community Service worker at the age of 21 with the Veterans Equity Center. It was there that I realized the importance of being strategic and how I must be part of the system to bring about change. I remember thinking that I would like to become a local legislator to impact my community because there is a need to have a seat at the table to represent the voices and concerns of the people.

As a result of my community service, I received one of the highest awards in Community Service from the Chancellor of California State University in 2001. Alongside the National Network for Veterans Equity (NNVE), my colleagues and I created Student Action for Veterans Equity (SAVE) and worked on the national campaign for equity for the Filipino Veteranos. In 2009, our group of volunteers formed the Bill Sorro Housing Program (BiSHoP), to address the housing issues for low to moderate income families and individuals. I managed the program for four years and assisted in strengthening the program's capacity. To date, BiSHoP has served over 1500 clients and continues to be a resource for the Filipino community. Currently, I am the Community Engagement Associate for Forest City facilitating the creation of partnerships for community development, such as affordable housing, jobs, open space, and youth development.

Working in the nonprofit sector for 14 years taught me the importance of working with the government whether at the national or local level. Also, the experience of serving our elders taught me to persevere in pushing the agenda to help our elders achieve social justice. In October 2015, the Filipina Women's Network (FWN) recognized me as one of the most influential Filipina Women globally. I have emerged as a critical political and policy leader in Daly City, the place I chose to call home.

I have served on several boards in various capacities. I served on the SamTrans Citizen Advisory Committee, the Daly City Personnel Board, the board of Senior Disability Action(SDA), the Bay Area Water Supply Conservation Agency (BAWSCA), Association of Bay Area Governments (ABAG), South of Market Business Association (SomBa), City/County Association of Governments (C/CAG) Affordable Housing Committee for Daly City, South of Market Business Association, Skyline College President Council, North County Fire Authority Board and the Pre-Hospital Emergency Medical Services Group (JPA) Board.

My Leadership Context

In February 2016, I learned about the San Mateo Democratic Central Committee. The Committee is comprised of (1) "elected members," who are elected by Democratic voters in the five County Supervisorial Districts in the primary election in an even-numbered year, and (2) "ex officio members," who are the County's Democratic state and federal legislators. Both elected and ex officio members are allowed two alternates who may vote if the elected members are absent. Besides, any Democrat in the County may become a non-voting Associate Member. In 2016, neither the elected members had one person of color representing the diverse, multi-ethnic communities of San Mateo County, specifically Daly City where I was raised.

San Mateo County has twenty incorporated cities, the largest of which is Daly City. The estimated population of San Mateo County is 771,410 as of July 2017. According to the California Department of Finance; Daly City has realized an annual increase of 1.2% in population over the past six years. In 2012, the population estimate was 102,593. Over 52% of this population was Asian Pacific Islanders, but there was not one Asian Pacific Islander in the Central Committee representing Daly City. This was disconcerting to me. So, I ran for one of the elected seats of the San Mateo Democratic Central Committee in the summer of 2016. Despite having never run for a political office, I had experienced running for school positions during my high school and undergraduate years, but I had never been on the same ballot for the primary elections as the next President of the United States.

Learning to Campaign

I learned what it took to reach out to voters, received assistance from a mentor who created my flyers, and started my campaign. From the hills to the flatlands, I hit the ground running. I used some of my funds to prepare flyers that summer. During those six weeks, I woke up at 5:30 in the morning and dropped off my leaflets in the district with a high proportion of Democratic voters. I made sure I was strategic because I had such a limited time until election day. I did this every day before I went to work in San Francisco. Each morning I was dripping in sweat from going up and down the stairs of homes in Daly City. These homes did not have just one level; the door front was often on the second level. I tried to make sure I did not fall down the stairs. I started to think of it like boot camp.

A month after I decided to run for the San Mateo Democratic Central Committee, my fiancé proposed. It was unexpected and another complicating factor in the back of my mind as I knocked on doors to introduce myself. Despite this unexpected change in my marital status, I felt that I needed to represent people of color by running for the committee. I knew that if I won, I would be breaking barriers for the people of color who held liberal views in Daly City. During this process, I learned to ask for endorsements from elected officials to support my run for the Central Committee. Since I was new to the political arena, I found it nerve-wracking to ask for endorsements and funding, but I knew this was part of the process if I wanted to reach my goal. I went to events with local elected officials, and my mentor introduced me. I would ask if they would support my candidacy. I received endorsements from four influential people that evening and re-connected with an Assembly member whom I had met years ago. I needed to be bold, introduced myself, and discussed the reasons why I was running for the Central Committee. I had to have my elevator pitch precise and pristine. I had an official website that would list the endorsements of local elected officials in San Mateo County who said yes to my request for their support.

Losing My First Election

The results were counted on the night in June 2016. I remember entering the headquarters of one of the candidates for District Supervisor and already was feeling down because I had seen results on my phone which did not bode well for my candidacy. Part of me just wanted to go home and rest, but the other part of me knew it was essential to be present for the candidate for the District Supervisor. When the results came in, my heart sank. I did not win. I felt all the hard work I had done had been wasted. However, I tried hard to push feelings of defeat out of the way. Instead, I focused on the broader race for the next presidential race. After two election parties for other friends, I went home tired, and a bit saddened. It was my first attempt to become an active voice on this elected committee, and I had failed. I did not reach my goal. I let the Facebook community and others know about my loss and received kind words of encouragement. I took the leap to go beyond my comfort zone, and although I failed, it did not mean that all hope was lost. In other aspects, I considered it a win. The experience allowed me to expand my network of support and engage with community members and voters. I gave it the best that I could. I gave my full effort and took the step to initially qualify and get myself to go out there and campaign. I felt crushed, but I knew I would not let this bring me down. I took this chance to reflect on what I had done and what I had learned from that first experience of running for a political office.

This low feeling after losing my first try at being elected was followed by a high feeling one week later. I had a conversation with a couple of community leaders who advised me that the election for the City Council of Daly City was upcoming in November 2016. The reason why it was timely was that two seats would be open, meaning two incumbents would not be vying for their positions.

Understanding Daly City's Local Government

I had been a resident of Daly City. As an American citizen, I paid my taxes, benefited from local services, such as access to libraries, schools, community service centers, hospitals and medical centers, U.S. postal service, and economic and community development. Daly City is a General Law City (authority is outlined in the California Government Code) governed by a council-manager form of government in which the elected five-member City Council (1) chooses a Mayor from among themselves and (2) appoints the City Manager. The Mayor presides at council meetings, represents the city in intergovernmental affairs, and facilitates communication between elected and appointed officials. The City Manager oversees an Executive Leadership Team that operates eight departments employing approximately 475 staff with an annual estimated budget of $150 million. For a summary of the Daly City form of government, roles of the City Council, and the roles and responsibilities of the mayor in relation to the City Manager, go to www.dalycity.org[1].

Deciding to Run

Life propels one in so many different directions. Ever since I was 21 years of age, I wanted to serve at the local level as an elected official. I wanted to impact the communities around me. I prayed long and hard, reached out to mentors and femtors. I had long conversations with my family and checked in with my soon-to-be husband. My fiancé encouraged me and said this was a dream of mine that I should pursue.

I prayed to discern the direction that God has for my life. I felt that He was opening doors and affirming that I should trust the path that had opened up. At first, my mother did not approve of me wanting to be in public office. Her words were, "Live a simple life, and focus on your family." I think like any mother she was overprotective. She knew that there could be issues, for which I would be ridiculed, and that I could not make everyone happy. My passion for serving could not be swayed even by my mother. I had a chance to give back and become a local legislator in the city that is over 30 percent Filipinos, and many other people of color. I am the type of person that once I make a decision, there is no turning back. I needed to consider taking this decision carefully.

I listened to my mentor and followed his advice. In April of that year, I attended a training program for Asian Pacific Americans who wanted to run for elected office. I used the information from that program, also known as a political boot camp. I

---

[1] http://www.dalycity.org/About_Daly_City/City_Profile/Form_of_Government.htm

was the first candidate to file my papers. I remember feeling excitement as well as anxiety about letting the public know that I was going to run for office. I thought I was being discouraged when a Daly City clerk stated, "You are my guinea pig as you are the first to register." She also mentioned that "One does not always win the first time." I remember leaving that room feeling inspired to prove this naysayer wrong. I knew that this would only be one of the discouraging experiences I would encounter. Knowing negative energies were likely to surround me, I had to be intentional about countering such negativity.

I realized that the scariest moments are when I gain the most growth and also when I let my conviction lead me. Enough people believed in my candidacy, and I won.

Challenges when Running for Office

As I ventured into running for a Daly City Council seat, I knew I needed to start meeting the residents one-on-one by knocking on their doors and introducing myself. Like my initial experience of running for office, the experience was nerve-wracking. I had to reiterate my years of being part of the community, going to all the public schools in the community from elementary through high school, and then finishing my bachelors and my master's degrees. I had to remind people that I grew up in Daly City, stayed there and that I wanted to give back to the community that has raised me.

Every door was different, and I never knew what I might encounter. I recall one incident when after I knocked and the door was opened, I introduced myself, and much to my surprise received a very positive response. They wanted to learn what I stood for and then commented: "Oh, you are so young to be running for City Council." Before I said goodbye, they affirmed their support for my candidacy. One barrier continued, they said. I looked very young. What could have been a compliment, instead became a question about my ability.

A Vietnam Veteran shared the story of his Filipino wife who unfortunately had passed away. While I was very empathetic, when he said he locked the doctors in the wife's hospital room to ensure that the doctor did everything he could for his wife, I felt a bit unsafe and did not know whether I had put myself in danger.

As a young woman, I needed to be aware of my surroundings. While campaigning, I had to show courage. Once, while walking to meet residents, I encountered a man in his front yard holding a butcher knife. He just stood there, looking dazed and confused. I did not continue my campaign walk that day. However, each day, I would work at my full-time job and during my lunch break trying to reach ten houses. I knew that every person I connected with mattered. November 8th was the goal-line. I kept reminding myself that I was doing this for the community I loved and wanted to support and bring forth change.

Keeping Negativity Out of Mind and Out of Sight

When running for office, there will be moments of self-doubt and people will try to persuade you to stop. Moreover, there will be people who will agree with you. There will be people who will convince you to stay in the race. This is where awareness of the opposing forces is crucial. You must push out the negative thoughts and have positive thoughts even when faced with opposing evidence. I made sure my signs were up and that I reached every corner of Daly City.

Sometimes, I would find my signs vandalized, written on, torn-down, or ripped up. When that happened, I would put up a new sign and keep on moving. I would not let these deterrents derail me from what I wanted to accomplish.

Learning to Ask for Help

I have always been a self-reliant and independent person. I think it comes from being the eldest in my family and with only one sister. I try to rely on myself and try to do best without asking for assistance. One thing I had to learn when running for office was to ask for support in my race for City Council. The hardest thing to do was to ask for money. However, all my mentors and the training stated that this was part of what I needed to do. I learned to swallow my pride and asked for help, at first, from close family members and friends, and later on, from strangers that I met on the campaign trail. This was another eye-opening experience. I am so grateful for every person that gave me money and their time to support me. I really could not have done this without the fantastic help of my supporters.

Run Filipina Run

I think running for office is one of the hardest things I have ever done in my life. It is physically, emotionally, and mentally draining. Your mind is always thinking of the things that need to be done. While you are thinking of the next fundraiser, you are also preparing for the next debate with other candidates. People continuously judge you, and you are always on the move. I learned lessons while running for political office and now that I have won a Daly City Council seat and been selected by my fellow council members, to be Mayor of Daly City, I reaffirm that first and foremost my mission to serve my community.

I am grateful for the endorsements made at that time by State Senator Mark Leno, State Assembly Member Phil Ting, Daly City Vice Mayor David Canepa, and Councilmember Ray Buenaventura.

After taking the oath of office for Mayor of Daly City in December 2017, I detailed the priorities that I hoped to carry out. My focus would be on economic development, particularly mixed-use developments, affordable housing, human services for youth and seniors, and a new hotel. I want the community to know their voice is represented and they have access to their local government.

After all of this, I am extremely humbled. I grew up in Daly City, and this is my hometown. It is a real honor to lead my community and to serve as a role model for young people.

ROXANE MARTIN NEGRILLO

SENIOR PLANNING DIRECTOR, PHD, AN OMNICOM MEDIA AGENCY
GLOBAL FWN100™ 2017

Moving Mountains

'You have been assigned this mountain, to show others that it can be moved.' In 2007, I started my media career as a senior planner in Abu Dhabi where my experience consisted of handling Nestle and Procter & Gamble brands for Fast Moving Consumer Goods (FMCG) in the Philippines. Fast forward to 2018 in Dubai, I am currently a Senior Planning Director specializing with accounts in various industries including automotive, fashion, technology, airline, property, retail, telecommunications, and consumer electronics.

I am the only Filipina in the media industry in Middle East with a senior management position. Through the years, I have had various powerful positions where I have represented my company in regional meetings in Europe, traveled the world for career advancement, and won Filipino and international awards for leadership. I have also been in many challenging situations where my leadership role had been undermined because I am a woman, an Asian, and a Filipina. I still remember how a non-Filipino receptionist told me before a meeting "I should congratulate you, because for a Filipina, you have a very good title." I have a term for such statements, and it is *complisult* (part compliment, part insult). These *complisults* do not bother me anymore. I have learned to embrace them for they are part of my identity as a woman leader in an international arena. I have learned to accept that we cannot always control situations that come our way. As Stephen Covey said: "10% of life is made up of what happens to you, and 90% of life is decided by how you react." I have become more mature in handling situations, staying positive even in the face of adversity. I have used my position of being "unique" as my greatest asset; I come across as a strong-willed female leader who is neutral, fair, and objective. I have focused my energy and used my leadership to inspire others. I know it is possible to be successful based on merit while keeping my integrity intact. I have created my own path, and I intend to leave a trail that can serve as a legacy for future Filipina women leaders to follow. Currently, my priority is not just to advance myself but also to build a sustainable pipeline of global Filipina women leaders. It is not impossible to move mountains. You can, as I have done, turn your fear into courage, convert challenges into opportunities, set your own goals, and most importantly have faith in yourself.

My Leadership Foundation

I came from a family that encouraged education and success. My parents would always tell my sisters, brother, and me to take our studies seriously in order to prepare for a bright future. They were right. I am glad that I listened to them. It was in primary school that I learned how to raise my hand and ask questions. It was in high school when I gained confidence in volunteering to be a stage director and when I was motivated to run for the student council. It was in the university that I realized the value of team effort, that collaborating with my classmates, brainstorming for ideas, finding common ground, rehearsing together for a presentation; also meant having each other's backs. We celebrated success a lot, whether it was my parents taking me to Jollibee after I got awarded with a medal or eating a footlong hotdog with my university classmates in Asturias behind UST after receiving the top grade of 1.0 for a marketing report.

Growing up was for me an upwards and onwards experience including leadership and achievements. At a very young age, I was preparing checklists for a stage play, forecasting the concert ticket sales required to achieve a sufficient profit for the student council to buy lockers for the school, or merely delegating tasks and roles for our thesis. In retrospect, all those moments served as training ground for me to become a leader. I acted like other leaders who have worked hard to prepare themselves for leadership, and leadership was not an easy mountain to move.

Leadership Styles

The kind of a leader you will turn out to be is always a question. Understanding different leadership styles is a tool for becoming an effective leader. I have found Daniel Goleman's article "Leadership That Gets Results" in the Harvard Business Review (2002) very useful. Goleman identifies six leadership styles that can be used in various situations to motivate, engage, and drive business results. These styles are: (1) Visionary where the leader mobilizes people towards a vision; (2) Coaching where the leader develops people; (3) Affiliative where the leader creates harmony; (4) Democratic where the leader forges consensus through participation; (4) Pacesetting where the leader sets high standards for performance; and (6) Commanding where the leaders demands immediate compliance. Most leaders gravitate toward one or two styles depending on the task or situation to be managed.

In deciding which leadership style fits the situation, one needs to stay objective and not to be swayed by subjective preference based on what is the easiest. There is a need to take a step back and evaluate the situation based on several factors, including team experience, strengths and weaknesses, the complexity of the task, timeframe, risk, available resources, and cost implication.

I have learned, it is okay for a leader to consult others for advice. No one needs to have all the answers all the time. One must practice humility to be an effective leader. The lack of ego is something that people appreciate, respect, and emulate.

I am inspired by my mentor, Ramon "Bong" Osorio, former VP and Head of Corporate Communications at ABS-CBN and currently President of the Public Relations Society of the Philippines. Before Sir Bong was the former chair of the Communication Arts department of the University of Santo Tomas for 17 years. He had a profound influence on my life. As his former student, I witnessed how he genuinely liked providing service to people, how committed he was in educating his students, and how he commanded respect of others. Because of his encouragement, I decided on a career in advertising. His "enjoy and love your job" attitude has motivated me to keep going. From him, I learned that personal values and integrity should always be intact and should never be compromised no matter how tough the situation.

Leadership Development

Great companies invest in leadership training and assessment of their leaders. I was fortunate to have been part of a great Dubai-based company with a long history of leadership training for its managers and directors. In their program, leaders were assessed on their leadership style, their responses to the organizational climate, and their competency in achieving the goal of having a balanced portfolio.

Using Feedback

Receiving feedback on one's leadership style is crucial. I believe that a leader's style can make or break a team. The style of leading a team has a direct impact on the overall atmosphere inside the team, and this also strongly correlates with team performance. Since we all have blind spots, we need credible feedback to become aware of how we perform as leaders. We must have an open mind in digesting the feedback, taking everything; the good, the bad, and the ugly. If we take things constructively, we will enable ourselves to evolve, change, and become better leaders. Leadership is a work in progress, requiring constant learning, evolving, and reflecting on ways we could have been better. In the face of failure, leadership is about deconstructing what went wrong and applying lessons learned so we could do things differently the next time.

I like receiving feedback about myself. As a leader, I tend to do self-evaluations frequently. However, I know self-evaluation is not enough since it might be biased. Sometimes I surprise people by asking them what they think of my leadership, how I can be better in what I do, and their advice for me. I do not ask random people, but those whom I think are unbiased, credible, without vested interests, and trustworthy. Here are a couple of feedbacks I received:

> I am so glad we have worked on the same team the past year because you have taught me more than I had learned in my past three years in media before I joined this company. (August 2014.) Gaby Bekhazi, a colleague working on my team at CARAT MENA.

> Roxane is extremely detail oriented and is very professional in all interactions within and outside the agency. She is incredibly hard-working, knowledgeable about media and can credibly support her point-of-view with facts, experience, and knowledge. She knows when to be firm to achieve results and when to embrace an opinion expressed by others. She is a pillar of strength for her team, the agency, and all of her clients respect her. (May 2016.) "Leaders for Growth" survey conducted by Hay's Group when I was Head of Planning for Al-Futtaim Group.

The feedback I received from the "Leaders for Growth" program, indicated that my most dominant leadership styles were Coaching and Affiliative. These leadership styles both focus on people and relationships. Coaching is about developing capability by focusing on the person and not on the task. My team perceived me as a credible and trustworthy leader who could develop their skills, provide them with support and ongoing feedback, and most importantly, identify growth opportunities so they could reach their career aspirations. Affiliative style is very effective when dealing with employees in highly stressful situations. To be effective, affiliative style requires honesty, transparency, and empathy.

Being an Authentic Woman

Data from Columbia Business School's Heidi vs. Howard study showed that "Success and likeability are positively correlated for men and negatively correlated for women." When I read this, I could not help but pause. If such a statement were true, then somehow it had negative implications for women. I remember a very powerful advertisement from 2013 by Procter and Gamble Philippines for its Pantene shampoo brand. The advertisement addressed gender stereotypes in the workplace. The narration for the advertisement stated:

> When a man is assertive, *he is a boss*. But when a woman leads, *she is bossy*. When a man engages in dialogue, *he is persuasive*, but when a woman steps up to be heard, *she is pushy*. When a man brings work at home, *he is dedicated*, but when a woman who's also a mother spends extra time at home working, *she is viewed as selfish*. When a man takes care of his outward appearance, *he is neat*, but when a woman takes care of her looks, *she is vain*. When a man is confident, *he is smooth*, but when a woman shows confidence, *she is a show-off*.

Sadly, women are often judged through a different lens. We live in a world where double standards are common, and stereotypes hold back women from leadership roles. But it is up to us women to challenge it. Let us not be comfortable with status quo. Sometimes we are trapped in an inferiority complex thinking we do not deserve to be equal, and we then undercut our own value. We should stop feeling we are less than equal. "When you get a good woman leader, she is every bit as good as a man... good leaders are gender-neutral." (Jack Welch, CEO of General Electric.)

I still live in United Arab Emirates (UAE), where there are over 200 nationalities and where the expatriates outnumber the local Emiratis who comprise only 20% of the total population. About 700,000 Filipinos live and work in the UAE. Despite this number of Filipinos, there are not many Filipino leaders and very few Filipina women leaders in the professional workforce.

It often has observed that Overseas Filipino Workers are mostly in administrative roles and not in high-ranking executive positions. Even some of the most virtuous people have an unintentional and subconscious bias based on nationality. As noted above, I had my fair share of *complisults* (partly compliment, partly insult) as a Filipina women leader working overseas. When a male director joined the company, he was surprised that there was a Filipina director who had the same title as he had, so he asked if I was getting paid the as he was. What he did not know was that I was getting paid *higher* because I have more experience. His ego could not handle this since he had a low opinion of Filipinos, his maid at home was a Filipina so he questioned why a Filipina should be a director, at the same administrative level. He started politicking against me inside the office to prove that he was better. Instead of confronting him, I focused my energy on achieving better business results and motivating my team. After a year, that guy left the company while I remained for a few more years.

Living outside the Philippines for more than ten years modified how I behave as a Filipino. Being exposed to different cultures has made me more tolerant and open-minded but also influenced me to feel a closer attachment to my home country and take pride in my Philippine upbringing. I have been prouder to be a Filipino when I am outside the Philippines. Each time I have been asked about my country of origin after a successful presentation or participation at an international meeting, I would say with a broad smile that I am from the Philippines. I remember a specific incident when I was in Hamburg, Germany for a Europe, Middle East, and Africa (EMEA) directors' meeting. When I showed my passport during check in at a five-star hotel, the front desk officer who was a Filipino was surprised to check in a Filipina at their hotel. He was so happy to have met me that he introduced me to his supervisor and his European colleagues. I did not know him but I felt his sense of pride and recognition, he was celebrating that a Filipina director checked in at the hotel where he was working.

Frequently people would also make assumptions about me, thinking that I had lived in Europe for many years and even received my education there. I would politely correct these assumptions and proudly say that I have been raised in the Philippines and add that my parents worked hard to give me a wonderful education for which I am thankful.

I have observed that it is easy to evolve, change oneself, and forget about one's origin when in a foreign country as an expatriate. I have seen how some people have changed their persona in order to assimilate with their host country culture. For some, assimilation has positive benefits and may provide a sense of independence and increased self-confidence. Yet, for some people assimilation has served as a mask for pretension.

For me, there are no fake accents, no fabrication, or delusion of grandeur, and no pretensions.

I am brave enough to be my authentic self, being completely comfortable with who I am, speaking my mind, giving feedback, and sharing opinions sincerely and with integrity. That is how I want people to respect and follow me as a leader.

My motto is: Do not be afraid to be you. Own it. Be your authentic self.

Motherhood, a Wave of Change

My son at a very young age has been exposed to my achievements. He traveled with me to India when I received the Women Leadership Achievement award by the World Women Leadership Congress in 2016. He accompanied me for my photo shoot for the 100 Most Influential Filipinos in the Gulf by Illustrado magazine in 2015. He was also with me in Canada and accompanied me onstage when I was recognized as one of the 100 Most Influential Filipina Women in the World by Filipina Women's Network (FWN) in 2017. He was a presenter and I was part of the judging panel for The Filipino Times awards in the UAE in 2017.

The gender gap is wider for working moms. Employers often hesitate in hiring working moms especially those with young children. There is a preconceived notion that working moms could not give one hundred percent attention to their work because they are often distracted by family-related tasks.

It has been observed that mothers tend to underestimate their worth and undermine their value. There is a sense of guilt at not having enough time to do everything. There is a stereotype that mothers, especially with young children, are struggling to find the balance between work and personal life. Although this might be true for some individuals, it has become a sweeping generalization that hurts all working moms. This is not a fair generalization as I know many moms who are very successful in managing both their work and their family.

I agree with what Sheryl Sandberg, COO of Facebook said about being a working mom: "Keep your foot on the gas."

The start of my career advancement coincided with raising my son, and this has proved challenging at times. For instance, it often meant taking him to the office when the nanny was ill or waking up three hours early while on a business trip to Europe to call my husband and remind him to take our son to nursery school on time.

While it has not always been easy, being a mother and equally being a working professional has taught me so much more than if I had not done them together. Having a child has never been an impediment to my effectiveness as a leader. On the contrary, it has boosted my work ethic and fueled my productivity as I do a balancing act between my professional and personal life.

There are certain realities that I have learned to embrace, such as multi-tasking, staying extremely organized, and as much as possible, planning one step ahead. For everything I have realized that quality over quantity is key. Rather than counting every moment that I have missed with my family, which turns into guilt, I maximize the time I have and appreciate every moment. Equally, I approach every aspect of work with productivity, efficiency, and results, rather than spending time at my desk putting in the 'hours.'

As my son grows up to be a young man, I would like to impart a specific set of values in him. These values include that women should be: treated as equal, listened to emphatically, and respected; and their contributions to the society should be valued.

Pay It Forward

As I grow older and become more successful in my career, my desire for social responsibility has also grown. It was strengthened even more when I became a member of Filipina Women's Network last year and I have met these extraordinary women from different walks of life, each one telling inspiring stories of bravery, courage, compassion, and humility. These Filipina women leaders deserve to be embraced and celebrated.

I have an unabashed admiration for leaders who are committed to social responsibility, whether as part of an organization or as individuals. My friend and confidante, Antonio Chedrawy, the Chief Financial Officer at OMD is very actively involved in humanitarian efforts; and he finds time from his busy schedule to participate. I have known him for many years, and he has been very supportive of charity projects for the benefits of the Filipino community, including giving donations to orphanages and homes for the elders. We both participated, along with other multinational colleagues in building a water tank at Suplang, Batangas under the Planet Water Foundation in 2017. Antonio is an inspiration in our industry and has supported me with sound advice both professionally and personally. He used to tell me that a great leader appreciates everyone's contribution and always stays positive no matter how challenging the situation might be.

Currently, I am getting more involved in social service work with the Filipino community in the UAE. Together with my fellow leaders at FWN and from other organizations, we are committed to building a strong and stable work pipeline for Filipinos in the Middle East. I am a volunteer lecturer and trainer for the Filipino Training and Development program, that is a social learning and skills upgrading program aimed at supporting the marginalized OFWs in the UAE.

A Woman's Worth: Knowing Your Value

That women tend to settle for less in the workforce is well-documented. Many of us are considered emotional human beings who are easily pleased. We feel lucky to be given a chance to contribute more time in the company and we do not mind expanding our role. We are given more tasks, but our pay remains the same. When the going gets tough, we are unable to manage and we become overworked, we start complaining. We must stop whining and start acting. We should begin to take charge.

When I started working in the Middle East ten years ago, I was still single, and I felt lucky to be earning more than double what I was receiving back home. Because I was new in the country, I was not aware of the salary brackets, and when I compared my salary with other Filipinos in the field, I thought I was doing well.

I was wrong for I was comparing apples to oranges. I discovered one day when my male colleague who had the same title as he accidentally left his salary certificate on a printer that was accessible to everyone. I went to the printer to take a report I printed. When I saw his salary certificate my jaw dropped. I was deeply shocked to find out that he was getting paid twice my salary even though we were both managers. I doubted myself and felt that maybe I was not competent and qualified for the job to earn only half of what my male colleague was getting, I felt hurt that perhaps they did not like me and this is their way of pushing me out. I felt discriminated against because they think of Filipinos as a lesser race hence they do not view someone like me as equally qualified. A lot of negative thoughts started racing through my mind and I was ready to explode.

I wanted to confront our general manager about his unfair treatment, but because I was young then, I did not find the courage to do it. Instead, I spent months putting my head down, minding my own business, and continuing to do my daily tasks. I worked quietly and continued to perform my duties very well. I told myself that great things happen to those who wait and when the time is right, I would negotiate and claim what I deserve.

I was fortunate that my direct supervisor, a Lebanese gentleman named Andre El Ghawi had strong faith in me and he had been championing my capability internally and externally to the clients. When the company underwent a massive restructuring, I found the perfect moment to discuss my compensation. The new management was selecting very few individuals who they would keep as the business shifted to new ownership. I was one of the very few who got chosen to stay. I did not say "Yes, thank you for keeping me," instead I used this as leverage to negotiate from a position of strength. I was aware that often in the face of organizational change out of fear of losing our job, we tend to impulsively accept anything being offered to us, even if we are being shortchanged.

I prepared myself days before I sat at the bargaining table. I wrote down a list of my accomplishments in the company and highlighted the most tangible ones that were directly linked to business profitability. I reminded myself: Do not overexplain, be as concise as possible. Do not be too soft on providing justifications as to why you need a raise, but also do not be so hard that you end up burning bridges. When you negotiate, be objective and try not to be emotional. State the facts firmly but diplomatically. Research industry benchmarks concerning compensation because you will be equipped to negotiate better since you know the market value of your contribution. Your end target is for management to realize your value in the company, that you are a strong asset, and most importantly that you are irreplaceable. Be courageous, for it is better to have tried and fail than to live a life with regrets for not even attempting it.

Sometimes women shy away from asking for a raise or promotion because we fear getting rejected. That is why preparation is very important. Prepare for both the best and the worst that could happen. To mitigate the worst, always have a plan B. This means that you should also consider looking for other opportunities that would match what you are expecting and what you deserve.

At the bargaining table, I told the CEO that I believe I was being undervalued in the current structure of the company. That I was handling the most important client, but I was being remunerated the least. I explained several facts that showed how my salary was not commensurate with the scope of my responsibilities. I mentioned that I was only asking for what I deserve as per industry average and nothing more. I was careful not to go over the top, so the management would understand how sensible my request was.

I told myself that I was ready to walk if the discussion turned sour. Fortunately, the new management agreed to adjust my compensation, so it was at par with the rest of the managers. Since then, I promised myself never to underestimate my abilities and undercut my value. See Sidebar 1 for a description of what I do currently.

My leadership story is still a work in progress. I am still young, and I know I will still evolve with more experiences and knowledge. But one thing is for sure, that I will stay true to myself and always be proud of my Filipino heritage.

My Leadership Advice

Here is my advice on becoming effective female leaders:

1. Do not lead like a man but lead like a powerful woman. Being a female leader gives you an advantage so trust your natural instincts. Go with your gut. Take a leap of faith.

2. Stay authentically humble. Do not fake it. Leadership is not about ego or power tripping. It is about being able to manage up, down, and sideways so that the people who work with you and the business can thrive in ways that drive value.

3. Be strategically agile. Learn to adapt and adjust your leadership styles based on different business and team climates. Keep evolving for the only thing constant in this world is change.

4. Before you can, you must believe you can. It starts inside you, that inner drive that brings you out of your comfort zone, that pushes you to your limits and expands your horizon towards professional success and personal fulfillment. Build a strong sense of purpose in your life that would serve as a strong foundation for resilience and persistence.

"Among Tier 1 international media agencies handling blue chip brands and usually dominated by Westerners and Arabs, Roxane Negrillo currently holds the most senior role of any Filipino."

SIDEBAR 1: SENIOR MANAGING DIRECTOR RESPONSIBILITIES

A Senior Planning Director in a media agency is responsible for managing a portfolio of clients and taking the lead in developing successful media and communications campaigns built on data-driven insights, strategy, and planning to achieve business and marketing objectives. She leads in driving innovation and media excellence across various paid media touchpoints and is primarily accountable for managing the client relationships and maintaining the profitability of the account.

Focus:

- As Managing Director, she is the authority for all media campaigns. She directly leads the media team using a governance approach that guides, supervises, and optimizes the implementation of holistic media campaigns.

- She develops and implements frameworks for integrated and collaborative planning among the company, clients, and external partners.

- She leads strategic media conversations to improve performance against set objectives and strengthen accountability.

- She identifies and manages strategically relevant long-term media partners for clients, makes decisions, and improves productivity of the business.

Among Tier 1 international media agencies handling blue chip brands and usually dominated by Westerners and Arabs, Roxane Negrillo currently holds the most senior role of any Filipino. During her 10 years in the UAE, she has worked with more than 100 international brands from various industries such as Fast Moving Consumer Goods (FMCG), aviation, telecommunication, automotive, finance, technology, fashion, retail, food, and real estate.

GEORGITTA 'BENG' PIMENTEL PUYAT

Chairman, Philippine Orchard Corporation
Filipina Women's Network, Board Member *(2018-2021)*
GLOBAL FWN100™ 2017

Volunteerism: A Life's Journey

'*Que Sera Sera*, Whatever will be, Will be' was a song I often sang as a young girl because I often wondered about my future. I sang this during the parties that my parents would host with music and dancing in my childhood home in Cotabato, Mindanao. My parents were leaders in their respective fields so the guests were their medical and pharmaceutical colleagues, Rotarians and their Rotary Anns, and close family friends and their children. Imagine ladies in their fine dresses and gentlemen in their suits socializing out in the lawn, while inside the house a portable film projector showed movies for the entertainment of the guests.

My name is Georgitta Pimentel Puyat, and my mission in life is volunteerism. I am the wife of a wonderful man, a mother to four sons and a daughter, mother-in-law to three daughters-in-law, and a grandmother to three precious grandchildren. I am a co-founder of a company that innovates products for the benefit of disadvantaged farmers and their families. I am a member of various socio-civic organizations that aim to educate, enrich, and most importantly, empower. I am a leader who thrives on hard work and inspires others to use the best of their abilities. And most importantly, I am a lifetime **Volunteer** who selflessly gives her time, talent, and resources to charitable and community-based activities.

Early Inspirations

I believe anyone can be a volunteer. For myself, volunteerism is a lifetime commitment. My first experience with being a volunteer was helping my parents

Ramon and Florecita Pimentel, my biggest inspirations and the foundation of my life mission of volunteerism. My siblings and I grew up in a strict household, where academics and extracurricular activities were encouraged. During our summer vacations, we would drive to the mountains of Upi and stay in our vacation house where the weather is like Baguio. Back then, there was no electricity so we would light our gas lamps when the sun sets. On Saturdays, we would watch the Tiruray tribe folk come down from the mountains in their colorful attire, bearing their beautiful baskets full of produce and crafts to be sold at the Market. Back then, it truly was an Age of Innocence.

My late father, Dr. Ramon Casiño Pimentel, Sr., was a pioneer doctor, from Balingasag and Tagaloan, Misamis Oriental. He left his gentrified family and traveled in search of a place to set up a medical practice. He took Pre-Med in Silliman University in Dumaguete, graduated from the UP College of Medicine in Padre Faura, Manila, and completed his residency at the Philippine General Hospital. He eventually chose to set up his medical practice in Cotabato after he married my mother. At aged 10, I used to travel with him in his old Buick car, or sometimes on the Minrapco buses, to see the wonders of Cotabato and visit patients who lived in barrios far away from his practice. It was on these trips with my stern, but kind, father that I was exposed to the beauty of nature and the need to preserve the unique culture of our province. It was so peaceful then that we could travel with no fear of being ambushed or being kidnapped. My responsibility on these trips was to be my father's assistant and to look after our expenses. Patients often paid us in kind, with live chickens, fresh eggs, and other local products that would then make an appearance at our dinner table.

My mother Florecita Muñoz Santiago Pimentel, currently living strong at 101 years old, is a vivacious woman who is very much the life of the party. She studied to be a Pharmacist at the University of Santo Tomas, Manila and is originally from Betis, Guagua, and Minalin, Pampanga. Her family relocated to Malabang, Lanao del Sur (a town adjacent to Marawi City) when her father became the town's municipal judge. My mother met my father in Lanao del Sur while he was traveling. After settling down in Cotabato with my father, she became an active member and leader of various socio-civic organizations. She was the longest-serving president of the Catholic Women's League Archdiocese of Cotabato. She was the proprietor of a pharmacy and soda fountain and was the sole local distributor of Magnolia Ice Cream products. She established Cotabato's first Puericulture Center Maternity Ward, which later became a hospital. I would walk to the Center every day after elementary school to spend an afternoon in the presence of women in need of prenatal care while I did odd jobs for the Center.

Enjoying New Activities

Growing up, I loved to try new activities and excelled in them, whether it was in track and field, or declamation contests. I consistently got high marks in my studies. My parents sent my siblings and I to public schools because the local teachers had received training from Americans. My classmates were a mix of Muslim and Christians and my best friend, Ruth, had Muslim-Christian parents. This love of new experiences was encouraged by my membership to the Girl Scout Movement of the Philippines (GSP). Some of my best memories were attending camps all over Mindanao and in the Girl Scouts National Campsite in Baguio City. It was through the Girl Scouts that I met many of my future peers.

Getting a College Education

This love for new and diverse experiences became the basis for my work ethic and moral standards that ignited my passion for volunteerism and that I continue to uphold. At age 14, I graduated high school as class valedictorian with top honors. In my valedictory address, I spoke of a time in the future when the Philippines would face overpopulation and lack of jobs. I could not imagine how relevant that speech was to today's situation. At the age of 14, I fearlessly boarded a boat by myself on a three-day journey to register at the University of the Philippines (UP) in Diliman. The world beyond Cotabato beckoned and I was ready to venture out. I was 15 years old, young by today's standards when I enrolled in UP Diliman as a freshman. My elder siblings Ramon Jr. and Yaying were also at UP as students. To help keep busy, I joined the UP Concert Chorus whose members included those with the world-renowned UP Madrigal Singers.

Building Lifetime Connections

Intrinsically entwined to my life as a college student was living in all-female dorms. In my first year, I stayed in the Ilang-Ilang Residence Hall, which housed female scholars from the provinces. We later then moved to Kamia Hall for the second and third years and then to Sampaguita Hall for our senior year and post-graduates studies. Our batch called ourselves the "*Tadidins*," a term with no real meaning, but often said with fond exasperation. Despite our individual journeys with some choosing to emigrate and some to stay in the Philippines, we still keep in contact and have reunions at locations all over the world.

I joined as a sophomore a Society of Dramatics and Fine Arts called the Sigma Delta Phi (SDP), the oldest Greek Letter Society for women at UP. Through SDP, I gained an appreciation for the Theatre. It is a tradition for the sorority to do annual productions, and this became a highlight of the student calendar. These productions gave me many life skills that I learned through osmosis, such as looking for sponsorship, fundraising, stage-managing, and play-acting. I acted in three different productions, portraying the film roles of Doris Day in 'The Pajama Game', Rita Moreno in 'Bye, Bye Birdie', and Natalie Wood in a Tennessee Williams play called 'This Property is Condemned.' Because of these musicals and stage shows, I gained a following and I was approached to be the singer for the official jingle of Cathay Pacific Airways. Much like the Tadidins, my sisterhood with my fellow Sigma Deltans transcended the decades and made a profound impact on my life. It was through the Sigma Delta Phi sorority that I later gave back to the university. We had fun and that made all the difference.

Learning from a Master

My most significant influence during my college years was my future mother-in-law, Eugenia Guidote Puyat. She was the Philippines' third Certified Public Accountant and a member of Zonta International, a global organization of professionals that aim to empower women and girls worldwide. At that time, she was the President of the Zonta Club of Manila, the premier Zonta Club in Asia. Originally as a ploy by my future husband to have me watched while he went to Wharton, my mother-in-law took me under her wing and brought me to her club's service activities. I was involved in the restoration of the now-defunct Puerto Real Gardens Aquarium and the planting of orchids and white roses in Intramuros. Lola Gening, as she was lovingly called by her grandchildren, brought me to her other volunteer endeavors, such as the *Asociacion de Damas de Filipinas*, a Catholic orphanage, and the Jovita Fuentes Music Cultural Society. As President of the Society, my mother-in-law helped set up scholarships for Philippine musicians to study abroad. Beneficiaries of this scholarship have included Jose Contreras (Piano), Julian Quirit (Violin and Conducting), and Lourdes de Leon Gregorio (Harp and Piano).

Marriage and Children

I met my future husband, Alfonso 'Jing' Guidote Puyat when I was 14 during the summer vacation before my last year of high school. He was on a trip with his Upsilon Sigma Phi fraternity brothers to see much of the Philippines and to visit as many Sigma Deltans in their home provinces. When he was in Cotabato City to visit my older sister Yaying, neither of us was very impressed with each other. We met again in my freshman year at UP when I became a Muse of the Yakal Residence Hall. Jing, a photojournalist from the Philippine Collegian, UP's official newsletter, was sent to get a picture of me for publication. Jing was late for our appointed meeting, and I was livid because I was going to be late for a class in a far away building.

During my sophomore year, Gari, Jing's fraternity brother, brought him to Kamia Hall to invite me for a double date with my sister for the Upsilon Cocktails at the Penthouse of the Manila Banking Corporation. Jing and I were the chaperones and he had, most importantly, a white Mercedes Benz that would be our transportation for the night. There was dancing, but Jing was not fond of dancing, so we ended up talking at length. Something must have clicked because he suddenly found me very interesting and that I could carry on a conversation that made sense.

Jing began courting me after I was accepted into the SDP. At one point, he said to me while we were conversing on the steps of the Arts and Sciences Building "I want you to be the mother of our future 12 children!" I was speechless! I felt he was so presumptuous and he was not even my boyfriend yet. I avoided him for weeks until he wore me down with his persistence through *haranas* [serenades] with his fraternity brothers outside my dorm window. He did not tell me that he deferred his acceptance to Wharton Graduate School in Pennsylvania. Someone close to Jing whispered to me that he already missed his first semester. I finally said yes to him so he could go for his Master's degree.

Our early courtship was marked by his time in Wharton and my continuing education in UP Diliman. Volunteer work was a constant with university projects and time for my future mother-in-law's projects. I would spend time with his family for Sunday lunch, and he would call so we could talk. He also frequently sent me love letters by slow mail. It was a long-distance romance, but Jing came home when he could from Pennsylvania, often in time to see me perform in the year-end production, as well at Christmas and summer breaks.

No couple has a perfect relationship. Jing believed in the traditional role for women in the home and told me before we were officially dating that I should consider changing to Accounting because I would be a housewife, taking care of our children and the finances of our business. This infuriated me as I was a young feminist who wanted to be a lawyer and to be told just to be a housewife did not sit well with me. When I graduated in March 1967 with an AB Political Science, I decided to enroll for a Master's Degree in Sociology instead of taking Law, because I knew it would be more practical and that sooner or later, Jing and I would be married.

When Jing finally returned from Wharton, I was still completing my Master's degree. He had a job waiting for him in a new company set up by his father, so he needed time to get used to his new position. Meanwhile, I had the opportunity to participate in the *Binibining Pilipinas* Beauty Pageant. He was not in favor of me joining the pageant, but I had made up my mind, packed my bags, and left for the Araneta Coliseum where all the candidates were housed for the duration of the pageant. Being a participant of the *Binibining Pilipinas* was a Trial by Fire because I had to learn as the pageant progressed. It was more than learning how to pose or how to give a good interview. It was also about philanthropy because, through the *Binibining Pilipinas* Charities and the Philippine Charity Sweepstakes, we would later promote the Philippine Tuberculosis Society for Indigent Patients. Jing soon came around to the idea of his future wife being a beauty queen when his family came to support me. Back then, there was only one titleholder, the Ms. Universe Crown, and all the other finalists were runners-up. In the end, I did not win (the winner was Charina Zaragoza), but I still have my runner-up trophy. Even now with the pageant so many years in the past, a few fans still remember me from that pageant year.

On December 16, 1968, Jing and I decided to get married a month later. We wanted a simple wedding, but our parents objected. They convinced us to postpone for another month so we could prepare for a proper wedding. Jing, along with my future in-laws, came to visit Cotabato City to formally ask my parents for my hand in marriage. Jing's father, the late Senate President Gil J. Puyat, was very much involved and allocated his mornings to work on the details of the wedding. We exchanged marriage vows on Sunday, February 16, 1969, in Santuario de San Jose in Greenhills, followed by a big reception at the Manila Polo Club in Makati. The next day, we left for our four-month, round the world honeymoon, a gift from Jing's parents. During the trip, I saw many wonders hand in hand with my new husband.

When we came back from our honeymoon, we moved to the Eugenia Puyat Apartments in Quezon City, where Jing's siblings lived after they were married. We settled into our new domestic life and I was pregnant with my first son, Ramoncito, our honeymoon baby. Unfortunately, I was cautioned by my parents not to come home to Cotabato City for security reasons as I was now married to the Senate President's son and trouble was starting to brew.

Searching for My Purpose

Four years into my married life, my husband and my two young boys were my priority. But I was restless. I was seeking something that I knew was very important to me as a person. I did volunteer work for the Philippine General Hospital and the Orthopedic Hospital for Children. I also joined The National Citizen's Movement for Free Elections (NAMFREL), an election watchdog unit known for non-partisan election monitoring. It was a frightening experience with goons entering into the West Rembo Makati Voting Stations. We guarded the ballot boxes with our lives and prevented them from being snatched before they were brought to the Municipal Hall for canvassing.

I felt like I could be doing more and many of my alumnae sisters from Sigma Delta Phi felt the same way. We started to gather together to rekindle our fellowship and called ourselves the "Wednesday Group." We met in each other's homes for cooking lessons, lectures, and of course, reminiscences of days when we were campus queens, frat sweethearts, ROTC Corps Sponsors, and campus theater luminaries. One day, a Sigma Deltan posed this question at a gathering, "What do we do now that we are out of UP Diliman?" A discussion followed and we decided that it was only right to give back to the university that had given us so much. We then established the Sigma Delta Phi Alumnae Association (SDPAA) with Celia Diaz Laurel as its first President. Its goals were to raise funds, support the service endeavors of the alumnae association, and promote sisterhood amongst the alumnae members.

Entrepreneurship and Giving Back to Indigenous Groups

To raise funds, we organized small bazaars in the homes of the sorority sisters. My sister Yaying and I joined and sold *Inaul* [silk] *malongs* woven by Maguindanao women, baskets from the Tiruray tribe, and woven *tinalak* cloth and brass figurines from the T'boli tribe. These products made by indigenous tribes from Cotabato Province would become popular with our friends. Local buyers and exporters would purchase our entire stock to be resold elsewhere. This was the springboard for BasketHouse Philippines, Inc., a business venture set up by my siblings, my mother, and myself as the company President, to promote, sell, and export the wares of the indigenous tribes of Mindanao. This was a genuine effort to give back to the Tiruray tribe who protected and evacuated my parents and their friends from Japanese soldiers during World War II. The soldiers were seeking people like my father because he was a doctor.

One day, Jing told me that he was happy that I did not follow his dictates that I should be a mere housewife. He told me I was like his mother and that it made him proud and that he respected me more for it. I was teary-eyed from the frank comparison and told Jing, "Just make sure you earn enough to support the family and me including my many charities as I will be devoting much of my time and resources on them." Since then, my family has been my most prominent supporters of all my endeavors and they have started to do volunteer work with me. I was so lucky I have my family's loving encouragement.

A Mother's Story

A mother's story is always different with each child. Having given birth several times, I have run the gamut of wonderful highs and devastating lows. The birth of my first child, Ramoncito, had no complications. My second child, Cocoy, was born during the arrival of two visitors to the Philippines, Pope Paul VI and Typhoon Yoling. It was a difficult birth, and I had to be immobilized. Later, I was informed that my uterus had failed to contract and I was in danger of bleeding to death. It took several hours before I was stable enough to be wheeled out of the delivery room. My next child, Deo, my little angel in heaven, is the one most people do not know about. He was born premature and died days later on Halloween. After five years of living in the Eugenia Puyat Apartments, we moved to our current home in Makati City, where my next child, Noel, was born. His birth was the easiest though his toddler years were a bit of a hardship because roughhousing with his eldest brother resulted in a broken leg. Niño, my fifth child, was born with health problems that caused him to be confined to his room through most of his early childhood. He was called the 'Boy in a Bubble' by most of my friends that knew of his condition. He mostly outgrew this as he got older. When Niño was six years old, he offhandedly asked: "When will the stork deliver my baby sister?" Jing and I saw this as a sign from the Lord that we could try for another baby. In 1987, Bea, my last child, and only girl was born. Bea's birth was received with jubilation, and several congratulatory messages came with the message: "At last, a Princess!"

My pregnancy with Bea was difficult during the last two months as I developed high blood pressure. When my due date came, I had to be monitored frequently, and the results indicated that my blood pressure was lower when I was in a fetal position. So, my OB/GYN doctor had me give birth in that position. After the delivery, I seemed to be fine. Three days later, I developed Post Eclampsia and slept for three straight days. While I was comatose, I was keenly aware of what was happening around me. I could hear the movements and the chatter of my children, and I could listen to the cries of my baby girl. But I slept on with my husband at my side. The moment I woke up, Jing held my hand and whispered. "Beng, you are very lucky. The Lord did not want to take you to his bosom yet. Maybe you still have a lot to do in this world."

Road to Service and Advocacy

After I recovered from my Post Eclampsia, I did some deep soul-searching. My near-death experience triggered a desire to work twice as hard. Every day was so important because I felt I was on borrowed time. Maybe the Lord's plans for me took time to align. Aside from my work with the SDPAA, I joined three prominent organizations at roughly the same time during my pregnancy with Bea: The Philippine Philharmonic Orchestra Society (PPOSI), Zonta International (ZI), and the UNIFEM National Committee Philippines (Now UN Women).

Sigma Delta Phi Alumnae Association, Inc.

Betty Go Belmonte, founder of the Star Group of Publications, was elected as President of the SDPAA in 1986. After she was elected, she asked me to help organize her Board as many of the alumnae were strangers to her, and she trusted my judgment. During Betty's term, the Alumnae Association was incorporated into a non-stock, non-profit organization with the Securities and Exchange Commission (SEC), and I was elected Treasurer.

In 1993, I was elected Chairman and President of the Alumnae Association. At the same time, my husband Jing was also the President of the Upsilon Sigma Phi Alumni Association. The only project we cooperated on was to jointly celebrate the Sigma Delta Phi's 60th and the Upsilon Sigma Phi's 75th anniversaries at the Manila Hotel.

The Creation of the SDP Outreach Trust Fund, Inc. (OTFI)

During the year of the 60th Jubilee Year of SDP, the SDPAA launched the year-round Outreach Trust Fund Drive. The proceeds were to be placed in a Trust Fund with the special proviso that only the interest earnings would be used to fund the Association's outreach projects. When the SDP Outreach Trust Fund, Inc. was established, I was elected the founding Chair of the Board of Trustees. Among the projects, the OTFI subsidized were: medical missions, scholarships for the UP College of Social Work, support for the Philippine General Hospital and the National Orthopedic Hospital, and the community development of Purok Libis, an informal settler's area beside Diliman.

Philippine Philharmonic Orchestra Society, Inc. (PPOSI)

In 1985, a group of business leaders established the Philippine Philharmonic Orchestra Society, Inc. (PPOSI), a private non-government organization whose aim is to support and finance the Philippine Philharmonic Orchestra (PPO), the premiere Orchestra of the Philippines based at the Cultural Center of the Philippines. Headed by the late Senator Edgardo Angara, this was a response to the Philippine Government's lack of funding for arts and culture programs. I was asked by the PPOSI Board to be the founding Chair of the PPOSI Ladies Committee and was later elected Member of the Board of Trustees. We were the workhorses of the Society and used our collective resources to promote the music of the PPO. We actively searched for new subscribers for the PPO Concert Series and started outreach performances in public spaces. We also sought funding to finance services for the musicians; including rehabilitating the musician's lounge, providing new uniforms, and granting scholarships for the foreign studies of the musicians.

In 1987, the PPOSI Board of Trustees launched the Orchestra Endowment Fund (OEF) to augment the retirement fund of the PPO musicians. I was Coordinator of the OEF. One unique fundraising idea of the Ladies Committee was the inception of the Home Concert Series, a special series of 14 concerts hosted in the homes of foreign ambassadors. These concerts featured highly acclaimed Filipino artists such as Evelyn Mandac, Rowena Arrieta, Otoniel Gonzaga, Andion Fernandez, Oscar Yatco, Liza Macuja, Celeste Legaspi, Ryan Cayabyab, among others. The Home Concert Series was a successful venture for the PPOSI Ladies Committee with tickets to each event quickly selling out.

Zonta International

Zonta International would be the organization where most of the advocacy and service projects that I am most proud of were realized. These projects have helped women, young girls, and their families for decades. I joined the Zonta Club of Makati and Environs in 1986, and I was then the only member of childbearing age. This is why my fellow club members called Bea my "Zonta Baby."

I always held a position since the start of my membership. I chaired the club's Annual Charity Bazaar, an idea that stemmed from the small bazaars that I had participated in with my sorority sisters. We were the first to use a credit card system, and the proceeds were used to sustain the club's various socio-civic projects. In 1992, I co-established and managed for seven years the East Rembo Livelihood and Skills Training Center, a multi-awarded service project that taught women, especially mothers in search of extra income, new skills such as sewing, dressmaking, and embroidery. The Center was featured in a 15-minute documentary for the TV program 'NEGOSIETE' and would later be a model of other livelihood centers in the Philippines. After I became President of my Club, our presence in the Livelihood Center would expand to include an award-winning adult literacy program and an informal continuing education for the youth program, in partnership with the Department of Education, Culture and Sports (DECS).

My most significant contribution to the club came at our darkest hour. Our old Community Center situated in Kalayaan Avenue, Makati City, was to be demolished to give way for a major road construction. With the help of my husband Jing, we had a meeting with local officials and secured a 1,000 square meters property in Fort Bonifacio, Taguig with a lease of 1 Peso a year for 25 years, renewable for another 25 years. On this property, we built our new two-story Zonta Makati and Environs Community Center. The Center became the permanent hub for the club's socio-civic activities in Makati, Taguig, and other nearby areas. The Center has preschool for the local community, a medical and dental clinic, and livelihood training for women.

In January 1997, I co-established the Zonta Makati and Environs Psychological Center for Sexually Abused Children, ages 3-17 years, in Marillac Hills, Muntinlupa, one of the legacy projects of our club. This was a response to the lack of government facility that provided mental health and wellbeing services to young girls who were the victims of rape, sexual abuse, and sex trafficking. Initially, it was a challenge to fund, but I was able to negotiate a monthly subsidy of PhP 50,000 from the Philippine Amusement and Gaming Corporation (PAGCOR), which supported the project for many years. The Psychological Center is staffed by volunteers and employs two full-time psychological therapists. They provide a variety of services including psychological support, family counseling, cultural field trips, and workshops on Women's Health, Women's and Children's Rights, Violence Against Women and Children Issues, and provide Legal Support to prosecute their abusers. For 21 years, the Psychological Center has received numerous rewards for service and advocacy from Zonta International as well as annual citations from the Department of Social Welfare and Development (DSWD), recognizing the Center as the longest-serving NGO-based project in Marillac Hills. At any given time, 200-300+ girls are sent by DSWD from all over the Philippines. To date, the Center has helped about 4,500 girls on their road to recovery.

UNIFEM PHILIPPINE NATIONAL COMMITTEE (NOW UN WOMEN)

I cannot remember the exact year I was recruited into the United Nations Development Fund for Women (UNIFEM) Philippine National Committee. My membership was passive, and I attended meetings only when I felt like going. I was not getting much satisfaction and I let my membership lapse two years, thinking that my name would be taken off the roster. In 2000, I was nominated to the Board, elected Vice-President, and tasked to be the Chairman of Government Relations. I would later be elected President for two biennia (2002-2004 & 2004-2006) and then Chairman for another two biennia (2006-2008 & 2008-2010).

My predecessor, Erlinda Panlilio, sent me a note one day saying that I should study the revised Recognition Agreement from UNIFEM Headquarters. After reading the draft, I requested more documents, including the original 1997 Recognition Agreement. The new agreement would require National Committees to contribute a minimum of US$ 50,000 per year. This upset the Board as it was unrealistic given the Asian Economic Crisis. The consensus was to break the relationship with UNIFEM Headquarters and disband the Philippine National Committee. I stood up and told the Board we should not give up.

UNIFEM Philippine National Committee has the distinction of being the only one in a developing country. Per report of the UNIFEM, we were the fourth biggest contributor among the 17 National Committees worldwide. We had been very diligent with meeting the mandates set by UNIFEM and giving up would be a waste. I proposed sending a position paper to UNIFEM Headquarters and it was quite a relief when they agreed to our request for an exemption from the revised Recognition Agreement.

Funds accumulated by National Committees are typically sent to the United Nations Development Programme (UNDP), and are then allocated to various UNIFEM supported projects globally. A unique feature that was granted to us was that funds raised by the Philippine National Committee be allocated by the UNDP to UNIFEM sponsored projects in the Philippines. One of the projects is PATAMABA, a network program that help improve the personal, social, and economic well-being of home-based workers. Home-based work was done by 98% women between the ages of 18 to 75 from 34 Philippine Provinces. The program provides the cottage industry workers with legal assistance, medical, maternity, retirement, and other benefits; as well as promoting stable employment.

Over the years, volunteerism has diversified my interests. While each of the organizations that I am part of has different aims, they all aim to give back through service and advocacy. No physical reward could match the gratification of knowing that people are changing their lives for the better.

Expanding Leadership to the World

Zonta International has been my organization of choice since my late mother-in-law introduced Zonta to me when I was a college student. After 32 years of active membership, I have served in many leadership roles in club, area, district and international levels.

In biennium 2010-2012, I was elected as Governor of District 17 (D17) with 72 clubs in six countries in Asia (Philippines, Thailand, Hong Kong, Macau, Singapore, and Malaysia). The District Governor is the direct link between the district and the

Zonta International Board, tasked to ensure oversight and governance over the district, and to report to the International Board regarding Zonta matters.

Along with my trusty red suitcases, I braved the harsh winter of Chicago, Illinois in order to attend the Governors-Elect Orientation/Training, as well as to visit Zonta International Headquarters. One of the things that had made a profound impression on me during my Governor's Training was the Lesson from the Geese. They always fly in a V-pattern formation allowing them to travel faster and further during their migration. When one strays from the formation, its flight quickly becomes difficult until it returns to the formation. Those in the rear honk their encouragement and when the leader gets tired, she goes to the back, and the next goose in line takes its place. This lesson became the inspiration for my biennial theme of "Women Empowering Women: Re-focusing on Zonta's Core Mission." I reasoned that if we were to change the world, we need to educate ourselves on the key mission and values of the organization.

After my Governors' Training, I wrote down what the district needed to do as I had about half a year to prepare before I was officially installed. This brought out the acronym T.E.A.M.S.H.I.N.E., a collective of goals set to enhance, empower and immerse the members of D17 with the core values and spirit of the Founders of Zonta International. By the time I was installed as D17 Governor during the ZI Convention in San Antonio, Texas, I was ready to face the members of D17 with its new District Board and a new direction.

The first order of business for the biennium was the training of Club Members. Since D17 is a large region with clubs from multiple countries, mandatory extensive training seminars were scheduled in Makati City, Bangkok, and Hong Kong for new members, club presidents, district committee chairs, and district board members. It is standard protocol to train the new district board and the committee chairs but it is a new practice to give club presidents an extensive refresher course on the objectives and policies of Zonta. By educating ourselves first, we were setting ourselves up as agents of change.

During the seminars, new practices were adopted like using public relations for visibility and public awareness, focusing on service projects that prioritize the benefit and empowerment of women and young girls, and increased use of members' diverse skills and talents. The most significant goal we asked of clubs was to promote the Legislative Awareness and Advocacy Committee (LAA) whose aim is to promote advocacy activities for gender equality, women's rights, and other matters that concern women. After their training, the 72 clubs have initiated advocacy efforts and service projects became more creative and focused.

I feel that I am one of the most travelled Governors in Zonta as I have journeyed the length and breadth of the Philippines from Laoag in the north to the islands of the Visayas, to the far south in Zamboanga for official D17 functions. My travel has extended to clubs in Hong Kong, Singapore, Malaysia, and Thailand, and even to the Zonta International Convention in Torino, Italy where one of my red suitcases finally gave up.

A highlight of my term as Governor was the 16th Zonta International District 17 Conference held in Sofitel Philippine Plaza in Manila. Dianne Curtis, the 2010-2012 ZI President attended the conference and complimented saying that our District conference was on par with an International Convention. The District Board ratified a motion to give 90% of the surplus funds earned from the conference back to the 72 clubs to be used for their service projects. The excess funds were to be divided equally. This was a first in the Zonta world.

By the end of my term as D17 Governor, I sat back and was amazed at all that we accomplished in 2 years. Membership has increased more than 20% and 5 new Zonta Clubs were chartered. 100% of the D17 clubs donated to the Zonta International Foundation, which supports international service projects in marginalized places in need of Zonta presence. We also pride ourselves with supporting hardworking young ladies who are leading the way in their respected fields and nominating them for accolades maintained by ZI. A rare feat that D17 managed to do was win a clean sweep of all the ZI awards. At ZI Convention in Torino, 2 Philippine Zonta clubs were awarded 2 of the Top 3 Zonta Clubs in the world.

I would describe my style of leadership, as very much like a seasoned conductor at the helm of an orchestra. It is only with the common goal and cooperation of the musicians that a performance can be harmonious. Proper attention and due diligence to the work is key as well as giving everyone room to grow creatively. There is also a need for singing, dancing, and merrymaking.

Epilogue: A Sentimental Journey

A close friend of mine once said to me while I was at a low point in my life, "Go into the world, do well and do good. Go into the world not just for yourself but also for others. When you link your journey with others, you will learn to love yourself and rise closer to God."

After the FWN Global Summit in Toronto, Canada, I extended my stay in North America to visit friends and relatives in the US. My cousin Lito would drive and we planned a road trip starting in Toronto, stopping by Buffalo, New York, visiting a cousin in the Poconos in Northeastern Pennsylvania, and ending in New York City. After a couple of days of rest and visiting Niagara Falls with my daughter-in-law's relatives, I left Toronto with much-improved spirits and half a suitcase full of gifts for my youngest grandchild, Cristiano.

The City of Buffalo has a special meaning to Zontians worldwide because it was where the first Zonta Club was chartered on November 8, 1919. It is the first US city you encounter once you cross the Canadian border. With 32 years of Zonta membership under my belt, I have always wanted to make a pilgrimage to Buffalo, so having the opportunity to do so near the Centenary of Zonta International was serendipitous. Our first stop was the old Buffalo Hotel Statler in the city center where the first Zonta Club held their meetings. Outside the hotel was a commemorative bronze plaque that noted Zonta's establishment. Our next stop was the Forest Lawn Cemetery to find the final resting place of Marian de Forest, a notable journalist, a playwright, a suffragist, a significant force in the women's progressive movement, and the founder of Zonta International. The weather that day was cold and windy, that made finding our last landmark more challenging. It took us more than an hour to find Delaware Park, north of the Forest Lawn Cemetery, to see the "Spirit of Womanhood," a bronze sculpture made by Larry Griffis and dedicated to Marian de Forest. When we asked for directions, it seemed like only the women knew where it was located. We eventually found it on top of a hill near a lake. The "Spirit of Womanhood" is a tall, elongated woman full of aspiration while the circle in her hands represent the world, eternity, and the cycle of life. As we approached, she seemed larger than life.

As I pondered my life's journey, I felt the weariness that I was experiencing lift away slowly. A lifetime of volunteerism is never an easy path, but I have many reasons to be grateful. My husband, children, daughters-in-law, and grandchildren are all in relatively good health. My mother, a miracle herself, is still alive at 101 years old. Many of my friends are in contact, thanks to modern conveniences like Viber and Facebook.

With one last look at the "Spirit of Womanhood," we drove off to continue our journey. Ever onwards we went, I am reminded of the lesson that awards, material riches, positions, and status in society are quickly forgotten when we are gone. But it is the footprints of service that we work on while still alive that many people will remember. I would like to think that I did something good and maybe people will remember me for the footprints I will leave behind.

LUCILLE TENAZAS

Associate Dean and Henry Wolf Professor
School of Art, Media and Technology
Parsons School of Design
GLOBAL FWN100™ 2013

A Class of Her Own

Original Interview and Words Mikhail Lecaros
First published in Adobo Magazine (March - April 2014)
Updated by Lucille Tenazas, July 2018

Blessed with an almost effortless dignity and a design sense that has earned her accolades all over the world, adobo Design Awards 2014 Head of Jury Lucille Tenazas is in a class all her own.

When it comes to the work of Lucille Tenazas, one is immediately struck by the precise manner that the designer's chosen elements convey information while avoiding the tendency towards over-embellishment that despoil many a contemporary work. Meticulous allocation of visual real estate notwithstanding, the voice and – more importantly – the intelligence behind each piece ring true and clear, communicating the intended message (and, by extension, the artist) more effectively than any number of superfluities.

Given the thought that must have gone into some of her pieces and the deftness of their execution, it is no surprise that Tenazas is at the top of her game. As a graphic designer, Tenazas has done work for clients as diverse as the San Francisco International Airport, Rizzoli International, the Neue Galerie Museum for German and Austrian Art in New York, and a number of non-profit organizations and institutions, as well as city, state and federal agencies. Highly-sought as an educator, Tenazas regularly gives design talks, seminars and workshops all over the world, in addition to being the Henry Wolf Professor in the School of Art, Media and Technology at Parsons School of Design in New York.

With over 30 years under her belt and a number of active projects going on at any given time, Tenazas is one practitioner who shows no signs of slowing down. Of course, the artist herself is amused by the notion that designing is the only thing people expect her to be up to all day long.

"They have this perception that I don't have a life outside of design," she laughs. "They think that that's all I do, I live, breathe, eat design, I mean I'm serious about what I do, but that doesn't preclude me living my life and enjoying other parts of my life. Sometimes they're surprised that I have kids, that I'm married…maybe the seriousness with which I view my work makes some people think that I'm a workaholic, but I'm not!"

Of course, seeing as Tenazas is the recipient of accolades like the American Institute of Graphic Arts (AIGA) Medal in 2013 and the National Design Award in Communications Design from the Smithsonian Cooper-Hewitt National Design Museum in 2002, one could be forgiven for thinking that it was mere "seriousness" that got her to where she is today, but that would only be half the picture.

Simply put, any artist is so much more than the mere sum of their works and, as *adobo* was privileged to find out, Tenazas is no exception, proving every bit as fascinatingly multifaceted – if not more so – than any single design.

The daughter of a civil engineer father and a mother who taught high school social studies, Tenazas grew up in the Philippines, attending the College of the Holy Spirit from kindergarten to college. The second of six children, Tenazas' creativity was fostered from an early age by her parents. Despite having the conventional expectations of wanting their daughter to be a lawyer or doctor ("You know, it would be great if there was an appendage to your name, like 'Atty.' or 'Dr.'!"), they supported her in her artistic pursuits.

Unfortunately, Tenazas' father would pass away when she was 16 years old, meaning he never saw the heights that his daughter eventually reached with her talents. Tenazas started small, joining school and local publications' competitions, slowly gaining a reputation in her circles for her abilities.

ADOBO How did your parents express their support for your art?

TENAZAS My father would just sit and watch while I worked on my art projects, he'd be drinking his beer, and he would wait for my mother because she always got home a little later from her teaching – around 7 or 8pm. After dinner, the dining table would be cleared, and I would then lay all my art supplies, but I think what was interesting to me was that he would always sit by me. He would sit quietly and watch what I was doing, and his presence was enough of an encouragement. Every once in a while, he would lean over and say "why did you use red for this?" and I would continue what I was doing and without even lifting my head, continue working and say, "I like it. I like making it this way." I think that the atmosphere I had at home, the encouragement of my parents, albeit not overt, by not so much putting their foot down, or making it into a situation where "you have to do this, or else!", and then continuing with the artistic work at school where I was held to a certain kind of standard. I was regarded as the class artist, volunteering to do art-related projects, doing the lettering and calligraphy for diplomas or certificates and so on. So my track, in a way, was pre-determined for me.

ADOBO So they never tried to change your mind?

TENAZAS My father was always planting seeds in terms of what was culturally acceptable and what was a viable profession—he was not alone in assuming that the arts was not a legitimate profession. You needed to be either a doctor or a lawyer to make money. And you know, who are you to question this? Being raised in an authoritarian culture, it wasn't my place to question what my parents said so I just quietly plodded along, engaging in work that interested me. But I think that at a certain point your parents can no longer question or dissuade you or do anything other than support you. And so I think, in a way, my parents were of that thinking that 'she cannot be swayed, so we might as well just follow what she's doing.'

ADOBO Tell us about when you realized there was a living to be made from your designs.

TENAZAS When I was at Holy Spirit, there were always these on-the-spot painting competitions and held at the various institutions, primarily the University of Santo Tomas (UST) in Manila, which had a robust Fine Arts program. These were typically day-long competitions starting in the morning and ending in mid-afternoon. Participants were given a theme and then fanned out around a certain perimeter within the campus and set to work. I participated in these competitions all throughout my college years. On my first try, I received an honorable mention, but in my senior year, I was one of four winners of the top prize. My brother, who was studying engineering at UST at the time, was hovering around while the judges made their decision. When my name was called, they gave me this envelope with cash – 400 pesos! We were so excited, my brother and I, that we took a cab home, instead of taking the bus. When we got home, my Mom asked, "how did it go?" And I said, "Well, you know, I did my best," and she saw from my face that I was disappointed. Then I turned around and I handed her the fat envelope! It was something I did all by myself in a short amount of time under very constrained circumstances. It was like (professional) design – there was a deadline, there was a theme, there was a project brief, whatever it is, it conforms to all these things that prepared me to actually enter the profession, and then be rewarded for it at the end of the day. So I've saved that envelope. It brings me back to how I was then, and in hindsight was a precursor to the work ethic that I have to this day. When I look back at my family albums – what I was doing then and how things like this prepared me to be at this stage of my work in my life, it is interesting to note this trajectory.

ADOBO We understand that you worked in a pharmaceutical company before you decided to go to the States to study. What was that like?

TENAZAS I had a full-time job as a marketing designer at a multinational company then named Smith Kline & French (now known as GlaxoSmithKline after several mergers) in Cainta, Rizal for three years. The work I produced there was what I submitted when I was applying to design graduate school in the United States. I received several letters of rejection to what I realized was quite a narrow body of work. We're talking vitamin labels, drug brochures, exhibition graphics for medical conventions, that kind of thing. Within the context of my work then, it was actually quite good, but taken independently, it did not have a lot of creative merit. Having been produced within a corporate design system, it was "prescriptive"—no pun intended, and did not have a point of view.

I eventually made it to San Francisco, at California College of Arts and Crafts (CCAC, now CCA) where I was accepted as a second degree design student in the undergraduate program. I spent my first few months undertaking design courses and building a new portfolio, and this was what got me accepted in the MFA Design program at Cranbrook Academy of Art in Bloomfield Hills, Michigan. So I think for me, my going to graduate school in the US was one of those seminal points because what it gave me was not just the opportunity to be better at what I did, but also to look deeper into my motivations and make me a critical thinker. So suddenly you were confronted with "It's not enough for your work to look good. It's not enough that it's pretty, but that it transcends formal resolutions and engage in more critical and provocative ways."

When I look back on my earlier work, the concept was not something I paid attention to. It was more about making things look good and putting things together in a very interesting way, but when you get deeper into it, what does it really mean?

I guess at the time, the people who saw my work didn't ask those questions anyway. And in the Philippines, that's what I think is missing. I'm curious about the standards creative people have in the cultural context of the Philippines. Because advertising, to me, having to deal with consumer culture, often addresses the lowest common denominator. You're supposed to sell something at all costs. So you have to compromise these high ideals of making something look too sophisticated or too elitist. This is what I'm interested to know: at what point or at what level do people have to dumb down the work? This is often the norm and true in many cases of creative work, especially in the field of advertising.

ADOBO You've mentioned being a collaborative partner rather than a hired gun when it comes to your design work. How did that come about?

TENAZAS In high school and in college, I was involved in design and literary extracurricular activities: the school yearbook and the literary paper. I was always the art director, but I developed a collaborative relationship with the editor. I think what was really a great experience for me was that my relationship with the editor and with writing, specifically, was cemented in that the editor trusted in my contributions. Going beyond my role in determining the art and photographic direction, I considered myself on equal footing with the editor and contributing writers. I'm not a writer, per se, but I took particular interest in the content. So eventually when I started working professionally and looking at my work, I gravitated to the design of books and publications. Over the years, I've worked with various authors and they're sometimes not prepared to confront a designer who actually pays particular attention to the content. Eventually, I started working on projects where people would come to me and they'd say "We don't know what the content is. I know it's going to be about this, but what do you think? You're the designer. Let's collaborate on it" even before the content is generated. I respect writing. I'm interested in it because my work is very linguistic. When people do connect with me, it's not about me saying "I'm the designer and you're not." I'm more interested in setting the tone for a collaborative process, "You're the writer, but we each can learn from the other's approaches." And I think as soon as you establish that relationship, there is a lot of respect and it moves on to integrity and freedom to do what you want to do for them because they know that you're being very thoughtful about their work.

ADOBO How do you deal with difficult clients?

TENAZAS They could profess they love you, they love your work, and I'm thinking, "What is your gut feeling, Lucille"? Here's my bottom line: If I like the person and I can actually have an intelligent conversation with them over lunch, not to discuss work, but just having a normal conversation with another human being, I may consider taking them on. But if there is some concern or issues that raise flags-- I mean you know, there are people who rub you the wrong way, or they're aggressive, I'm not going to put myself through this. It's more trouble than it's worth, so why do it? So at that point, you just trust your instincts.

I'm also very patient – I'm not an imperious person. I sort of look at the situation and just say, "You know, I want to be able to do a good job on this. I want this to be a project that we're both happy with." And they respect you for that. They do see your commitment. To me, my best weapon, in any relationship, in any of my projects, is that I'm very enthusiastic about my work and what I can contribute to issues others are concerned with. Assessing the other person becomes a reciprocal exercise "now, is this the kind of person we want to work with?" I'm doing the same thing too. I want them to think whether the relationship is a mutually beneficial one. I mean, I have every opportunity to judge them in the same way that they're judging me.

I think when people see themselves as being an important part of the process, it's great – it's gratifying for them. They didn't have to go to design school, but I always assume that they are experts at what they do. I can guide them and involve them in my thinking process: "Now this is what I'm showing you. Observe this, and take a look at this. Tell me what this adds up to." I encourage them. I look for smart people who don't feel threatened. They know they've arrived at what they've done because they've earned it, so they can admire and respect equally smart people who are accomplished. There's no insecurity involved, there's no need to be NUMBER ONE all the time.

ADOBO The funny thing is, if the client really does know everything and has all the answers, then what does he need you for?

TENAZAS There is often a very interesting dynamic at play about what role one affects when they're in the position of hiring someone. Though I know that my services are valuable and are worth something, what I hope to gain from a designer-client relationship is an opportunity to expand their understanding of the world, and the impact design has in it. Perhaps, it is my continuous involvement as an educator, simultaneously with my creative practice, that gives me an optimistic view that we are all continually learning from others.

It is often said that the only way one knows what it is they like is when they see something they don't like. I try to come from a position that is not about dichotomies or scenarios that are polarizing, but encourage a discussion where nuance and the articulation of uncertainty and doubt can be unraveled and discussed.

I'll give you an example-- When I was in the Philippines last year, I did a master class for designers and creative directors at the Ayala Museum, and there was a participant who asked me the same question, like you: "You know, I work for this ad agency, and I really feel that we're at the bottom of the totem pole there. We're kind of just service providers, dealing with account executives whose role is to be the liaison between the client and the designers." They often push the latter to unreasonable expectations to satisfy the client. And so they now have to present the ideas to the client, right? And so this person says, "After this class, I have to go back to work and battle it up with this guy, yet again."

I understood what he was going through, but I didn't know the context. All I could tell him was "You really have to defend your ideas. Say it without any kind of anxiety, without any kind of tension and say, you know, let me just clearly state what this is about and the rationale behind it." I saw him and he looked defeated. Poor guy. But anyway, on the last day of the class, he does his presentation, and we have a reception/ cocktails, picture taking, etc. This guy walks over to me, and he said, "I just want to tell you that when we talked that first day, I went back to my office, remember?" And I said, "Yeah, I know." And he said, "Yeah, and I just stood my ground, and I talked with this account executive and explained the design concept in a clear way, and he was just taken aback, and it's kind of interesting because he went "Tell me what you have in mind." And I was, wow, that was a quick turnaround! It's not the kind of thing that you change overnight. But something must have happened to this guy for him to actually assess a situation and look at where he stood, thought about what I said, or what he felt he got from the class and then just did it! So I was quite impressed.

ADOBO It must have made you feel good at some level, to have given him his moment of clarity. Do you get that feeling from teaching?

TENAZAS (laughs) This happens a lot to me. I was giving a lecture many years ago in Miami, and there was a person from the host organization who picked me up from the airport, and we had a typical conversation about what he did, his role at the organization, the kinds of projects he worked on, etc. When I reached my hotel, he dropped me off, and that was it. End of the story. I see him again, years later, at some design conference, and he walked up to me and said, "My life changed after that conversation." Maybe I was giving some advice; I don't even remember. I was just asking questions about where he stood in his work, in his life, in his relationship, and maybe that triggered something. I planted a seed. It didn't have to be something that was a profound thing, but it was profound for him. So as a teacher, and I have been teaching now for over 30 years, it happens to me that when my students have me, they get intimidated, they may get "oh, she has high standards" or "she's just a little too critical" or whatever, and some of them don't perform as well, some of them don't get it. But I realize many years later, I would get a phone call or get an email, and they would say "you may not remember me but I was one of your students in 19__, but I have always remembered what you said." So I know that it's not an immediate feedback of what I have done but perhaps a comment that served to plant a seed.

ADOBO Okay, on that note, do you remember the first class that you ever taught?

TENAZAS The first class I taught was actually at my alma mater, College of the Holy Spirit the year after I graduated from my college. I was a senior in the Fine Arts Dept., majoring in Advertising and one of my teachers, a nun, was being sent on an academic scholarship to Japan for three years and she needed students she trusted to take over the three classes that she was going to leave behind. So she appoints three of her students, me being one of them – and we hadn't even graduated! I was flattered of course for being chosen, as did the other two, and she assigned me the most difficult one because it was a theoretical class as opposed to a studio course– Aesthetics – and so I just said, "Yeah, I'll do it." She provided us with reading lists, the syllabus and her lesson plans to get us up to speed. So I show up after the vacation break, no longer in uniform and I'm assigned to teach the class a year below me. I had been the president of the student Fine Arts Organization, so the students knew me. I walk into the classroom in my "civilian" adult clothing, and they greeted me, and said, "Oh, hey, hi, Lucille! You've graduated, congratulations! Do you know who our teacher is?" I said, "Well, actually, it's me." We were only a year apart, so that threw them off, but it was a learning experience (laughs).

ADOBO How did you do?

TENAZAS Well, it threw me off, too, because I didn't think of myself as a teacher and there was only one year separating us, so I thought, how would they see me? How would they regard me? Was I credible teacher inspite of my inexperience? It was a steep learning curve. I mean you know, the lesson plan was there, the syllabus, the curriculum, etc... so my first teaching experience was really about catching up. When you're a student, you could coast through some of that, but as a teacher, you're supposedly the font of knowledge so I had to do double work, even triple or quadruple work. So you could consider this experience a "baptism by fire" but it was a valuable one. I taught in an adjunct capacity while working full-time for three years, before I left for the US. But the first studio class I taught was also at my alma mater, CCA in San Francisco, when my teachers offered me the opportunity to teach in 1985 and return to the bay area after working in New York for close to 4 years. I stayed for 20 years and became the Founding Chair of the MFA in Design before leaving in 2005 to live in Rome, Italy.

ADOBO How different was it to teach in California?

TENAZAS As a young design teacher, I think my mindset was to treat the classroom like a design studio. I took on the role of the art director, and in my mind, the students were my design assistants. My initial projects replicated those of a studio and in a sense the students were in competition with each other, vying for the successful design solution that best responded to the problem at hand.

But over time, I realized conducting a class in this way was a dead end because I was not interested in giving them commercial work. Over time, I realized that I needed to provide more opportunities for them to develop their personal voices, propose projects that are more open-ended, and be more experimental. I was more interested in knowing how they thought by mining their personal history so that I was developing in them, a point of view. So it wasn't about the client, the client was *them*. There were a couple of reasons why I changed my way of teaching. 1) I was confronted with returning students who were much older and had more life experiences. I realized that these were not your typical 18-year old college-age students, so I had to figure out ways to approach design thinking through a much more inclusive lens. 2) Even if I was in my 30s at the time, it was quite a humbling experience to have students articulating their ideas in unique ways and to realize that even as one has the role of the teacher, it is a shared experience and a journey both of you are on. So lessons can be learned on both sides in different ways. I was keen to learn from the experiences they brought with them, and it was more important for me to develop in my students a unique voice, filtered through their cultural backgrounds. It is through shared experiences that designers develop empathy and the ability to respond to a design problem; however different it is from one's own.

ADOBO Tell us how this ties into your concept of the cultural nomad.

TENAZAS The cultural nomad versus the cultural tourist. We all have been tourists at one time or another. We take pains not to act and look like a tourist because the association is one of a superficial connection to a new environment, resorting to typical interactions without going deeper into the new experience. We don't have to be in a new geographic location to be considered a tourist—all manner of new situations present themselves to us where we may initially feel disoriented, uncomfortable until we figure out ways to adjust and acclimate ourselves. So, in a meta-sense, we are "tourists" when we enter a new relationship, start of a new job, go to a party where we don't know the host, etc. There's a fear of absorbing a new place because it's an unknown quantity, whereas a nomad allows herself to weave in and out of situations and assess, and stand not apart, but try and let herself be absorbed into the situation. And I'd like to think of myself as one.

I use this analogy because it reflects what a designer does when confronted with a new project. As designers, we are often called upon to look critically at an unfamiliar environment, first assessing the situation, and then orienting ourselves within it as we develop a relationship and understanding of what was initially foreign territory. Cultural nomads synthesize what they pass through, are permeable to experience and are ultimately altered by it. The cultural tourist, on the other hand, remains separate and fundamentally unaltered by the experience of passing through a different terrain. If we imagine ourselves as cultural nomads, we set ourselves free to enter different territories. It is in this mindset that the designer of today is able to engender qualities of community, participation, and empathy. Especially when dealing with multi-cultural situations, we are moving, among, within, between cultures and one has to be flexible.

ADOBO How do you go about forming that relationship?

TENAZAS It's about empathy, which is a difficult word to describe because it means putting yourself in a position and to try and imagine what that is and how it feels. I ask my students the difference between sympathy and empathy. Sympathy involves feelings of sorrow in light of a personal loss or unfortunate situation that one feels in order to connect with others, whereas empathy doesn't necessarily have to involve that. It just means that I understand what you're saying but even if I have not personally experienced what you have gone through. It is the ability to put yourself in somebody else's shoes and imagine what they're going through in that situation. So there has got to be some way where there is a common language or a common understanding that we all connect with, and there's an engagement, and that I think is really the key. Even with just a brief conversation, it's a connection. That, to me, is what empathy is about.

ADOBO What do you tell your students about the love-hate relationship between art and commerce?

TENAZAS I tell them that when you're young, you don't have to be choosy and picky because at the beginning, you take on whatever gives you money and you're saving up. You need to have all these different levels of experiences anyway; it's not always perfect. But the important thing is for them to know what they are about, what they represent and what their values are. So when they get to the point where they say, "okay, this is not me anymore," they have to have the courage to say, "I can't stay here, this is dehumanizing," because at a certain point it's going to be harder to leave. People sometimes do these kinds of things where their five-day-a-week job is a drudgery, and then the fun, fulfilling work is on the weekends, right? I just don't understand that; life is too short to be doing work (that you don't care for) for the better part of the week. And that's the majority of people we know and that's because they have allowed themselves to be led on. It's important to take a stand and say, "this is really about me, this is my life, so why am I doing something else?" But for you to arrive at that decision, you would need to really know where you stand, what your values are. I'm talking about a kind of integrity, an identity of what you represent as a person and as a creative human being.

ADOBO In your experience, either in your professional or academic careers, how much did your background play into it? Like your race or gender, did either affect how people perceived you?

TENAZAS I'm often asked this question. But the thing is, when I arrived in the United States, the one thing that made me feel a sense of inferiority about my design work was the fact that I was older than my classmates. I had a degree back in the Philippines; I had worked for three years, so I thought that my returning to school was a remedial course, that my work was not as good, so it needed to be improved upon and that I will be up against younger and better-trained students.

And the second issue was that, since I'm from another country, my classmates had the benefit of a more focused design education, so their work is much more polished (I thought). Race or gender did not enter the equation since, in my mind, my facility with the English language enabled me to communicate and be understood. I never thought of race, I never thought of gender. It was really about two things: My coming from another context and being transplanted to another and being challenged by the thought of whether my work can hold its own. I'm sure I realized that I looked different, but it didn't really hit me. I just thought: If I could speak English and I could communicate, there shouldn't be a problem, right? I mean, they understood exactly what I said, I could talk to them, my work was strong, so why should there be a problem? Perhaps that was naïve on my part, but in a way, if you're not burdened by these issues, it does not get in the way of engaging with others who are different from you.

ADOBO Filipinos in other countries tend to have entirely different sets of problems.

TENAZAS Perhaps it's a case of arrested development. I left the Philippines as an adult and set off to discover opportunities that I did not have in my profession back home. There was an excitement and open-mindedness at this time in my life. I was different from someone who was transplanted to another country, uprooted and brought by their parents before developing their own sense of connection. I remember a situation where I was giving a lecture in Los Angeles, and a student posed a question, "Why is it that your work is not reflective of your Filipino culture?" I soon discovered that the person was a young Filipino-American yearning for a more visible and literal manifestation of the culture his parents had left behind. I countered with a series of questions, "What do you mean by that? Did you expect to see palm trees and tropical colors? Visual clues that hark back to the Philippines? He proceeded to say that he was doing research on ancient Philippine script called *alibata*, also known as *Baybayin* as a way to connect with his cultural background. I encouraged him to explore linguistic history and study its historical references, and perhaps in this way he can find relevance and meaning as a designer operating in the US, by bringing that level of cultural authenticity in his work from someone who wasn't born in the Philippines.

Speaking for myself, my work as a professional designer bears a strong linguistic approach. As well, my teaching has always concentrated on typography, form dictated by meaning. Language is central to my work, having learned English in the Philippines within a strict formal context, trained to speak it correctly at school while growing up in a multilingual household with voices speaking Tagalog, Spanish and Aklanon, the dialect of my parents. As with other Filipinos raised in a multi-lingual culture, I have crossed these linguistic frontiers constantly and automatically, so my knowledge of the constructions of grammar is often combined with the delicate nuances of hidden meanings that open themselves up to association. By questioning the authority of language and the relativity of meaning, I wanted to free myself of the colonial nature of my relationship with the English language, to subdue it and make it my own. It is no surprise that my work is layered and complex, manifesting the loosening and exploration of structural boundaries as a result of my multilingual and multicultural background. So that mindset can only come from someone who grew up the way I did. It may not be the issue for an American, because, for them, it's more fluid. There's none of that transition. It's much more of an intellectual or linguistic exercise, but that is, to me, the true layer, the true explanation of why my work is the way it is.

ADOBO Fair enough. It does come across a bit condescending, doesn't it, if someone expects that everything you do has to be reflective of a Third World upbringing?

TENAZAS But you see, that's the simplistic point of view. There has to be the understanding that I am the product of all these worlds, right? You don't claim one necessarily over another because you are who you are, formed by the experiences that you had growing up. The student from Los Angeles who asked me that question was experiencing a level of cultural hunger, and he wanted to impose it on me as a way to validate his efforts. He felt that my work was not successfully telegraphing my background that was satisfactory to him. But as I said to him, it is not that easy. You have to explore what you feel is the best way to do the work that is an extension of who you are. He's young, he's searching, he wants to know what that "lost" culture was, and wonders what he could have experienced had he stayed.

ADOBO What do you do in your free time?

TENAZAS Well, a lot. My family life is something I devote good quality time to. I have two sons in their young 20s, the older one lives and works in San Francisco, and the younger one is still in college in New York. My husband, Richard Barnes is an artist and photographer and being with another creative person engenders a constantly evolving creative life. We have a collaborative relationship, very kind, critical, in a positive way and deeply respectful of each other's work. He's very active in his work and constantly travels on assignment as well as pursues personal projects. We were able to live in Italy for a year because he was awarded the Rome Prize and was a fellow at the American Academy, so the experience greatly benefited our sons and expanded our understanding of the world.

ADOBO How did you find that understanding in the places you've lived in?

TENAZAS I've returned to Italy several times over the years and during the time we lived there, my observations at street level derived from walking and slowing down have made me acutely conscious of the layers of history and the seemingly effortless juxtaposition of ancient, with modern amid the insistence of everyday life. I get less and less concerned about running into the next museum, into the next baroque church or archeological site. I realized that if I just calm down, just walk the streets, and then absorb what the street life is about. I think that is the product of being comfortable alone. I like the fact that I'm no longer intimidated by not having company, so there are things that I like doing by myself. Part of that is this journey of walking around the neighborhood, with the unpredictable discoveries and optimism that there is constant interest in the most mundane things. I enjoy planning my lunch of the day, and if I'm by myself, I choose a place depending on my mood, even if it's just to think about the day and clear in my head. It doesn't have to be expensive. But the conditions have to be right. That it's nice and quiet if I want to be in a quiet place that I have to savor the food, whatever it is. I like being conscious of it. To me, it's appalling when somebody says, "I just eat at my desk." Are you kidding me? You eat at your desk? And this one person says, "Oh, I only eat for sustenance." And I say, "What do you mean? You don't eat for the pleasure?"

ADOBO Having lived in so many countries, what do you miss about the places you've lived and worked in?

TENAZAS There are little slivers of memory that hit me, but I try not to regret anything and that all the experiences are actually cumulative and they evolve, they change, you kind of edit out certain things. I have a different life and have made it in such a way that it is also portable. It can go anywhere in the world, and I trust that connections made along the way define one's sense of belonging. My feelings about what constitute a "home" are constantly changing and I try to find experiences that are uniquely mine in whatever city or country I visit.

A few years ago, I was invited to give a lecture and conduct a week-long workshop at a design university in Istanbul. During one of the sessions, I asked a student, "Take me to the place where you like to go for coffee. Don't take me to a Starbucks or the mall. Where is the local hang out? Take me there." I enjoy these discoveries. When you ask for these authentic experiences, I feel it's a sign of respect and an appreciation for the local culture-- they feel that you are one of them. That's the nomad in me, again, the cultural nomad.

ADOBO Your work is distinctive for never pandering. Tell us about your take on the role of understatement versus spoon-feeding.

TENAZAS It wasn't always that way because when I was a young student, the important thing impressed upon us by our teachers was that the role of the designer was to make things clear, to articulate things so that people knew the answers to questions, solve the client's problems. But the more that I thought about what I was doing, I realized that it was a much more interesting to be provocative and to leave some things out so that you are not necessarily spoon-feeding or giving out answers because it doesn't come out as a conversation. You're just handing things down, and you're saying, 'here it is, this is the answer to the problem.' It is critical to assume that the audience or the person who's looking at your work is equally intelligent and can decipher clues that you leave behind. That open-endedness makes them appreciate it more since they are able to leave their stamp on it through their own unique interpretation. And to me, that is the most valuable thing. It's a trust that you give the other, someone you don't know, because you never know who's going be confronted with your work. I feel confident in setting the stage for many interpretations to occur-- my work will live on beyond me, and it will continue to have a life depending on how many people are confronted with it and interpret it.

This interview of Lucille Tenazas first appeared in Adobo Magazine, March - April 2014 issue. Adobo is a bi-monthly magazine that reaches a wide spectrum of communications professionals in advertising, design, and media. It is based in Manila and has a worldwide circulation of 60,000.

LILY TORRES-SAMORANOS

Immigration Attorney, Asian Pacific Legal Outreach, US
GLOBAL FWN100™ 2016

A Hymn of Praise to Failure

"Failure is Success in Progress..."
- **Albert Einstein**

Hot tears ran down my flushed face, while I quietly contemplated my life. I felt the heat from my pulsating body because of anger. I wanted to scream, but instead stifled a sob. I was angry, very, very angry. I was angry at God, as I realized that life is not fair.

As I was standing in front of the kitchen sink full of dirty dishes, I looked through the window above that sink. I stared at the blue sky and the brown lawn outside. And I swore under my breath, that for as long as I live in this world, I would never be dependent on anyone for my survival. I swore this oath as I continued to hold my sobs. My identity as a Filipina was sealed, but I was determined that being a Filipina was not the issue. Then I mapped out my life with precision while looking over a sink that was almost too high for me to see over. I was eleven years old.

Herstory

I had been raised in a privileged household back home in the Philippines. Both my parents were lawyers. Although not wealthy, we were prosperous. My mother later told me that we were not very wealthy, because my father refused to take bribes. I glowed with pride knowing my dad had integrity. We had a busy household with maids, nannies, and a driver. My father had an armed bodyguard. Even in my innocence, I knew he was influential and connected.

In my young and carefree life, my single chore was to get out of bed and get ready for school. My sisters and I were given a lot of luxuries. If I were too sleepy to brush my teeth, a maid would brush my teeth. If homework was due, I would coerce the maid to do it for me. It is rather embarrassing to admit such behavior on my part. At that time, my only ambition was to have a great childhood.

My parents provided a comfortable life for me and my two sisters. We had ballet classes, Hawaiian dance classes, badminton lessons, attended private schools, had tutors, took great vacations, and enjoyed all the extravagant trappings of an upper middle-class existence. We even had a washing machine. In the sixties Philippines, ownership of that modern appliance was a total luxury. It was a status symbol. Life was very good. I knew that when I had grown up, my parents would arrange my education and eventually my marriage. Since I was painfully shy when I was young, this was an ideal arrangement with me. I felt secure, protected, and proud of my background and heritage, and had no fear or worries. Yes, I thought with innocence, my life was mapped out.

The End and Beginning

Then that life abruptly ended. My father passed away when I was ten years old. It was unexpected, but the pressures of thinking a civil war might erupt and that Martial Law would be declared was too much for him. He was horrified that the Marcos Regime would rule the country. He was the Executive Director of the Philippine Veterans' Administration. The marriage of politics and military was a huge part of his everyday life since he had been a Lieutenant Colonel after WWII. He had a close relationship with President Magsaysay, who perished in an airline crash under suspicious circumstances. My father was vying to be the Secretary of Defense under the Magsaysay administration, but this was not meant to be. My father lived and breathed politics all the time. The military industrial complex was alive and well, and the Philippines was a "banana Republic."

My socialite mother panicked because she knew that my father had unscrupulous enemies in the country. My father was at the polar opposite of the Marcos Regime. My father's old friends were gone. My mother tried to maintain our lifestyle, but I knew that it was different. The late-night parties with a variety of interesting people and politicians stopped. The almost weekly offering of food, live animals, fruits, and vegetables as homage to my father from the townspeople in the province halted immediately. He was the town's one and only lawyer who would help them with their legal problems. Visits to a wealthy friend's private beach were not to happen again. The lavish and exotic excursions ended. There were fewer maids. Then Martial Law did become a reality. That was a dangerous and tumultuous time in my country's history.

Leaving the country was nearly impossible.

The Seed of Determination Planted on Fertile Ground

But my mother, a very strong and determined woman, got us out of Philippines as improbable as it was and settled us in California. That whole experience was almost miraculous. All along I thought it was a temporary move. We left behind a considerable amount of assets; an American car, hectares of rice fields, a fish farm, land for homesites, an apartment building, an ancestral home in the Province, another house under construction in the suburbs of Manila, stocks and bonds, and my parents' pensions. My mother only brought her jewelry with her. I thought we would be back after things settled. I did not realize that we could leave the Philippines if we could only show that we had assets to secure our return. In California, we lived at our relative's home for a short period before striking out on our own.

My mother forged ahead, and she never looked back. Her motto was "Never look back, but only go forward," and it became my mantra as well. It was a lesson in humility and gratitude. Now looking back, it was actually an important lesson in detachment. This was a lesson I did not know would serve me well in the future. I saw my mother in a very different light. I regarded her with awe because of her spirit and bravery to face insurmountable challenges.

Adversity, Thy Name Is Many

Gone was our strong protector. I deeply resented that we lost everything. But the young heal easily; and life had to go on. At eleven years of age, I learned to provide housekeeping to my relatives in exchange for housing us. Although the change was drastic, I did not question it. My chores were endless, but I did not mind. I woke up at 6:00 a.m. to prepare breakfast, and went to bed at around 11:00 p.m. after all the chores and school work were done. After school, I did laundry for everyone, and hung up all the wash, since we could not use the dryer because the electricity was too expensive. I ironed the clothes. I mowed and watered the lawn, did the dishes, cleaned the house, made up all the beds, folded the heavy bedding, vacuumed the carpet, took out the trash, and helped prepare dinner. I became a very efficient housekeeper.

There were no maids, no money, no connections; and I could not wait to move out.

We did not have time to mourn our losses while we were at our relatives' house; we were too busy. For the first time, I experienced hunger, sadness, and yearning for a life that could have been. I knew I had to change my expectations, and be strong. I had to do this not just for me, but for my family. My mapped-out life was being redrawn against my wishes.

Looking back at that experience, it was truly a teachable moment. The work ethics ingrained in my youth at that time, could not have developed but for the hardships that we endured. Even at that age, I knew that I could have chosen differently and rebelled; but I knew instantly that it would only disrespect my mother and only lead to a self-destructive existence, which would have ended in some kind of failure. I could not do that to my mother who had sacrificed so much. We did not come to a new country for me to self-destruct. I also realized that this was my life and not hers. My choices mattered very much. If I had to remedy our impoverished circumstances, I felt responsible for solving that challenge for myself and my family.

I was no longer shy. I was highly ambitious. I firmly resolved to be a lawyer and to fight for inequality and social justice.

My First and Eternal (S)Hero

Sadly, I saw my beautiful, accomplished, and highly educated mother morph into a struggling immigrant woman, who took any odd jobs that she could find to support her daughters. At the high point of her life in the Philippines, she had entertained a princess from Indonesia at the Malacanang Palace, the "White House" of the Philippines. She never married again. I like to think this was because she was loyal to my father, but I think the reality was that she could not stand to be with any man she had to be subservient to ever again. For every piece of jewelry she had to create, and every piece of army salvage clothing she had to sew, and for all the low and humble jobs that she took, I realize she made the ultimate sacrifice in order to give her daughters a secure environment to pursue their dreams. She swallowed her pride and took any job so she could send us to private school. Now as an adult, I applaud her for the extraordinary effort it took for her to buy a fixer-upper Victorian house in a decent and safe neighborhood for her three daughters. She is my eternal (s)hero.

I wanted this exceptional woman at my side when I walked down the aisle. From her, I learned to be a strong woman, who would not be dependent on any man for anything. This was contradicting the stereotype of a subservient Filipina. My mother was never subservient. I wanted to emulate her bravery, strength of character, and steely determination.

It Takes More Than Good Grades

Because of the discipline, I developed at a young age growing up in America, and lack of childhood activities, the library became my sanctuary. I read books that gave me varied vicarious experiences. I got lost in the world of books, and it fueled my desire for knowledge. I loved the learning. I strove to get the best grades, and it paid off. The tragedy of my young life became the anchor that rooted me to become an outstanding student, which earned me scholarships and grants at the University of California (UC) Berkeley. Only in America could a dream of obtaining an excellent education by hard work alone without any money be realized. I was paid to go to both UC Berkeley and law school at UCLA, as long as I maintained a decent grade point average. Only the very rich and elite could have this type of education in the Philippines. No matter how brilliant a poor person was, it would have been extremely challenging to attain a higher education of this caliber.

But my early struggles were nothing compared to what followed in the next chapter of my life. Becoming a lawyer was an arduous task. But it was not the work required to become a lawyer but the isolation I felt in pursuing this career. I had never felt so alone, and navigating law school was a constant balancing act. Suddenly law school did not appear to fit into my life's roadmap.

A Pattern Became Clear

There were many times that I was off balance from the get-go in my pursuit of a legal education and career. Despite my experience with inequality during my rushed childhood in America, I still wanted to believe in meritocracy. I wanted to believe that everyone was playing on a level playing field, and that if you worked hard enough, the reward would be automatic. I badly wanted a different reality. In my naivete, I assume that life could be fair even when I personally had faced challenges. After all, I did work hard, and I was rewarded with a full scholarship and several grants in law school and Berkeley.

I detested law school, not because of the hard work, which I expected but because I was the only Filipina in my class of 300 students. I felt different. I had no mentors. I believed at one point that being a Filipina was the problem. I wanted to quit the first semester, crying to my mother about my "struggle" and how everything was unfair. She sat me down in the kitchen area, and she calmly told me while continuing with her cooking:"so quit. I do not like you being so miserable." With mouth opened and eyes bulging out, I stared at her aghast for a moment, before I regained my composure. Then, I muttered, "You didn't raise a quitter." We looked at each other, and I quietly walked out of the kitchen. For the first time, I realized that whatever I did with my life, whether I failed or succeeded; she would support me. I knew I would never dare to push her tolerance to the limit. She knew me so well. I had inherited her rebellious streak. The following week, I was back in law school determined to graduate and become a lawyer. My mother and I never talked about that night, and I never spoke to her about quitting ever again. My mother unintentionally (or perhaps not) reset my compass, and I quickly readjusted the course of my roadmap once again.

It was at this time during my adult life that I realized there was this "constant pattern" in my life's roadmap that I could not seem to escape. When I moved here from the Philippines after the sudden death of my father, I noticed that I was the only Filipina in my grammar and middle school. It was the same when I graduated from a small class of social welfare majors at UC Berkeley; and once again, when I graduated as the only Filipina in my class of 300 law students at the UCLA Law School. When I accepted a position as a Deputy Public Defender in an office of 110 attorneys in a densely-populated, high-crime city, I was the first, and only Filipina there during my entire 25-year tenure at that office. I currently work at a nonprofit Asian legal agency as an immigration attorney in San Francisco; but when I was initially hired, I was again the only Filipina in the staff of 30 attorneys.

From the beginning, the challenge of being different has been a constant theme in my life as an immigrant in America. As always, I hated the fact that I stood out because of my skin color, my accent, and my demeanor. I thought, what if I could have just blended in? Life would have been easier. I saw it as a challenge that I was not born here and had to assimilate. I loathed that word "assimilate." I felt I have to surrender some part of myself and identity. I felt cheated that it was always I, who needed to make concessions. It was only later that I learned to adapt and combined both cultures through "acculturation." The blending of both cultures without denying either one was an excellent way for me to express myself completely. I have embraced two very different, but equally significant cultures. I relish and value both of them. It took maturity and self-reflection to realize it and comfortably adapt to both.

The Dark Nights of The Soul

It was through the adversities in life that led me through painful self-examination, in what many called the dark night of the soul," that I have learned to accept my imperfect self lovingly and developed strength of character and bravery. At this point, I have had many "dark nights of the soul" episodes. Some provided me with "A-Ha" moments, and some just did not make sense at all. There were times that I questioned what I had done to offend God. I concluded that when one is desperate for answers, one becomes spiritual and clings to metaphysics for explanations.

Later, I learned that it was just to be, as it should be, as it could be, and as it would be. It was the detachment from hate, fear, regrets, and negativity that prompted me to move forward without looking back at weakness, pain, and suffering. It became a lifelong lesson in knowing when to let go.

The taunting and malicious teasing of my classmates when I was young; the sexist and racist attitude of professors, judges, bosses, and other authority figures during my professional years; and the fierce competition of my colleagues made me question myself and my self-worth. I felt that their attitude was a reflection of my failure and maybe less than stellar performance as a lawyer. But, I was reminded by my older and much wiser mentor, a senior attorney in my office, that life is unfair. He told me " You should expect this. It is time to put on the big girl pants and fight the battle; however, you choose to fight it." But I asked if being belittled because one is different supposed to be expected? Then Cole, an African-American mentor, explained the politics of being a person of color; and to see beyond the black and white (no pun intended) superficiality in life's journey. That conversation woke me up. No one was going to pat me in the back when I had my victories. The playing field was never equal, and I had to learn the game well just to survive, let along triumph. Through these experiences, my resolve had gotten stronger, and my will had become fiercer.

No Woman Is An Island

One final lesson I learned was not to be bitter. Throughout my experiences in life, I learned to change the circumstances I did not like, instead of letting the negative circumstances change my persona, my moral fiber, and my very essence. Adverse circumstances have challenged my morals and even my belief in humanity had I allowed it. I tried to let go of the bitterness that could have easily engulfed me. I realize that I would be giving away my personal power to an unhealthy experience, and so concluded I would never give my power away to a callous adversary or to an undesirable endeavor.

I strove not to be so bitter as to lose my faith in humanity. I learned to be strong and even brave at various times, and I also learned the importance of trusting others in times of need. As I grew into maturity, I learned that I could lean on people for support when my world crumbled.

It is a valuable lesson to learn to trust and depend on those who love me. I do not have to face the troubling times alone. I was fortunate to surround myself with people who had seen my weaknesses but did not judge me for them. Unlike Job's friends in the Bible, who berated, criticized, and ultimately blamed him for his suffering, my friends and family made sure that they did not point out my mistakes and what caused my fall from grace. Instead, they generously offered their shoulders for moral support and even monetary assistance. I learned that the cliché is true "No Woman Is an Island." My friends of every color, race, and religion picked me up when I was down, and held my hand while I took baby steps back to my reality. I need to acknowledge my glorious women friends who surrounded me with unfailing love, like Margaret, Alice, Mattie, Marie, Margo, Cathy, Jane, Riz and especially my two wonderful sisters, Rhoda and Chloe. They are women warriors with battle scars, who taught me survival, strength and love. It humbled me but also renewed my faith in humanity.

Mine is an immigrant story of survival, adaptability, and resilience. Through the highs and lows in both my personal life and professional careers, I have learned to rely on my upbringing as a Filipina to meet the challenges and obstacles in my path, including my struggle with my bittersweet legal career. I have learned that the problem is not being a Filipina, but my misguided belief that the opinions of some negative and biased people or bad experience mattered. Important note to self: stay away from destructive people and what they are selling.

It has always been and always will be my opinion that valued the most.

It was not unusual when I started my career as a lawyer in the 80's to be mistaken in a courtroom full of stodgy old white men as the court interpreter or the court clerk. I too have had my many me-too experiences. I had been likened to a flight steward when I wore my blue power suit; called a "babe" by jailers when I visited my clients in jail or prison; been told that I won my cases because of my short skirts or pretty outfits; and heard other offensive comments regarding my appearance. As exasperating as it was, I saw this as an opportunity to change the expectations of man, and to show society how to break the barrier of race and gender. I wanted to teach them to embrace a different perception of women of color. I learned to see race and gender as an advantage instead of a failure. The challenge was great and many times I almost quit; but then, something inside me prompted me to try harder, to win impossible cases, and to develop my own style of litigation. I quickly developed a dark sense of humor, because the pain and suffering I have witnessed and experienced in my legal career would have been too much to bear without it. Humor became my friend and salvation. Now, I effortlessly laugh a lot, and I laugh out loud; and most of all, I laugh harder at the most absurd odd little things in life!

Through my own immigrant experience and my overcoming the norms of societal expectations, I have developed resilience. I have learned to recover quickly from contrary expectations of a "Filipina" woman in our American society. I took the strength and advantages of being a "Filipina" woman to the courtroom. In essence, unexpected deals and negotiations and positive jury verdicts were all achieved by using all the attributes of good lawyering including the sensitivity and creativity brought on not only by my training as a lawyer and but also as a Filipina. I am after all – a total package.

My Resolve and Paying Forward

My whole life, I have tried to mentor young women and advance the cause of women in our society, not just by words, but by examples. I made myself visible by working in a male dominant legal field and by starting a charity in a remote province in the Philippines called, "The Abandoned and Suffering Children of the Streets." I joined the Circle of Filipino-American Rotarians of Northern California (CFAR), I have been active in my community and society in general, with a goal of service to others. My intention is not purely altruistic; it is also personal, because by serving others, I learn to be stronger.

Like my mother, I try to be strong so that others can be strong. That is the secret that I want people to know; that being strong for others, makes you strong for yourself. When there is fear, focus on service. Both my parents were the epitome of bravery, and I continue to strive to walk in their footsteps.

I hope that I have given all of you a glimpse of my character based on my personal journey and lessons learned from epic failures. Remember, it is better to make mistakes than not to try at all. It is only then that the true core of character is strengthened from the fires of painful experiences, that one can obtain the lessons, ethics, and values of what matter most in life. I realize that hard work is nothing without integrity; perseverance is useless without a just cause, and strength is a curse without kindness. After all that has been said and done, I just want to be able to go to bed at night, at peace with my soul, myself and conscience that I have not been a quitter, and I have done the best I have each day. I can look those I love and know (family, friends, and even strangers) straight in the eye and tell them, I tried to do my best and the right thing with kindness. As for adapting to situations, again, I do believe it is better to be kind than to be rigid and right. When I look at the pattern in my life, I hope it continues; because I have learned to like it and live it.

In Retrospect

As I look back at my eleven years old self, I would have told her, "Right on sister!" Be mad, be angry, be on fire, and keep on keeping on. But do not dare stop there. Learn to fight for yourself and for others to make the playing field be as level as possible. Learn to forgive yourself and smile, because life can be ridiculous. Life is not meant to be taken seriously, but it should be experienced to the fullest. You will have a plethora of emotions when dealing with your challenges, but if you pay attention, you will also have the skills to take a situation, and with the help of God, and with those HE/SHE has benevolently put in your life to support you, you will figure it out. But first of all, love yourself and give thanks always for the good, the bad, and the ugly in your life, because there will be moments of the bad and the ugly which will make the good sweeter. Do not be afraid to make choices, because the last thing you want is for life to make the choices for you. The worst thing to happen is to be caught in a cycle of inaction. A life spent without experiencing failure means a life unspent; because this world is imperfect, and it is impossible to expect perfection in life. Sometimes, when you fail; you will feel like a total failure, and the pain will hurt so badly, you will just want the world to end. You need to realize that it is only the end of THAT world, and a new one is just beginning. You will make mistakes, and you will fail, but you will also learn to get up taller than before. Just do not forget to get up, even if it hurts you. You will not only survive; and in some instances, you will even triumph!

The most important note to self: there will be interesting detours and potholes to avoid in life's journey, be flexible and do not stick to the roadmap!

LEONOR S. VINTERVOLL

NORWEGIAN CIO FORUM A/S
FILIPINA WOMEN'S NETWORK BOARD MEMBER (2018-2021)
GLOBAL FWN100™ 2015

Janteloven and Leadership

While sitting at the breakfast table, I remember my husband asking, "What happened to your meeting with the first Ambassador of the Philippine Embassy in Oslo?" He was curious. He expected to see enthusiasm, as he witnessed how I always tried to convince visiting politicians from the Philippines on the benefits of having an embassy in Norway. For the first time, I snapped at him and said, "I am done with community service." His response surprised me. He said, "Well, good decision!" He has always been supportive of what I do and has high respect when it came to my advocacies. He was and is my number one supporter. To say I was surprised is an understatement, and I wondered what made him feel that way.

CHOOSING FAMILY LIFE OVER WORK

It was tough to give up the opportunity of a lifetime: an assignment at the head office of Norconsult A.S. in Oslo, Norway. However, a complicating factor was giving up the care of my son to a kindergarten. A one-year-old child usually goes to a kindergarten as nannies are not available and not affordable. I gave it a try for one year. I requested for a part-time position that was not granted. In the end, I had to quit as I chose my son and my family as my top priority.

From 1974 onwards, I worked my way up the organization from being Executive Secretary of Norconsult A.S. Philippines to being Executive Assistant with travel from the Philippines to Oslo to being Treasurer of Norconsult A.S. based in Oslo, Norway. For 11 years, I gained valuable experience with the company. I traveled from the Philippines to Oslo to conduct business. I took a one year leave of absence that became three years to move to the UK when my husband was assigned there. Upon my return to Oslo, Norconsult offered me back my position that I did for a year. And then, I had to make a decision between continuing to work full time and spending more time taking care of my young son. This decision was huge. It was a life crisis for me as I enjoyed my career.

At that time, women were considered the primary caretaker of the home and family, and women were held responsible for raising the children. Paternity leave was not available then, not even in Oslo. My husband's paycheck was more substantial than mine. If this happened today, the decision to continue working would be easier. Perhaps, I would not have felt the need to leave my job since my husband could have taken leave to help with childcare. Nowadays, fathers have an equal opportunity to avail of paternity leave, as much as 90 days in Norway.

Learning to be Entrepreneurial

> Continuous learning is the minimum requirement for success in any field.
> - **Dennis Watley**

Quitting meant that I would lose my steady income, and because I was accustomed to working, to stop working was out of the question. As an alternative, I thought about starting a business. Establishing a business from the ground up terrified me. There was so much that I did not know. All I had was my experience working with managers, managing directors, and the executives who ran the company. My knowledge was the theories I learned in the university. I took a course called "Doing Business in Norway" from the *Norsk Teknologisk* Institute (Norwegian Institute of Technology.) The information and knowledge I learned from that short class gave me the courage to open my business.

Full of courage and ready to take a risk, my first step was to approach the Norwegian Import from Developing Countries (NORIMPOD). I sought financial support from them to start an import business, bringing in products from the Philippines. Fortunately, they granted financial assistance. With part of the funds, I attended the Philippine exhibit at the Center for International Trade Expositions and Missions (CITEM), the export promotion arm of the Philippine Department of Trade and Industry. I found beautiful handicrafts for home decorations made out of cloth, paper, and wood. I bought and exhibited these products at a Norwegian national exhibition of wholesalers. I have always been fond of the arts and designing interiors and I thought I could start my import business. In addition to my new-found courage, luck was on my side. The products were marketable in the Norwegian market and I would have suppliers from the Philippines. I would have flexible time to take care of my son while managing my small company. It was a risky but adventurous move. The first two years were fantastic. My company, Philippine Import Export, (PHIMEX Norway), participated at the yearly Norwegian Trade Fair for wholesalers, and this brought me clients from all over Norway. I was proud to be an importer of Philippine products and contribute to the Philippine economy and industry. The business gave me flexible time to balance work and family life. As more and more clients patronized my business, I had to order more products wholesale. However, I experienced a drop-in product quality causing financial loss. It was not possible to send back the products, and my demands for replacement were never addressed. I hired a quality control person based in the Philippines, but that did not work. Close supervision during the manufacturing process, and before the goods were shipped, was crucial. That meant that I would have to travel to the Philippines, an impossible feat, given my situation. I could not leave Norway as the demands of my husband's job did not allow him to provide care for my son in my absence. There were still some measures I could try to save the import business, such as hiring someone to ensure the quality of goods, but that would take funds that I did not have.

To stop the continued loss of funds, I decided to close my fledgling business. Sadly, my first attempt at business had failed. I asked myself whether I should return to working for a company.

> I'm convinced that about half of what separates the successful entrepreneurs from the non-successful ones is pure perseverance.
> - **Steve Jobs**

I refused to admit I was a failure. I realized while running PHIMEX that I enjoyed going to exhibits and finding unique items that I knew people would like. So, I decided to shift my business plan from wholesale import to retail sales. I established a boutique called Gifts and Interiors, located in an upscale area with other shops and restaurants on the harbor side of Oslo, Gifts and Interiors was the only boutique of its kind in the mall. We specialized in high-end products for interior design, such as designer curtains sourced not only from the Philippines but from worldwide wholesalers. I had made connections with global suppliers when I went to various trade fairs and exhibitions and when I was running PHIMEX. The Gift and Interiors shop became quite fashionable. For three years, the boutique performed very well, and we were showing a profit every year. On the fourth year, the situation changed. I started losing money. When I looked for the reason, I discovered that our inventory was losing valuable items. I questioned whether they were being misplaced and asked whether they were stolen. It was disheartening to think that my employee was stealing from me. One day, I had to attend a community meeting, which prevented me from being at the boutique that day. My only employee was left by herself to sell products and close the shop. This presented an opportunity for me to confirm my suspicions. I returned just before closing. When I met her at the door, she was carrying two bags filled with goods from the store. I caught her in the act and it was such a disappointment. I trusted this woman, and she was robbing me blind.

As a small business owner, I did not have the funds to hire more than one employee. In retrospect, I worked long hours to pay my employee's salary and provided benefits, including paid leaves. As I evaluated this turn of events, I realized that I ended up working for my employee instead of her working for me. I did not want to hire a new employee. And that incident spurred my decision to close the boutique. This was officially my second attempt at being an entrepreneur and my second failure. I may have failed a second time, but I knew that I would overcome these failures. I was going to persevere and use my passion for succeeding as a businesswoman and as a person. I knew that there must be another way. I am not a quitter!

Finding the Courage to Continue

> Success is not final; failure is not fatal. It is the courage to continue that counts.
> - **Winston Churchill**

Destiny provided a third opportunity for starting a business. An opportunity opened in 1998. I met a Filipina who was a manager at Malaysian Airlines. We became good friends, and she offered a promotional price for air tickets exclusively for the members of the Philippine Women's Organization (PWO) in Norway, an organization that I had founded and led. To my surprise, I surpassed the sales of their top sales agent in Norway. She believed that I would excel in sales and marketing and with her endorsement and encouragement, I trained on the Amadeus booking system.

I started my travel business in 1998, that I continue to this day. My business partner manages the day-to-day operations and I receive my share of the profits. I mostly market to Norwegians and book group tours to the Philippines. When I first started, making travel reservations booking through the internet was non-existent; thus, travelers depended on travel agencies like mine. I was feeling satisfied; business was booming and most of all, I found the travel business to be fun. My days were hectic, juggling various responsibilities: looking after my son, family, the travel agency, and performing community service. I could have employed more personnel, but that would mean I would have invest more capital, and I was not willing to do this. With the increase in income, I started investing in real estate, mostly in the Philippines. I bought condominiums and rented them long-term. I did not invest more in Norway aside from our investment in an expensive villa because of high taxes.

In 1998, many migrants could not get jobs in Norway and were dependent on the Norwegian Social and Welfare Department. In an annual report I submitted to the Migrants Office, I recommended that "instead of giving the migrant a daily allowance without requiring them to work, the government could subsidize any company willing to provide 'on the job-training' to a migrant. After the training, the company could employ the migrant or not." My idea would elevate the migrant's self-esteem as it would allow them to work for pay instead of receiving a handout from the Social Office. The politicians adopted my idea, and the government issued a directive to implement it. Once the program was in place, I registered my travel agency as a company that would accept migrants for on-the-job training. The subsidy idea helped many small businesses like mine and trained unemployed immigrants. The migrants were not only Filipinos, but some were also other nationals.

My Desire to Render Community Service

I have been asked why I devote so much time to my community. I was blessed to have the opportunity to migrate and work in Norway, fall in love and meet my husband, and have a family. I volunteer to give back to the community that stood by me during my journey. If my actions and contributions can help another Filipino and give them the opportunity I received, the time and energy spent is worth it.

Two other factors made me add community service to my crowded schedule. "You don't need to thank me, you have done it yourself. If you did not excel, I would not have recommended you." These are the words of Mr. Kaare Hagness, the Director who endorsed my assignment and transfer to Norway. I call him my "guardian angel." He believed in me and changed my life. And I would like to follow his example by giving opportunities to my fellow Filipinos.

When I first moved to Oslo in mid-July 1981, I did not get involve in community activities. This changed in 1985 when I saw a travel agency advertisement that promised that in addition to travel to Cebu to scuba dive, you could buy a Filipina wife for 10,000 kroner (about US$1,234). I was shocked. And I did not like the implication that Aage, my Norwegian husband could have had the opportunity to buy me as a mail-order bride. Together with the first Filipino Community in

Norway and in Mid-Norway, we decided to take action against this travel agency. The community rallied in front of the International Airport in Oslo to stop this trip to Cebu. I initiated a letter campaign and got hundreds of signatures to stop this travel agency. Unfortunately, my husband was assigned to London, UK, and my son and I accompanied him and thus I could no longer be actively involved with the Oslo community. However, the group in Mid-Norway did file a case and won! The travel agency was closed down. Returning from London to Oslo in 1989, my community service continued. And in 1990, I was asked by the Executive Director Ms. Inger Axelsen of the Immigrant Office in Oslo to organize a Women's Organization as she had a project involving the different women's national groups and organizations in Oslo. To speed up the formation of the Philippine Women's Organization, I took the initiative to draft the organization's constitution and by-laws. These documents were reviewed and ratified at the next meeting by the Filipina women who had joined the group. Thus, the Philippine Women's Organization was established in June 1990.

As stated on the PWO's website, our aim is to serve the community, work towards integration, and contribute to the Norwegian authorities position that emigrants are not a liability but an asset to the society. PWO's mission is to advocate for women's and children's rights and welfare. PWO respects women's responsibilities as well as men's. PWO believes that migrants' diversity is useful for Norwegian society. Statistics Norway reports that in 2017, immigrants made up 14% of the population in Norway, with Filipinas being the largest group of non-EU immigrant women. In Norway, 80% of immigrants from the Philippines are women.

Thirty years of continued, dedicated community service may seem hard to believe, but for me, it has become a part of my life. I have felt personal satisfaction every time I made someone happy; by helping solve some of their problems or making their lives more comfortable. It made me feel good to help my fellow *kababayan* [countrymen]. In community service, however, setbacks do happen.

Leadership Test: Someone Took Credit for My Work

When someone took credit for my work, I felt defeated. I resolved not to let this get me down, and strove to turn this to my advantage. That resolve turned to a sense of injustice when I realized that a woman who had claimed to have done a lot for the community, in reality, had only led a Philippine Independence Day celebration. Worst, she took credit for the all the work I had done with the Filipino community. I was outraged.

The Philippine ambassador to Sweden tried to make me feel better, by apologizing and saying, "Leonor, you should not be disappointed because you are a family member of the Embassy!" I felt her sincerity and accepted her apology. Her gesture of goodwill helped me calm down and assess how to move forward.

That situation made me realize that quitting one type of leadership is sometimes necessary and could lead to other opportunities for community engagement. To sustain a leadership position in such an environment was very challenging. I was disappointed at the turn of events, but one can expect these things to happen. My most significant lesson was that if someone wants to take credit for my work I needed to be clear about my contributions whenever there is an opportune moment. I would consider it a form of flattery (*Someone wants to be you*), look on the bright side (*I must have done something good*), and outdo yourself (*Go for the next leadership challenge*).

Leadership Test: Fighting for What Is Right.

> In a matter of principle, stand like a rock.
> - **Thomas Jefferson**

I worked with and led the Filipino Community in Norway for five years, and together with the Council, pioneered the most attended event of the community, the "Fiesta Filipino." When I decided to stand up for my principles, I did not get the positive results I was hoping for. In September 2016, I was deeply disappointed. The FilCom Council I once respected unwisely supported an act of misconduct against a council member. The treasurer of Filcom discovered that the media officer had unauthorized access to the Filcom bank account and removed the access. When the council learned about the treasurer's action, the council issued a resolution to provide the media officer access to the bank account and made a decision to remove the treasurer without due process. The media officer stated that it would be ugly; and threatened me by indicating his willingness to kill for FilCom, if I chose to take the treasurer's side. No one deserves to be threatened in such a way especially when fighting for what she believes is the right thing to do. Despite the admission of irregular actions by the media officer, and without a quorum at their meeting, the council supported the media officer even though they knew it was unjust. Compassion for the media officer, who was jobless and dependent on social welfare was the primary consideration, rather than doing the right thing. During the election, those who admitted that they were aware of the irregular actions did not attend and did not to participate in the new elections. They had already decided that they would remain as advisers. After the elections, I was told that the votes were already in place. No one reported on the problem. No one acknowledged the injustice and the error of the decision. That was the end of my involvement with the group. At some point,

I had to decide when enough was enough. We no longer shared the same vision, mission, and goals. To fight for a principle was no longer relevant.

Feeling Burnt Out

I started to feel unappreciated. I began to count the many ways I had provided service to the Filipinos/as in my community, the many times I attended to and hosted visiting dignitaries, the lobbying for recruitment of nurses and engineers from the Philippines, and the visits to political, social offices, and even far-away prisons to help two Filipino inmates and their families. I started to feel burnt-out. I realized why my husband said: "Good decision" when I snapped at him "I am done with community service."

Surviving Community Service

It was time to re-assess my expectations about community service. I had to remind myself why I cared about the Filipino community in Norway. Making a difference gave me satisfaction. My checklist for surviving community service are as follows in no particular order:

- Learn to deal with cultural myths and stereotypes. Among Filipinos, there is a belief in the crab mentality. The stereotype explains why no crab escapes from a bucketful of crabs. As the saying goes, the other crabs pull back any crab trying to escape. This might be similar to an interpretation of the Norwegian concept of *janteloven* [no one is better than the others]. These stereotypes might explain why leadership of community service activities is problematic. Your leadership view might not align with the community. Community members will have different opinions about community matters depending on what they think is beneficial for them.

- Understand the constraints of the community. The top priority of many overseas Filipinos is financial gain. Some hold two or three jobs leaving little time for volunteering.

- Recognize that expectations will vary about who is a leader and how that leader should behave. People will expect perfection from a leader. Sometimes one mistake can ruin a leader's reputation. People expect the leader to delegate but expect the leader to work for the community. People expect the leader to be first to arrive and last to leave any event. When something goes wrong, people are likely to blame the leader so the leader must be prepared to be a "shock absorber."

- Develop the habit of listening first before talking, think of criticisms as constructive, and deal with an issue before it leads to more problems. Willingness to listen is a way of showing care, empathy, and compassion.

- Respect is a two-way process. As a leader, you show respect to others by giving them a chance to express their views and opinions. As a leader you gain respect by being transparent and accountable, providing good results, and finding the courage to say "enough is enough."

- Be authentic. Set the course with sincerity, courage, and selflessness.

- Be positive. Give hope, instead of just delivering facts.

- Be ethical. Set your standards high and bring others along to meet those standards.

Giving My Best

The good you do today may be forgotten tomorrow but do good anyway; Give the world the best you have and maybe it never is enough but give your best anyway!
- **Mother Teresa**

The Au Pair Program Between Norway and the Philippines

As I have said earlier, I diverted my attention and focused my energy on researching the Au Pair Program in Norway, a project I started under the auspices of the PWO, a year before the arrival of the new Ambassador. I decided I will outdo myself.

Au pair means 'on equal terms.' Norway has endorsed the Council of Europe's Agreement of 24 November 1969 on au pair placement, which defines and standardizes the conditions for au pair placements. Au pairs are neither students nor domestic workers but belong to a special category for the purpose of cultural exchange. The services that the au pair performs can consist of light housework and childminding, but au pairs are not considered domestic workers. The au pair's working day is limited, and the au pair given an opportunity to participate in learning the Norwegian language and in recreational activities. An au pair's residence permit is only good for two years.

Au pairs are single women and men, usually between 18 and 30 years old, who experience a type of cultural exchange arrangement with a European host family, where they are considered a 'temporary' member of the family. As a minimum, the au pair is guaranteed free board and lodging, lives with the host family during the entire stay, has his/her own room, and receives pocket money. The au pairs pay for their travel to the host country and the host family covers the travel expenses for the au pair's return home.

In 1998, the Philippine government unilaterally banned the au pair program because of reports of sexual abuse, exploitation, harassment, and withheld wages in some parts of the world. But in Norway, the au pairs continued to arrive from the Philippines. Some of them first went to Denmark on a tourist visa then looked for a host family to sponsor them as au pairs. Norway, and other countries ignored the ban and continued to issue au pair visas. This practice opened the door for Philippine airport officials to benefit from "escort" services.

When departing from the Philippines, travelers could be offloaded from the plane before is departed, subjected to review of more travel documents by the immigration officer at the airport, and sometimes denied boarding their flight. To avoid being offloaded at the airport in the Philippines, travelers with au pair visas paid for the services of an "escort," an airport official who would help them get past Philippine immigration. Escort fees are reported to be between P20,000 and P30,000 [US$375] in 2008.

After 2010, three countries were allowed to receive Filipino au pairs before the lifting of the ban. In February 2012, the Philippines government lifted the ban and issued new guidelines for au pairs going to Europe, including Norway. The procedures were simplified under the new guidelines. Under the new rules, au pairs are required to submit only an authenticated contract of engagement (authentication usually by the Philippine diplomatic post at the destination); a passport with a valid au pair visa; and a certification from the Commission on Filipinos Overseas. Since au pairs are not considered overseas Filipino workers, they do not need to go through the Department of Labor and Employment (DOLE) or the Philippine Overseas Employment Administration (POEA.

Researching a Position Paper to Lift the Ban for Au Pairs in Norway

I received complaints as well as requests for help both from host families and au pairs, and as a leader, I felt compelled to do something. So, I established an au pair agency, interviewed au pairs, host families, and helped au pairs with their problems. It took me more than a year to finish my fact-finding report. My findings became the basis for the position paper I submitted to the new Philippine Ambassador in Oslo, Her Excellency (HE) Ambassador Elizabeth Buensuceso. The Philippine Ambassador took immediate action and, along with the Philippine Foreign Affairs department, developed guidelines that resulted in the lifting of the ban in Norway. I was told that the position paper that I wrote was used as the basis to lift the ban for all of Europe. Representing PWO, I was interviewed and I contributed the justification for improving the Au Pair Program. The Labor Union is still challenging the sustainability of the Au Pair Program in Norway. One of the issues is the perception that only affluent families could afford the au pair program. This is not correct as we know that middle class families are benefitting from the program. Our work to justify the continuation of the Au Pair Program continues.

LEADERSHIP AND *JANTELOVEN*: CONTRIBUTING AND BENEFITTING

Leading and dealing with the overseas Filipinos require strong determination to move forward, understand different perspectives, and accept different behaviors. Many challenges exist for those of us who migrate and live overseas. Being an overseas Filipino is not easy. In Norway, to succeed requires learning Norwegian and adjusting to cultural norms, such as *janteloven*, a word which can be interpreted as being egalitarian or that no one is better than the others and that might mean that individual differences are not tolerated in order to maintain peace. Retaining one's Philippine national identity while assimilating into the host country's culture is a challenge. For Filipinas, there is an added challenge of improving our image and of gaining respect.

Like being an entrepreneur in a foreign country, leadership in community service takes courage and the ability to remain comfortable in times of distress. The more you can cultivate being at ease during challenging times, the greater the likelihood that your leadership will contribute to the greater good and will benefit the community. The sense of fulfillment in performing community service as a leader is gratifying. It is, however more complicated than running a small business. Serving as a role model means that expectations are extremely high. One small shortcoming has a big impact on your credibility and integrity.

To succeed in community service, one must think about contributing to the greater good.

- Put others first; set aside any thoughts about yourself. Draw out the best in others; do not expect others to look up to you. Motivate your constituency, give credit to those who deserve it, and provide feedback to improve performance.

- Focus on your objectives, on why you perform community service. Approach goals with an open-mind and good conscience. Set high standards for yourself first and then others.

- Expect that with good intentions come with disappointments. Learn from the failures. Be open to new opportunities.

- Be authentic to your convictions and principles. Be mindful about ethical leadership.

Leading for Impact

CHRISTINE AMOUR-LEVAR

Co-Founder of Women on a Mission
Founder of HER Planet Earth
GLOBAL FWN100™ 2016

Finding Your Profession of the Heart

'To every man there comes in his lifetime that special moment when he is figuratively tapped on the shoulder and offered a choice to do a very special thing; unique to him and fitted to his talents; what a tragedy if that moment finds him unprepared or unqualified for the work that would be his finest hour.' This quote by Sir Winston Churchill, probably the most influential person of the twentieth century, a man who so embodied resistance to tyranny that he was called by many 'the largest human being of our time,' is a constant source of inspiration in my leadership journey.

While how I view myself as a Filipina woman leader is still very much a work in progress, Churchill's statement resonates deeply with how I feel about my evolution over the last few decades. From my early years growing up in Manila and Paris, to attending university in Tokyo and working on multiple continents as a young professional, from navigating the heartache of my divorce from my ex-husband to finding love again as a single mother of two young children, and being blessed with two more healthy children; the journey has been formative and not without many challenges, pitfalls, joys, and sorrows. But ultimately, as Churchill so eloquently stated, I believe the voyage has prepared me for that special moment in my life where I am called to do something with more significance and more meaning than the sum of my experiences to date.

Childhood and Growing Up

I feel very blessed to have grown up in a loving, multiracial, multilingual and multicultural home. My mother, Eloisa Araneta, is a proud Filipina who studied and lived abroad for several years before meeting my father upon her return to the Philippines. My father, Bernard Huni, is a French and Swiss dual citizen, who was also a military commando during the French-Algerian war (France's equivalent of the Vietnam war) and who subsequently enjoyed a successful international career in shipping working in France, Tahiti, the Philippines, Hong Kong, and the United Kingdom. As a result of growing up with cosmopolitan parents, living in Asia and Europe, I am the product of an international education, which has helped me navigate the vagaries of a global career and a life across many borders.

When I was five years old, my family and I moved from tropical Manila, where I was born, to a small town outside of Paris, near Chantilly. At the time, my father had decided to pursue a business opportunity with one of his uncles in France, and, he uprooted the whole family. Soon after we arrived, I started my schooling at a local public school. The French education system seemed strict and punitive compared to my American-style kindergarten in Manila. Despite the beauty of the short European summer months, the cold and dark winters required some adjusting. We lived in a big house on the edge of a dark forest and occasionally I felt a little isolated. Furthermore, I could sense my mother's longing for the support of her family and friends back in the Philippines, but it also did not help that my father was often abroad on extended business trips.

Despite these challenges, after many months, we finally adjusted to this new life and found many things to enjoy and love about France. Eventually, we made the most of our five years there, before moving back to the Philippines.

Upon our return to Manila, I studied at the Lycée Français and after a few years there, transferred to the International School of Manila where I graduated with honors and an International Baccalaureate Diploma. Then two months after my 18th birthday, I moved to Tokyo to attend University.

Prior to that moment, I had never set foot in Japan and did not even know much about this country's great history and culture. I had also never studied the Japanese language and did not even enjoy Japanese cuisine. The truth was I had no desire to go to Japan and was tempted to return to Paris. Of my 200 classmates at the international school in Manila, I was the only one who ended up going to Tokyo for university. The majority of my friends went on to study in Europe or in the United States. Going to Japan was entirely my parents' decision. They believed that I would benefit from this unique life experience and from the added bonus of learning the Japanese language.

So, off I went to the land of the rising sun, without really knowing what to expect. I could never have foreseen the kind of massive culture shock I was about to experience. During my freshman year at university, I lived in a strict all-girls dormitory run by stern Japanese nuns. All activities were severely regimented, and everyone had to be up and dressed, ready to clean the dormitory communal areas, such as toilets and showers, every morning at eight AM sharp. Having grown-up with a somewhat privileged lifestyle in Manila, with maids and drivers at my beck and call, this change in my life took some serious readjustment. Additionally, I often felt frustrated because despite studying the language for hours every single day, I was unable to communicate in Japanese until about six months into my stay. It was only after I spent two weeks working on a Japanese farm on the southern island of Kyushu, where I was forced to speak the language regularly and without any other foreigners in sight, that I finally made a breakthrough with the language. I came back to Tokyo dreaming in Japanese. And based on this particular case, I can confirm that total immersion really does work.

In the end, my time in Japan turned out to be a genuinely humbling but incredibly rich and formative experience. Upon graduating cum laude from Sofia University in Tokyo with a Bachelor of Arts degree in International Business and Economics and a minor in the Japanese Language, I stood at the threshold of new beginnings, about to venture into a new life. I felt a deep sense of anticipation and excitement. Which direction should I go? What career path should I embark on? I felt the world was my oyster.

My Guiding Principles

There are four things that I would like to share in this chapter, principles that I hope will help guide younger women as they start in their lives and their careers:

- The first is to think of your life and career in terms of your BRAND.

- The second is the importance of having GRIT in anything you do.

- The third is to think of FAILURE AS AN OPPORTUNITY for growth.

- And the fourth is to FIND YOUR PROFESSION OF THE HEART and use that to uplift others.

I will expand on the above, pulling in examples from my life that have shaped me as well as people and experiences (both successes and failures) that have profoundly changed me.

Own Your Brand

The first concept is to think of your life and career in terms of your own brand. What is your Brand? Your brand is being true to yourself. Aligning your career choices with your values and not the other way around. Go after your dreams, even if you do not know yet what that dream looks like, and it may take many years for you to find what you truly enjoy and excel at. Whatever you do, choose to do something you are genuinely passionate about. You will find joy and fulfillment by living life this way.

Steve Jobs once said: "Have the courage to follow your own heart and intuition because they already know what you truly want to do with your life. Everything else is secondary."

In my case, sports have always been a big part of my life. I was very athletic and competitive as a child and teenager. Growing up, I played football, tennis, basketball, touch rugby, swimming, and could never stay still. Thus, it was not a coincidence that I ended up working for Nike, on and off for about 11 years, in four continents and many cities.

Throughout my life, when it came to picking jobs, I followed my heart. Even the work I do with my two non-profit organizations, Women on a Mission and HER Planet Earth, has a competitive athletic element that is entirely in line with my desire to challenge myself both mentally and physically. Another reason I started these philanthropic organizations was that I wanted to help women who are less fortunate than me. I feel incredibly lucky to have lived a privileged life and believe that with such good fortune, comes great responsibility. Since 2012, I have been determined and driven to make a difference in the lives of women who are deprived of the most fundamental freedom, the right to live in peace and happiness with their loved ones, the right to education and self-accomplishment, the right to thrive in harmony with nature, the right to live with respect and decency, and the right to dream. Ultimately what drives me is the desire to create a world where human rights and environmental integrity can blossom and prosper.

And as you go through life, it is important to remember that every single one of your actions shows who you are and what you value, just like a brand: Be it the jobs you choose, how you conduct yourself with others, even what you post on social media. The choices you make throughout your career and your personal life, contribute to building your brand, image, and legacy as a person. To do that well, you need to become relentlessly focused on what you do that adds value to your profession and your chosen focus in life. This means staying relevant and continually trying to learn and grow while still being true to your core values and aligning your brand with the choices you make.

Having Grit

Secondly, GRIT. GRIT is courage, resolve, persistence, and it is not giving up when the going gets tough. Having GRIT is that subtle difference between people who are successful and people who are not. Simply put, the path to success and to achieving your goals is to take massive, determined actions. Everything I have ever achieved would have remained merely an idea if I had not had the necessary GRIT to follow through and to turn my ideas into reality.

As a result of GRIT, I feel I have built a meaningful life and career thus far, while also raising my four children. I certainly would not be sharing my experience with you today in this book about leadership, if I had not taken chances, pursued my dreams, and put hard work behind each of these initiatives.

I had four job offers before graduating from my university in Tokyo. I knew I needed to find a job quickly if I wanted to stay in Japan because a student visa without a confirmed job offer meant you had to exit the country. So, six months before graduation, I sent out 60 curriculum vitae (CVs). On many occasions, I even hand-delivered them if I could, and this while still attending classes at the university and working two part-time jobs.

Thankfully, within a few months, I was gratified to have four serious job offers, from well-established companies. In the end, I picked the one that did not necessarily pay the most, but it was the job that offered the most significant opportunities to learn and to use my Japanese, plus exposure to many industries. It was the job that interested me the most.

Thus, I started in a fascinating industry, advertising, working for an agency called McCann-Erickson; Japan's most significant international advertising agency. I was their first non-Japanese recruit in their university-hire program. A few years later, this first job, coupled with my passion for sports, led me to a dream international marketing job at Nike's world headquarters in the United States.

GRIT and hard work have been a part of my life ever since. From succeeding at Nike where I was their youngest regional PR manager at age 23, to transfers internationally with them, to taking other chances in my career, and to reinventing myself several times, GRIT was with me every step of the way.

When I ran my own retail business in Singapore for three and half years, it took GRIT to make it work. Moreover, it was not easy. However, running my own business was one of my best leadership lessons. I learned a tremendous amount about myself, about people, and about managing a small business. These were invaluable life lessons, I still apply today, in my work with my two non-profit organizations.

When I decided to embrace freelance writing as a journalist a few years ago, even though I had not been trained as a writer, I found many closed doors. Nevertheless, I pushed on, because I enjoyed writing. Today I am a regular contributor to various international publications including the Straits Times Newspaper of Singapore, the Manila Bulletin Newspaper of the Philippines, the Huffington Post, and Forbes Asia. A few years ago, I also published my first book about post-motherhood fitness and aspirations, something that has given me much pride and contentment.

Having GRIT always bears fruit and it comes back to you in countless ways.

Another example of this is five years ago, based on a contact I made through my charitable work, I was offered an exciting and challenging consultancy job in the philanthropic and leadership development activities of a subsidiary of Temasek Holdings, Singapore's sovereign wealth fund. Today I am responsible for developing and implementing their brand Marketing and Corporate Communications strategy. The company employs over 600 people in Singapore and serves diverse international clients from multiple key industries.

Ultimately, there is no substitute for hard work, a good education, and a positive outlook on life. The good news is that any of us can develop GRIT if we stay focused and committed.

Failures as Opportunity

Thirdly, think of failures as challenges and opportunities for growth. Obstacles in life can only do two things, stop us in our tracks or force us to get creative. As difficult as it may seem, we all need to look at challenges as blessings, gifts that can be used to ignite our imagination and help us go further than we ever knew we could.

One of the lowest points in my life was the divorce from my ex-husband Mike after ten years of marriage. Throughout this painful time in our lives, we were both deeply concerned about our children's wellbeing. Thankfully we survived the experience, and we found a way to thrive and nurture our relationship as friends and as parents to the children.

The first thing we did soon after our breakup was to consult a child psychologist who advised us that living in proximity to each other would be less traumatic for the children. It would give them some form of stability, knowing that though they now lived primarily with their mother, their father was very close and accessible at any time. So, we decided to live in two separate flats but in the same building.

A few years later when I met my second husband, Steven, and remarried, instead of us moving away from this setup, he moved right in with me and my two children who were four and six years old at the time and Mike still lived a few floors above us.

Soon after, Steven and I had two children together, and during this time we all continued to live in the same building. The older children simply viewed their father's flat as the upstairs part of our home and would zoom up the service lift several times a day to see him when he was in town. Weekend sleepovers at his place required little, if any, change to their daily schedule. My two younger children often accompanied the older two to visit their "Uncle" in his flat upstairs. They felt equally at home and occasionally shared their meals with him. In their innocent eyes, he was an important member of our family.

Many people looked at our set-up and thought, "How bizarre. Why would anyone want to live this way, in such proximity to an ex-husband or an ex-wife?" The answer is simple. "It takes a village to raise a child." There is much wisdom in this old African proverb. The proverb is from the Igbo and Yoruba regions of Nigeria where people believe that raising a child is a communal effort. The responsibility lays not only with the parents, but also with the extended family, and in some cases, the community. And this is a proverb that my ex-husband, my husband and I took to heart, especially during the formative years of our children's upbringing.

In addition to the mother, the father, and the step-father raising the children, every other family member, and close friend has a role to play. The larger the community, the better for the child. Every member of this extended family can impart wisdom, values, and tradition that children are receptive to.

As one reflects on this unconventional modern living arrangement, it is obvious that it requires a certain type of individual who can look beyond the petty differences of opinions, the bruised egos, and the emotional volatility that inevitably come with any divorce. It helps if the second husband, as it is in my case, is not responsible for the breakup of the first marriage. Nevertheless, ultimately, it is about putting the children first and our feelings a distant second. Beyond the sense of failure, frustration, and self-pity that may dominate the emotions of the adults after a divorce, it is the children's fragile feelings and nascent self-confidence that really need to be placed at the center of this complicated situation.

We all lived this way for six years, and then as the children grew up, my ex-husband bought a flat ten minutes' walk from us. Today, even if we are not living in the same building anymore, we still feel part of the same village. And when I think back on some of these heart-warming moments during the formative years of my children's upbringing, I thank my lucky star that I had two admirable and unique men in my life to have children with. Both men have been able to put egos aside for the love, happiness, and well-being of the children.

What this experience has taught me is that from failure and pain, you can find success and hope. If you work hard to make the best of any situation ultimately, you will discover the silver lining, and you will be able to nurture it into something positive and beautiful. The learnings from this personal challenge have also helped me in my career and in my life. They have made me more optimistic and have taught me to always look for opportunities to improve a problematic situation. Tough times and failure teach us to trust ourselves more because ultimately, we are more resilient and capable than we think.

Finding Your Profession of the Heart

I am a great believer that you are attracted to people and projects in your life that you are genuinely interested in and that you have a passion for. Of course, in the end, it is up to you to seek out these opportunities, take some chances, and turn them into a real success. This is very much the attitude I have adopted over the years and how I have tried to lead my life. Along the way, I have learned a lot and thankfully I am still learning. Throughout my journey, I have stumbled many times, but ultimately, I have crafted my own unique path in life. And what I have come to realize is that success is profoundly personal and cannot be measured as a number or qualified as a position. Living with awareness and purpose; choosing to do things that make a difference in the lives of others has helped me find my own brand of leadership.

Ultimately, I believe that if your actions inspire others to grow, you are a leader. In the words of motivational speaker Simon Sinek, "Leadership is not about being in charge, leadership is about taking care of those in your charge." This is the kind of leadership that resonates with me and guides me in my current profession as a marketer, philanthropist, and adventurer.

Today, I feel extremely fortunate to have found a way to bring together my passion for sports and adventure, with my desire to empower women and protect our beautiful planet via the two non-profit organizations I founded, Women on a Mission and HER Planet Earth.

Women on a Mission primarily supports and empowers women who have been subjected to violence and abuse; more specifically women survivors of war, survivors of domestic violence, rape, and other forms of abuse. We support them by raising awareness and funds for organization and charities that champion such women and advance their position in the world.

HER Planet Earth is a women's advocacy movement that supports underprivileged women affected by climate change. Poor people, and women, in particular, are among the most vulnerable to climate change and environmental degradation. Among the world's 1.3 billion poor people, the majority are women.

Both entities fundraise by organizing challenging expeditions to off the beaten track locations around the world. Expeditions are self-funded by each participant who help raise funds through their networks, friends, and contacts for our partner charities. We also organize events, workshops, and talks as ways to increase visibility and raise more funds for our chosen charities.

One of the most satisfying moments in the last few years working on these philanthropic projects was during my trip to Rwanda in Africa in November 2017. There I was visiting one of the charities we support, Women for Women International (WfWI). Rwanda is a fascinating country that has risen from the ashes of a civil war, to become one of the fastest growing economies on the African continent. After the 1994 genocide, Rwanda lay in ruins. Hundreds of thousands of corpses were piled up on roadsides. Churches and schools were destroyed; offices and businesses plundered. Above all, the nation was traumatized by the horrific crimes that had decimated the population. Because most of those killed were men and because many male perpetrators fled to neighboring countries, approximately 70% of Rwanda's post-genocide population was female. Faced with ensuring their families' survival, women stepped up and ended up playing a significant part in the country's reconstruction.

As one proud graduate from a program, we funded told me, "I am no longer poor. I can now support my family by making bricks and selling them as part of my cooperative. My children go to school, and we have enough to eat. I have you and your team of women to thank for my good fortune." Her honesty and gratitude deeply touched me. The women we met in Rwanda are courageous, determined, hardworking survivors of a decimated generation. They told us their stories through song, dance, and with tears in their eyes and in so doing, they touched our hearts forever.

What is wonderful for me to realize is that because I took a chance and did something outside of my comfort zone through Women on a Mission and HER Planet Earth, my life has been enriched in countless ways. The encounter in Rwanda was profoundly moving, and I have been blessed to have experienced countless other such moments in the countries I have visited and where I have worked with women's groups that Women on a Mission and HER Planet Earth supports. The opportunity to change lives is a privilege and taking that mission to heart has expanded my vision of the world.

Being at the core of Women on a Mission and HER Planet Earth has allowed me to push myself beyond my limits on multiple occasions and truly test my leadership capabilities. Managing teams under pressure on challenging expeditions to some of the most inhospitable places in the world such as the Arctic, the Antarctic, deserts in the Middle East and Africa, and mountains in the Himalayas, has taught me valuable lessons of humility and resilience.

Indeed, when I migrated with the noble Nenets reindeer herders of Siberia in minus 30 degrees Celsius temperatures, the simplicity and purity of their way of life reminded me of the importance of community and family for survival. When I traveled through the Himalayas and spent time with the proud Sherpas of Nepal and with the serene people of the Kingdom of Bhutan, their kindness and generosity inspired me to be a better person. When I met Jordanian Bedouins on the plains of Wadi Rum and when I witnessed the sheer force and beauty of the Lut desert of Iran, a piece of my soul was captured in the vast emptiness of these magnificent regions. When I stood on the rim of a bubbling volcano with the Afar people of the Danakil Desert of Ethiopia and when I rode across the Atlai Mountains of Mongolia with the mighty Kazakh Eagle Hunters, it ignited in me a passion for living that I had never felt before. And finally, when I was lucky enough to reach the summit of a mountain that had never been climbed by anyone else before on the coldest, windiest, and most remote continent on this planet, Antarctica, it was one of the most empowering and unforgettable experiences of my life.

As I reflect on these magnificent journeys that I have been blessed to undertake, I realize that some of the experiences that at the time felt like the most miserable and desolate were, in fact, the most formative and enriching. I understand that my greatest achievements came in the face of the greatest adversity, and that true growth only comes from challenge, from stepping away from what is comfortable and stepping into the unknown. This is not simply true of travel. No matter where you are in the world you can seek and find adventure by opening your mind and exploring your own limits.

In the final analysis, I believe that everyone has a distinct mission that has the capacity to inspire others. For me, self-improvement comes mainly from helping others, because humans are neurologically wired to gain personal dividends from altruism. That is why it is so important to invest time and effort to find the meaning and purpose of your existence and find a way to lead a life that matters, a life that empowers and uplifts others with kindness and true generosity of spirit. This is what will give you the greatest satisfaction in life. It does not happen by chance. The choice is yours to make.

Throughout the last few years, one of my guiding principles has been that "we rise by lifting others." For me personally, empathy is at the core of good leadership. Innately in all of us, I believe there is a desire to be good, to be fully alive, and to find meaning in life. What is that meaning? What is that purpose? Could it simply be to love what you do and to feel that you are making a difference? That is where it all begins.

Setting up Women on a Mission and HER Planet Earth has allowed me to find my profession of the heart, that intersection where passion and ability come together for a greater good. That realization has given me fulfillment, peace, and happiness. It is as if everything that I have done in my life thus far has prepared me to do this extraordinary thing, unique to me and fitted to my talents. This is what Churchill once described as his "finest hour."

In the end, what I hope readers will take away from this chapter is that life is a series of opportunities, that if you pursue with passion and determination will allow you to unleash your full potential and find your profession of the heart. Our achievements grow according to the size of our dreams. So, if there is something you want to try out, do not hold back, go after it with all your heart. Do not be afraid to take chances with courage and make them happen with GRIT and hard work. And most importantly, continue to invest in the meaning and purpose of your existence, but do not choose someone else's definition of success and ask yourself these questions:

- What is YOUR Mission in life?
- What are YOU truly passionate about?
- What are YOUR unique gifts and abilities?
- What could YOU do to make more of a difference?

We are indeed all fortunate, and because of this we should be driven by a great sense of responsibility and a desire to give back. Ultimately, I encourage you to challenge yourself, to seek out different and difficult adventures and experiences, that will help you push your life to limits you have never imagined.

WOMEN ON A MISSION www.womenmission.com

Founded in 2012, Women on a Mission (WOAM) is a non-profit organization, headquartered in Singapore, which aims to raise awareness and funds for women survivors of war and to support and empower women who have been subjected to violence and abuse. WOAM has raised close to 1 million USD to date to support organizations that advance the position of women around the world.

WHAT DRIVES US

We firmly believe that we should do our part to help people in need, and as a result contribute to making this world a better place. In our hearts, we know we can make a difference, one woman at a time.

HOW WE DO IT

Our work combines challenging expeditions, inspirational campaigns and fundraising events, TED-style motivational talks as a means to raise awareness and fund for our charity partners.

OUR EXPEDITIONS / EVENTS

Nine successful challenging expeditions to remote locations (Everest Base Camp in Nepal, Wadi Rum Desert in Jordan, Tsum Valley in Nepal, Siberia in Russia, Angkor Wat in Cambodia, the Lut Desert in Iran, the Kingdom of Bhutan, the Danakil Depression of Ethiopia and the Altai Mountains of Mongolia)

Nine major fundraising events with over 1000 guests (combined)

On the ground motivational talks, leadership & entrepreneurship training, gender equality awareness workshops reaching over 800+ women in Singapore, Nepal, Iran, Bhutan, Rwanda and Mongolia

Over 40 companies & organizations have partnered with us, donated and sponsored our initiatives and events since 2012

WHO WE SUPPORT

Our fundraising efforts are specifically directed to the millions of women and girls displaced or widowed by decades of violence in war-torn regions. Our support to date has allowed 500 women in war-torn countries to participate in year-long training programs, giving them the knowledge and skills to rebuild their lives. Our contribution has impacted more than 1000 women in communities around the world. Common discriminatory practices, amplified by extremist groups, often make it dangerous for women to seek education, healthcare services, employment, or, in some cases, even to leave their homes.

Our partners are existing well-established non-profit institutions that have excellent programs and structures in place dedicated to serving the underprivileged. In particular, we have established long-standing ties with.

  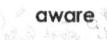

'We Challenge Ourselves to Empower Women'

1 in 3 women
experiences sexual or physical violence in her lifetime

2 million
WOMEN & GIRLS are trafficked annually

Up to 50%
of sexual assaults are committed against YOUNG GIRLS worldwide

2/3
of children denied primary education are GIRLS

17%
Women's nominal wages are 17% lower than men's

HER Planet Earth

www.herplanetearth.com

Founded in 2017, HER Planet Earth is a global women's advocacy movement, headquartered in Singapore, that promotes a deeper connection between women empowerment and the integrity of the environment. HPE has raised close to 100,000 USD to date for organizations and programs that empower and educate underprivileged women and engage them in environmental issues and conservation activities.

'Empowering Women for a Healthier Planet'

WHAT DRIVES US

We believe women are Gamechangers with unique knowledge and solutions to move the needle on sustainability. We aim to inspire women to become policymakers and agents of change to achieve social and economic equity and a healthy and thriving planet.

HOW WE DO IT

HPE's strategy is to organize and promote campaigns and activities to increase visibility of the movement, and to raise funds for programs that empower and educate underprivileged women, and engage them in environmental issues and conservation activities.

WHY WE DO IT

At the heart of sustainable development is a respect for all fundamental human rights as well as accountability to the earth and future generations. Climate change and environmental degradation are barriers to sustainable development, augmenting existing inequalities. Gender often remains the untold story behind climate change.

In many countries, women are among the most vulnerable to climate change and environmental impacts, partly because they make up the larger share of the agricultural workforce and tend to have access to fewer income-earning jobs. The destructive forces of nature, warped by rising global temperatures, manifest in cyclones, floods and other extreme weather conditions, which can act as negative force multipliers in societies already riven by inequality.

The onset of droughts, accompanied by heightened food and water insecurity, also have a disproportionate effect on those least able to deal with the resulting increased social strains. While climate change is a global phenomenon, its impact is not spread across a level playing field. Its effects are felt locally, and poor people suffer the most. Among the world's 1.3 billion poor people, the majority are women.

OUR URGENT CONCERNS

Reduce plastic waste

Reduce CO2 emissions

ENDANGERED SPECIES

Protect endangers species

OUR URGENT CONCERNS

HON. THELMA B. BOAC

President, Governing Board of Trustees,
Berryessa Union School District, San Jose, CA
Professional Leadership Coach, Santa Clara County Office of Education
Filipina Women's Network Board Member 2014-2018
U.S. FWN100™ 2007 and GLOBAL FWN100™ 2013

Filipina: Leave Footprints That Last

When we first enter this world and breathe our first breath of life, we cry our hearts out. I have always wondered about this mystery of life. Perhaps it is the precursor to the kind of life that we all must lead. Or perhaps it is life's way of telling us that the road to mortality is full of bumps and holes, and it will be up to us to jump over the bumps and smooth out the holes. Life is full of tears and laughter; it is also full of great promise. It is the longing of this promise that leaves footprints and gives our life meaning.

Life's Surprises

In this chapter, I reflect on life's interruptions, obstacles, and failures that I encountered. These were unexpected and completely changed the direction of my professional and personal life. The struggles, failures, and tragedies were life-changing experiences that ended my complacency of being a classroom teacher and helped me discern what is my true purpose in life. Being in the classroom during those seven years was a dream come true. At that time, I had no other professional goal or ambition but to remain in the classroom and be with students. I was satisfied with who I was and what I was doing. What was most satisfying was that I also fulfilled the dream of my adoptive Filipino parents in the U.S. as well as my biological parents in the Philippines that I was to go to college and become a professional. I was the first in my family to reach that goal and was extremely grateful to God that my adoptive parents were there to witness the fulfillment of a lifelong dream. I would like to think that I was a good, if not a great teacher. Thankfully, someone else thought so too.

Accepting Life's Little Interruptions

Three years into my marriage, my youngest sister died suddenly in the Philippines leaving two little children without a mother. Her passing filled me with anger for quite a long time. I found myself asking: why? I began to question my faith in God and suffered in silence. We thought about adopting the little children and bringing them to America. To my disappointment, my brother-in-law who is the father would not agree. The children were twelve months and three years of age. Though deeply disappointed, I understood the father's objection. At the same time, my husband and I were also planning to start a family of our own. We laid out several plans as we tried to have our own children. I was still coping with my sister's death. It was affecting me personally and physically. After much counseling with a close friend, I decided to immerse myself in work, involve myself in our church community, and join community organizations. My professional life changed, I was no longer in the classroom and given more administration and supervisory responsibility. I became Department Chair, Head of Testing, Resource Specialist for English Language Learners, and was wholly responsible for the Title 1 budget of one million dollars. This may not sound like a great deal of money, but to a single school, this was huge.

Life's little interruptions in my life are frustrating. The most devastating disruptions are those that are life-altering; those that interfere with your best-laid plans. Not doing something about them is crippling to the soul and mind. Instead of responding with curses and cries, I tried to remember that God is present for every moment and experience. I learned to accept that there is a reason for everything even though at times I faltered.

Growing to be Influential

In a high school with a population of four thousand students, at the time the largest high school in Northern California, where the third largest student population were Filipinos, I became the role model for our students, and the "go to" teacher for parents. I became their personal advisor and counselor. Because I was fluent in Spanish, Spanish speaking parents would seek me out for advice on navigating the school system. I saw many parents during Sunday mass where I served as both Lector and Eucharistic Minister. I was invited to various community events and became a recognizable figure in the community. Organizations recruited me to head scholarship programs benefiting graduating high-school seniors of Philippine ancestry in Santa Clara County. I received many community service awards from various organizations including the California state legislature. It was a common sight to see me in the company of elected officials. Being immersed in my work and conquering my anger helped ease the pain of losing my sister. I began to see the value of my work and involvement in the community, and this became extremely important as I advanced toward future endeavors.

Realizing Who I Am

My husband and I continued to wait to become parents. We waited for three years, six years, ten years, and on and on! We consulted with specialist after specialist! Being a woman and a Filipina and not being able to become a mother is tragic! There were hurtful comments and positive comments as well, but also ridiculous ones. Through it all, my in-laws were wonderful. They never pressured me. They understood how I was feeling. And for that, I loved them dearly. Then, there were my mom and dad, always hopeful. "Never lose faith and continue to pray," my mom would say to me. "Success will come." Success never came. The true realization that I would never be a mother came as I was lying in the hospital for a biopsy, not the first time, and the doctor would not give me any more anesthesia because she felt it was too dangerous. I endured excruciating pain. I vowed I would move heaven and earth and go through whatever painful steps that were necessary. Not trying hard enough was not on the agenda. I wanted to be able to live with myself. It was that critical for my sanity. And try I did. And pray I did. The devastating feeling of accepting I would never be a mother was overwhelming and tears flowed freely and numbed the pain. Being crippled by what I believed was my own failure was not in my veins. As difficult as it was, my goal was to rise above it. Then, as if some divine intervention enveloped me, I surrendered and accepted my fate. The many years of trying and hoping came to an end. The Good Lord must have a plan for me, I said sadly. My husband Dan, waiting patiently in the waiting room, saw me weak as I ambled slowly towards him. The expression on my face revealed a thousand words. He had a comforting smile on his face. His first words to me: "God has a plan for you and me. It's okay not to have our own. He knows best." All I could do was cry.

An Awakening, Never Forget

I reflected on what my mom said, "success will come." I continued to look deep down at myself and tried not to pay attention to others who looked at me with pity. Recognizing that I had to heal myself, I began the process of healing. But there were times when people made it difficult. Questions were mean-spirited. "Whose fault is it, yours or your husband?" Some failures are bigger than others. This was a huge one because it was more public and carried a greater stigma. I continued to focus my energy into my work and community commitments. Grateful for the gift of having the ability to build relationships and partnerships with the staff, I focused on moving forward. Thanks to my parents they prepared me for this type of leadership. Mom and Dad were active in the community in Grover Beach, California, where I grew up. The Filipino community was a close-knit community. Mom was President of the Filipino Women's Club of San Luis Obispo County, and Dad was active in the American Legion. Many of the men were the *manongs* [older brothers] who came to this country in their youth in the 1920's and loved this country with all their heart and soul. The majority of these *manongs* fought in World War II and settled in the agriculturally rich San Luis Obispo County. Through hard work and possessing a strong work ethic, these *manongs* were able to buy land and fulfill their dream of farming their own land. Many of the *manongs* had not been to the Philippines for many years, but they held on to the most precious of their heritage; Filipino cultural traditions and kept it alive for future generations. Through hard work and perseverance, the Filipino Cultural Center was built in Grover Beach in 1968 and is still thriving today. They never had a chance for a good education, but dream they did. What a legacy! What a footprint!

My adoptive father was among these *manongs* who was able to fulfill his dream of owning his own land. My adoptive mom, who was my biological aunt, was a World War II war widow whose husband was missing in action in the Battle of Bataan. Her two very young children died just before the Americans liberated the city of Manila. She came to America after the war and met and married my Dad. They were not blessed with children of their own. They adopted me when I was ten years old.

From my beloved adoptive parents, I learned how to cultivate and nurture partnerships, how to respect other people's opinions, and how to work collaboratively for the good of the community. I benefited from this knowledge, and this is the reason perhaps why I was tapped for leadership positions at my school. I accepted the position of being the head of testing and the overseer of the entire bilingual program with 80 teachers under my leadership.

Greatest Failure

What I considered to be my most significant failure in life was my inability to have a child. Nothing was more painful than this. It is debilitating for any woman, and I am no different. Psychologically and socially it affected me profoundly. I am thankful for my deep devotion to my faith that helped me get out of this misery. I thought of my adoptive mom who lost everyone including her two very young children during World War II. For a mother to lose everyone so dear to her would be earth-shattering. But she turned it into something positive. Guided by her faith and a vision for the future she left the Philippines and came to America where she found a new life and, ultimately, success. If my adoptive mom could endure such tragedy, then who am I not to be able to do the same? As Eleanor Roosevelt said, "You've got to look fear in the face." Mom did just that. That was the inspiration that lifted my burden. Just as I was beginning to heal, another devastating blow hit me. My mom, the woman who I love with my whole heart and soul, died suddenly of a massive coronary at the young age of sixty-seven. This incredible woman who had been my comforter, my consoler, my savior, my beloved mother was no longer with me. The loneliness and the intense grief was suffocating. I asked myself, "How much more could I take?" I felt lost, confused, and defeated. I was struggling to pull myself together. She was the mother who had brought me to America when I was ten years old, adopted me, sent me to college, and gave me the skills to make something of myself. Her words to me, "You are my little girl." "Make your stay in America impactful and meaningful." "Use your talent." "Leave a legacy." Inspirational words I live by every day that continue to define my hopes for the future.

Staying on Course

Recovering from the sudden death of my mother took time. Moving on with life required a great deal of support. I tapped my network of support; counselors, social workers, trusted friends, and family members. These people helped get me out of a rut. Having people to talk to other than the people at home was a life booster. I felt like a prisoner in my sorrow and I knew that prolonging the agony and wallowing in self-pity was not healthy. I needed a new beginning and to start living again. My beloved mom did not stop living when she lost her first husband and her children. I decided to get a master's degree in Educational Leadership and Supervision. My new responsibilities at school and studying at the same time to become an administrator kept my mind from the devastating loss. It was school during the day and the university in the evening. It was challenging! Settling in with this new routine was therapeutic.

Reading books on leadership and implementing new techniques and skills during the day was energizing. The objective was to concentrate on being successful in my new endeavors. Failure was not an option. I witnessed school administrators struggling with their responsibilities. And some, unfortunately, felt they failed. However, in my view, they did not fail. They just got too anxious and forgot to build trusting relationships and partnerships with the people with whom they worked. According to Fullan (2001), "We must try to build good relationships even with those who may not trust us" (pg. 42). Studies have found that when leaders have a positive attitude, the people they work with are likely to have a positive attitude and produce more. I am no stranger to failures. It is what you do with failure that makes the difference. Failing at something builds character, a kind of tenacity, integrity, and persistence. It is what gives your life meaning. It becomes the stepping stone to success.

Divine Intervention?

Not long after my mother's death, I received word that my brother-in-law in the Philippines, the husband of my deceased younger sister, had died suddenly. The two children were now legally orphans. The decision to adopt the children and bring them to America was a no-brainer for my husband and me since we had wanted to do so years earlier. By this time the children were already in their early teens. The age did not matter to us since it was also their wish to live in America with their aunt and uncle. The adoption papers began immediately, and within six months the paperwork was completed. I traveled to Manila to pick up the children and brought them to America. Ironically, we arrived in San Francisco on Thanksgiving Day. The children met their new dad for the first time. Their arrival brought memories of traveling alone in 1960 when my adoptive parents waited anxiously for me. The cycle of life had come full circle. The significance of Thanksgiving Day when we arrived was not coincidental. I honestly believed that God had, in His perfect timing, made this family miracle possible. It was God's will.

The Children

What had been long anticipated finally become a reality. We were now parents to two young teenagers. Imagine the adjustments on both sides. Our son, Roland, was the quiet one and our daughter, Maria Rosalie, was the talkative one. The adjustment period did not last very long though our daughter, Maria Rosalie, had more difficulty adjusting. I discovered her palms and feet were always wet. I attributed it to nerves and living in a new environment. Just imagine leaving her beloved grandparents, her relatives, and friends behind. Then, all of a sudden, living in a new country with people she barely knew. This brought tears to my eyes and vivid memories of when I first arrived in America as a lonely and scared child. Dan and I had to adjust to being new parents as well, having been just the two of us for many years. But we got through the challenges of being parents to teenagers together. I must admit, that at times, I was too anxious for our two teens to be successful that I might have pushed them too hard. There were times when my husband would remind me that in the classroom I was a teacher, but outside the school, I was, above all, a mom! A hard lesson to swallow but he was right. Looking back, having a teacher for a mom must have been frustrating for them. I am grateful to grandparents and relatives who helped raise them and helped provide a good foundation. Respectful and motivated, both graduated high school and went on to college and careers. As parents, we were not perfect and I am sure we made mistakes along the way. Dan and I raised them with love and support. Roland and Maria Rosalie grew up to be a fine young man and young woman with much love and affection for their mom and dad. We feel truly blessed. These children are now grown up, with families of their own. My husband Dan and I are the proud grandparents of three precious little girls and one boy. Indeed, I believe my adoptive mom would have been proud. She was right when she said to me at one time, "success will come." Now I know what she meant.

Understanding Failure

A success story cannot be fully appreciated until it has faced trials and tribulations. To know success, one must experience failure. Failure is a chance to start over again, and it can lead to many wonderful things. The sweetest success comes only as the result of the most difficult challenge, the kind that requires one to reach down deep inside and fight with everything you have. Anchor (2010) believed success is about using that downward momentum to propel ourselves in the opposite direction. It's not about falling down, it's about falling up (pg. 127). Being open to failure is opening one's heart to possibilities that are still waiting to be conquered. I needed to do just that and opened my heart and started looking forward. There is that wonderful life after failure. It is called success and acceptance and it goes hand in hand with failure. That is Life! The goal is to stay focus but flexible; to keep on trying and not give up. It took these very difficult experiences for me to understand that failure is unavoidable in life. This understanding fueled my desire to take risks in my career and move forward. I learned quite early that there are people who might want to derail one's career advancement. But I had every confidence that if I failed the first time, there would be another chance. I decided to nurture an attitude of no fear of failure. I credit my mom for my conquering the fear of failure. Every success I have achieved has been because of her. It started with my fear of playing in front of people during piano recitals because I was afraid of making mistakes. My stomach would turn nervously in anticipation of performing in public. Mom told me the audience would not notice the mistakes. "Just continue playing and don't stop," she would say. "Mistakes offer you a chance to improve the next time." She made it sound easy. Every day I think of my beloved mom. She made me the woman I am today. Her loving memory is the reason why I continue to tap my potential, all in her honor.

Reaching my Potential

Before completing my master's degree in Administration and Supervision, the position of Villa Principal in the largest high school district in Northern California became available. Aware that the "Boys Club" of the district controlled the decision makers, I knew that my chances for that position would be very slim. There were rumors that the Head Principal would not favor my candidacy. Since the principal would make the final decision, I felt this new endeavor would be futile. I decided not to apply. Not surprisingly, there were many eager applicants, and the majority were male. But considering that a district of 28,000 culturally diverse students had very few people of color as administrators and not all mirrored the student population, I eventually decided to take the risk of applying and going through the interview process. If I did not succeed, it would not be the end of my career. Failing to try would be more of a failure. And regret was not something I wanted to burden myself with for the rest of my life. I turned in my application. The interview process was extremely lengthy. I had to hurdle four steps, and each step included a different group of people. I was able to advance to the next step, and to the next, and to the next. The process lasted about two weeks. Finally, I made it as one of the finalists and the only female. The final decision did not come quickly. I considered it a success just to undergo the grueling process. If I did not get the position, it would not be a horrible disappointment. There would be other opportunities.

A week later the Head Principal paid me a visit in my office. Before she sat down, her first words were, "Congratulations, you are the new Villa Principal"! I found out later that staff members, including some of the administrators, lobbied the Head Principal in favor of my appointment. This was totally unexpected. I was already prepared to accept defeat. Still, I was headed to uncharted territory to be in a leadership position in a school of over 4,000 students where the learning community and students depended on me for guidance. All I could say to the Head Principal was "thank you!" At the first staff meeting in the fall, as a tradition, newly hired and newly assigned personnel were introduced to the entire staff. When the Head

Principal introduced me at the end, I was stunned. The entire audience screamed, clapped, stood up, and gave me a standing ovation. I was filled with humility and could barely speak as a result of the overwhelming response. The Head Principal was as surprised as I was. During my many years at the high school, I could not recall an audience ever giving a new administrator a standing ovation. The director of our wellness program came up to me after the staff meeting and said this was the "first" ever. And she had been at the school since it opened in 1976.

The AHA Moment

News spread quickly throughout the community. Filipino organizations were elated that there was now a Filipina principal at the high school. The impact on the community was significant. The community felt they finally had "success." There was now a voice where there was none before. It was a new beginning! I was encouraged by the community's support. I was mindful of the implications of being in that position. The success I experienced was an "AHA" moment. I did not doubt that my appointment as Villa Principal encouraged other Filipino teachers to aspire to be instructional leaders and school administrators. That was my hope and goal. I was honored to be a role model and to be at the decision-making table. Community-based organizations began to invite me as a resource person. I enthusiastically supported tutoring centers where students could review for college entrance exams and have a place to get help with homework and counseling.

I was more than honored to share my success. Success included giving hope to the Filipino community. If failure is a life-changing deal, so is success. It was important to me to view success without the ego. Ego is harmful and a distraction. Furthermore, ego can be a cause of derailment. A reflective person has much to gain by having patience, persistence, and flexibility, the ingredients of success. They are also the essential assets for acquiring emotional intelligence. The best success comes from reflections, reconsideration, editing, and acceptance of suggestions that are different from our own. Success is a journey. It is not the victory that pleases us but the struggle that was behind the victory; the journey that we took to get there. The most significant successes have been preceded by the biggest failures. The journey to success is never over unless you stop looking forward. The only thing stopping us from going ahead is the fear of failing. Failure is inevitable in life, and it is up to us to overcome these challenges and use them to our advantage. What I have gone through in my life only strengthened my resolve in dealing with the many uncertainties of life. As Winston Churchill said, "Success is not final, failure is not fatal: it is the courage to continue that counts." The world does not stop revolving, so we must not stop evolving. Our Creator gave us the brains and the intelligence to use our human capacity to make good. It would be a huge mistake if we did not take advantage of using our God-given gifts for the good of others. If we do, we will be forever blessed.

A few years later after my appointment as Villa Principal, I was promoted to be Principal of Silver Creek High School in the same school district. The district superintendent called me at midnight and expected an answer immediately. The first thing that came to my mind was my beloved mom's words, "leave footprints." Without hesitation, I accepted the promotion. I considered this to be a chance for me to learn and grow. So, I welcomed the challenge. It would also be great for the Filipino community. I knew of the many responsibilities and challenges that came with the position, the hard work and the long hours, and the many hats I would be wearing. The Filipino community was very proud. I was a success in their eyes. I was proud to be the only Filipina high school principal in Northern California. To the Filipino community, this was quite an achievement. Unbeknownst to me, other members of the community, including the Filipino community, were already planning the next move on my behalf. I can describe my tenure as principal in this way: "It was the best of times, it was the worst of times," from the book, "*A Tale of Two Cities*" by Charles Dickens. It was the hardest, most physically mentally demanding, intellectually challenging but best job in the world!

A Chair at The Decision-Making Table

Being a high school principal gave me the opportunity to be at the decision-making table. Finally, my voice mattered. The principal is the CEO of a school. We hire and fire personnel when necessary. The position itself is a very high profile. Principals work collaboratively with the city and other elected officials, serve as a resource person for different agencies, and participate in many events with the community. We are sought out as a resource by politicians. We become politicians ourselves as we are the face of the school community. We are public figures visible to the community. It is not strange that principals consider themselves successful, for the pathway to get there require a great deal of patience, perseverance and, at times, sacrifice. We are survivors. Survival is built into our DNA. It is part of the very fabric that makes us into who we are. As human beings, we were not just made to survive. We were made to thrive. And thrive we do. We get out of our comfort zone and make our voices heard.

What Retirement?

After almost four decades in education, I decided to retire. No more twenty-four hours, seven days a week work schedule. But this was not to be. When you have built a reputation and your community knows who you are and respects you, you are always sought after. The job offers came left and right. I accepted a part-time job as an adjunct professor at San Jose State University and the National Hispanic University, supervising and mentoring graduate students working on their California teaching credentials. Later, I accepted the position of Professional Leadership Coach, also known as Professional Expert by the Santa Clara County Office of Education coaching newly promoted principals and school administrators. I expanded my influence to the greater community. After my retirement was made public, I was recruited to run for the Board of Trustees in the Berryessa Union School District where I reside. Running for public office was never in my best-laid plans. This was something totally new. People were eager for me to run and ready to support me. The spirit was willing, but the flesh was not. Being very much a private person, the new endeavor was too public for my taste. The whole idea did not appeal to me.

Venturing to the Political Scene

As an elected official, I would have a guaranteed seat at an even bigger table. It was this desire to have a voice and leave a lasting footprint that finally motivated me to run for public office, as a board of trustees of the Berryessa Union School District in San Jose, CA. I was the first Filipina to be elected and the only woman on the board of five people making critical decisions regarding the education of children in our local community. The road to a successful election is never smooth. There are many ups and downs to overcome, and hurdles got higher and higher and more challenging to face. The alternative of giving up was not acceptable to me. Footprints can leave an imprint and empower the next generation of leaders. Sidebar 1 highlights my leadership impact as footprints that I am proud to leave behind.

I am My Mother's Legacy

As Leymah Roberta Gbowee of Liberia said as she accepted the Nobel Peace Prize, "you can never leave footprints that last—if you are always walking on tiptoes." Inspiring words to live by. Empowered women never walk on tiptoes. They have their feet firmly planted on the ground. Leaving footprints that last is our legacy for the next generation of women leaders, especially Filipina women leaders. "If at first you don't succeed," my mother said to me, "try and try again until you do. But one thing you should never do in life is give up." A difficult lesson to learn, but it was the advice I followed throughout my life and career as an educator and elected official. At age ten in America, attending school was a huge challenge. Frightened and ashamed that my English was not perfect, I remembered standing next to my chair as punishment, towering over my classmates, forbidden to sit down until I pronounced "Connecticut" correctly. Once I finally did, I saw eyes glaring at me like owls in the night. A little girl trembling but not defeated. The only brown child in the class. No one to run to for comfort at school. Comfort was my mom, at home. "This is just a temporary setback," she would say. "Failure is not a bad word. You can turn this into something positive someday." The nuns taught me courage and resilience. But it was my mom who taught me that when I am down, it was up to me to get back up. She taught me confidence. There were many times I felt like the smallest player on a huge stage and could not wait to get off stage. But I had confidence that the steps I take and the footprints I leave behind will have a permanent impression on those I hope to inspire and empower. I am my mother's legacy. Building a legacy is not just constructing a beginning and an end; it is a process, a lifetime journey. Our lives deserve to be remembered. It is our footprints that will decide how we are to be remembered. Our voice is power. We must never accept silence, for silence means acceptance. In the words of Dr. Martin Luther King, Jr., "Our lives begin to end the day we become silent about things that matter." There is great need to be cognizant of the world around us.

The United Nations has created seventeen Sustainable Goals to make our world a better place. We cannot turn a blind eye to these goals. We can all do something to make a difference. Begin in your own community. Educate students well. Train and mentor. Elect public officials who are sincere and dedicated to the preservation of our planet. Be ready to give support. Help those who are in need both in our own community and the world. Use your voice to make an impact. Discover the potential that lies within you. Leave footprints so others can follow. Get involved in the election process and run for public office. The enjoyment of life has a little fear in it. Leaping into it requires courage. Everything we do in life is a leap of faith. So, run Filipina run! A seat at the" bigger table" awaits you. Your footprints will be remembered forever by those whose lives you have touched.

❋

"I would like to thank our district personnel, teachers and staff for their dedication to our number one client, our STUDENTS!"

SIDEBAR 1: MY LEADERSHIP IMPACT

I am a member of the Governing Board of Trustees of the Berryessa Union School District in San Jose, California. All Governing Board of Trustees are elected by the voters every four years. I am the first Filipina elected to the Board and the only female of a five-member team. The most important responsibility of being a trustee of a school district is to be a leader and champion for public education. Four decades in public education as a teacher, a high school principal, an adjunct professor, and a professional coach for the Santa Clara County's newly promoted school administrators have prepared me for this very critical decision-making body. I have great pride in what the team and district have accomplished together.

YEAREND ACCOMPLISHMENTS

My tenure as President and Member of the Governing Board of Trustees have been built on trust and respect. Accomplishments this year to name a few:

- Selected a new superintendent (female)
- Developed and adopted policies, curriculum, and approved the budget
- Oversaw facilities issues
- Successful Implementation of the Bond ($77 Million) passed overwhelmingly by the voters to improve school facilities (completion 2019)
- Adopted collective bargaining agreements (two-year term) a rarity these days
- Continued strong Professional Development to implement newly adopted curriculum
- Approved and implement Dual Immersion Program (K-1st grade) Mandarin and Spanish
- Approved more intervention opportunities for struggling students
- Continued strong Professional Development for all teachers and staff

OUR COMMITMENT

This past year, the Suspension Indicators for our students of almost 8,000 were in the Medium category. The district declined in this category by 1% overall. The following subgroups declined in the suspension category: English Learner, Asian, Filipino. The following declined significantly: Socio-economically Disadvantaged, Students with Disabilities, African American, Hispanic, White, and Pacific Islander. On the English Language Arts (SBAC) test, all students scored HIGH (16.2 points above Level 3). More work needs to be done with the Socio-Economically Disadvantaged students. They did not reach Level 3 but did increase by 3.3 points. English Learners increased significantly (by 32.6 points). On the Math test, all students scored HIGH (9.5 points above Level 3. Subgroups increased their score this year: ELL, Socio-Economically Disadvantaged, Special Education, Asian and Filipino. The African American subgroup and English Learners increased their scores significantly.

As Governing Board of Trustees, we are committed to a vision of high expectations for student achievement and are accountability driven. We share strong beliefs and values about students' ability to learn and of the system and its ability to teach all children at high levels. To continue supporting student success, the district (with Board approval) added critical personnel to support student's academic, social and emotional well-being: social workers, counselors, psychologists, speech therapists, teacher assistants, translators, more hours for nurses, office assistants, custodial staff, ground monitors, etc. all to assist teachers, keep students safe and help them succeed.

WILMA 'AMY' EISMA

SBMA ADMINISTRATOR AND CEO, PHILIPPINES

GLOBAL FWN100™ 2017

Moving Beyond Power and Position

My journey to leadership and service began in 1993, when in an act of youthful daring, I decided to walk up to Dick Gordon, then chairman of the Subic Bay Metropolitan Authority (SBMA), to join his corps of volunteers for the conversion of the former US Naval Base into the first free port of the Philippines.

The SBMA had been newly created then for the daunting task of maintaining the eight-million dollars' worth of infrastructure turned over by the Americans, replacing the 40,000 jobs lost upon the closure of the said base, and transforming the area into a commercial, tourism, and investment hub.

But the most pressing challenge of the time was to rebuild the area from the devastation of the second largest volcanic eruption of the 20th century, the 1991 catastrophe of Mt. Pinatubo that wrought havoc in Subic and the rest of Central Luzon, damaging crops, infrastructure, and personal property, totaling at least 10.1 billion pesos, plus an additional 1.9 billion pesos in 1992 due to post-eruption ash falls and *lahar* flows.

Being idealistic, I rose to the challenge of helping my neighborhood community. To my delight, the boss, as we called Gordon, not only accepted me in his staff but even let me into his inner circle. That inner circle made me cocky! Arrogant!

As a 22-year old fresh Ateneo Law School graduate from Olongapo City, I never had imagined working side by side with the SBMA founding chairman, riding helicopters, negotiating contracts with the World Bank, and joining trade and business missions all over the world. I was on top of my game, or so I thought. "Aim high," he exhorted us all. And so we young ones did.

Then came the biggest blow to my tender and impressionable ego; I flunked the bar exam.

That definitely blindsided and brought me back to the ground with a thud. It jolted me back to terra firma after flying ever so high that I lost sight of the ground. But determined to pick up the pieces of my shattered ego, I salvaged what I could from that most trying time of my young adult life.

Yet it was then that I realized my first real life lessons: the lesson to move on and fight back when life knocks you down, the lesson not to dwell on temporary failure but to stand up and move on, the lesson that your time to fly on your own would come, and finally, the lesson that I should never ever allow myself to be cocky again.

Moving Beyond Failure

And so I moved on and worked harder. I learned to walk the talk, as Gordon did. I focused on rising on my own merit and capability and stayed as close to the ground as possible. Awakened by a new sense of maturity and humility that could only come from hard lessons learned, I weaned my ego from vainglory. Painfully I realized that to be smug was to make myself a hostage to the ego.

In hindsight, that was also my very first lesson in leadership, and that is, those who have the most power should be the most humble.

Yes, humility strips a leader of the trappings of power and privilege. It frees her from that constricting sense of entitlement and allows her to share her authentic self with others. It shows her strength, not her weakness as a leader. But most of all, it inspires rather than discourages those around her.

After my stint as a volunteer and lawyer for the SBMA, I moved to the private sector and for 15 or so years, soaked up international corporate business practices, won awards and accolades, honed my leadership skills, and learned every lesson in the corporate environment.

These lessons served me in good stead through the years, lessons like responsible stewardship as a leader and inclusive growth for all stakeholders. In organizing a number of farmers' cooperatives, I came to know the wisdom in the Chinese proverb, "Give a man a fish and you feed him for a day; teach a man to fish and you feed him for a lifetime." In striving to bring the best of myself to the task at hand, I brought out the best in others. And in bringing out the best in others, I inspired them to become even better.

Then came another jolting experience. Philippine President Duterte appointed me as SBMA administrator and chief executive officer in December 2016, and eventually as its chairman and administrator some nine months later. It was a job I never asked for, lobbied for, or applied for because I was happy where I was. In fact, a couple of months earlier, the Business Civic Leadership Center of the US Chamber of Commerce based in Washington, DC had chosen my company's CSR programs, which I had developed, as one of its top five honorees in the Best International Community Service category, besting 7,000 other US companies worldwide.

And so I made a pilgrimage to the Shrine of Our Lady of Manaoag in Pangasinan so I would not get appointed. But when I got the fatal call one morning, that pit in my stomach told me that it was destiny, that the Universe must be telling me something. Being born, bred, and raised in Olongapo City, I thought the message was: it was time to come home.

And so I did.

Taking a New Road

Unheard of in any change of administration in Philippine government, I did not bring my own retinue of secretaries, executive assistants, or staff to my new office. I did not want to judge the people of SBMA without their having proven their worth. Doing so would demoralize the ranks and send the wrong signal that I did not trust any of them or that none of them was good enough for me.

Instead, I only brought me and myself alone because to me, my job from the very start was clear: to provide leadership and vision, moral compass and heart.

I also brought with me homegrown values of hard work, discipline, integrity, and passion, as well as the leadership lessons I learned during my volunteer days; work ethic and values that had served me well in the corporate world and which I knew would serve me even better in the public sector, values that defined my authentic self and molded my heart and my character.

I had no other goal but to make my father proud by making a difference in the lives of others. It was he after all who had wanted me to become a lawyer, ignoring my incessant pleas to come home to Olongapo when things got tough during my first year at law school.

In achieving that goal, I let integrity and transparency guide my way rather than any personal agenda because my only agenda then, as it is now, was to help my community, my home, and my people to have a better life. (See Table 1 that shows how impact indicators during my administration are trending upwards.)

Unfortunately, the road to leadership in government is not paved smoothly.

At the outset, I found myself in conflict with those whose agenda was questionable. It was tough and disruptive, polarizing the Agency into factions. Such a workplace was simply not my cup of tea because all I had wanted was to do my job to the best of my ability and to do it honestly and thoroughly.

Things became so bad that I had wanted to take the easy way out and quit. However, the overwhelming love and support of my people, my board of directors, the local and national government leaders, and even strangers spelled the difference between quitting and fighting on.

And so, I stayed on.

It was then that I realized why there was so much jockeying going around for that position, why the wannabe and would-be crossed swords for it and why many would not hesitate to compromise themselves to get it. The answer was simple. There were great power and prestige in heading a government agency and holding sway over 67,452 hectares, which according to the Finance Magazine was Asia's "Fastest Growing Trade Zone in 2017."

Why, it would almost seem like playing God over the fate of a prestigious government agency with some 2,600 government employees and a free trade zone with 10,000 residents, over 1,700 local and foreign investors with US$9.1 billion worth of investments, more than 128,000 workers, and which contributed some 19 billion pesos to the national economy.

But unbeknownst to many, this very same position is not all fame and glory. It also brings with it a most grueling test of character and leadership that the untrue and false-hearted would easily succumb to. Indeed, power is overwhelming and intoxicating and has its own pitfalls. As an acid test of character and leadership, it can bring out the best or the worst in people.

Becoming a Man for Others

Yet leadership in government is not about power but service, service that goes beyond the boundaries of age, creed, politics, geography, gender, and social class; service that embraces the common good rather than any personal agenda or interest; service that is ever-ready to be given with nary a thought to one's convenience, comfort, or need.

In treading the path of service in government, I now find myself wielding power and position yet ironically moving beyond them because public service to me is all about becoming "a man for others." In the course of my daily routine, I have become acutely aware that the true meaning of leadership is dutiful stewardship over people, resources, skills, systems, communities, and environments. I have also learned that beyond power and position is a rich and meaningful life of service where fulfillment comes from the largely inner satisfaction of knowing that you serve honestly and thoroughly.

In this job, I take to heart the words of American politician Margaret Chase Smith (Statement, 11 November 1953; also in Declaration of Conscience, 1 June 1950, p. xi):

> My creed is that public service must be more than doing a job efficiently and honestly. It must be a complete dedication to the people, and to the nation with full recognition that every human being is entitled to courtesy and consideration, that constructive criticism is not only to be expected but sought, that smears are not only to be expected but fought, that honor is to be earned, not bought.

This is what drives me today, as I strive to leave a legacy most worthy of my father's name, a legacy that I hope would make him beam with pride, as he used to do at my every achievement, a legacy that no other but only I, his favorite whom he had egged to become a lawyer, could present to him.

And so I strive to build a future that my nephews and younger generations deserve. I continue to dream of building physical infrastructure like new roads, bridges, and communities to serve people and move resources. At the same time, I continue to endeavor to build soft infrastructures like jobs, skills, work values and ethics, reliable services, good governance, and a quality of life that everyone deserves.

Driven by Malasakit

Today I demand from my team the kind of service that is driven by *malasakit*, which inspires them to take up the plight of others as their very own, to expand their concern and responsibility beyond their own backyard to include the rest of the community and environment; service to stakeholders that begins and ends with integrity and character and above all, with the Filipino value of *malasakit*.

Consequently, I have adopted *malasakit* as the core principle and anchor of all my strategic initiatives and objectives, and integrity and character as the moral compass to guide my Agency and people. I am convinced that there is no other way to fulfill my mandate without these principles as our core values because with integrity and character as our compass, we shall never lose our mooring but instead anchor all our efforts on what is fair, honest, and just. With *malasakit* at the top of our minds and deep in our hearts, we shall be driven to achieve productivity and teamwork, and serve others with passion and love.

Malasakit was what made Subic rise in 1992 when some 8,000 individuals responded to the clarion call for volunteers after the Subic Naval Base, which was America's largest overseas military installation outside its mainland, was turned over to the Philippines government. From near and far, and from all walks of life, these volunteers came. Together they marched through empty streets to protect offices and housing units from looting. Together they shoveled ash fall from rooftops, highways, and ports, helping to remove remnants of Subic's past as a military base that was devastated by Mt. Pinatubo and to make way for Subic's new beginning as the country's first free port.

I know all this because I was among those 8,000 volunteers who heeded the call of the hour at a time when thousands of Filipino base workers had just lost their jobs, and we all had nothing, literally nothing not even a roof over our heads.

Still, we found something within us to give so that we could rise again. And that something was *malasakit*.

But what is *malasakit*? To this very day, no English translation for *malasakit* that totally captures its meaning comes to mind. The closest English word I can think of is empathy, but *malasakit* means more than merely feeling what others feel, which is how empathy is defined in dictionaries. It is also more than just a strong sense of civic duty because *malasakit* is a sense of oneness with whoever is in need without being asked or required. It is given voluntarily and it springs naturally and spontaneously whenever the occasion arises.

Today *malasakit* is Subic's message to the Filipino nation and people. It is our message to the world. Which is why I never tire of calling for *malasakit*. With great conviction, I bring the same message of *malasakit* wherever I go regardless of time or occasion and across audiences, ranging from public and private leaders and employees to teachers, students, and parents and to my fellow Filipinos here and abroad.

I echo the same message even during trade and business missions and investment roadshows abroad for how else can I tell the story of Subic without recounting the story of our volunteers and their *malasakit*? How can I succeed in attracting investors to our free port without letting them know that *malasakit* drives us to care for their businesses and industries as our own and as American businessman Henry J. Heinz once said, "To do a common thing uncommonly well..."

And so I will continue to call for *malasakit* until I am old and gray because I have seen how it can protect our coasts and rivers and the rest of our precious environment. I have witnessed how it can galvanize a community into action and acts of untold bravery and heroism. I have known the transformative power of *malasakit* that can turn apathy into empathy, disunity into harmony, growth and development from devastation, and desperation into fulfilled hopes and visions.

Today *malasakit* remains as Subic's rallying point and inspiration. Based on *malasakit*, we clean our own surroundings, streets, rivers, and coasts. We pick up pieces of trash we see along the way. We plant our own trees, take care of our mangroves, and even keep track of our bat population. We follow traffic rules even in the absence of any law enforcer. We preserve the cultural heritage of our indigenous community even as we send them to skills development programs to widen their livelihood and job prospects. We observe road courtesy, put out fires, and rescue those in distress beyond our community because we care for one another and because *malasakit* is our lifeblood.

And we do all these without asking for anything in return; save perhaps that others would also have the same *malasakit* for our community, our home, and our people; and that they, too, would discover the greatness that awaits them because of *masalakit*.

Moving Onto the Future

Today I carefully listen to the stirrings of not only my mind but mostly my heart where my life purpose resides, and that is, to spread the message of *malasakit*. I clearly see a vision of what I want to be and what I want to do; not for myself but for the future generation. I welcome the unfolding of each day as another opportunity to further my goals and dreams for the people I intensely care for and for a community I will always call home and where I will spend the rest of my life.

And as I continue moving beyond power and position, I find myself wanting less for myself but more for others, focusing on the moment but working passionately toward the future.

That future is where I know that my big audacious dreams can and will come true but only if I plant today the seed that would one day make them a reality; only if I succeed in inspiring others to reach higher than what they see today and to bear the torch that would light our shared path to that future, a future that may seem intangible at the moment but serves as the basis of our Agency's strategic initiatives and objectives, a future that will define our direction for the long term but will shape our day-to-day strivings.

Charting that future is undoubtedly a challenge, a challenge that has to be taken up with dedication and determination, a challenge that has to be tackled one day at a time until that future becomes today, a challenge that we can only overcome with *malasakit*.

And so I go back to how Subic has risen from the ashes of Mt. Pinatubo because of volunteerism and *malasakit*. I go back to my message of *malasakit* because this is what will empower a people to hold on together in the face of any obstacle to the future. This is what will subsume the self for the higher good. This is what will transform the strength of one into the strength of all.

At the end of the day, knowing that my call for *malasakit* has made the future better and brighter for my people and my community and that I have done well by my father's name is what matters most to me.

❋

Table 1: Subic Bay Metropolitan Authority (SBMA) Impact Indicators

IMPACT INDICATORS	BASELINE (As of Q1 2017)	LATEST INDICATORS (As of Q1 2018)	VARIANCE
Financial			
Revenue	727,676,474.73	777,475,069.35	7%
Operating Income (EBITDA)	431,522,540.34	349,935,256.37	-20%
Net Income*	46,768,716.47	-49,183,376.26	-205%[1]
Business & Investment			
No. of Existing Locators	1,355	1,586	17%
Committed Investment for the Quarter	PHP480,346,576	PHP866,282,960	80%
Total Cumulative Committed Investment	PHP496 B	PHP497 B	0.38%
Import & Export (in US$)			
Import Value	384,449,721	490,346,528	28%
Export Value	536,363,345	590,366,601	10%
Job Generation			
Total Freeport Workers	115,272	134,104	16%
Contribution to the National Economy			
LGUs' 2% Share of 5% of GIE*	150,467,202.96	147,224,078.18	-0.20%
Government's 3% Share of 5% of GIE	225,700,804.44	220,836,072.27	-0.20%

[1] Causing the decrease in Net Income was the higher US$ & JP¥ FOREX rates for the quarter under review. Were it not for the losses in revaluation, as driven by currency prices, the Agency's Net Income would have grown by 35 percent, instead of registering a decrease of 205 percent.

BIR Collection	326,802,891.45	197,383,282.94	-40%
BOC Cash Collection	4,219,944,955.98	4,821,041,338.89	14%
Dividends to the Nat'l Government**	0	0	

* Gross Income Earned
** Actual payments made to the Bureau of Treasury / Payment schedule, as set by the Department of Finance, is at the end of Q3 2018

Port of Subic

Port Revenue	PHP 285,933,129	PHP 285,437,603	-0.20%
Containerized Cargo Volume	33,012 TEUs*	41,328 TEUs*	25%
Non-containerized Cargo Volume	1,826,519 MTs**	1,515,421 MTs**	-17%
Gross Registered Tonnage	6,866,378 GRT***	7,390,281 GRT***	8%

* Twenty Equivalent Units
** Metric Tons
*** Gross Registered Tonnage

Tourism

Same-day Visitors*	1,958,344	2,306,495	18%
Tourist Arrivals**	409,377	427,869	5%
Hotel Occupancy	66.67%	69%	2.33%
MICE Events	59	80	36%
MICE Participants	18,755	80,808	331%
Sports Events	15	23	53%
Sports Participants	13,350	13,750	3%
No. of Cruise Ship Arrivals	0	6	
No. of Cruise Ship Passengers & Crew	0	15,100	

* Those who arrive & leave on the same day
** Those who stay for one or more nights

ANNABELLE MISA HEFTI

Psychologist
GLOBAL FWN100™ 2015 & 2016

Stepping over *Stolpersteine*

The setting was an elementary school ground in Cebu. The children were playing various games. A group of girls stood around playing *Piko*, a game where one person jumps with one foot to push a stone to the next square while avoiding the other stones. It was a game of skill. I liked playing Piko as a child. I was also good at it. I was known for kicking my stone above the opponent's stone wherever I wanted it. I would play *Piko* through the lunch breaks at school. I simply loved it. I was the "champion," and I had to live up to expectation. I knew why I was hooked. I liked winning. It felt good. I did not win all the time, definitely not, but I tried again, maybe not harder but I never gave up. In games, I consider myself as a gracious loser. I was in it for the fun but not necessarily to win. This is where failure eludes me. I refuse to be bitter if things do not turn my way. I just move on.

Moving on is a choice I have made. We can choose to be miserable and wallow in self-pity for failing to win or we can learn from the situation and indulge in self-encouragement. I consider losing in *Piko* a temporary setback. Setbacks come in many forms, such as hurting comments, a missed train, and incidents that cause emotional and physical pain. Setbacks are by definition temporary. The determining factor is not what happened but how you choose to respond.

Attitudes are Shaped at Home

Unlike many Filipino families, my father, Papa Maying, held the family's purse strings. He did the budgeting and planning. My father started to manage his life when he was only 12 years old. He left his hometown to study in the city. He worked his way through high school and college. Despite the rigors of study and work, he still was involved with school politics. He became the first president of the student council at his university. To make an impression, he delivered his acceptance speech in Spanish. These were during the years of American occupation. Taking the initiative and leading were easy for him. I absorbed his self-confidence and self-assurance by being around him. These are traits that have nourished my self-worth from my early childhood. I learned much just by growing up under my father's wings.

Get an Education

Papa Maying knew what he wanted and he wanted an education. He grew up in a quiet town 100 km from a big city. He knew that if he stayed in this sultry seaside town, he would remain poorly educated with little opportunities. He left his hometown and ventured to reach the city on foot. The trip took one week. He related to us the trials and challenges he faced and how he stood up to these challenges to pursue his goals and ambitions. His attitude was that he could overcome any challenge.

Be Positive

My mother, Mama Conching always described her childhood as happy. She lived until she was 97. When people asked what her secret for longevity was, she said without pausing, being positive. Two words that gave her 97 years! My Mom did not know fear. She just went ahead with what was in front of her. She was 66 years old when she went to Switzerland for the first time and wanted to explore. My son was only six months old at that time, so I could not accompany her. She simply said, I will go alone. I bought her a two-week Eurail Pass and helped her map out her itinerary that included Italy and France. She managed on her own and returned beaming. She talked about the people she met and how kind people were. An Indian couple with a baby took her under their wings and she traveled with them from Paris to Lourdes to Rome. On one of our trips to France, I suggested she join me in drinking some red wine. By the way, soft drinks were more expensive than wine. She quickly agreed and then she slept for 10 hours that night. The next evening, she asked if she could have wine again.

Learn from a Painful Lesson

My two older brothers always played together. For them, three was a crowd, and I was brushed aside when I wanted to join them. They said, they were playing boy's games and I should go back to my dolls. I did go back to my dolls, but not for long. I remember this incident very well. I broke one of my smaller dolls and I went to my oldest brother Wins who was kind-hearted. I asked him to fix the doll. He said he would need some cloth that we did not have. I tore up a white pillowcase and gave it to him. He said it was wrong. With a little coaxing, he fixed the doll anyway. When my father arrived home, he asked about the torn pieces of cloth. Wins did all the talking and he got the beating. I felt bad. I look back to this incident as a reminder that manipulation at the expense of others is never acceptable.

Celebrate Being Smart

My father used to hold "spelling and arithmetic contests" with our cousins and us. This was during my elementary schools years. I usually won the spelling contests and some of the Arithmetic games. This may be how I earned the "bright one" reputation in the family. My cousins deferred to my opinions. My two older brothers accepted that my intellectual level, was above theirs. When I was in my third year in college, my cousins asked me to take the Career Eligibility Civil Service examination with them. I was supposed to pass them some answers. We all passed. I was glad for they depended on this eligibility for their future.

Model Healthy Attitudes

My parents were my role models for success. Failure was just a word but not a possibility for my parents. Their message was that there are stumbling blocks, *Stolpersteine*, along our paths, but these are temporary. Dad emphasized the need to have alternatives. When the first option did not work, it was time to move to the second option. They now call these as Plan A and Plan B. The idea was not to sulk and feel defeated. There are many ways to Rome; my Dad used to say. Mom graduated Magna cum Laude with a major in Math. She never wavered. She believed in herself. This was a healthy environment to grow up in.

My experiences has shown me that building leadership starts early. When significant people in the family treat a child with importance and respect, the child develops a positive image. This is key to self-confidence and self-esteem. These qualities are key to positive character development.

Resilience, another important leadership quality, also starts early. When a child possesses a healthy attitude about his/her ability to recover from adversity, this child will not whine or retreat, but will keep his/her head up and face the situation. The child might ask for reassurance that is it alright. The child does not see this as a failure, but simply something that did not work out. The child will forget about it and move. Resilience also means letting go. When a child does not harbor negative experiences, this child does not dwell on inner unrest but instead builds resilience, a quality much needed in adulthood.

Adjusting to Swiss Life

After my graduate studies in Counseling Psychology in California in 1976, I took a trip across the U.S. as the first leg of my trip back to the Philippines. I met Walter, a Swiss, during a Greyhound bus trip. Walter went to visit the Philippines. I was working then at the Guidance and Counseling Center at UP Diliman. After two years, we got married. We moved to Rüderswil in the Emmental Region, in Switzerland. German, French, Italian, and Romansh are the four official languages in this small country of 9,000,000 inhabitants. We live in the German-speaking part. I speak High German which I first learned at the Goethe Institute while the locals were conversing in Swiss German. When I first moved to the Emmental Region, I asked for a miracle so I could carry on a conversation in Swiss German with my dinner guests. I wrote about this wish for a gift of tongues in *Bending Without Breaking* (2017).

I live with my spouse Walter and our two sons in the Emmental, a farming region in Switzerland. The population of Rüderswil is 2500. The small village has one main street where the Town Hall, a Cheese Dairy, a Post Office, and a primary school are located. The houses are spread out in farmsteads. There is hardly anyone on the streets even in summer. Rüderswil, like other small towns in Europe seem to be perennially in "air raid" mode, empty and deserted.

I have always been a city person. Living in a *barrio* was something that even my family in the Philippines could not do. I reminded myself that this was my choice. There were many challenges: new language, being a stranger in a foreign place, career and job issues, new surroundings, and a new and diverse cultures. What I needed was to focus. Priority was learning the language, nurturing a family, and establishing my roots. This meant finding friends and making connections. Isolation is the last thing a migrant should endure. What I learned from my parents was to optimize. I was ready for the challenges. I focused my mind on the good things around. The rural surroundings with its rolling hills and vast greenery were a welcome change from my life in the cities. I conditioned and trained my mind to think and feel positive. This was the first and probably the most crucial step for my successful integration into my new home. There were no failures. I took a step forward before a setback was in view.

Leadership in Migrant Communities

Living in a foreign-language country is very challenging for any migrant. Not only are there multiple languages, as is the case in Switzerland, but also a variety of dialects. Even with my basic High German, it was intimidating not to understand what was being said around you day in and day out. Learning the language was a priority for cross-cultural integration. The need to learn the local version of German spoken in Switzerland, was identified by all of the respondents I interviewed in 2007 (See Hefti, 2007). Yet, insufficient attention to both language and culture continues in migrant training orientations and assistance programs.

In *Migrant Issues in Switzerland* (Hefti, 2007) I discussed the issues faced by Filipina migrants in Switzerland. I drew upon my work in a Counseling Center for Foreign Women and as a psychologist in a private office. The Filipinas interviewed had a positive attitude about their lives in Switzerland and understood the need to bridge cultural differences. (See Sidebar 1 for one of my cherished success stories story at my work at the Counseling Center for Foreign Women.)

In the section that follows, I will share my observations as a participant, founder, and leader concerning associational life in Switzerland. Over the years, I have seen associations come and go. In cases where I initiated the formation of a group, only to watch it falter, I sometimes blamed myself for the failure. I have come to realize that associations have complex life cycles and that they are organic. In the beginning there is excitement and energy and that later there can be a need to shut-down and move on when the short-term goals have been met.

Understanding Associations

Migrant communities all over the world are very diverse and bring their languages and cultural mindsets to their host countries. The Filipino migrant community is as intercultural as other communities. Filipinos come from many regions with their own languages and dialects. With these multi-linguistic backgrounds, come the similarities and differences in habits, norms, and practices. These cultural values become the thread that brought migrant communities together to form associations. However, differences in Philippine languages, professional interests, and political motivations tend to pull the Philippine groups apart resulting in numerous Overseas Filipino Associations (OFAs). In Switzerland, there were about 73 OFAs for an estimated population of only 14,647 in 2005 (Bagasao, 2007). OFAs include cultural groups, sports groups, professional associations, and hometown associations. There were associations of Bisdaks, Bibaks, individuals from Batangas, Ilocano groups, and Aguman Kapampangan. In other European countries, in the U.S., and in other countries with Filipinos, a similar pattern emerged. The results is a failure to work together for an ill-defined common good. Organizations go through several stages of development and this has implications for leadership (Simon, 2002). Simon identified the following stages: grassroots or invention stage; start-up or incubation stage; adolescent or growing stage; mature or sustainability stage; stagnation or renewal stage; and decline and shut-down stage. The organizational life cycle is not necessarily sequential but each stage of development requires leadership that is attuned to that particular organizational life cycle.

Being a Founder

Seven years after I arrived in Switzerland, along with two other Filipinas, I founded a women's group, the *Samahang Pilipina* [Pilipina Association]. It started as cooking and eating meet-ups. Soon other *Samahang Pilipinas* were formed in other cities. Loneliness and being alone had put us together. The original groups in Bern, Luzern, and Zürich have existed since 1985. In 2015, a few of the founders met to assess the success or failure of the group after 30 years.

Being a Horizontal Leader

I have always believed in horizontal leadership. I believe in equality. I may have been called the 'Chair' in an organization, but I liked consensual planning and execution. *Samahang Pilipina* Bern has had several presidents. I was more the person behind the scenes.

There were many *Stolpersteine* or stumbling blocks to running a hometown association. Community-based groups tend to be very personal. People join because they are seeking familiarity and they want to belong. Based on this expectation, the group structure tended to be loose and undefined. Many were named presidents of these groups. The bigger groups have elected board members. Community-based groups are non-profit organizations and board members work voluntarily. It takes dedication to provide much personal time to the association.

Expanding to Embrace the Broader Migrant Community

Organizing comes naturally to me. After I founded *Samahang Pilipina* in Bern and encouraged organizers in other cities to do the same, I felt the migrant community was broader and more multicultural than merely being a Filipina group. I initiated the Migrant's Women Forum in Bern. The membership was not big. In addition to Filipinas, several nationalities were represented including Brazilians, Thai, Japanese,

Malaysian, Turkish, Kurds, Vietnamese, Palestinian, Kenyan. The group functioned well for a while. We focused on addressing migrant issues and needs. We held workshops that dealt with our identity issues. Many herstories unfolded in these workshops. We joined rallies and other events relevant to migration. These were our efforts to make our group visible. However, within a four year period, many left the group. Only about six stayed, and we became a group of friends without a common goal or purpose as an association. I consider this a failure on my part. Looking back, it may be that I was not cognizant of the diverse needs of this group of strong women. A few of these women were refugees. Some were hardcore activists. Some like me lived a privileged life. Within this constellation, each of us had their own agenda and priorities were hard to define.

The dissolution of the Migrant's Women's Forum was a learning experience. I learned that I have to be conscious that I was leading more than a group, I was leading a gender-based group; a female group! Although there were lesbians in these groups, they were female in their emotions and attitudes. I had to reorient my approach to working with women's organizations. When I worked as Director of the *Zentrum* 5 Integration Center for Migrants in Bern, I managed the activities with assistance from the Turkish, African, and Spanish women. I learned to deal with the different women by adjusting to their specific national backgrounds. I discovered I could easily relate with the Latinas and laugh heartily with the Africans. However, I had to be patient with what I perceived as the stand-offish attitude of the eastern Europeans and the central Asians. I felt my leadership qualities were honed working with women representing diverse ethnicities, languages, and motivations.

Expanding to Network Filipino Associations Across Europe

The issue of "Fortress Europe" was already evident in the early 1990's. Migrant groups learned to work to address their concerns. The first Europe-wide conference was held in Kerkrade, the Netherlands in 1991. The theme was "Facing the Challenges of Fortress Europe." This event was attended by Filipinos and Filipinas from about 10 European countries. One of the offshoots of this conference was the creation of a women's organization, called *Babaylan* Philippine Women's Network in Europe in Barcelona, Spain in 1992. The conference "Empowering Filipina Women in Europe" was attended by close to 100 Filipinas. It was truly empowering to be part of this milestone event. Many participants returned to their host countries and started Filipina women's associations. For the next two decades, Filipina leaders and country representatives had a biennial summit meetings in different European cities. At this point I would like to refer back to Simon's (2002) life cycles of non-profit organizations. *Babaylan* went through the first two stages, Invention and Start-up, quite fast since the formulation of goals for the network were quickly outlined. Plans for action were identified and enthusiasm was high. Within five years Filipina women's groups were active in many European cities. In the late 1990's *Babaylan*-Philippine Women's Network in Europe was visible. Filipinas were sitting on official committees and commissions representing the migrants. The group was growing, consistent with the fourth stage of organizational development. There was a sense of accomplishment. The fifth stage of sustainability became a challenge. After 10 years some country and local groups became complacent. Attendance at conferences declined. I became a passive member at this time. My work at the migrant center was quite demanding and I had to make priorities. I was still active with *Babaylan* Switzerland. I must mention that membership in European or global groups can be onerous. By the time one is engaged at the European level, one had been involved at the national and local level. At the local level, there is direct contact with the grassroots and the daily struggles are demanding. Many leaders remain at the local level for practical reasons of time and financial management. NGO leaders have to give their own time and expense to the organization. *Babaylan* Europe is now at the sixth stage of experiencing Stagnation. It needs to reorient its goals and develop updated strategies. It needs to involve newer, dynamic and maybe younger members. It needs to think and do things outside the box. This might call for new leadership to reclaim the passion and dream of a united European women's group.

One of the things that *Babaylan* Europe did well at the start was holding an intensive two-week Seminar on Gender Sensitivity in Rome and was attended by 25 country representatives from all over Europe. This was one of the most rewarding and learning seminars I attended. It was an excellent starting point for women working together as women. We became aware of the many women's issues, struggles, and hopes. We had an understanding of what we were talking about. We did not disagree on these issues. Anyone who has attended an intensive gender sensitivity workshop will never support any event that displays women as objects, be it a fashion show, or posing in front of cars at an Auto Saloon, or worst of all a beauty pageant. We understood the conditioning of becoming a "Maria Clara" in the Filipina personality. For me, a deep understanding of patriarchy helped me make sense of women's docility. *Babaylan* Europe started good and functioned well. In the 1990's *Babaylan* predicted the migration crises that the world is facing today.

At this point I think *Babaylan* Europe did grow but it did not develop the maturity necessary to sustain its members' interest and commitment. Their was lack of creativity in adjusting the goals to changing needs of migrants in Europe. In every organization, personalities always play important roles. This is especially true in women's groups. Women tend to take issues personally and do not forget negative experiences. Sometimes the damage from negative perceptions is irreparable. Issues should be opened up for discussion, as early as possible. This was difficult to pursue at the European level. Distances were a problem. Maybe today's modern technology can make communication more efficient.

Many migrant groups have folded having reached the fifth stage and are in Decline and Shutdown. When personalities clash, group rapport is missing, communication breaks down, and gossip mostly about untruths prevail, the opposing party forms another group. The dispute continues. Conflicts in planned activities trigger bitter relations. Community relationships are impaired and mistrust pervades the air.

Across the globe, Philippine migrant organizations are struggling for sustained existence and are dealing with low membership and identity problems. A few low-key and less visible organizations seem to be surviving better.

Leaders of Philippine community organization need to be prepared to face many issues. The organizational structure is usually informal and goals are not wholly defined. These conditions call for an emotionally resilient leader. Resilience might be the key to successfully leading such a group. Filipinos possess a collective self-esteem and this means that looking good as a group is vital to their cooperation. The leader has to be a role model for positive personal and social values. Despite setbacks at the organizational level, success stories by individuals who have joined these organizations are not uncommon (see Sidebars 2 and 3).

Success is an Attitude

Success has different meanings for different people. It depends on one's goals. When I moved to Rüderswil, my personal goal was nurturing my family, establishing roots, and learning the language. I also had a goal of being active in my profession. I wanted to advocate for women's rights and migrant's rights. I had goals of developing migrant associations. I have succeeded in meeting most of these goals. When I faced challenges and results that did not turn the way I expected, my reactions were varied. Sometimes, I felt devastated. Sometimes, I blamed myself for failing to make the right decisions. I felt crippled. If you have felt the same way, let us be reminded that the challenges should not overwhelm us; instead, we should turn them into opportunities. Failure is just a word.

We can always start over again. This is the stand of a confident person. This attitude is what we need more of. I leave you with the words of Nelson Mandela: "Do not judge me by my successes. Judge me by how many times I fell down and got back up again."

Samahang Pilipina Bern was founded in 1985. The purely Pilipina organization was sustained for 30 years. The founders met for one weekend in 2015 to reflect and assess the years past. The first part of the workshop was to share each other's migrant stories. Tales of struggles, happiness, and resilience poured out. The outcome of this workshop is a book entitled Bending without Breaking: Thirteen Women's Stories of Migration and Resilience.

SIDEBAR 1: A SUCCESS STORY OF AN INDIVIDUAL

One of my cherished success stories at my work at the Counseling Center for Foreign Women in Bern, Switzerland was the eventual empowerment of a Filipina victim of domestic violence. Laura took four years to leave her abusive husband finally. She was out of breath the day she appeared with her two small daughters armed with only one bag. From the look on her face, I knew this was the final run. I accompanied Laura and her two small daughters to the women' shelter where they stayed for ten months. During this time, the Social Worker and I, worked on her self-worth and self-esteem. Laura first focused on learning German and later entered formal training to become a vocational nurse. The daughters did well in school and became professionals. Laura did not narrow her lived experiences to victimhood. She chose to rise to claim her dignity. Such success stories are not without support. She had our social service team to guide her to independence. We were individual leaders who made a difference in many of our client's lives.

SIDEBAR 2: SUCCESS STORY OF AN ORGANIZATION

"It was the saddest day of my life. A little boy, barely three and a half years old, and a little girl one year younger than him were clutching their milk bottles under their arms. The little boy asked me, "Where are you going mother? Can I come?" I did not manage to answer, I just turned my back and walked away slowly. I tried to hold back my tears and my emotions. I remember the mumbling and crying of my children, with my mother and the rest of the family comforting them."

That was 1981. "A Lady in the White Apron" is the chapter written by Alice Javier. Hers' is a success story. She worked as residence housekeeper in foreign embassies in Bern. She stayed longest in the residence of the Norwegian ambassadors. As a college graduate, she mastered her craft easily. Alice has earned the reputation of a good cook. In 2013, Alice was awarded The King's Commemorative Medal. It is a medal granted to persons who served at Norwegian Foreign Service Missions and others in special service. This was in appreciation for Alice's 30 years of service.Alice has been active with Samahang Pilipina Bern for years. She is a present member of the board. *www.sapil-schweiz.ch*

SIDEBAR 3: SUCCESS STORY OF FORMING *BABAYLAN*-PHILIPPINE WOMEN'S NETWORK IN EUROPE

In Chur, a city nestled in the mountains of Graubunden, Adora Fisher founded the Balikatan group in 1993. *Balikatan* was a member of *Babaylan* Switzerland that brings the issues of Switzerland to *Babaylan* Europe. As with most groups, Balikatan started with fundraising events. They were able to form their own choir and dance troop. In time, Adora gained the attention of the local officials. *Balikatan* became an integration center for migrants. The services included German classes, a meeting point for women from different nationalities, children's programs and various workshops. Adora's basic goal was "to get migrant women out of their anonymity." She was awarded "*Dunnapreis*" or Woman of the Year 2006 in Chur. She said she is very proud of this citation as she is the first migrant to receive this recognition. *Balikatan* celebrated its 25th year Jubilee with pomp and pride. *www.balikatan.ch*

CATHY SALCEDA ILETO

Sr. Director for Corporate Marketing, at Sutherland
Vice Chair, Information Technology and Business Process Association
of the Philippines (IBPAP)
GLOBAL FWN100™ 2015

Filipina *Delikadesa* = Waves of Positive Change

Throughout my career, I have realized the distinctly Filipina quality of *delikadesa*, that involves creativity, agility, resilience, and resourcefulness, has helped me through the many challenges I encountered. *Delikadesa* is about orchestrating and gently, but persuasively, communicating an opinion. It is getting everyone together and giving them a new set of lenses to see things and say "can we do this together?" It is gentle but powerful, just as women leaders should be.

Whatever it is I embark on, I find this insatiable urge to create positive change by leveraging this Filipina quality with my expertise in marketing and communications. *Delikadesa* has given me the drive, ability, and courage to disrupt multiple industries.

As a builder, I was part of the original team that established the Information Technology and Business Process Association of the Philippines (IBPAP); the enabling association for the information technology and business process management (IT-BPM) industry in the Philippines. The IT-BPM industry has created 1.2 million jobs and an additional 3.68 million jobs outside the industry for the Philippines and generated approximately USD 23B in revenue for the country in 2016. IBPAP has been a catalyst for the industry's growth for the last decade. I currently serve the IBPAP board as its Vice Chairperson and head the industry's Technical Working Group on Country Competitiveness tasked with driving country and industry promotion.

As a leader, I head the Marketing, Communications and Public Relations functions for the Asia Pacific at Sutherland. Aside from being an integral member of the leadership team, I play a strategic role in ensuring the success of Sutherland's unique provincial model in the Philippines. (See Box 1 for more information about IT-BPM, IBPAP, and Sutherland.)

As a woman, I am passionate about advocating for women's empowerment. I believe we have the power to create lasting change and I find fulfillment in watching women grow and thrive in leadership positions through the programs I have championed, such as Sutherland's League of Extraordinary Women.

One lesson I want to pass on to the next generation of women in leadership is *delikadesa* which is a leadership quality I developed throughout my professional career from across multiple industries including media, telecom, pharmaceuticals, and IT-BPM. *Delikadesa* is an essential quality that remained constant amidst change and is critical to my being a woman leader.

Let me tell you first about the beginnings of my communications career. I had the opportunity to learn about the activities inside the newsroom and out in the field covering economic development. It was this *delikadesa* that helped me succeed in accomplishing the goals I set for myself.

Finding My Passion

At the age of 23, while engaging with business conglomerates and scions in the Philippines, I found a natural inclination and passion for corporate communications and social responsibility. I found joy in creating business features focused on the environment, education, and the economic impact of various industries. Later in my broadcast media career, I had the opportunity to become the executive producer of my news program on the country's largest cable news network.

At that time, it was more lucrative to have a job on the trading floor, but I chose to follow my passion for helping businesses and individuals communicate the work they do to create positive change. It was 1996 and what I told myself was this: "My passion is being able to communicate and influence." I wanted to try a career in media. I set my sights on this dream, which was to be a creative instrument in leveraging the power of media as an influencer to create positive change.

Having been assigned to cover the business sector and the economy at large, I sometimes found myself faced with situations that challenge my integrity: How do I report on stories truthfully? How do I keep my moral compass sound? These were internal conflicts I had to face in addition to simply meeting my deadlines. As a communications professional, it is ultimately *delikadesa* that helps one balance doing the right thing while ruffling the feathers of powerful stakeholders.

One day, while covering the telecom industry, that was considered a sunrise sector at that time, I met by happenstance the Corporate and Regulatory Affairs

Head of one of the leading telecom companies. I did not know, I was going to be offered a job by the same executive to help build their corporate communications capabilities. It was such a dynamic and exciting sector that I did not think twice about leaving the glamour of broadcast media. I told myself: "This is my opportunity to create sustainable communications programs that will impact communities and industries across the nation."

I realized then that my five-year experience with media could help me become effective in my new role as a corporate communications executive. I knew that this company had a well-oiled corporate communications organization within. They had a nationwide breadth and reach, and I felt that it would help me grow professionally as a communicator. I had an insatiable urge to be a full-fledged communications practitioner. I already had a solid foundation in media and working with this telco, would add public relations and corporate social responsibility to my core competencies. The career move helped me become well-rounded but also developed my agility, the ability to move with quick, easy grace.

Expanding My Expertise

After almost five years of building my corporate communications career with this telco company, I was offered a position with the world's leading pharmaceuticals company to serve as its Corporate Communications Head, in charge of both its internal communications, employee engagement, and external affairs. It was here that my expertise in communications expanded further into areas such as internal communications, crisis management, and public affairs. Since pharmaceuticals are a highly regulated industry, I found myself meeting Congressional policymakers whose decisions impact the business environment of the pharmaceuticals sector in the country. I also became the face of the company responding to media inquiries at the height of the discussions concerning the Cheap Medicines Bill. I was also responsible for creating a positive employee experience and engaging the local communities through medical missions and other similar projects. My programs earned accolades including the prestigious Gold Quill and Anvil Awards for the many communications campaigns I helped develop for the organization.

Some of the challenges I helped address were: "How am I going to defend our brand?", "How do we keep our brand relevant?", "How do I work with all these stakeholders and regulators?". While these proved to be the most challenging issues I faced during this time, these issues were also pivotal in my growth as a communications executive.

I have strengthened my understanding of the Filipina value of *delikadesa* as a result of overcoming these challenges. *Delikadesa* is about using creativity, agility, resilience, and resourcefulness to accomplish goals while keeping my moral compass sound. This *delikadesa* helped me move around, within and beyond my sphere of influence to create positive change.

Building on this, I found myself propelled into a leadership role in Information Technology and Business Process Management (IT BPM), a sunrise industry. At that time, I knew nothing about the outsourcing sector. I had covered bits and pieces of the Business Process Management industry during my career in media, but I had very little knowledge of the entire ecosystem.

The role offered to me was to create a 360-degree marketing communications campaign to position the Philippines as the preferred IT BPM investment destination in the world. This was a tall order for someone with little knowledge about the different facets of IT BPM.

I was told that my role was part of a blueprint, which was an industry roadmap that outlined priority actions that the industry association had to execute to fulfill the very lofty goal of one million jobs by the year 2010.

Expanding My Impact

The facet of the role that attracted me the most was the piece on country marketing that translated into a global opportunity for me; I could market the Philippines to the world. With this new opportunity, comes new learning as a leader. Aside from *delikadesa*, I learned the importance of having a desire for positive change, not just to a single company, but more importantly to a whole community, industry, and a country. The potential for people-level impact and national economic development were tremendous.

It is important for a leader to possess a limitless desire for new challenges. I find motivation in these kinds of opportunities that push me beyond my limits. For this job, I had a chance to pioneer industry-wide initiatives to promote the Philippine country brand; something I have never done in my past roles.

As the IBPAP Executive Director for External Affairs, I found a stronger purpose in my professional life and intensified my passion to uplift the Philippines IT-BPM brand globally and to help create millions of jobs for Filipinos without them having to leave their homeland and their families.

I feel that I have contributed immensely in growing this industry over the last decade.

Today, I am in my second term as a Board of Trustee at IBPAP where I provide much-needed oversight for country and industry marketing as well as government affairs. I currently serve the IBPAP Board as its Vice Chairperson, as well as the head of its Technical Working Group (TWG) on Country Competitiveness. I am tasked with providing oversight on key high impact programs that position the Philippines as the premiere IT-BPM investment destination in the world. With this leadership role that I currently have in the industry, I'm able to continue building a country marketing legacy in several ways. In 2017, the TWG on Country Competitiveness conducted a country and industry brand audit and a revamp of the Philippine IT-BPM brand value proposition, with the objective of being able to effectively market the Philippine IT-BPM industry to the world with a more relevant message. The new tagline "Philippines: Innovative Human + Tech" is about the Philippine brand of creative service that brings heart into the cold digital space, warmth in the distant voice, and humanity in technology. As the BPO industry moves forward toward the intersection of innovation and digital, the new country narrative was built on the premise that a career in IT BPM could be a dream for every Filipino, from the Metro to the countryside. The entire country moves from being just proficient in English to being well-versed in digital and innovation, and finally, where the country continues to connect people to improve business. It has been a joy working on the brand audit with the leaders of the industry and partners from the government. It was a learning experience for all of us who were involved in this initiative.

Looking back, I have indeed come full circle. The very first country and industry brand was my brainchild back in 2007 as the very first Executive Director for External Affairs at then BPAP. The previous country and industry storyline was "Experience Excellence. Experience the Philippines."

Fast forward to a decade later when I have been appointed by the Board of IBPAP to head the country brand refresh and audit which I had developed with key stakeholders in the industry and launched in 2017. I have also come full circle, in the sense that, I would be back in this industry association, not as a full-time Executive Director, but as a Board of Trustee providing oversight on country competitiveness. Country Marketing is something very close to my heart and is my way of giving back to an industry and a community that continues to be very good to me.

Building on Mentorships

It has been a remarkable journey for me. I have been blessed with mentors and executive sponsors who provided support and guidance as I matured within the industry. One of my role models is an influential woman figure within the IT-BPM Industry, fellow GLOBAL FWN100™ awardee (2014), Ms. Karen Batungbacal De Venecia, one of the founders of IBPAP and the very first Board of Trustee who provided oversight in the area of government affairs. She was my Trustee-in-Charge when I was an Executive Director for External Affairs at IBPAP. It was because of her guidance that I was able to accomplish life-changing initiatives for the industry. One of the efforts that both Karen and I collaborated on was the amendment of the women at work provision of the Labor Code. We were both very passionate in lifting the restrictions on women working at night, as well as ensuring women's safety and well-being in our industry.

After ten years, I am back at IBPAP and working again with Karen, this time as my fellow Board of Trustee at IBPAP. Karen continues to serve on the Board representing the Global In-House Centers.

It is important that we nurture our work and personal relationships with our role models. These healthy mentor-mentee relationships provide the motivation to overcome both personal and professional challenges. Since Karen's mentorship has been such a positive influence on my own personal and career life, I have asked myself how I could ensure that other women have access to mentors and executive sponsors. I also believe that women should support other women in more ways than one. It is very disheartening to see women who are very critical of their fellow women. I have encountered some women seeking advice and consolation about being tormented or bullied at work by fellow women in the company.

Empowering Women

In my own small way, I wanted to change this and create something that allows women to empower other women, especially in my workplace. I wanted to bring women together through a platform that will enable healthy conversations and that hopefully would lead to a more robust women community. A community that would nurture their careers and propel them forward. I wanted a program that would help women back up other women.

Resilience is developed when women are empowered to speak and when they have a women community and sisterhood to run to for support. I have been through so many challenges in my professional career, but because of my fellow women supporters I have become resilient and confident as a leader.

I launched a women's empowerment initiative at Sutherland called "The League of Extraordinary Women" inspired by a woman I admire, Sheryl Sandberg. She is an American technology executive, activist, and author of the book *Lean In*. She is the Chief Operating Officer of Facebook and founder of Leanin.org. She is an inspiration to me because she can balance the many facets of her life. One example that resonates with me is when she championed the proposal to change state law and allow women in the third trimester of pregnancy to park in accessible parking spaces.

No one, particularly men, thought about the need for this, but she did because she empathized with the problem. She was able to communicate why it was important and leveraged her leadership role to move the needle for the advocacy she believed in.

As I have indicated, the "League of Extraordinary Women" draw inspiration from women leaders who empower other women, such as Sheryl Sandberg. The program entails working closely with the site leadership and site councils of the Sutherland organization, as well as primary functional heads.

Establishing thought leadership programs and pushing for an advocacy, requires being true to your passion and utilizing creativity, agility, resilience, and resourcefulness, combined with *delikadesa*. It is the Filipino quality of finding something in nothing. In finding the gaps and seeing the opportunity in those situations. It is that unchartered territory where as a woman, you can act through it with *delikadesa* rather than facing it head-on with "fire, hell, and brimstone." *Delikadesa* is about orchestrating and gently, but persuasively, communicating an opinion. It is getting everyone together and giving them a new set of lenses to see things and say: "Can we do this together?" It is gentle, but powerful, just as women leaders should be.

SIDEBAR 1: MY LEADERSHIP IMPACT

My impact for the industry would be recommending and influencing policy changes to ensure a sound business environment. I am proud of the passage of the "women at night" provision of the Labor Code to ensure women's safety even when working at night. The code required BPO centers to have separate toilet and lavatories, dressing rooms, sleeping quarters, and a nursery for women.

I have contributed to the increased profile of the Philippines that resulted in winning two National Outsourcing Association Awards for the Best Outsourcing Destination in the World during my term at the IBPAP in 2007 and in 2008.

For Sutherland, it was my leadership and partnership with human resources (HR) that allowed us to win Employer of the Year at the influential ICT Awards in 2016 and the launch of the first woman initiative or community called the League of Extraordinary Women (LOEW).

TESTIMONIALS

"Cathy is successful leader because she has a clear purpose, a clear vision of where she wants to take her organization; and aligns this vision with the needs of the community and beyond that, the country."
- **Maria Cristina H. Concepcion**, President & CEO, Business Process Outsourcing International

"Cathy has been an instrumental figure in the development if the Philippine IT-BPM Sector. She has leveraged her expertise in marketing and branding to propel the IT-BPM Industry to where it is now."
- **Jonathan Defensor De Luzuriaga**, President, Philippine Software Industry Association

"Cathy is the epitome of a Modern Filipina Patriot… her tireless efforts to elevate the stature of the IT-BPM industry, her passionate pursuit to create a unique Philippine country brand, and her relentless desire to achieve inclusive growth in the countryside are but some of the highlights that come to mind when I look at the year just passed where I had the privilege of working with her directly. "
- **Rey Untal**, CEO and President of IBPAP

"The energy, talent and time Cathy devotes to country promotion and job creation has truly been unparalleled. Our country is really fortunate to benefit from Cathy's untiring efforts to create both a Philippine brand and more high value jobs in the countryside."
- **Benedict C. Hernandez**, Accenture

"Cathy is relentless when it comes to elevating the Philippine country brand as the premiere location for knowledge work. Our country and our industry owe a lot to this young, rising, beautiful, brainy, creative leader. We are very fortunate to have in our team."
- **Karen Batungbacal**, Senior Vice President, Optum Global Solutions

"An avid advocate for promoting women empowerment at work, Cathy is an energetic proponent for developing women in leadership roles through her League of Extraordinary Women initiative at Sutherland. These initiatives will go a long way in enhancing the society at large, BPO industry and strengthen the nation. "
- **Shridhar Aiyer**, Vice-President HR, Sutherland

"Cathy is extremely passionate about everything she does, especially promoting/developing provincial areas of the Philippines. She has a passion for change, while executing with a touch of class."
- **Jennifer Kavanagh**, Site Head for Sutherland Taguig.

"Cathy made it her personal mission to catapult the Philippines as a formidable player in the global IT-BPM industry. Armed with a lethal combination of unbridled passion, dedication, intelligence, and charisma, she built a career centered on social impact and love for the Country."
- **Charlene Chan**, formerly the Corporate HR Head of Sutherland, IBPAP Executive Director for Talent Development.

"One thing that sets Cathy apart—she is able to influence everyone in elevating the sense of urgency on all her initiatives. She always gets things done."

- **Beng Coronel**, Pointwest President, and President of the Healthcare Information Management Association of the Philippines (HIMAP)

"Up close, Cathy is an admirable leader in every way. A true patriot, beautiful inside and out Cathy is firm yet sensitive and compromising, and passionate yet open minded."

- **Miguel del Rosario**, Head of the Animation Council of the Philippines.

WAFA 'MARILYN' R. QASIMIEH, Ph.D.

Senior Executive Cultural Consultant,
Islamic Affairs and Charitable Activities Department (IACAD),
Mohd. Bin Rashid Center for Islamic Culture, Government of Dubai
GLOBAL FWN100™ 2014

Ambassador of Peace and Humanity

'In recognition of your excellent service to humanity in improving your surrounding communities through outstanding civic and charitable stewardship, you are hereby celebrated and honored with the highest distinction at the 2nd Annual SPMUDA Global Awards and World Water Day 2018.' 23 March 2018.

I was honored by the statement above from the Southern Philippines Muslim and Non-Muslim Unity and Development Association (SPMUDA). SPMUDA is a non-profit civil service organization that is affiliated with the United Nations Department of Economic and Social Affairs and that supports the United Nations sustainable development goals. SPMUDA's mission is to build a better world with universal peace and to deliver humanitarian assistance to the needy. SPMUDA identified volunteer Goodwill Ambassadors with responsibility for promoting understanding and friendship that promote the welfare and benefit of the poor and the needy. SPMUDA has branches in 197 countries. I serve as a goodwill ambassador for both the United Arab Emirates and the Philippines and as a board member and deputy minister for finance.

Not Born with A Silver Spoon

My success in life has not been achieved through good luck but through hard work and determination. Even at an early age, I had ambitions. I wanted to get out of poverty and I knew I would have to work hard to achieve my dream.

I was born in 1964 the fifth in a family of nine children in Lambunao, Iloilo. I am not ashamed to say that I was born poor. My past is a part of my present and will always be a part of me. I would not be where I am today if I had not gone through all the difficulties I have faced. My parents tried to make sure we had food, shelter, and clothing. My parents worked extremely hard to support and sustain the studies of their children. I did not feel any shame in helping my parents nor any shame in sharing the poverty of my parents. Their situation motivated me to push even harder, with the hope of pulling my entire family out of poverty.

Despite our poverty, I persevered and earned a college degree. In 1984, I graduated with a bachelor's degree in Science, major in Forestry, from the West Visayas State University. I worked as part-time cleaner in the library and was paid Pesos 1.50 per hour, or a total monthly pay of Pesos 53. It sounds like a pittance but it was extra money for basic necessities at home and school in the 1980's. It helped me buy what I may needed without asking my parents. I did everything in my capacity to earn what I could to augment the little money I had. I learned from a very early age that work is noble and essential for survival.

After graduation, I worked for several years with the Department of Environment and Natural Resources as a Forester in Roxas City. I had always wanted a better life not only for myself but also for my parents and my siblings. In 1986, at the age of 23 and full of youthful ambition, and ready to take on any challenge despite the fear of the unknown, I moved to Dubai and became an overseas Filipina worker (OFW).

From the Bottom Up

While in Dubai, I worked for several companies. I eventually joined the Islamic Information Centre as their librarian and lecturer. I found that empathizing with people who were searching for the truth came naturally to me. When my son Omar was eight months old, I accepted a position to work for the Government of Dubai's Department of Islamic Affairs, later renamed the Islamic Affairs and Charitable Activities Department (IACAD).

At IACAD, I rose through the ranks. I worked as an Administrative Assistant, a Senior Advisor, and an Executive Cultural Consultant. Three years ago, I was promoted to Senior Executive Cultural Consultant.

Finding Time for Higher Education

In 2001, I began to study Islamic Fundamental (Usool Al Deen) at the Preston University in Ajman, UAE Campus. Despite my very demanding schedule as a working mother, wife, and business person, I made time for my studies and attended school at night in order to realize my dream of completing higher studies in Islam.

In 2014, I obtained a PhD in Humanity. The studies required a working knowledge of English and Arabic.

Finding Joy in My Work

My job became my joy and pleasure, a chance to help better lives for others and most importantly, an offering to Allah God Almighty. At work, I always was enthusiastic and diligent. I showed initiative, faced my challenges, and worked harder every year. From day one, I vowed to respond to the call of duty with heart and compassion.

My position with the Government of Dubai and my ability to speak Arabic has enabled me to serve as a link between the Filipino community and the Arab world. Working in the Government for almost two decades has been a test of aligning my competencies with their requirements and qualifications. I have acted not only as an employee but also a friend.

As Senior Advisor in the Islamic Affairs and Charitable Activities Department of the Government of Dubai, I play a key role in formulating strategy and executing key educational and humanitarian initiatives. My career in this Department has been characterized with dignity and integrity.

In many ways, I am told by my colleagues that I epitomize "the spirit of advocacy: passionate but deliberate, visionary but realistic, committed but imbued with a sense of alertness and operational dexterity." When I was younger, I had no idea about what advocacy entails and how to get involved. As I grew older, I started to learn and my advocacy grew to involve causes for social welfare, humanitarian, leadership, and education. It is not easy, but because of the full support of my family and the Filipino community here in the Gulf region, I am able to face any challenge with a positive attitude.

I feel blessed that my formal job involves being an advocate for peace, education, and community service. I am inspired by the efforts of other leaders who have made great strides in promoting cultural diversity. Being exposed to different communities and different nationalities is the best training I received. I have met a variety of people and listened to their problems, celebrated their victories, and appreciated their achievements. Many of these people probably do not realize that they have helped me develop awareness on how to approach cultural differences.

SEEKING THE TRUTH

My most important personal transformation happened in 1989 when I converted to Islam and become a believer. My Arabic name *Wafa* means faithfulness or loyalty.

My acceptance of this *deen* [religion] opened new doors for me, not only for spiritual growth, but also for emotional, social, and even professional growth to me the most precious treasure that Allah granted me in Dubai. Soul-searching experiences helped me understand the needs of other people who are seeking the truth. I felt the need to give back to the community that I now consider myself a part of, and thus my drive to push harder in my effort to help more of my compatriots. My efforts have been recognized by my department and I am a five-time recipient of the Best Employee of the Year Award for the Edification Administration under IACAD.

I am grateful to Allah God Almighty for all the blessings He has bestowed upon me and for His help in granting me success in my endeavors. Indeed, I came to Dubai for a better life, and indeed Allah has blessed me with more than I even asked for. But of all the successes that I have attained, nothing can compare with the blessing that Allah God Almighty has given me when my parents and two of my brothers and one sister, together with their families have converted to Islam. Now, I feel that I have somehow given back to my parents a little of what they have given to me, and that I can still continue to give them rewards by all the prayers and good deeds that I intend to do until we finally meet again.

My Leadership Tips

In reflecting on the challenges that I have faced and the accomplishments I have achieved, I have come to believe that leadership is created by the ways we behave, react, and interact. Harmonious relationships are important to our leadership and are connected to our effectiveness. We are born with unique skills, talents, and wisdom that need to be nurtured and developed. We need to invest time, effort, and resources in our leadership development. Think process not position, because leadership is a process, not a tittle. It is about leading with others in ways that establish direction, create alignment, and build, build, build commitment.

Believe in Yourself

You need to believe in yourselves, believe in your abilities, and believe in your ideas, including new ideas. As for me, I always had faith in my capability to achieve things that I dreamt of and this faith gave me patience, determination, and the wisdom to know that whatever I dream, I can turn into reality, of course, with God's will. As life has gone on, problems have come my way. However, whatever happens I do not run away from the challenges, but instead, I face them headlong. My desire for success in each task is greater than the hurdles that have blocked my path. I focus on where I want to go and persist in working hard to reach each goal.

Work Towards Your Dreams

My success started with dreams followed by identifying goals and achievements. Dreams cannot be bought. A dream is nothing without perseverance, determination, creativity, initiative and patience, because hurdles and obstacles are part of the road to success. The road to success is always under construction. Goals are the guide that spring from your dreams, they are the pillars that keep you grounded, they serve as the inspiration that keeps you going in the face of problems that seem insurmountable. I think that the fear of failure may be the key to success. So much so, that if we strongly desire something, we shall be able to see the positive aspect of all things. We can reverse a 'bad fortune' and turn it into a golden opportunity that brings success.

Write Your Success Story

I usually get an invitation to be a guest speaker at graduation ceremonies and forums in the Philippines and in Dubai attended by young Filipinos and youth from other countries. I have voiced the following: Never be discouraged. Never hold back. Give everything you have. This is not the end but the beginning of another journey. Just as I was able to rise above my circumstance, just like other success stories, you can make your own story and create a happy ending. You are the author so let it be a good story. The world needs your talents, and the world is shrinking and is becoming one big city where you can explore your possibilities and write your own story of success despite failures. You invested a lot in your education; a lot of effort, time, and pain. In addition, your husband or wife, your children, and other people invested in you, trusting in your capability to change the direction of your life, and perhaps uplift their conditions as well.

The biggest tools to success are hard work, dedication to the job at hand, and the determination to win. We should always do our best in whatever we are doing. It will be a consolation that in case you cannot make it, for some reason beyond your control, you know that you have applied your best and are prepared to derive lessons from the experience and accept it as a learning opportunity.

Be Self-Aware

I have emphasized the importance of utilizing the resources at hand. I remind others that some have different skills and talents. Some have money. Some have patience. Some have kindness. Some have courage. Some have love. Some have the gift of long-suffering. Whatever it is, try to figure out what are you going to do with what you have. You have to figure out how you can use your values and skills to help you achieve success. Keep in mind that there will always be opportunities that will suit your situations. This is a fast-paced life, and technology constantly changes the pattern of life. The door is always open, keep opening it more.

We all have our own quality of wisdom and intelligence and we will be given appropriate opportunities and challenges. It is up to us to try and overcome the challenges and grab the opportunities. Some successful people say, success consists of going from failure to failure without the loss of enthusiasm. Pick yourself up and try again, just like all champions do. Keep trying until you succeed.

Acknowledging Awards

With all the accolades that have been showered upon me during the past, I am grateful that there are people whose support and commitment made a difference in my life. In receiving these awards, I acknowledge leaders who were my inspiration and role models. I hope to be an inspiration and role model to the next generation of leaders.

The Philippine Government has honored me with two major awards that any Overseas Filipino Worker dreams to receive. These are the *Bagong Bayani* [New Heroes] for Community and Social Service (2011) given by the Bagong Bayani Foundation, Inc. and *Banaag* [Ray of Light Award] (2010)under the Presidential Awards for Overseas Filipino Individuals and Organizations, Commission on Filipinos Overseas. The *Banaag* Award was for my tireless efforts in assisting distressed Filipino workers in the UAE and extending financial assistance to impoverished Filipinos in my hometown of Iloilo and other regions. The award included recognition for the role I played in facilitating the airlifting of OFW's from war-torn Libya.

In 2015, 2016, 2017, I received the Influential Filipino in the Gulf award from *Illustrado* as part of their championing the image of Filipinos abroad in their slogan of '*Taas Noo, Filipino*' and their vision of 'Helping the Filipino flourish – global vision, native soul.' In 2016, Lalaine Chu-Benitez, *Illustrado's* Editor-in-Chief, made a statement about the 100 Most Influential Filipinos in the Gulf (MIFG) that resonated with me:

> They are able to shape, not only our collective consciousness, but also the way our community moves forward in this region. Whatever fields these Filipinos excel in, they are at the forefront. They pave the way. They represent the Filipino. We salute all the Filipinos out there. *Taas noo, Filipino!*

One of my most cherished certificates of recognition is from Calinog National Comprehensive High School in Iloilo. In 2018, I attended their commencement exercise with the theme "K-12 Learners: Ready to Face Life's Challenges. The certificate reads in part "for being invincible and beacon for those who hope."

My success can be traced back to the trust and faith that others had bestowed in me. When I am trusted to carry out a responsibility, I always give it the best I can. People have confidence that I will do an excellent job. For example, in 2016, I was given the responsibility to serve as Chairperson for two of the Philippine Consulate's biggest community events in Dubai: the Independence Day and the *Bayanihan* Festival.

The key to success is being positive. I promise myself that I shall work untiringly and relentlessly because I am very optimistic that my reward will come from God on the day of reckoning. And for all our collective efforts, I pray that we all be rewarded together.

"The Government of Dubai has entrusted Wafa with the management and operation of an 8-room center to benefit the Filipino community regardless of their religious orientation."

SIDEBAR 1: GLOBAL HUMANITARIAN WORK

As a Global Humanitarian leader, Wafa has used her influence to help the poor and provide support for education and community building projects in the Philippines. These projects included: school supply donation for 350 students at Pacalundo Elementary School and 1,742 students at Matina Aplaya Elementary School in Lanao Del Norte. Mindanao & Ricardo Memorial Hospital Lambunao, Iloilo received 20 Wheelchairs.

She is the woman behind the multicultural day, blood drive, day International Women's day, tree planting day, clean up the world day, and international labor day. She provided leadership in "FASHUNITY" combining fashion and unity, an annual event in Dubai, that gathers more than 52 countries in a weeklong display of national pride.

SIDEBAR 2: ARABIC CLASSES AND LIVELIHOOD TRAINING

The Government of Dubai has entrusted Wafa with the management and operation of an 8-room center to benefit the Filipino community regardless of their religious orientation. Arabic classes are taught not only to Filipinos but also to expatriates living in the UAE. Every year, more than 500 students have graduated from these Arabic classes and these graduates have found better working opportunities in the UAE.

The center is also utilized for skills training and livelihood courses. More than 1,000 trainers from different Filipino organizations have benefited from this initiative. These organizations include PINOY, SMPII, OFCEA, CADD, PINAS, TROPA, TEACHER, PHOTO WALK, POLO OWWA FOR INTRE-PINOY, and FILIPINO COMMUNITY.

SIDEBAR 3: SCHOLARSHIPS

For Wafa, who is a product of the government-run West Visayas State University in her home province of Iloilo, education is empowering as ignorance and mediocrity may lead to broken dreams of Filipinos. In the Philippines, she has supported a high school in Iloilo province. For five years, she has provided scholarships to more than 120 secondary school and university students from Caninguan National High School and Panuran National High School in Lambunao Iloilo.

SYNTHESIS

Maria Africa Beebe, PH.D.

Pinay, Pinay saan ka pupunta? Nandito na ako.
Filipina, Filipina where are you going? I am now here.

In the Philippines, "*Where are you going*" [Saan ka pupunta?] is an informational greeting. The response to the greeting could be a lift of the eyebrows, a smile, pointing with the lips, a vague "There only" [*Diyan lang*], or naming a specific geographic place such as Davao, Dubai, Norway, Canada, or America. "Where are you going?" can also be an existential question: What is your higher purpose? Where is your life headed?

FILIPINA IDENTITY

Filipina is the feminine form of Filipino, the term used for people who are from the Philippines; or are descendants of people who are from the Philippines. In "A Filipina in a Word, a Filipina in the World," Tuminez (2015, p. 449) suggested this leadership advice "Be proud of your identity. No matter where in the world you go and no matter how high up you rise in the business and political world, do not lose touch with who you are and where you come from. Do not be ashamed of your beginnings, no matter how humble they may be."

Filipina identity in the global environment is complicated. As a result of many cultural and ethnic influences from Spain, China, Japan, Malaysia and the United

States; many Filipinos today find themselves negotiating their identity as global citizens whether they stay in the Philippines or migrate to another country (Hess & Davidson, 2010).

In retelling the indigenous myth, of *babaye*, Lilia Quindoza Santiago's story was that the first woman was born from the nodes of bamboo at the same moment, but separately from the first man. "As a person born whole and separate from man, the Filipina legitimately owns her own body and herself and can chart her own future and destiny." (Basu, 1995, p.7). On the other hand, Gonzales' (2007) research at the Mimosa Leisure Estate in Manila suggested that Filipinas are considered desirable due to their perceived submissiveness and service-orientation.

In the Philippines, women have been active in community engagement, and social and political action, including people power during the Marcos regime resulting in the end of the Marcos dictatorship. Women have helped vote in two women as national presidents: Corazon Aquino and Gloria Arroyo-Macapagal. From the fight against Spain to peasant organizations from the 1930s, worker movements in the 1950s and 1960s brought about some beneficial legislation, including higher wages, health benefits, more extended maternity leaves, equal pay for equal work, and the Philippine Development Plan for Women (Basu, 1955). Recently, Ileto (2018) and her colleagues successfully spearheaded the "Women at Night" amendment to ensure the safety of women who work at night.

In some places in the diaspora, the prevailing narrative about Filipina women blurs the distinction between "Filipino" as the name of a national identity and "Filipino/a" as the generic term for designating a subservient class dependent on foreign economies (Rafael, 1997). Liebelt (2008) cited other authors who noted that being "Filipina" was equated with being a caring maid vulnerable to exploitation and abuse (Gonzales, 1998; Ignacio, 2005; Parreñas, 2001; San Juan, 1998; Tadiar, 2004). According to Ebron (2003), the terms Filipinos and domestic work are synonymous in Italy. Other writers have noted that the job of a domestic worker is a position that carries with it trust, respect, and responsibility; qualities which have been recognized as essential to leadership. Liebelt (2008) concluded that some Filipina domestics who work in the diaspora "conceive of themselves as cosmopolitans who reach out beyond their cultural, religious, and ethno-national origins; to feel at home in the world despite their working-class occupations and non-elite status." They are 'working class cosmopolitans' (Werbner, 1999).

Leadership Repertoire for Global Competence

FWN Founder and CEO Marily Mondejar highlighted the historical perspectives of leading and rising with FWN. Quesada, who first joined the FWN board in

2010 and is currently FWN President, explained her hopes for continued FWN sisterhood, dialogue, and impact while Puyat clarified why she is responding to the FWN challenge. The authors in *DISRUPT 3.0. Filipina Women: Rising* continue to shape the conversation concerning the leadership repertoire of Filipina Women leaders (FWL). Their leadership repertoire includes: developing leadership; building leadership legacy; leadership and entrepreneurship; being first and foremost; and leading for impact. In the synthesis that follows, themes and examples are drawn from the chapters in these categories.

Developing Leadership

Filipina Women Leaders (FWL) have developed their leadership readiness from early childhood socialization, student leadership, love of learning, and the influence of mentors and femtors. These FWL showed qualities of self-awareness from their early childhood. Laxamana recognized that her leadership journey started when her third-grade teacher "planted the seed of self-confidence" and was cultivated by school activities. Mayo learned to be resilient when her parents allowed her at a very young age to live with her grandparents until their untimely death when she was ten years old. "In my life," wrote Ocampo "I have been resilient, resourceful, understanding, and loving. I am part of the culture that I inherited from my parents, and it forms the foundation of why I have succeeded and led so well, especially across different cultures."

Love of learning manifested in participation in specialized training, continuing education, and higher education. For example, Winterhalter and Zeldes completed their doctoral studies. Every FWL attended continuing education courses relevant to their professions. Two specialized training programs for migrants are worth highlighting because of the impact on some of these Filipina Women Leaders.

- Migrants' Associations and Philippine Institutions for Development (MAPID). Funded by the European Union from 2007 through 2010, MAPID was implemented by the Scalabrini Migration Center in the Philippines, the Commission on Filipinos Overseas (CFO), the *Fondazione per le Iniziative e gli Studi sulla Multietnicità* (ISMU) in Italy, and the University of Valencia (UV) in Spain. MAPID aimed at: (a) understanding of the migration-development nexus; (b) promoting transnational development; (c) building the partnership between migrants' associations in Italy (and Spain) and key Philippine institutions to promote development in their home country. MAPID, according to Mayo, was pivotal in her leadership development and those of other Filipino migrants in Europe.

- The Leadership and Social Entrepreneurship (ALSE) program at the Ateneo School of Government. The goal of ALSE is to inspire and train Overseas Contract Workers (OFW) to be new business leaders. The LSE Program is a joint initiative of the Ateneo University School of Government (ASoG) and numerous emigrant organizations. Calaguian and Salinel give credit to ALSE in Dubai for their becoming social entrepreneurs in their adopted country.

"Even though I did not know of Kotter's (1998) work then," Winterhalter wrote: "I may have unknowingly followed his steps to organizational change. That is, I communicated my need to finish college soon (establishing a sense of urgency), discussed each major decision with everyone in my life that was going to be affected (forming a powerful guiding coalition), and planned our actions together (empowering others)." Winterhalter chose to stay in higher education because she felt that "this was a space where I could truly make an impact because I love what I am doing." In Zeldes' quest for the truth about historical trauma in the Filipino American community, her goal in making a documentary film was "I wanted Filipinos and Americans to know this happened in America. I realize that there is still much to be done that requires my leadership."

From developing their leadership to helping other women achieve their leadership potential, these FWL have a clear understanding of their purpose and passion and heed the call to "pass-it-on" (Salinel). Young has acknowledged that "because I missed on mentorship, I made it my goal to make a difference for others through mentoring. Mentoring felt good and made me want to reach as many people as I can." Grateful for the help they received from mentors, coaches, and people who believed in them; these women have femtored, coached, and developed the leadership of their *kapwa* in their professions.

BUILDING LEADERSHIP LEGACY

Several FWL discuss leadership values and qualities that have been taught by subsequent generations and their hope that the next generation will surpass their legacy. Two sisters, Añonuevo and Eustaquio-Syme recounted the story concerning their mother who began her career as a grade school teacher and then moved on to a government position as an auditor assigned to the Central Bank of the Philippines. "She accomplished this while successfully balancing a career and raising a family." She further indicated that "our mother impressed upon us that having a career of her own provided her with financial and psychological independence." Her mother's advice helped both sisters face adversities; Añonuevo when her husband died at age 40 and Eustaquio-Syme when she moved to Canada alone and without encouragement.

Bian and Stalder have daughters whom they are grooming to take over their family business. Bian at eighteen years of age decided she would build her own school. She has built not just one but several schools as part of the Joji Ilagan International Schools. Bian's mother told her: "you are a headstrong woman and so confident of yourself. One day, you will be a star!" Bian's daughter echoed that "Dream big, aim high because you can do it." "Another thing I have learned from my mother is going after opportunities even if it means having to step out of my comfort zone. It has been my experience that opportunities remain just opportunities until they are acted upon." Stalder's early beginnings differ from Bian. At age seven, Stalder experienced a #metoo moment from an extended family member. Her response was to show courage and resolve. Stalder wrote: "We are what we are now because of the decisions we have made, the choices we have taken. Every decision made has far-reaching consequences, not felt at the moment, but felt at some time yet to come." Stalder's daughter echoes this "Our legacy is created from the choices and decisions we make in life. How we live and love and how we touch others through our lives creates a legacy of respect."

Murry reminded us that based on her experience "we should never forget the intricate pathways we experience through our life. Taoist thinking reminds us that adversities and failures will only ensure the gates for success will open. Whether you are already a leader or just about to start your path to leadership, remain open, think outside the box, and have courage in redefining your own pathway." Murry's daughter added that her mom sets a high standard, and is thoughtful, fearless, and resilient. The daughter admits to realizing how central social justice is to her mother's work; as shown by her mother's empathy and respect for humanity.

In an effort to spend more quality time with her ten-year-old daughter, Dr. Teh has brought her to meetings, workshops, the hospitals, and even in the operating room. One of Teh's prescriptions for leadership is: "We must empower our girl children and help them realize that there are opportunities everywhere and that financial security does not come only as wives and mothers. It is what we can offer to the world that matters."

Leadership and Entrepreneurship

Several FWL have shown that being entrepreneurial is integral to their leadership. Abiva noted that "One of the challenges of being a woman and an entrepreneur is that many men in the high-tech industry of Educational Multimedia and Technology try to put you in your place by testing you and trying to see if you really know what you're talking about. Men traditionally dominate the technical niche." As a Filipina Champion of the Geeks, Abiva has climbed mountains both literally and figuratively. As head of a family business in the Philippines established by her parents, Abiva emphasized the need for "a succession plan" that includes having people who are qualified to run the business as opposed to family connections. As an Angelpreneur, Abiva has provided the technical know-how and mentoring for the success of aspiring entrepreneurs.

Go-Chiu and Tang who came from entrepreneurial families in the Philippines have demonstrated in their stories the role of innovation in profits. Go-Chiu's parents "emphasized the values of discipline, hard work, filial piety, and trust as the keys to success especially in dealing with people." While growing up, Go-Chiu did not ask for these tasks to be given to her but was trusted to accomplish them. She said, "I responded with a willing mind and an open heart to do what I was asked to do." In the process, Go-Chiu "proved to my father and the people surrounding me that a woman at the helm can steer the ship to safe harbor through the rough seas."

Tang wrote, "I have been a CEO for most of my life, but the road was not always perfect." Inspired by her family's entrepreneurial spirit, with strong role models and getting a systems perspective from her internship, she started her own business right after graduating from college. Betrayal by her then husband made her grieve and then decided that she alone can break her cycle of despair. She rose from her grief, took a leap of faith, and with hard work, good communications, honesty, and empathy, became a beautypreneur. Tang emphasized the need to be open to learning, innovation, and change.

Montano and Quintos attempted to make their mark overseas; Montano by moving to the US to work in the healthcare industry and Quintos by moving to Taiwan to work in the information and communication technologies. However, both decided that their purpose in life is best served back in the Philippines despite potential setbacks and risks of starting over again. Montano, who survived being buried alive after an intensity 7 earthquake in Baguio City, has found her social enterprise niche in capacity building in emergency training and disaster preparedness. After writing her first book *Abroad Me: 22 Success Strategies for Young Overseas Filipinos*, Quintos decided to take charge of publishing it and eventually setting up a company that advocates migrant adaptation, financial literacy, and even gender equality.

After focusing mainly on financial security, Calaguian found her road to her *Ikigai*, the Japanese concept of "a reason to jump out of bed each morning." Calaguian discovered her "passion in social entrepreneurship, empowering those within a marginalized sector of the community, people with disability" in Dubai, UAE.

Despite making a difference as an international banker while based in Milan and then in London, Romulo decided to become a restaurateur. Romulo developed a 5-year financial plan based on Strengths, Weaknesses, Opportunities, Threats (SWOT), and a comprehensive marketing plan for her family who owned Romulo Café in the Philippines. Opening a restaurant was beyond Romulo's comfort zone since she was used to the more structured routine at the bank. Romulo concluded that "The training, skill-set, and disciplines I had acquired during my banking career helped me manage the day-to-day operations of the restaurant. Having a financial background allowed me to manage the bookkeeping, accounts, and profit and loss of the company with ease. Having run a global business previously, I had experience in start-up projects, people management, and product development; all skills that I have been able to apply in the restaurant."

Being First and Foremost

Some Filipina Women Leaders have exceeded expectations, disrupted the status quo, and broken the glass ceiling as they became first and foremost in their fields. Torres-Samoranos believed at one point that being a Filipina in the U.S. was the problem. She noted that:

> I was the only Filipina in my grammar and middle school and when I graduated from a small class of social welfare majors at UC Berkeley. Then I graduated as the only Filipina in my class of 300 law students at the UCLA Law School. When I accepted a position as a Deputy Public Defender in an office of 110 attorneys in a densely-populated, high-crime city, I was the first, and only Filipina during my entire 25-year tenure at that office. I currently work at a nonprofit Asian legal agency as an immigration attorney in San Francisco; but when I was initially hired, I was again the only Filipina on the staff of 30 attorneys.

Negrillo is the only Filipina in the media industry in the Middle East with a senior management position. Negrillo is a Senior Planning Director specializing with accounts in various industries including automotive, fashion, technology, airline, property, retail, telecommunications, and consumer electronics. Vintervoll researched a position paper to lift the ban for assignment of Au Pairs to Norway. She was told that the position paper was used as the basis to lift the ban for all of Europe. Puyat stated that despite problems as a volunteer, it is the positive outcome and people-level impact of being a volunteer that has kept her going. For example, when she was Governor of District 17 of Zonta International, they won all of the ZI Awards offered annually during her biennium term including the Young Women in Public Affairs Award, The Jane M. Klausman Women in Business Scholarship, and The Amelia Earhart Fellowship. Tenazas, an artist based in New York and a self-proclaimed cultural nomad, in 1996 became the first non-New York-based national president of the American Institute of Graphic Arts (AIGA).

Barker, a child of an Overseas Filipina Worker, moved to the UK and rode the business roller-coaster before she decided to run for a public office. Barker made history as the first Filipina woman to be elected as a Town Councillor and as a Borough Councillor in the UK. Manalo who won a Daly City Council seat and was selected by her fellow council members to be Mayor of Daly City, California declared: "I reaffirm that first and foremost my mission is to serve my community."

Carrion was one of five generous individuals from the Philippines and longtime members of the Rotary Club, who was inducted into the prestigious and exclusive Arch Klumph Society in 2018 at the Rotary International. Carrion's goal is to have more "women contribute significantly towards creating a happier home, an environmental sounder community, and a kinder world." Carrion continued: "It is when we have stretched our limits, broken through our glass ceiling, and grasped what we thought was beyond our reach, that we become avatars or the very embodiment of the causes, aspirations, and ideals we ultimately live for." Jose became the First Filipino doctor to make it into the Surgeon's locator list of Intuitive Surgical, the maker of the Da Vinci Surgical System. Jose's explanation is apropos to most of these Filipina women leaders: "I became first and foremost in this field by exceeding expectations, by sheer determination and hard work, by overcoming challenges, and by staying focused on my goal."

LEADING FOR IMPACT

Several Filipina Women leaders exemplify the impact they have on other people around them. As leaders, they have gotten results by getting their team, peers, constituents, and stakeholders to do what is right. As leaders, they have provided certainty, guidance, vision, and a solid commitment. As leaders, they value *malasakit* and get everyone together through *delikadesa*.

The leadership reach of Filipina Women Leaders has gone beyond their professional fields to include their social engagement and policy advocacies. Amour-Levar has "intentionally aligned her career choices with her values" and has considered it a privilege when an opportunity to change lives opens up.

"Life is full of tears and laughter," Boac wrote, "it also full of great promise." Boac concluded that "it is the longing of this promise that leaves footprints and gives our life meaning." Boac encourages women to "get involved in the election process and run for public office. Leaping into it requires courage. Everything we do in life is a leap of faith. So, run Filipina run! A seat at the bigger table awaits you. Your footprints will be remembered forever by those whose lives you have touched." Qasimieh indicated that she believes her "success can be traced back to the trust and faith that others had bestowed on me. When I am trusted to carry out a responsibility, I always give it the best I can. People have confidence that I will do an excellent job." "And, for all our collective efforts," Qasimieh prayed "that we all be rewarded together."

Hefti recounted that her parents were her role models for success. The message from Hefti's parents was that there would be stumbling blocks, *Stolpersteine*, along our paths, but these are temporary. In Moving Beyond Power and Position, Eisma asserted that "those who have the most power should be the most humble." Eisma explained: "One way of showing humility is *malasakit*, oneness with whoever is in need. Without being asked or required, *malasakit* is given voluntarily and springs naturally and spontaneously whenever the occasion arises."

Ileto equated *delikadesa* with waves of positive change. "*Delikadesa*," as explained by Ileto, "is about orchestrating and gently, but persuasively, communicating an opinion. It is getting everyone together and giving them a new set of lenses to see things and say 'can we do this together?' It is gentle but powerful, just as women leaders should be." Ileto believes that *delikadesa* has given her the drive, ability, and courage to disrupt multiple industries.

Rising to Global Leadership

The readiness for global leadership of Filipina Women Leaders consists of the dimensions of global competence identified by Hunter and Hunter (2018). These leaders are self-aware, open-minded, attentive to diversity, and risk takers; these leaders balance historical perspectives with global awareness, demonstrate intercultural capability, and collaborate across cultures. These leaders demonstrate their character strengths in virtues that are common across cultures (Patterson & Seligman, 2004). These are humanity, transcendence, wisdom, courage, temperance, and justice.

ACKNOWLEDGEMENTS

This book required a collaborative effort that was made possible by the following:

- Marily Mondejar, Founder and CEO of Filipina Women's Network, provided executive oversight.

- Thirty-eight contributing authors shared their leadership reflections, narratives, vignettes, setbacks, outcomes, global competencies, and success stories; whether *en route* to Dubai, London, Davao, Manila, New York, San Francisco, or elsewhere in the world.

- For book cover design, Lucille Lozada Tenazas, Global FWN100™ 2013 and Henry Wolf Professor of Communication Design & Associate Dean of Art, Media and Technology, Parsons The New School for Design.

- Anne Quintos, Managing Partner, PageJump Media and Global FWN100™ 2016 served as our layout designer and provided an extra set of critical eyes.

- Edwin Lozada, President of the Pilipino American Writers and Artists (PAWA), Inc. whose work in *DISRUPT 1.0* and *DISRUPT 2.0* provided a template for *DISRUPT 3.0*.

- Georgitta "Beng" Puyat for underwriting the printing of the limited edition.

- Noel Puyat, Henry Cureg, and Edna Cureg for ensuring a smooth printing process.

- James Beebe, our external reader who read the whole book and gave us his invaluable advice. James Beebe, Ph.D. is finishing his latest book *Qualitative Inquiry: Quest for Understanding*. James is a retired professor in the Doctoral Program in Leadership Studies at Gonzaga University and, prior to that he retired as a U.S. Foreign Service Officer with USAID serving in the Sudan, Philippines, Liberia, and South Africa.

- Our peer reviewers provided comments, recommendations for improvement, and suggestions for edits – Elizabeth Bautista, Gloria Caiole, Wennie Conedy, Lirio S. Covey, Kristine Custodio, Sonia Delen, Maria Hizon, Bambi Lorica, Elena Mangahas, Marie Claire Lim Moore, Rocio Nuyda, Melissa Orquiza, Gizelle C. Robinson, and Benel Se-Liban. Although we publicly acknowledge our reviewers, the identity of the reviewers was not disclosed to the authors.

- The daughters who commented on their mother's narratives: Nicole Bian (Joji Ilagan Bian), Alex Murry (Rebecca Murry), Joie Emelline Teh (Catherine Teh); and Diana Stalder (Dina Dela Paz Stalder).

- For giving us permission to quote her poem, "*Babae Kami*," Marra PL Lanot; a poet, essayist, and freelance journalist. She has published articles and columns in newspapers and magazines on the arts, culture, and politics. Her latest work is *Cadena de Amor: New and Selected Poems in English, Filipino, and Spanish*.

- Franklin M. Ricarte (Draft Orange), Social Media and Tech Guru updated the Filipina Leadership website http://www.filipinaleadership.org/ and provided various media communications support.

- For Chapter 1 permissions and photos: Al Perez, Ana Julaton Photo Collection, Angelica Berrie, Benjamin Pimentel (INQUIRER.net), Bessie and Eppie Bangalan, Christina Macabenta Dunham, Cora Manase Tellez, DIY Awards, Drew Altizer Photography, Eve Ensler, Evelyn Dilsaver, Farren Associates and Masterworks, Filipina Women's Network Photo Collection, Francine Maigue, 2015 Face of Global Pinay Power, Franklin M. Ricarte, Gani Ricarte Photography, Genevieve Jopanda, Giovannie Pico, Photo by Adam Berwid and Era Coniendo, Institute for Image Management, Kelsey Escoto, Lito Gutierrez (Philippine Daily Inquirer), Judge Lorna Schofield, Lucille Tenazas, Tenazas Design, Marily Mondejar Photo Collection, Mary Kate Stimmler, California Lieutenant Governor Mona Pasqual, One Billion Rising, Rowena Romulo, 2017 Face of Global Pinay Power, Consul General Rowena Sanchez (Philippine Consulate General San Francisco), San Francisco Chronicle (Claire Joyce Tempongko photo), San Francisco City Hall, Sheroes Monologues: Elena Mangahas, Gloria Ramos, Marily Mondejar, Maya Ong Escudero, Sol Manaay, Colonel Shirley Raguindin, California Chief Justice Tani Cantil Sakauye, TOWNS Foundation, V-Day, and Webex and Cisco.

- Colleagues from the Global Networks read the introduction and synthesis and gave comments and feedback; Jerri Shepard, Ed.D., Gonzaga University; Robert Bartlett, Ph.D. Eastern Washington University; and Mark Beattie, Ph.D., Washington State University.

- FWN Filipina Leadership Global Summit (12-17 September 2018) Steering Committee and Committee Chair, Leonor Vintervoll for bringing in sponsors.

- Oxford University, Oxford Philippines Society, Cafe Romulo, Councillor Cynthia Barker, and our London connections who helped with our DISRUPTing Oxford book reading event and with planning some of the FWN Leadership Summit.

- Amaze Studios, Barry Cox Photography, Don Paolo Studios, Jiggie Alejandrino & TEAM OSS, Moments.no, Cameron Bowman, Dawn Eicher, and Kelly Lotosky for the photographs of the FWN Board members.

- Ramar Foods International and Wells Fargo for their unwavering support.

- Forest City and Megaworld International for supporting the FWN Leadership Summit.

Other *kapwa* global Filipinas too numerous to mention here who gave us support in spirit and cheered us on.

Maraming salamat!

Appendices

Appendix A

References

AIM, Center for Bridging Leadership. (2015). Bridges of peace in Mindanao. Metro Manila, Philippines: Asian Institute of Management.

Archer, D. (2012). The psychology of beauty. Retrieved from https://www.psychologytoday.com/intl/blog/reading-between-the-headlines/201206/the-psychology-beauty

Baker, K.G., Gippenreiter, J.B., 1998. Stalin's Purge and its impact on Russian families. In: Danieli, Y. (Ed.), International Handbook of Multigenerational Legacies of Trauma. Plenum Press, New York, NY, pp. 403e434.

Bagasao, I. (2007). Filipinos in Europe: Economic contributions, challenges and aspirations. In F. M. Hoegsholm (Ed.), In de olde worlde: Views of Filipino migrants in Europe (pp. 28-57). Quezon City: Philippine Social Science Council and Philippine Migration Research Network.

Baker, K.G., Gippenreiter, J.B., 1998. Stalin's Purge and its impact on Russian families. In: Danieli, Y. (Ed.), International Handbook of Multigenerational Legacies of Trauma. Plenum Press, New York, NY, pp. 403-434.

Bass, B. M., & Bass, R. (2008). The Bass handbook of leadership: Theory, research, and managerial applications (4th ed.). New York: Free Press.

Basu, A. (Ed.). (1995). The challenge of local feminisms: Women's movements of local feminisms. New York: Routledge.

Bautista, Maria Cynthia Rose Banzon. (2002). Migrant workers and their environments: Insights from the Filipino diaspora. Unpublished manuscript.

Beebe, M. A. (Ed.). (2016). DISRUPT 2.0. Filipina women: Daring to lead. San Francisco: Filipina Women's Network.

Beebe, M. A. (2017). The leadership repertoire of select Filipina women in the Diaspora and implications for theorizing leadership. In J. Storberg-Walker, & P. Haber-Curran (Eds.), Theorizing women & leadership: New insights & contributions from multiple perspectives (). Charlotte, NC: Information Age Publishing.

Beebe, M. A., & Escudero, M. O. (Eds.). (2015). DISRUPT 1.0. Filipina women: Proud. loud. leading without A doubt. Philippines: Filipina Women's Network.

Bichsel, M., Bugayong, L. K., & Fen, L. C. (2017). Bending without breaking: Thirteen women's stories of migration and resilience. Switzerland: sR Book Design.

Block, P. (2009). Community: The structure of belonging. San Francisco: Berrett-Koehler.

Bob Parsons Quotes. (n.d.). BrainyQuote.com. retrieved august 2, 2018, from BrainyQuote.com web site: Retrieved from https://www.brainyquote.com/quotes/bob_parsons_477657

Branine, M., & Pollard, D. (2010). Human resource management with islamic management principles: A dialectic for a reverse diffusion in management. Personnel Review, 39(6), 712-727. doi:https://doi.org/10.1108/00483481011075576

Brave Heart, M.Y.H., DeBruyn, L.M., 1998. The American Indian Holocaust: healing historical unresolved grief. American Indian and Alaska Native Mental Health Research 8 (2), 56e78

Brown, D., & Kothari, D. (1975). Comparison of antibiotic discs from different sources. Journal of Clinical Pathology, 28(10), 779-783.

Bruner, J. (1999). The process of education. Massachussetts: Harvard College Press.

Bryman, A., Collinson, D. L., Grint, K., Jackson, B., & Uhl-Bien, M. (Eds.). (2011). The sage handbook of leadership. London: Sage Publications.

Buchholdt, T. (1996). Filipinos in Alaska: 1788-1958. Anchorage: Aboriginal Press.

Byrne, R. (2006). The secret. UK: Simon & Schuster.

Cain, S. (2012). The power of introverts. Retrieved from https://youtu.be/c0KYU2j0TM4

Cain, S. (2013). Quiet: The power of introverts in a world that can't stop talking. New York: Broadway Paperbacks.

Calbay, R., De Leon, M., & Lising, P. (Eds.). (2015). Cyberpreneur Philippines: Online business start-up guide. Taguig City: PageJump.

Campbell, C.D., Evans-Campbell, T., 2011. Historical trauma and Native American child development and mental health: an overview. In: Sarche, M., Spicer, P., Farrell, P., Fitzgerald, H.E. (Eds.), American Indian and Alaska Native Children and Mental Health: Development, Context, Prevention, and Treatment. Praeger, Santa Barbara, CA, pp. 1e26.

Canfiield, J. (2015). How to get from where you are to where you want to be. New York, NY: Harper Collins Publisher.

Cantwell, M. (2017). The hidden power of not (always) fitting in. Retrieved from https://youtu.be/cnooCepNZv4

Center for Creative Leadership. (2015). Benchmarks by design.

Choy, C. C. (2003). Empire of care: Nursing and migration in Filipino-American history. Durham: Duke University Press.

City of Daly city: Form of government. Retrieved from http://www.dalycity.org/About_Daly_City/City_Profile/Form_of_Government.htm

Collins, J. C. (2001). Good to great: Why some companies make the leap... and others don't. New York: Harper Business.

Commission on Filipinos Overseas. (2013). Stock estimate of overseas Filipinos as of December 2013. Retrieved from http://www.cfo.gov.ph/images/stories/pdf/StockEstimate2013.pdf

Commission on Filipinos Overseas. (2017). 2015 CFO statistics on Philippine international migration. Retrieved from https://www.cfo.gov.ph/images/pdf/2017/2015compendiumstats-insidepages-2017-06-29.pdf

Covey, S. R. (2003). The 7 habits of highly effective people personal workbook. New York, NY: Simon & Schuster.

Crawford, A., 2013. "The trauma experienced by generations past having an effect in their descendants": narrative and historical trauma among Inuit in Nunavut, Canada. Transcultural Psychiatry 0 (0), 1e31.

Crick, F. (1970). Central dogma of molecular biology. Nature, 227, 561-563. doi:10.1038/227561a0

Cuyegkeng, M. A. C., & Palma-Angeles, A. (Eds.). (2011). Defining Filipino leadership. Philippines: Ateneo de Manila Press.

Daud, A., Skoglund, E., Rydelius, P.A., 2005. Children in families of torture victims: transgenerational transmission of parents' traumatic experiences to their children. International Journal of Social Welfare 14 (1), 23e32.

De Jesus, M. (2005). Pinay power: Theorizing the Filipina/American experience. New York: Taylor and Francis Group.

De Mello, A. (2012). Rediscovering life: Awaken to reality. New York: Image Books.

Dean, J. K. (1994). The praying life: Living beyond your limits. Nashville: B&H Publishing Group.

Dickens, C. (2004). A tale of two cities Project Gutenberg. Retrieved from https://www.gutenberg.org/files/98/98-h/98-h.htm

Doronila, M. L. C. (1989). The limits of educational change: National identity formation in a Philippine public elementary school. Quezon City, Philippines: University of the Philippines Press.

Ebron, G. (2002). Not just the maid: Negotiating Filipina identity in Italy. Intersections: Gender, History and Culture in the Asian Context, (8).

Ethnologue: Philippines. Retrieved from https://www.ethnologue.com/country/PH

Evans-Campbell, T., 2008. Historical trauma in American Indian/Native Alaska communities: a multilevel framework for exploring impacts on individuals, families, and communities. Journal of Interpersonal Violence 23 (3), 316e338.;

Follett, M. P. (1924). Creative experience. London, UK: Longmans, Green and Company.

Follett, M. P. (1949). Freedom and co-ordination: Lectures in business organization by Mary Parker Follett. London: Management Publications Trust, Ltd.

Gallo, R., & Montagnier, L. (2003). The discovery of HIV as the cause of AIDS. New England Journal of Medicine, 349, 2283-2285. doi:10.1056/NEJMp038194

Gardner, H., Csikszentmihalyi, M., & Damon, W. (2001). Good work: When excellence and ethics meet. New York: Basic Books.

Gentry, W. A., & Eckert, R. H. (2012). Integrating implicit leadership theories and fit into the development of global leaders: A 360-degree approach. Industrial and Organizational Psychology, 15, 224-227. doi:10.1111/j.1754-9434.2012.01434.x

Gentry, W. A., Eckert, R. H., Stawiski, S. A., & Zhao, S. (2016). The challenges leaders face around the world: More similar than different. (White Paper). Center for Creative Leadership. Retrieved from https://www.ccl.org/wp-content/uploads/2015/04/ChallengesLeadersFace.pdf

Gone, J.P., 2013. Redressing First Nations historical trauma: theorizing mechanisms for indigenous culture as mental health treatment. Transcultural Psychiatry 50 (5).

Gonzales, J. L. (1998). Philippine labour migration: Critical dimensions of public policy. Singapore: Institute of Southeast Asian Studies.

Gonzales, V. V. (2007). Military bases, 'royalty trips,' and imperial modernities: Gendered and racialized labor in postcolonial Philippines. Frontiers: A Journal of Women's Studies, 3, 29-31.

Greenleaf, R. (2002). In Spears L. (Ed.), Servant leadership: A journey into the nature of legitimate power and greatness (25th Anniversary ed.). New York: Paulist Press.

Greenleaf, R. (2008). The servant as leader. Retrieved from https://www.essr.net/~jafundo/mestrado_material_itgjkhnld/IV/Lideranças/The Servant as Leader.pdf

Gungwu, W. (1997). Global history and migrations. New York: Harper Collins Publishers, Inc.

Gupta, V., Surie, G., Javidan, M., & Chokker, J. (2002). Southern Asia cluster: The organizational and societal worldviews and their foundations. In B. Pattanayak & V. Gupta (Eds.), Creating performing organizations. Sage: New Delhi, India.

Gutierrez, L. (2010, August 24). Filipina women's network in US marks glass-ceiling breakthroughs. Philippine Daily Inquirer.

Hamermesh, D. S. (2013). Beauty pays: Why attractive people are more successful. Princeton: Princeton University Press.

Hefti, A. M. (2007). Migrant issues in Switzerland. In F. M. Hoegsholm (Ed.), In de olde worlde: Views of Filipino migrants in Europe (pp. 301-317). Quezon City: Philippine Social Science Council and Philippine Migration Research Network.

Hill, N. (2014). Think and grow rich. Aristeus Books.

House, R., Javidan, M., Hanges, P., & Dorfman, P. (2002). Journal of World Business, 37, 3-10.

Hunter, C. K., & Hunter, W. D. (2018). Global competence model. Retrieved from https://globallycompetent.com/global-competence-model/

Hutchens, D. (2002). Shadows of the Neanderthal: Illuminating the beliefs that limit our organizations. Singapore: Cobee Publishing House.

Hutchens, D., & Gombert, B. (2011). Listening to the volcano: Conversations that open our minds to new possibilities. Singapore: Cobee Publishing House.

Ignacio, E. N. (2005). Building diaspora: Filipino community formation on the internet. New Brunswick, NJ: Rutgers University Press.

International Ergonomics Association. (2018). What is ergonomics? Retrieved from http://www.iea.cc/

Javidan, M. (2010). Bridging the global mindset to leadership. Retrieved from https://hbr.org/2010/05/bringing-the-global-mindset-to.html

Justices of the peace act, R.S.O. 1990, c. J.4. (2018). Retrieved from https://www.ontario.ca/laws/statute/90j04

Karenian, H., Livaditis, M., Karenian, S., Zafiriadis, K., Bochtsou, V., Xenitidis, K., 2011. Collective trauma transmission and traumatic reactions among descendants of Armenian refugees. International Journal of Social Psychiatry 57 (4), 327e337.

Kotter, J. P. (1998). Leading change: Why transformation efforts fail. (pp. 1-20). Boston, MA: Harvard Business School Publishing.

Kellermann, N.P., 2001a. Psychopathology in children of Holocaust survivors: a review of the research literature. Israeli Journal of Psychiatry Related Science. 38 (1), 36-46.

Lasar, C. (2016). Toto O. Quezon City: PageJump Folio.

Legaspi, A. (2017). Ang pag-ikot ng salapi sa panahon ni JLC. Quezon City: PageJump Folio.

Liebelt, C. (2011). In Berglund E. (Ed.), Caring for the 'holy land': Filipina domestic workers in Israel. Oxford and New York: Berghahn Books.

Lindenauer, S. M., & Oneal, E. (2016). Paralyzing summer: The true story of the ann arbor V.A. hospital poisonings and deaths. Ann Arbor: University of Michigan Press.

Macansantos, F., & Macasantos, P. (2015). Philippine literature in the Spanish colonial period. Retrieved from http://ncca.gov.ph/subcommissions/subcommission-on-the-arts-sca/literary-arts/philippine-literature-in-the-spanish-colonial-period/

Mehl, E. M. (2016). Forced migration in the Spanish pacific world: From Mexico to the Philippines, 1765–1811. Cambridge: Cambridge University Press.

Members (immigration and refugee board of canada). (2018). Retrieved from https://irb-cisr.gc.ca/en/members/Pages/index.aspx

Mendenhall, M. E. (2008). Leadership and the birth of global leadership. In M. E. Mendenhall, J. S. Osland, A. Bird, G. R. Oddou & M. L. Maznevski (Eds.), Global leadership: Research, practice, and development (pp. 1-17). London and New York: Routledge.

Mendenhall, M. E. (2008). Leadership and the birth of global leadership. In M. Mendenhall, J. Osland, A. Bird, G. Oddou & M. Maznevski (Eds.), Global leadership: Research, practice, and development (pp. 1-17). London, New York: Routledge.

Mendenhall, M. E., Osland, J., Bird, A., Oddou, G. R., Stevens, M. J., Maznevski, M., . . . Stahl, G. K. (2018). Global leadership: Research, practice, and development (3rd ed.). New York: Routledge.

Mohatt, N. V.; Thompson, A. B.; Thai, N. D.; Tebes, J. K. (2014). Historical trauma as public narrative: A conceptual review of how history impacts present-day health. Social Science & Medicine 106.

Nasir, N. S., & Cobb, P. (2007). Improving access to mathematics: Diversity and equity in the classroom. New York: Teachers College Press.

Wick, D., Mark, L., & Greenhut, R. (Producers), & Nichols, M. (Director). (2001). Working girl. [Motion Picture] 20th Century Fox.

Ocampo, J. M., Plankey, M., Zou, K., Collmann, J., Wang, C., Young, M., Kassaye, S. (2015). Trajectory analyses of virologic outcomes reflecting community-based HIV treatment in Washington, DC 1994–2012. BMC Public Health, 15, 1277. doi:http://doi.org/10.1186/s12889-015-2653-x

Ocampo, J. M., Smart, J., Allston, A., Bhattacharjee, R., Boggavarapu, S., Carter, S., Young, M. (2016). Improving HIV surveillance data for public health action in Washington, DC: A novel multiorganizational data-sharing method. JMIR Public Health and Surveillance, 2(1), e3. doi:10.2196/publichealth.5317

Peacocks. (n.d.). Retrieved from https://www.nationalgeographic.com/animals/birds/group/peacocks/

Peterson, C., & Seligman, M. (2004). Character strengths and virtues: A handbook and classification. Washington, DC: American Psychological Association / Oxford University Press.

Pimentel, B. (2007, October 25). Kuwento Kuwento: Marily's Mission. Inquirer.net.

Pless, N., Maak, T., & Stahl, G. K. (2011). Developing responsible global leaders through international service learning programs: The Ulysses experience. Academy of Management Learning and Education, 10, 237-260. Retrieved from https://www.researchgate.net/publication/257227589_Pless_N_Maak_T_Stahl_G_K_2011_Developing_responsible_global_leaders_through_international_service_learning_programs_The_Ulysses_experience_Academy_of_Management_Learning_and_Education_10_237-260

Poitier, S. (2000). The measure of a man. San Francisco: Harper San Francisco.

Quintos, A. (2014). Abroad me: 22 success strategies for young overseas Filipinos. Taguig City: PageJump.

Rafael, V. L. (1997). Your grief is our gossip: Overseas filipinos and other spectral presences. Public Culture, 9(2), 267-291.

Reiche, S., Bird, A., Mendenhall, M. E., & Osland, J. S. (2017). Contextualizing leadership: A typology of global leadership roles. Journal of International Business Studies, 48, 552-572.

Rich, R. (2013). The Great Recession: December 2007–June 2009. Retrieved from https://www.federalreservehistory.org/essays/great_recession_of_200709

Roffey, B. (1999). Filipina managers and entrepreneurs: What leadership models apply? Asian Studies Review, 23(3), 375-405.

San Francisco District Attorney's Office. 1998 Homicide Survey.

San Juan, E. (1998). From exile to diaspora: Versions of the Filipino experience in the United States. Boulder: Westview Press.

Santiago, L. Q. (1995). Rebirthing babaye: The women's movement in the Philippines. In A. Basu (Ed.), The challenge of local feminisms: Women's movements of local feminisms (pp. 110-130). New York: Routledge.

Shouk, A. A., & De Leon, J. P. (2017). Blue whale game link to two Dubai suicides? Retrieved from https://gulfnews.com/news/uae/crime/blue-whale-game-link-to-two-dubai-suicides-1.2212432

Simons, G. F., & Fennig, C. D. (Eds.). (2018). Ethnologue: Languages of the world (21st ed.). Dallas, Texas: SIL International. Retrieved from http://www.ethnologue.com

Sotero, M., 2006. A conceptual model of historical trauma: Implications for public health practice and research. Journal of Health Disparities Research and Practice 1 (1), 93e108

Statistics Norway. Foreign citizens by citizenship and sex. Retrieved from https://www.ssb.no/256015/foreign-citizens-by-citizenship-and-sex.1-january

Statistics Norway. (2017). Key figures for immigration and immigrants. Retrieved from https://www.ssb.no/en/innvandring-og-innvandrere/nokkeltall

Stevens, M.J., Bird, A., Mendenhall, M.E., & Oddou, G. (2014). Measuring global leader intercultural competency: Development and validation of the global competencies inventory (GCI). In J. Osland, M. Li & Y. Wang (Eds.), Advances in global leadership (Volume 8 ed., pp. 99-138). Bingley, UK: Emerald.

Tadiar, N. X. M. (2004). Fantasy-production: Sexual economies and other Philippine consequences for the new world order. Manila: Ateneo de Manila University Press.

Tedx Talks (Producer) (2017). The hidden power of not (always) fitting in Marianne Cantwell. [Video/DVD] Retrieved from https://www.youtube.com/watch?v=cnooCepNZv4

Tracy, B. (2017). Eat that frog!: 21 great ways to stop procrastination. Oakland, CA: Berrett-Koehler Publishers.

Tuminez, A. S. (2015). A Filipina in a word, a Filipina in the world. In M. A. Beebe, & M. O. Escudero (Eds.), DISRUPT. Filipina women: Proud. loud. leading without a doubt (pp. 436-452). Philippines: Filipina Women's Network.

U.S. Citizenship and Immigration Services. (2016). Bringing children, sons and daughters to live in the united states as permanent residents. Retrieved from https://www.uscis.gov/family/family-us-citizens/children/bringing-children-sons-and-daughters-live-united-states-permanent-residents

U.S. Citizenship and Immigration Services. (2017). Green card for immediate relatives of U.S. citizen. Retrieved from https://www.uscis.gov/greencard/immediate-relative-us-citizen

U.S. Citizenship and Immigration Services. (2018). Green card for family preference immigrants. Retrieved from https://www.uscis.gov/greencard/family-preference

U.S. Citizenship and Immigration Services. (https://www.uscis.gov/greencard/family-preference). Green card for family preference immigrants. Retrieved from https://www.uscis.gov/greencard/family-preference

University of Oslo Museum of Cultural History. (2016). The Gokstad grave. Retrieved from https://www.khm.uio.no/english/visit-us/viking-ship-museum/exhibitions/gokstad/3-gokstadgrave.html

Valdes, C. ". (2017). Educating women leaders: Transformation in women's colleges. Mandaluyong, Phil: Anvil Publishing.

Washington Post. (July 14, 1977). Nurses Convicted in Poisoning Case Nurses Convicted in Poisoning Case

Wexler, L.M., DiFluvio, G., Burke, T.K., 2009. Resilience and marginalized youth: making a case for personal and collective meaning-making as part of resilience research in public health. Social Science & Medicine 69 (4), 565e570

Wheatley, M. (2006). Leadership and the new science: Discovering order in a chaotic world. Oakland: Berret-Koehler Publishers, Inc.

Wilcox, R. K. (1977). The mysterious deaths at Ann Arbor. New York: Popular Library.

Winn, M. (2014). What is your ikigai? Retrieved from http://theviewinside.me/what-is-your-ikigai/

Winterhalter, E. T. (2016). Physical learning spaces and college students with ADHD. (Unpublished California State University, Northridge, CA.

World Economic Forum. (2017). Global gender report gap 2017. (). Geneva: World Economic Forum. Retrieved from https://www.weforum.org/reports/the-global-gender-gap-report-2017

Zeldes, G. A. (Director). (2016). That strange summer. [Motion Picture]. USA.

Zeldes (archive research):

https://www.nytimes.com/1977/03/14/archives/2-nurses-will-seek-dismissal-of-trial-lawyer-in-the-va-hospital.html

https://www.nytimes.com/1977/12/20/archives/new-trial-ordered-for-filipino-nurses-judge-assails-the-prosecutors.html

http://ticklethewire.com/2011/02/03/looking-back-at-the-mysterious-murders-at-ann-arbors-veterans-hospital-what-went-right-and-what-ultimlately-went-wrong-in-the-case/

http://www.videoethno.com/JVE_1_Issue1.php?un=alumitge@msu.edu

Appendix B

Additional Web-Based Resources

Filipina Women's Network. 2007-2018. Interviews with FWN100™ awardees.
The Filipina Women's Network interviews its Top 100 Most Influential Filipina Women awardees as part of its time capsule project with the objective of documenting the contributions of Filipina women to society to inspire future generations.

Filipina Women's Network. 2007-2015. FWN Global 100: The 100 Most Influential Filipina Women in the World. Filipina Women's Network has published the Filipina Leadership Summit magazine from 2005-present. The magazine serves as a program and resource for attendees. The 2013-2018 issues showcase the Global FWN100™ Most Influential Women in the World.

AAUW. Barriers and Bias: The Status of Women in Leadership. This report examines the causes of women's underrepresentation in leadership roles in business, politics, and education and suggests what we can do to change the status quo. Retrieved from https://www.aauw.org/research/barriers-and-bias/

Comprehensive Assessment of Leadership for Learning (CALL) Assessment. CALL measures key practices across the district that impact school leadership.
Download various papers that CALL researchers have written. Retrieved from https://www.leadershipforlearning.org/research.

Institute for Intercultural Communication. 2014.
Retrieved from https://intercultural.org/intercultural-training-and-assessment-tools/
Provides a list of selected intercultural training and assessment tool.

Kozai Group. The global competencies inventory (GCI). Retrieved from http://www.kozaigroup.com/global-competencies-inventory-gci/
Global Competencies Inventory measures three facets of intercultural adaptability in identifying personal characteristics related to successful performance in contexts where cultural norms and behaviors vary from one's own. This tool is generally used for purposes such as professional development, team building and succession planning.

Leadership Assessment Tool Inventory - Assess Your Skills. Retrieved from
http://www.kellogg.northwestern.edu/faculty/uzzi/htm/teaching-leadership.htm
These exercises assess ability to apply critical management skills to identify and solve key organizational problems.
Leadership and Management Development Strategy. Retrieved from http://www.exec.gov.nl.ca/exec/hrs/forms/Peer_Assessment_Form2_Forms_and_Applications.pdf
Developed to endorse learning and development opportunities to strengthen the leadership and management capacity of the Newfoundland and Labrador Public Service.

Najafi Global Mindset Institute. Global mindset inventory's three capitals.
Retrieved from https://thunderbird.asu.edu/faculty-and-research/global-mindset-inventory
The Global Mindset Inventory is an assessment tool for identifying one's capacity to lead and

influence individuals and companies in a global context, particularly those who are from a different culture.

Northouse Authentic Leadership Self-Assessment Questionnaire. Retrieved from
http://people.uncw.edu/nottinghamj/documents/slides6/Northouse6e%20Ch11%20Authentic%20Survey.pdf
This questionnaire contains items about different dimensions of authentic leadership.

Office of Personnel Management Assessment & Evaluation LEADERSHIP ASSESSMENTS
Retrieved from https://www.opm.gov/services-for-agencies/assessment-evaluation/leadership-assessments/
A suite of leadership tools that enhance self-awareness by measuring leadership effectiveness from multiple approaches.

Pew Research Center. 2015
Women and Leadership: Public Says Women are Equally Qualified, but Barriers Persist
Retrieved from http://www.pewsocialtrends.org/2015/01/14/women-and-leadership/

Via Institute on Character. Do you know your 24 character strengths? Retrieved from http://www.viacharacter.org/www/the-survey
The VIA survey was created to help individuals identify the make-up of their character strengths that are classified under six virtue categories. The survey can be taken online and is free of charge.

Appendix C

Suggestions for Workshop Activities to Enrich the Book Reading Experience as Stand-Alone Activities or as Part of a Leadership Course

1. ACTIVITY: LEADERS YOU ADMIRE.

Objective: To seek leadership characteristics through personal experience

Activity Description: Divide the group into small groups. Ask participants to share a story about the best or most influential leader they have read about in the book. After each story, identify leadership characteristics by asking the question: "What was it that made this person such an effective leader?" Then as a group, identify the traits that all the leaders seemed to share.

Check out: http://www.workshopexercises.com

2. ACTIVITY: STAND BY YOUR QUOTE.

Objective: To introduce leadership discussion and awareness

Activity Description: Place thoughtful leadership quotes from the women au- thors on the walls, making sure the print is readable. Ask the participants to walk around the room reading each of the quotes. Then have them stand by one quote that resonates well with their personal views on what makes a good leader (there can be more than one person standing by a quote). When all participants have se- lected a quote, have each explain to the group why her chosen quote is important to them--share a leadership insight.

Check out: http://www.workshopexercises.com

3. ACTIVITY: CHARACTER STRENGTHS.

Objective: To learn your character strengths

Activity Description: Great leaders have identified and clarified their core work- ing values. They understand how each of their core values translates into leadership behavior. Take the VIA survey to know your character strengths. Which character strengths do you share with any of the 3 or 4 women leaders? Are these character strengths unique to Filipino culture? Or to American culture?

Check out: https://www.viacharacter.org/survey/account/register

4. ACTIVITY: LEADERSHIP TIPS.

Objective: To find ways to strengthen leadership ability

Activity Description: Choose 2-3 chapters from the book. Compare and contrast the leadership story and the leadership tips and their implications for your own leadership experience. Make a list of intentional simple, on-the-job self-improvement strategies. For example, list ways of building meaningful work relationships. List ways of motivating others.

5. ACTIVITY: THIS I BELIEVE ESSAY.

Objective: To describe the core values that guide your daily lives

Activity Description: Follow the instructions for submitting an essay to 'This I Believe'. http://thisibelieve.org/guidelines/ Write and submit your own statement of personal belief. Reflect how you approach new challenges through your interpretation of the individual chapter readings.

Variation: Choose one of the women leaders and write a "This I Believe" essay from the woman's perspective--pretend you are that woman writing the essay. You may interview the author if possible.

6. ACTIVITY: LEADERSHIP THEORY AND PRACTICE.

Objective: To define your own leadership theory and practice

Activity Description: From two or more of the chapters, share which leadership theory or practice you found most valid to your work-life and explain why. If none of the theories or explanations spoke to your personal experience, feel free to challenge the theory and propose your own explanation.

7. ACTIVITY: REFLECTED BEST SELF.

Objective: To compose a portrait of you when you are at your best.

Activity Description: (1) Solicit feedback about your best-self from others—classmates, work or community service colleagues, clients, personal friends, mentors, family members. Give them at least 2 weeks to respond. (2) While wait- ing for their responses, you should engage in a deep personal reflection about the times when you were at your best, write three short stories that stand out as times when you were at your best, then identify patterns or commonalities that arise across those stories. (3) Review your best-self feedback from others and look for themes. (4) Revise the portrait of who you are at your best, incor- porating feedback from others with your own reflections. Your revised portrait should be a written description of the essence of your best-self. What are your key insights? What are the action implications for you, as you think about a) be- ing at your best more often, and b) making your best-self even better? Which of the women authors is most like your best self?

Check out: http://positiveorgs.bus.umich.edu/?s=reflected+best+self
Or
http://faculty.som.yale.edu/amywrzesniewski/documents/ReflectedBestSelfExerciseIntroduction2014Careers_000.pdf

Appendix D
FWN Award Categories

Behind the Scenes Leaders

This award category recognizes Filipina women who may not have the big title or corner office, but is a driving force behind the success of a social cause or life issue, a community organization's project or initiative; or her employer's organizational business unit or department. Someone who has gone beyond the call of duty to devote time, energy, and resources to advocate for those who need a voice, or support the organization she represents or works for.

Builders

Builders have demonstrated exceptional business impact at a large workplace environment; displaying deep passion for a cause through collaborative initiatives or alliances with nonprofit organizations on behalf of her own organization; demonstrates high potential and skill with measurable results at a government agency, or organization in the public and private sectors. "Buildership" is about building better organizations, leading broken organizations to adjust, repair, and re-align.

Continuing Influential

The Most Influential Filipina Women in the World™ Award may be received up to three times. Remarkable women were selected for the second time for continuing to be influential in their field, workplace and community. When selected for the third time in the future, awardee will then be inducted into the FWN "Always Influential" Hall of Fame.

Emerging Leaders

This award category recognizes Filipina women below age 35 who are making their mark in a leadership role, are on the pathway to principalship and building capacity across a system. Emerging Leaders have powerful mindsets and skill sets that drive achievement for their organizations.

Founders and Pioneers

This award honors Filipina women in their capacities as the chief executive, president, executive director or founder of a company, community organization, non-profit, or business venture that they helped start, build or significantly grow. This award category is for the trailblazers who have marshaled resources and applied innovative practices, processes and/or technologies in a new and groundbreaking way to address a significant business or organizational opportunity.

Innovators and Thought Leaders

This award recognizes women who have broken new ground in the global workplace, have delivered new and unique applications of emerging technology transforming the way people think, in the fields of sports, literature, the arts and pop culture, or have improved the lives of others by helping develop a product or service in the fieldsof science, technology, engineering, arts, or mathematics. This award category is also for someone who have either launched a new enterprise, a learning function, or completely overhauled an existing development or community initiative that has sparked a following.

Keepers of the Flame

Sustaining Pinay Power. As the excitement dies down and reality sets in, many will drop out and others will pick up the torch. The Keepers of the Flame are the caretakers, ensuring that the Pinay Power Vision is kept alive.

Nicole

This award honors Filipina women whose words, actions, and activism, inspire others to act and revolutionize society's way of understanding traditional beliefs and customs thus leaving behind a Filipino global imprint. "Nicole," who sparked an international dialogue about women's rights, national sovereignty, and international law, as she steadfastly pursued justice against her rapists, inspires this category.

Policymakers and Visionaries

This award recognizes Filipina women leaders who have demonstrated exceptional acumen combined with a forward-looking vision in the development or influencing of policies, campaigns or laws that impact business, industry, and society. Leaders who enrich the lives, careers and businesses of others; someone who shares the benefits of their wealth, experience, and knowledge; actions that significantly change how we think and live.

Biographies

MARIA A. BEEBE, PH.D.
EDITOR
🦎

INTRODUCTION
SYNTHESIS

Global 🦎 Katipunera 🦎 Educator

Maria A. Beebe, Ph.D. is an applied sociolinguist whose research interests include critical discourse analysis, women's leadership, and information communication technologies (ICT) for development. She has an M.A. in Anthropology and Ph.D. in Education from Stanford University. Maria co-edited DISRUPT 1.0. Filipina Women: Loud. Proud. Leading without a Doubt and DISRUPT 2.0. Filipina Women: Daring to Lead. She is the author of The Leadership Repertoire of Select Filipina Women in the Diaspora and Implications for Theorizing Leadership in Theorizing Women & Leadership: New Insights & Contributions from Multiple Perspectives (Storberg-Walker & Haber-Curran, 2017). Maria co-edited AfricaDotEdu to share lessons learned about the use of ICT for creating networks among universities in Africa. Maria has over 20 years of experience in international development, higher education, and the use of the Internet for teaching and learning in Afghanistan, Ethiopia, Liberia, Nigeria, South Africa, Tanzania, Uganda, and the Philippines. Maria has lived and worked in South Africa, Liberia, Philippines, Sudan, and Afghanistan. Maria had a six-week Fulbright specialist teaching and research award on discourse analysis and leadership at the Asian Institute of Management. Together with personnel from TechNation, Maria founded TechWomen.Asia. Maria created the PVO Global Networks to facilitate collaborations by global citizens and organizations for a sustainable world.

ANGELICA BERRIE

PREFACE: FILIPINA POWER

Angelica Berrie is President of The Russell Berrie Foundation, which has made transformational gifts to establish the Naomi Berrie Diabetes Center at Columbia University in New York, the Russ Berrie Nanotechnology Institute at the Technion in Israel, and the Pope John Paul II Center for Inter-Religious Studies at St. Thomas Aquinas University of the Angelicum in Rome. After the death of her husband, New Jersey sales entrepreneur, Russ Berrie, Angelica became Vice-Chair and CEO of Russ Berrie & Co., a global gift company known for its teddy bears and RUSS Trolls. She is currently Board Chair of the Center for Inter-Religious Understanding; the Shalom Hartman Institute North America (a center for pluralistic Jewish learning in Jerusalem); Co-President of American Friends of Ofanim (a nonprofit organization in Israel whose mission is to deliver high-quality supplemental education to children in the periphery using mobile classrooms); a member and past Co-Chair of the Jewish Funders Network. With her brother Lorenzo Urra, Angelica co-founded Global Nomad, an experiential travel design company based in Hong Kong. She co-authored a book on philanthropy: "*A Passion for Giving: Tools and Inspiration for Creating a Charitable Foundation,*" with wealth adviser Peter Klein.

MARILY MONDEJAR

MARILY: RISING

Fearless Leader 🌺 Grassroots Organizer 🌺 Community Advocate

Marily Mondejar has parlayed her success as a business leader and image consultant into founding the successful non-profit, non-partisan advocacy organization, the Filipina Women's Network (FWN). FWN has members in 28 countries and seeks to increase the influence of Filipina women as leaders and policymakers in the private and public sectors. Mondejar has steered the organization to a leading position in the Filipina women community worldwide. Ms. Mondejar's campaign to re-shape the Filipina image grew out her necessity to elevate the status of Filipina women. In 2001, an internet search for the word Filipina returned millions of hits, including "mail-order brides, sluts, exotic, sexy and submissive wives." Her plan was to highlight the leadership roles and economic contributions of Filipina women in corporate America, small business, public service, and the government.

As an executive coach and management consultant, she has provided counsel to the senior leadership of prestigious organizations. Ms. Mondejar is recognized for the Image 360®-degree assessment questionnaire, a method for measuring executive image performance and corporate reputation. She has delivered business, career, and image presentations in a variety of formats and has reached over 10,000 participants internationally. A select list of international and trade publications that have quoted Mondejar include *The Chicago Tribune, Dallas Morning News, AdWeek, Self, Allure, Working Woman, Black Enterprise, Academy of General Dentistry's AGD Impact, El Norte* (Mexico), *Cintermex Magazine* (Mexico), *Momentum* (magazine for Mercedes Benz owners), and various TV, radio and publications in the US, Philippines, Canada, and the UK.

Ms. Mondejar balances her professional life with advocating for other women in the business arena and serves on multiple boards engaged in public service, community, philanthropic, and professional development. She has been appointed to commissions and task forces by San Francisco Mayors Willie Brown, Gavin Newsom, and Edwin Lee.

A resident of San Francisco, she has raised two wonderful sons as a single mother and is a proud grandmother of three boys and adores her new great-granddaughter.

About the Contributing Authors

MYLENE ROMUALDEZ ABIVA

FILIPINA CHAMPION OF THE GEEKS

Educator 🏃 Positive 🏃 SuperWoman

Mylene Abiva is currently the President and CEO of FELTA Multi-Media Inc., a 50 year-old company that provides innovative instructional materials and educational devices for school technology. FELTA has been the Education Solution Provider of INTEL Education since 2012. Mylene occupies a throne in the Seat of Knowledge. She has been a president of the Philippine Marketing Association (2009), a Certified Professional Marketer, an Organizer of the Philippine Robotics Olympiad, an Ernst and Young Entrepreneur of the Year Philippines (2009), an ASEAN Business Leader in the Woman Category (2014), an ASEAN Woman Entrepreneur (2015), one of the 100 Most Influential Filipina Women in the World (2016), and an ASIA CEO Most Innovative Company (2016). Mylene has been a GO NEGOSYO Pioneer Mentor since 2005 for her Expertise in Marketing. She is a mother, a model entrepreneur, a mountain climber, and a master in multi-tasking. She is powerful, relevant, graceful, instinctive, and compassionate.

CHRISTINE AMOUR-LEVAR

FINDING YOUR PROFESSION OF THE HEART

Positive 🏃 Honest 🏃 Determined

Of French, Swiss, and Filipino descent, Christine Amour-Levar is a social entrepreneur, environmental advocate, marketing consultant, and author who passionately believes in women's leadership and empowerment. She grew up in Manila, Paris, and Tokyo. Christine lives with her husband and their four children in Singapore. After graduating from Sophia University in Tokyo, she embarked on a fulfilling career that took her across Europe, Asia, North and South America for brands such as Nike, McCann-Erickson, Philippe Starck, and her own Brazilian fashion retail business, Beijaflor. After selling her retail business in 2010, she wrote the motivational guide, *The Smart Girl's Handbook to Being Mummylicious*, published in May 2012. Today, Christine is the CMO of iRace Media, one of Asia's leading horse racing publishing and media companies. She also heads Marketing and Communications at Temasek Management Services, a wholly-owned subsidiary of Singapore's sovereign wealth fund, Temasek Holdings. In 2012, she co-founded Women on A Mission, the as a non-profit organization, and since 2012, she has led teams on challenging expeditions to the Arctic, the Antarctic, the Middle East, Africa, and the Himalayas to raise awareness and funds for women survivors of war and to empower and support women who have been subjected to violence and abuse. An avid believer in women as gamechangers she brings unique knowledge and solutions to move the needle on sustainability. Christine also set up #HERplanetearth in 2017, a global women's advocacy movement that promotes gender equality and the integrity of the environment.

Maria Victoria E. Añonuevo

Success Amidst Adversities
A Life Fulfilled

A significant part of Ma. Victoria E. Añonuevo's (Marivic) career was with Ayala Corporation and Ayala Land, Inc. where she rose from the ranks as Manager to Senior Vice President. Other senior positions she had with Ayala include: Member of the Management Committee, President and Group Head of Ayala Malls Group, Head of the Residential Business Group, Sales, and Marketing Group, and head of the Laguna Technopark, Inc., and Ayala Hotels, Inc. She was also President of the Philippine Marketing Association and the Marketing Opinion and Research Society. After retiring from Ayala Land, Marivic was appointed the Managing Director and CEO of the Millennium Challenge Account-Philippines, the local accountable entity of the Millennium Challenge Corporation, a United States foreign assistance agency established by the US Congress for poverty alleviation. Marivic provided oversight for a five-year $434m grant that funded community-based projects for the poorest of the poor municipalities in the Philippines. She worked as Senior Advisor to companies in various industries and a partner of CEO Advisors, Inc., a management advisory firm composed of current and former CEOs that helps organizations and enterprises address their business needs. She is currently Chairman and President, Mejora Ferro Corporation. Marivic is a BSBA and MBA graduate of the University of the Philippines and of the Program for Management Development of the Harvard Business School.

Cynthia Barker

Building My Political Backbone
Ethical ☸ Diplomatic ☸ Transformational

Cynthia Barker is best known as the first Filipino elected as a Borough Councillor in the United Kingdom. Her professional career as a businesswoman and a trailblazer in the recruitment, immigration, and healthcare training fields; eventually led to a political career. In 2016, Cynthia received a British Community Honours Award, endorsed by Her Majesty The Queen, in recognition of her outstanding voluntary contributions to British society, including promoting integration and building social cohesion through her community work and leadership. In 2017, she was recognized as one of the Top 100 Most Influential Filipina Women (FWN100™). She has a Councillor position in two local authorities and has a number of board roles as a Trustee at the Elstree and Borehamwood Museum, a trustee for Filipina Women's Association UK (FWA), a trustee at 60 Plus Club UK, and is the School Governor for Saint Nicholas School. She is President of the Rotary Club Elstree and Borehamwood.

JOJI ILAGAN BIAN

DREAMING BIG, GIVING THE BEST

Game Changer ❧ Gritty ❧ Chic

Hers is a life devoted to encouraging the potential of young people and developing human resources that have helped made Mindanao and Davao City a destination that can compete with the rest of the Philippines, if not, the world. *"My life is a tapestry of different weaves and colors symbolizing the very diverse experiences that I have: a wife and mother, an educator, a business leader, and a community worker,"* she said. Moreover, these experiences gave her a comprehensive perspective and understanding of the complexities of life. She recalls the early years were intense. Fresh from the University of the Philippines with a diploma in Hotel and Restaurant Management, she surveyed what services the city needs and found a niche in developing human resources in the hospitality and tourism sector. Her tenacity paid off, and as the economic conditions improved, she was able to train professional and highly skilled individuals for the hospitality and tourism industry. "I always knew that I made the right choice even at a very young age. I never run away from challenges. We have to fight for our dreams if we want them to come true. I meet them head-on and always emerge a winner," she said. And, she is indeed a winner.

HON. THELMA B. BOAC

FILIPINA: LEAVE FOOTPRINTS THAT LAST

Educator ❧ Professional Coach / Mentor ❧ Community Leader

Thelma was born in the province of Bohol, Philippines. She came to America at the age of ten and lived with her adoptive parents in Grover Beach, California. Her adoptive father, a World War II veteran, was one of the original *manongs* who immigrated to America in the 1920's. Thelma's adoptive mother, her biological aunt, came to America as a young war widow. Both parents were active in community affairs. Thelma received her BA degree from San Francisco State University and MA degree in Educational Leadership from San Jose State University. Thelma retired after a 37-year career in education. She continued her dedication to education at San Jose State University and The National Hispanic University, where she was an adjunct professor and supervised and trained graduate students entering the teaching profession. Thelma currently is a professional expert coach to newly promoted principals and school administrators for the Santa Clara County Office of Education. Thelma is seeking re-election after a successful four-year term on the Berryessa Union School District Governing Board of Trustees. She holds the distinction of being the first Filipina to be elected and the only female serving on the Board of Trustees, thus expanding her influence and commitment to youth and community. A sought-after educator and community leader, Thelma has been the recipient of many awards. She has been recognized by State legislative leaders and by various community organizations for her dedication to public service.

CRISTINA CALLAGUIAN

THE ROAD TO MY *IKIGAI*

Self-motivated 🎎 *Optimistic* 🎎 *Cause Motivated*

Cristina Calaguian is Founder and Managing Director of Dagaz HR Consultancy and Recruitment Company FZ Llc. She is a graduate of the University of Santo Tomas with a BA in Economics. Cristina has over 28 years of professional experience in the United Arab Emirates (UAE) and the Philippines. She initially established her reputation in the Philippines where she was a successful licensed stockbroker and branch manager for 11 years. After moving to UAE in 2003, she established DAGAZ, a Gulf-wide recruitment company that she manages as a social enterprise. DAGAZ focus is on supporting and empowering people with disability and helping them find work through Developmental Coaching. She is also a Certified Consultant of the internationally recognized Harrison Assessment tool and process. She is currently a member of the Board of Trustees and President of the Alumni Association of the Ateneo Leadership and Social Entrepreneurship program in the UAE. Cristina enjoys volunteer work and is a motivational speaker for Filipina workers. Cristina discusses cultural awareness as part of the post arrival orientation of the Philippine Overseas Labor Office in Dubai. She also discusses career management for visually impaired members of the UAE community. Cristina is a passionate advocate for self-management and personal development necessary to unleash an individual's potential and achieve career successes. Cristina is proud to be recognized as one of the GLOBAL FWN100™ GLOBAL 2017 Most Influential Filipinas Globally and Illustrado's 100 Most Influential Filipino in the Gulf.

MARIA ROSA 'BING' NIEVA CARRION, PH.D.

WHAT MAKES AN EFFECTIVE LEADER

Vibrant 🎎 *Committed* 🎎 *Happy*

During the last 17 years, Maria Rosa 'Bing' Nieva Carrion created, authored, and published thirty-five books. created, authored, and published thirty-five books. These books define who she is and what she believes in. She has stated that she views the books as "Embracing humanity by creating life-defining legacy books." The success of each book represents a milestone of her life's journey. She is the biographer of the former President Gloria Macapagal Arroyo, the late Jaime Cardinal Sin, and Senator Loren Legarda. In 2008, San Francisco California Mayor Gavin Newsom honored her at a reception at the San Francisco California Main Library where she donated copies of all the books she has authored to the City. In 2017, three friends and Bing, established My-Cord Philippines to promote mental health. She is CEO. The objective of My-Cord is to facilitate access by all Filipinos to counseling to improve their lives. In May 2018, she was honored with a Honorary Doctorate degree for public administration by the National Defense College in partnership with the Bethany Evangelical School of Theology. Bing considers being a mother and best friend to her children Aristoncito and Aryssa Maria and being a nurturing grandmother to her grandchildren Aidan Matthew, Adam Isaiah, and Alon as her most significant achievement.

WILMA 'AMY' EISMA

MOVING BEYOND POWER AND POSITION
Feisty 🦎 *Intense* 🦎 *Focused*

Lawyer Amy T. Eisma was born, bred, and raised in Olongapo City. From 1993 to 1998, she served as volunteer on the staff of the Subic Bay Metropolitan Authority (SBMA) Founding Chairman Richard Gordon. She then moved to the private sector and worked with a multi-national company as corporate, government, and regulatory affairs, community and farmer relations, and diversity and inclusion manager for 15 years. She succeeded in organizing 30 farmers' cooperatives and developed and implemented farmers' projects and programs, which won prestigious international awards including the Stevie Award, the International Business Award, and the Corporate Social Responsibility (CSR) World Leader Award. In 2017, Amy came full circle from being a Subic volunteer to being appointed by Philippine President Durterte as SBMA's Administrator and CEO, and eventually as Chair and Administrator. By the end of 2017, under Amy's leadership, SBMA's net income increased by 34 percent and several Freeport locators or SBMA clients undertook expansion projects that increased their investments by 203 percent. She has pushed a ten-point agenda consisting of policy reforms and good governance, sustainable development, safety and security, community engagement, locator service excellence, Subic Freeport development as gateway, Foreign Direct Investments (FDIs), and Micro, Small and Medium Enterprises (MSMEs), tourism as a star industry, infrastructure-building, and Freeport expansion.

MILA EUSTAQUIO-SYME

SUCCESS AMIDST ADVERSITIES
YES FILIPINAS CAN

Her Worship, her title as a Justice of the Peace, Mila Eustaquio-Syme is a graduate of College of the Holy Spirit, Maryknoll, and University of the Philippines. She completed an MBA from York University in Toronto. In 1982, she was elected President of the UP Alumni Association in Toronto. She noted with sadness, how degrees and experiences from developing countries were unrecognized. She was later elected Director of the Canadian Ethnocultural Council, an umbrella organization of more than 50 ethnic groups and was its first Chairperson of the Women's Committee. In her various capacities, she has lobbied and advocated for rights of immigrant and minority women, with attention to issues of stereotyping, mail order brides, violence against women, abuse against foreign domestics, racism, employment equity, and the lack of recognition for degrees from non-Canadian universities. In 1994, she was appointed a Member of the Immigration and Refugee Board of Canada, a position similar to an Immigration Judge. In this role, she has made determinations on refugee claims. In 2005, she was appointed Justice of the Peace for the Province of Ontario where she presides over the Bail Courts, offenses under the Highway Traffic Act, the Dog Owner's Liability Act, the Environment Act, the Fisheries Act, and Municipal By-laws, among others. She is a lover of dogs, and was heartbroken when she had to sentence a dog to death.

JANETTE NELLIE GO-CHIU

INNOVATOR BY HAPPENSTANCE
Devoted 兔 Passionate 兔 Innovative

Janette Nellie Chiu holds various positions in the field of business. She is president of GCH Holdings, Inc., the umbrella company of GCH Group of Companies with ventures in food, agriculture, and real estate. She also heads two foundations. GCH Foundation focuses on helping build healthy communities by focusing on health and nutrition projects and the Crocolandia Foundation Inc., that manages Crocolandia Nature Park and is involved in the preservation and conservation of Philippine wildlife and encouraging children to love and protect the environment. Nellie was president of Zonta Club of Cebu I from 2014 to 2016. Under her leadership, the Club implemented new ways to strengthen the advocacies on women and child protection, livelihood, and education. Nellie graduated with a degree in Business Administration from the University of San Carlos in Cebu City. In 2016, the USC Alumni Association recognized her with the Semper Fidelis Award for *Devotio* for her dedication to serving the community. During the same year, she was awarded one of the 100 Most Influential Filipina Women in the World by the Filipina Women's Network. By devotion, passion, and innovation, she has brought success to her personal, business, and community life.

ANNABELLE MISA HEFTI

STEPPING OVER *STOLPERSTEINE*
Invested 兔 Connector 兔 Traveler

Anny was born in Cebu, but she has spent most of her life away from Cebu. At the age of 16 years, she started her studies at the University of the Philippines in Diliman. Since then, Cebu has remained a transient destination. Work and study brought her to three continents. Anny now lives in Switzerland. Her work as a Counseling Psychologist made Anny aware of the significance of empowerment to many women's issues. When Anny served as Director of a migrant's center, *Zentrum 5*, in Bern, she saw the struggles of refugees, migrants, and the undocumented from all over the world. She was a member of the Federation of Swiss Psychologists (FSP), represented migrants at the Federal Commission for Equality between Men and Women, and was involved with the Commission for Adult Education Canton Bern. Anny is a founding member of two Europe-wide Filipino organizations; the Babaylan, Philippine Women's Network in Europe and the European Network of Filipinos in Diaspora (ENFID). Recently, Anny produced a book, *Bending Without Breaking*, a compilation of thirteen narratives by Filipina migrants in Switzerland of their migration and resilience.

CATHY SALCEDA ILETO

FILIPINA *DELIKADESA* = WAVES OF POSITIVE CHANGE

Agile ❦ *Advocate* ❦ *Unifier*

Cathy is passionate about advocating for women's empowerment and her chapter is about that journey from becoming empowered to empowering others. She believes we have the power to create lasting change and she finds fulfillment in watching women grow and thrive into leadership positions through the programs she has championed throughout her career. In 2015, she was honored with the FWN Builder award for demonstrating exceptional business impact in a large workplace environment. She has displayed a deep passion for a cause through collaborative initiatives or alliances with non-profit organizations on behalf of her own organization. Cathy was part of the original team that established the IT and Business Process Association of the Philippines (IBPAP); the enabling association for the information technology and business process management (IT-BPM) industry in the Philippines. She currently serves as its Vice Chairperson and heads the Technical Working Group on Country Competitiveness tasked with driving country and industry promotion. She is also the Asia Pacific Senior Director for Marketing, Communications, and Public Relations at Sutherland. Aside from being an integral member of the leadership team, she plays a strategic role in the organization by ensuring the success of Sutherland's unique provincial model in the Philippines.

JENNIFER MARIE B. JOSÉ, M.D.

THE WOMAN'S ROOM

Innovative ❦ *Thought Leader* ❦ *Passionate*

In March 2016, Dr. Jennifer Marie B. José received the Trailblazer Award from Da Vinci Surgical System for the outstanding achievement of being the first Filipino surgeon in the Philippines to perform 100 robotic surgeries. She was honored as one of the robotic surgeons world-wide recognized by Intuitive Surgical Inc. for their proficiency in robotics surgery. She performs robotic assisted hysterectomy, myomectomy, cystectomy, adhesiolysis, and urogynecology procedures such as sacrocolpopexy for suspensions and incontinence procedures. Dr. José is the first from the ASEAN countries to perform Robotics Sacrocolpopexy and done the procedure the most number of times. Dr. José is Vice-President Aesthetic Gynecologic Society of the Philippines. She has been recognized for her work in Training Cosmetic, Vaginal Surgery and Rejuvenation (Istanbul, Turkey) and is a Fellow of European Society of Aesthetic Gynecology, Head of the Urogynecology and Incontinence Center and Section Head, Urogynecology and Minimally Invasive Gynecologic Surgery at the Makati Medical Center. Dr. José is also Head of the Urogynecology, Comprehensive Pelvic Floor Center and Head of Robotics Gynecology at St. Luke's Manila. Dr. José is presently an International proctor of the Intuitive Surgical; the maker of the da Vinci Surgical System in robotic surgery and has been teaching robotic surgery in other countries, including Vietnam and Korea.

Leah L. Laxamana

Journey to Being Present: Making Friends with Fear and Uncertainty

Brave 🌀 Liminalist 🌀 Eternal Optimist

Leah is dedicated to promoting equity and empowering global communities. She has over a decade of cross-sector and international experience in social impact work helping organizations foster community engagement and pilot new initiatives. Most recently, Leah was at Twitter overseeing the company's @NeighborNest technology learning center for the community and implementing philanthropic initiatives. She previously worked with the Robert Wood Johnson Foundation as a National Urban Fellow, served as a volunteer with the Peace Corps in Honduras and worked with Korn/Ferry International. Leah is currently involved with various community programs advocating for the most vulnerable residents of San Francisco's Tenderloin and other disadvantaged neighborhoods. Leah received her BA in Social Sciences and Minor in Hispanic Studies from Ateneo de Manila University and Master of Public Administration from Baruch College of the City University of New York. She is a life-long learner and lover of languages, dance, and capoeira.

Juslyn C. Manalo

If at First You Don't Succeed

Compassionate 🌀 Spiritual 🌀 Pinay

Juslyn Cabrera Manalo is currently the Mayor of Daly City, CA and was elected as the first Filipina councilmember in November 2016 and appointed Vice Mayor in December 2016. She was the first Filipina in these roles in a city that is 30 percent Filipino. Juslyn was born in San Francisco, CA and raised in Daly City. In addition to being Mayor, she works for Forest City, a company that creates mixed-used developments nation-wide. Previously Juslyn worked in the non-for-profit sector serving the Filipino World War II Veterans and advocated for equity and justice for elders. She also managed the Bill Sorro Housing Program and assisted in its creation. Both her father and mother are Filipinos. Her mother Josefina Manalo immigrated to the U.S. in 1973, and her father immigrated in 1980. Juslyn received her undergraduate degree in Asian American Studies with a minor in Women Studies. Her graduate degree is in Public Administration from the School of Public Affairs and Civic Engagement at San Francisco State University. Juslyn is a board member to the following organizations: Senior Disability Action, Bay Area Waters Conservation Agency, South of Market Business Association, Skyline College President's Council, and the City/County Association of Governments of San Mateo County.

ANA BEL MAYO

FIVE DOLLARS IN MY POCKET

Simple ❊ Authentic ❊ Italiana

Ana Bel Mayo has lived for 28 years in Inzago, Milan, Italy. She is active in several associations that support the local Filipino communities as well as the broader community. Her passion for volunteering blossomed in 2009 after she participated in the Migrant Associations and Philippine Institutions for Development (MAPID) training course. This course had been organized by the ISMU Foundation, promoted by the Scalabrini Migration Center, and co-funded by the European Commission. The project promoted the capacity-building of the Filipino associations in Italy and Spain as well as the Philippines, while encouraging their transnational collaboration. The goal was to strengthen their role as co-development agents between Europe and South-East Asia. The Philippine consulate of Milan and the municipality of Inzago have given Ana Bel awards for her work with migrants. She was named as one of the 100 Most Influential Filipinas in 2016. Today Ana Bel is the councillor and treasurer of the association and president of the World Cities of the World Adda colors, and a member of the Council of Volunteers of the City of Inzago. Ana Bel is married to an Italian, Giovanni Riva who adopted her children and who took on the responsibility of securing their future. With her husband's help, Ana Bel continues to enjoy her advocacy work.

SANDY SANCHEZ MONTANO

INTENSITY 7

Compassionate ❊ Driven ❊ God-loving

Sandy has always exhibited quiet and gentle strength. Her early childhood was uneventful. She grew up in a farming province in the north of Luzon in the Philippines. She loved life and embraced everything that it had to offer. Sandy decided to study Nursing. Her student days in Baguio became a life changer for her when in July 1990, at 18 years old, she experienced one of the most devastating catastrophes ever to visit the Philippines. An intensity 7.7 quake struck. She was buried in the rubble for days. Sheer willpower pulled her through, and just as her hope was fading, she was rescued. This was a turning point. While working on her diploma in Nursing, she devoted her spare time to volunteering in community outreach programs and to teaching life-saving skills. She started a family and moved to the U.S. with the thought that this would be the course of her life. Her soul would not keep quiet though. She felt there was something she needed to do, having survived the 1990 quake. She and her family returned to the Philippines to answer her calling. Her passion for educating people to save lives is reflected by founding a social enterprise called Community Health Education Emergency Rescue Services (CHEERS). She continues to nurture, innovate, and work towards a resilient and sustainable community. Her work has been recognized both locally and internationally.

Rebecca Murry

Redefining Pathways

Resilient ❧ Patient ❧ Hard-working

Rebecca Murry, an architect for 20 years, shifted to teaching mathematics using a constructivist-based instructional approach. She believes students need to be encouraged to be curious not told what to think. Young mathematicians build understanding through peer discourse, making conjectures and generalizations, and reflecting on misconceptions. As a Math Coach at the United Nations International School, she implements STEAM/Problem-based courses and innovative math curriculum design. She has made international school presentations and conducted webinars in New York, Brazil, Spain, and Denmark focused on Blended Learning, STEAM & Project-Based math applications. She has facilitated Primary Maths in Qatar with the Educational Collaborative of International Schools and Harvard University's Research Schools International. She is a book reviewer for the National Council of Teachers of Mathematics and recently co-authored a book about linear measurement systems. She was the recipient of one of the 2017 Global FWN's 100 Most Influential Filipina Awards. She has a Bachelor of Architecture degree from Pratt Institute and a Master of Science in Education for Special and General Education from the Bank Street College's Graduate School of Education.

Roxane Martin Negrillo

Moving Mountains

Compassionate ❧ Fair ❧ High Integrity

Roxane Martin Negrillo is a media practitioner with over 17 years of experience in the Philippines and the Middle East. She was a cum laude graduate of the University of Santo Tomas Faculty of Arts and Letters with a degree in Communication Arts. Through the years, she has received recognition as a female Filipina leader. Her awards include Asian Young Women Leadership Awardee (Dubai, UAE) in 2015 by the Asian Women Leadership Summit; Global Women Leadership Awardee (Mumbai, India) in 2016 by the World Women Leadership Congress; Marketing and Advertising Professional of the Year (Dubai, UAE) in 2016 by *The Filipino Times*; one of the 100 Most Influential Filipinos in the Gulf (Dubai, UAE) in 2017 by the *Illustrado* magazine; one of the 100 Most Influential Filipina Women in the World (Toronto, Canada) in 2017 by the Filipina Women's Network. Roxane is a mother of a wonderful boy named Marcus Lance, with whom she spends most of her personal time. She is currently attending the Ateneo School of Government Leadership and Social Entrepreneurship (LSE) program and is a volunteer lecturer for the Filipino Training and Development Program. She is also a resident judge at *The Filipino Times* annual awards that aim to honor outstanding Filipinos in the UAE.

JOANNE MICHELLE FERNANDEZ OCAMPO

The Dynamics of Defining Success and Failure

Spirit ❧ Mind ❧ Heart and Soul

Joanne Michelle is currently a Project Director in Public Health Informatics at Georgetown University, and is working on HIV-related projects with the D.C. Women's Interagency HIV Study, Department of Medicine, Division of Infectious Diseases, and the Office of the Senior Vice President for Research and Chief Technology Officer. She also holds a part-time position focused on applied public health research with the Norwegian Institute of Public Health where she is an Advisor at the Department of Zoonotic, Food and Waterborne Infections. In 2014, Miss Ocampo helped found and since then has led the Next Generation Global Health Security Network as its Inaugural Coordinator. In 2017, Miss Ocampo was recognized as received one of the GLOBAL FWN100™ 2017 leaders awarded by the Filipina Women's Network for her mentorship, leadership, and work in global health security and public health. Miss Ocampo holds a bachelor's degree in Biology from Eastern Connecticut State University, and a master's degree in Biohazardous Threat Agents and Emerging Infectious Diseases, and a professional certificate in Business Administration, both from Georgetown University.

GEORGITTA 'BENG' PIMENTEL PUYAT

Rising to the FWN Challenge

Volunteerism: A Life's Journey

Inspirational ❧ Altruistic ❧ Goal-oriented

Georgitta 'Beng' Puyat is a lifelong Volunteer with a commitment to service and advocacy. As a member of the Zonta Club of Makati for 32 years, she has initiated and nurtured projects that have affected generations of women and families. She has worked with the East Rembo Livelihood and Skills Training Center and the award-winning Psychological Center for Sexually Abused Children (ages 3-17) in Marillac Hills. She was elected Zonta International District 17 Governor for 2010-2012. She was also the President and Chairman of the UNIFEM Philippine National Committee, a Trustee of the Philippine Philharmonic Orchestra Society and Chairman/President of the Sigma Delta Phi Alumnae Association. She is the Co-Founder and Chairman of the Philippine Orchard Corporation, whose mission is to help marginalized farmers improve their economic status through the introduction of innovative products that promote quality and sustainability. She graduated from the University of the Philippines Diliman with an AB degree in Political Science and finished a Masters in Sociology. She enjoys being with her family, especially her three grandchildren, and traveling. She is an inspirational, result-oriented leader whose life experiences shaped and directed her desire to be a 'Volunteer' for Women's Issues. She recognizes that an organization is only as good as its leader, her goal is to be the best leader possible in her quiet way.

WAFA 'MARILYN' R. QASIMIEH PH.D.

AMBASSADOR OF PEACE AND HUMANITY
Truthful ❀ Influential ❀ Optimistic

Filipina humanitarian Dr. Marilyn "Wafa" Roscales Qasimieh is perhaps the most influential Filipina working in the Government of Dubai where she is a Senior Executive Cultural Consultant Islamic Affairs and Charitable Activities Department (IACAD). Wafa takes pride in having been named as Ambassador of Peace and Humanity for the United Arab Emirates (UAE) and as a Member of the Board of Directors and Deputy Minister for Finance of SPMUDA, the International Organization for Peace and Development at Trans-Mundi Pax Humanitas (Trans-world Humanitarian Peace). She is also regional Chairman of Middle East African Network of Filipinos in Diaspora (MEANFID), former Country Chairman for UAE of MEANFID, and former Chairperson of Filipino Club-Dubai. In 1984, she graduated with a Bachelor's in Science degree, major in Forestry from the West Visayas State University. She worked for several years with the Department of Environment and Natural Resources as a Forester before she moved to Dubai in 1986. She studied *Usool Al Deen* at the Preston University in Ajman, UAE. In 2014, she obtained her Ph.D. in Humanity. She then joined the Islamic Information Centre as their Librarian and Lecturer. After that, she worked at the Department of Islamic Affairs where she rose through the ranks. The Philippine Government honored her with two major awards; the Bagong Bayani for Community and Social Service (2011) and Banaag Award or Ray of Light Award (2010). She is married with one son.

SUSIE QUESADA

SISTERHOOD, DIALOGUE, AND IMPACT
Strong ❀ Dedicated ❀ Genuine

Susie Quesada is a third-generation owner and President of Ramar Foods International. As the leader in Filipino and Asian Food, Ramar Foods manufactures authentic high-quality tropical ice cream, eggrolls, and sausages that bring the flavor of the Philippines to supermarkets and restaurants in the United States. Susie believes that food brings people together to do great things. She was awarded one of the 100 Most Influential Filipina Women in the US in 2007 and now serves on the Board of the Filipina Women's Network (FWN). The mission of FWN is to support the next generation of Filipina women leaders. Susie wrote about her leadership journey in "Mommyla, Popsy, and Me: Leading by Example" in *DISRUPT 1.0. Filipina Women: Proud. Loud. Leading without a Doubt*. Susie holds a BA in Multicultural Literature and Education from the University of California at Berkeley. She started her career in public education. Susie is an Alumni of Harvard Business School's Owner President Management Program Class of 2018. Susie spends her free time reading, cooking, traveling with her husband, and playing adult co-ed soccer in the San Francisco Bay Area.

Anne Quintos

Butterflies in the Gut: Leading Outside Comfort Zones

Passionate 🎋 Non-conformist 🎋 Strong

Anne Quintos is the Managing Partner of PageJump Media and is responsible for promoting design, drive, and direction to its various cross-media projects. Through her leadership, PageJump has expanded from print publishing to video, digital, and events production. Since co-founding PageJump in 2014, the company has received prestigious awards for its content, such as a National Book Award from the National Book Development Board. Before returning to the Philippines to manage PageJump, she worked for one of Taiwan's largest consumer electronics companies for eight years. Anne graduated cum laude with a B.A. Mass Communications from St. Scholastica's College in Manila and took graduate studies in Technology Management from the University of the Philippines, Diliman. In 2018, she participated in the Creative Enterprise Programme by the British Council. Because of her advocacy, creativity, and entrepreneurial spirit, she received an Obra Award for Community Building in 2015 and an Emerging Leader award by the Filipina Women's Network in 2016.

Rowena Romulo

Nothing is Impossible: From Banker to Restaurateur

Passionate 🎋 Determined 🎋 Courageous

Rowena Romulo is the owner of Romulo Café, the first international outpost of a family-owned food business established in 2009 in Manila. The restaurant draws upon the family legacy of one of the Philippines' international diplomatic figures, Carlos P. Romulo and offers food lovers a taste of the Philippines in the heart of Kensington, London. Since it opened in March 2016, Rowena has put Filipino cuisine firmly on London's foodie map winning the Time Out Love London award for most loved restaurant in Kensington, received 5-star and top ratings from food bibles like Timeout and Square Meal. Romulo Café was included in Harden's and the Tatler Restaurant Guides in 2018. In May 2018, Romulo Café retained its crown as Timeout's Most Loved Restaurant in Kensington and was a runner-up for Most Loved Local Restaurant in London. Before devoting her work fulltime to Romulo Café, Rowena was an accomplished Senior Banker with over 30 years experience in the financial services industry having worked at Citibank and JP Morgan with international assignments in New York, Milan, and London. Her last financial business role was as Managing Director of a Global business. Rowena is a wonderful example that it is never too late to start a new career.

RACHEL U. SALINEL

PURPOSE, PASSION, AND PASS IT ON

Passionate ❧ Assertive ❧ God-loving

Rachel Salinel is a freelance broadcast journalist who reports on the lives of Overseas Filipinos in the UAE on The Filipino Channel of ABS-CBN. Rachel is the Managing Partner of the Filipino Excellence in the Middle East (FEME) Connect Directory which she co-founded in 2015 with colleagues from the Leadership and Social Entrepreneurship (LSE) program of the Ateneo School of Government held in Dubai. The directoryas one of the factors in her selection as one of the 100 Most Influential Filipina Women in the World in August 2016 in Cebu, Philippines. She won *The Filipino Times* 'Journalist of the Year' award in 2015 and was named one of the '100 Most Influential Filipinos in the Gulf' by Illustrado Magazine for the period 2015 to 2017. She started her career as a reporter with a Japanese TV network bureau in Manila. Rachel co-hosted the Magazine TV Program "Kaya Natin Ito" in 1991 which aired on Channel 13 in the Philippines. In Dubai, she was a freelance Senior News Presenter of TAG 91.1 FM from 2013 to 2017. Rachel co-hosted with her husband Art Los Banos the FEME radio talk show on Dubai Eye 103.8 FM from October 2010 to February 2013.

DINA DELA PAZ STALDER

BLOW. FALL. BOUNCE.

Loving Yet Tough

Dina Dela Paz Stalder is the President and CEO of the Stalder Group of Companies. She grew up in San Pablo, Laguna and her parents were simple farmers. She is proud that Stalder Group of Companies earned a blue-ribbon award from the Laguna Lake Development Authority as an environmentally responsible business. In addition to employment, the company provides housing for employees. Her humble beginnings have contributed to her success despite the challenges and obstacles she has faced in life. She now owns a manufacturing plant in the Philippines that produces products that are recognized in the United States, Asia, and Europe. She serves in leadership positions for several charity institutions to help the environment and Filipinos in need. She lives in Manila, Philippines with her three lovely children as a single mother.

Nikki Tang

No Way to Go but Up

Focused ❊ Committed ❊ Empowered

Nikki Tang is a globally recognized leader in the beauty and aesthetics industry. Nikki's companies, DMark Beauty and DermAsia, provide unique beauty solutions and are at the forefront of revolutionizing the field of medical aesthetics in the Philippines. Besides being identified as a "Beautypreneur," Nikki Tang has become a multi-awarded global executive. Her latest awards include being one of the Filipino Women Network's Global 100 in October 2017. This honor puts her among globally recognized Filipina leaders tasked to be catalysts and increase the number of Pinay leaders through femtorship or female mentorship. Last year, Nikki became a fellow of the Royal Institute of Beauty Care of Singapore, a recognition of her continuous investment in human capital. Her company DMark Beauty was a finalist for SME Company of the Year in the Asia CEO Awards held in October 2017. More recently, she received the prestigious Presidential Award from the Philippine Dermatological Society, an honor she sees as especially meaningful, since it came from her premier clients. Nikki Tang is also known as a champion of women empowerment. She believes that a self-confident and well-educated woman will reach greater heights and lead others to succeed in any endeavor they choose. This is Nikki Tang — an executive who leads by example.

Catherine Teh, M.D.

Turning Struggles into Strengths

Resilient ❊ Compassionate ❊ Doyenne

Dr. Catherine Teh is a leader and pioneer in the field of HepatoPancreatoBiliary (HPB) surgery in the Philippines. She has been an active member of the Asia Pacific HPB Association and International HPB Association since 2001 and a member of its scientific committee since 2013. She is a co-founder of the Philippine Association of HPB Surgeons (PAHPBS), serves as secretary of the organization, and led efforts for PAHBPBS to be recognized as a national chapter by the IHPBA in 2016. She is the only woman among the founding members and in the council of the International Laparoscopic Liver Surgery Society (ILLS) formed in 2016. She is a member of the expert panel of the American Society of Clinical Oncology where she has responsibility for the development of guidelines for the screening, early detection, and treatment of colorectal cancer. Since 2010, she has led the Network of Colorectal Cancer Multidisciplinary Teams in the Asia Pacific Region and has developed a database for patients with colorectal liver metastases. She finished the healthcare leadership management program at the Harvard Medical School in March 2018. Dr Teh is a graduate of the University of Santo Tomas College of Medicine and Surgery Class of 1993. She completed General Surgery Residency at the Chinese General Hospital and Medical Center in the Philippines and fellowships at the Queen's Medical Center and Kings Mills Medical Center in England, the National Cancer Center in Singapore, the Zhe zhiang University in China, the European Institute of Telesurgery in France, the University of Louis Pasteur in France, and the *Centre Hepatobiliare* at *Hopital Paul Brousse* in France, among others.

LUCILLE TENAZAS

A CLASS OF HER OWN
Analytical ❦ Intuitive ❦ Critical

Lucille Tenazas is a professor and graphic designer based in New York. She is the Associate Dean in the School of Art, Media and Technology (AMT) at Parsons School of Design. Lucille was the recipient of the AIGA Medal in 2013, the most prestigious in the field, awarded by the American Institute of Graphic Arts (AIGA). The award was for her lifetime contribution to design practice and outstanding leadership in design education. From 1996 to 1998, she was the National President of the AIGA and was awarded the National Design Award for Communication Design by the Cooper Hewitt, National Design Museum. For her contributions to design, then Mayor Willie Brown declared May 15, 1996 as Lucille Tenazas Day in San Francisco. As principal of Tenazas Design, she has worked on projects for the San Francisco Museum of Modern Art, Stanford University Art Museum, San Francisco International Airport (SFO), the National Endowment for the Arts, and the Princeton Architectural Press. Her work has received numerous design awards and has been featured in many publications and exhibitions both nationally and internationally, including a one-person exhibition at the San Francisco Museum of Modern Art. Her work has been included in surveys at the Cooper-Hewitt National Design in New York and the Centre Pompidou in Paris. She has lectured and taught in the US and abroad and served on panels and juries where she provided expertise and critical evaluation of current movements in architecture and design.Lucille graduated with a Bachelor of Fine Arts in Advertising from College of the Holy Spirit Manila (CHSM) and studied at the California College of the Arts (CCA) in San Francisco. She holds a Master in Fine Arts in Design from Cranbrook Academy of Art in Bloomfield Hills, Michigan.

LILY TORRES-SAMORANOS

A HYMN OF PRAISE TO FAILURE
Resilient ❦ Strong ❦ True Believer

Lily Torres-Samoranos works as an immigration attorney at the Asian Pacific Legal Outreach, a San Francisco non-profit organization that provides legal services to some of the most disfranchised and indigent. She has been outspoken in the media about the Muslim ban and the current immigration policies that devalue human beings who are seeking relief from persecution in their respective countries. She represents adults and children from all over the world in immigration court during their removal proceedings, cognizant of seeking all types of relief for them. She has dedicated her legal career to social justice and the importance of ensuring due process to those facing legal challenges in criminal and immigration courts. As an immigrant and a person of color, Lily has personally experienced discrimination and injustice. Thus, she is determined to give voice to those who have none; courage to those who have no strength to face their legal situation; and compassion to those who are most despised and derided in society. Given the immigration crisis in the U.S., she sees her role as more crucial than ever. Lily is a community leader and a strong advocate, who strives to make the community for Filipinos and others in San Francisco and beyond a better place. Her great joy is sharing her life with her husband Reynold, and their three sons Ricky, Kaelan, and Brandon.

LEONOR S. VINTERVOLL
JANTELOVEN AND LEADERSHIP

Patient 🎋 Determined 🎋 Result-oriented

In close cooperation with three Philippine Ambassadors based in Sweden, Leonor Vintervoll served as primary contact for the Filipino community in Norway. As a leader, her successful lobbying resulted in a quota for recruitment of Filipino nurses and engineers and the lifting of the ban on the deployment of au pairs in Norway and eventually for the whole of Europe. As a behind the scenes leader, she was always ready to help, whether it was a Filipino with a problem in Norway or disaster fund-raising for the Philippines. Her experience as Lay Judge for 16 years on the City Court of Oslo and *Borgarting Lagmannsrett* (Court of Appeal) was a significant factor in her successful leadership in the community. Her dedication to community service was recognized when she was awarded one of the FWN100 Most Influential Filipinas in the World in 2015 and again in 2017. Awardees are inspirations for the empowerment of the next generation of women leaders. Leonor serves on the FWN Board of Directors and says that her fellow board members inspire and challenge her to higher levels of service.

EDITHA TIJAMO WINTERHALTER, ED.D.
SANGANDAAN

Pragmatic 🎋 Transformative 🎋 Explorer

Editha Winterhalter, Ed.D. is the perfect billboard example of a late bloomer succeeding. Although she began her professional career later than many, through grit and determination, she is now on a career fast-track at California State University, Northridge (CSUN). She has been at CSUN for twenty years. She is the Director of Administrative Services as well as Director of Risk Management and Insurance in the division of Administration and Finance. Before that, she was the Director of Academic Budget Management in the division of Academic Affairs of the university. Dr. Winterhalter is a full product of CSUN; having received all of her academic credentials from CSUN. She received her Bachelor's degree in Accountancy in 2003 and Master's degree in Education Administration in 2007. In 2016, she received her Doctorate in Educational Leadership with Distinction. Her dissertation is a qualitative study of the impact of physical spaces on the learning experience of college students with attention deficit hyperactivity disorder (ADHD). Editha chairs the National Executive Board of the International Society of Filipinos in Finance and Accounting (ISFFA), an organization whose mission is to provide mentors, leadership, and scholarship support to emerging Filipino professionals in the areas of finance, business, and accounting.

Myrna P. Young, MSN, RN, CNOR

Big Dreams, Broken Glass
Enthusiast 🎀 Educator 🎀 Inspired

Myrna Young like many of the bright, talented women from the Philippines, had big dreams of a successful personal and professional life. After succeeding in various nursing leadership roles since 1990, Young now enjoys a full and rewarding career as a Nursing Education Specialist and works at the prestigious Robert Wood Johnson University Hospital in New Jersey, USA. She further feeds her passion for helping people through community outreach and mentoring staff, colleagues, and students. Not only does Myrna surround herself with high-caliber talent, as in the Filipina Women's Network, the National Association of Clinical Nurse Specialists, and the Organization of Nurse Leaders; but she also volunteers her time with the Philippine Nurses Association of New Jersey, the March of Dimes, and various food banks. Myrna was named as one of FWN's 100 Most Influential Filipina Woman in the World in 2017. She received a Global Nursing Recognition award at the United Nations. Myrna has numerous publications, has membership in numerous associations, and continues to teach as her way of sharing her knowledge.

Geri Alumit Zeldes, Ph.D.

Was it Murder? Leadership in My Quest for Truth
Learner 🎀 Curious 🎀 Content

Geri Alumit Zeldes, Ph.D. is a tenured Professor in Michigan State University's School of Journalism. Geri has received a dozen best paper awards from international communication associations and more than a 100 honors and screenings for her documentary films and other scholarship. Her awards include the Dr. Suzanne Ahn Award for coverage of social justice issues from the Asian American Journalists Association, the Edward R. Murrow and Unity awards from the Radio Television Digital News Association, two national Best of Festival Awards from the Broadcast Education Association, a Top 25 Public Vote recognition for an exhibit in ArtPrize, three regional Emmys, and a handful of awards from the Society of Professional Journalists. She has also received awards from the Michigan Association of Broadcasters and Michigan Associated Press Editors' Association. In October 2017, the Filipina Women's Network recognized her with a "100 Most Influential Filipina Women in the World Award" in the Innovator and Thought Leader category. In 2018, Geri was added to the Diversity Champion Honor Roll. Geri has obtained grants to support her work as well as the work of her creative teams. She was invited to speak at two TEDx events and featured for her social justice scholarship on MSU's "Spartans Will" campaign.

Filipina Women's Network Board of Directors

Marily Mondejar, Founder and CEO
Susie Quesada, President
Maria Beebe, Ph.D., Chair of the Board
Maria Santos Greaves, Secretary
Amar Bornkamp, Treasurer

Lita Abele
Carol Enriquez, M.D.
Hon. Thelma B. Boac
Leonor S. Vintervoll
Georgitta Pimentel Puyat
Maria Roseni M. Alvero

About the Filipina Women Leadership Book Series

The Filipina Women Leadership Book Series project aims to fill the gap in the leadership literature that highlights the unique qualities of Filipina women whose culture, values, and faith make them effective leaders and managers. The leadership book series chronicles Filipina women's leadership skill sets, capabilities and expertise and how we contribute as active participants in the global workplace. The DISRUPT leadership series is a key component of our game plan to elevate the presence and participation of Filipina women in the public and private sectors.

DISRUPT Book Orders:

Book Launch: September 13, 2018 at
House of Parliament, United Kingdom

Book orders: https://www.ffwn.org/event-876425

- 1.415.935.4396
- www.filipinaleadership.org
- filipina@ffwn.org

Cover Design by **Lucille Tenazas, Tenazas Design/NY**

www.ingramcontent.com/pod-product-compliance
Lightning Source LLC
Chambersburg PA
CBHW031129160426
43193CB00008B/76